The Unsettlement of America

IMAGINING THE AMERICAS
Caroline F. Levander and Anthony B. Pinn, Series Editors

Imagining the Americas is a new interdisciplinary series that explores
the cross-fertilization among cultures and forms in the American hemisphere.
The series targets the intersections between literary, religious and cultural
studies that materialize once the idea of nation is understood as fluid and
multi-form. Extending from the northernmost regions of Canada to Cape Horn,
books in this series will move beyond a simple extension of U.S.-based
American studies approaches and engage the American hemisphere directly.

Millennial Literatures of the Americas, 1492–2002
Thomas O. Beebee

The Plantation in the Postslavery Imagination
Elizabeth Christine Russ

The Interethnic Imagination
Caroline Rody

Religious Liberties
Elizabeth Fenton

Between the Lines
Monique-Adelle Callahan

God's Arbiters
Susan K. Harris

The Unsettlement of America
Anna Brickhouse

The Unsettlement of America

TRANSLATION, INTERPRETATION, AND THE STORY OF DON LUIS DE VELASCO, 1560–1945

Anna Brickhouse

OXFORD
UNIVERSITY PRESS

OXFORD
UNIVERSITY PRESS

Oxford University Press is a department of the University of Oxford.
It furthers the University's objective of excellence in research, scholarship,
and education by publishing worldwide.

Oxford   New York

Auckland   Cape Town   Dar es Salaam   Hong Kong   Karachi
Kuala Lumpur   Madrid   Melbourne   Mexico City   Nairobi
New Delhi   Shanghai   Taipei   Toronto

With offices in

Argentina   Austria   Brazil   Chile   Czech Republic   France   Greece
Guatemala   Hungary   Italy   Japan   Poland   Portugal   Singapore
South Korea   Switzerland   Thailand   Turkey   Ukraine   Vietnam

Oxford is a registered trademark of Oxford University Press
in the UK and certain other countries.

Published in the United States of America by
Oxford University Press
198 Madison Avenue, New York, NY 10016

Library of Congress Cataloging-in-Publication Data
Brickhouse, Anna.
The Unsettlement of America : Translation, Interpretation, and the Story of Don Luis de Velasco,
1560–1945 / Anna Brickhouse.
pages cm
Includes bibliographical references and index.
ISBN 978–0–19–972972–2 (hardback)—ISBN 978–0–19–987559–7 (ebook)   1. Velasco,
Luis de, 1500–1564.   2. Translators.   3. Translating and interpreting.   4. Intercultural
communication.   5. America—Civilization—16th century.   I. Title.
P306.92.V45B75 2014
418'.02092—dc23
2014006354

1 3 5 7 9 8 6 4 2
Printed in the United States of America
on acid-free paper

For Bruce, Campbell, and Malcolm,
who love to share stories

{ CONTENTS }

{ LIST OF FIGURES }

{ ACKNOWLEDGMENTS }

Many friends, colleagues, and institutions have given me their support in the years since I started writing this book. My profound thanks go to the American Council of Learned Societies for a 2012 Research Fellowship that allowed me to work uninterrupted on this project in its final stage. I am grateful as well to the wonderful editors and production staff at Oxford University Press, especially Brendan O'Neill, Stephen Bradley, and Jayanthi Bhaskar. From the outset, I also had greatly helpful responses when I shared my work with a variety of departments and programs, and it is a pleasure to think back over the years and acknowledge these institutions in rough chronological order from beginning to end: the Departments of English at Penn, Rutgers, Vanderbilt, and Notre Dame; the English Department and Local Americanists at Maryland; the Department of English and *ALH* at Illinois; the Departments of Literature at UC San Diego and UC Santa Cruz; the Department of English at USC; the Dartmouth Futures Institute; the Penn State Center for American Literary Studies; the Departments of American Studies, History, and English at Indiana University; the English Department, the Humanities Center, and the TransAmerican Studies Working Group at Stanford; the Humanities Institute and the English Department at Rice; the Center for the Humanities at the University of Miami and the College of Arts & Sciences at Florida International University; the Humanities Center, the Americas Before 1900 Working Group, and LASER at Ohio State University; Omohundro Institute of Early American History and Culture; the Humanities Institute and the TransAmericas Research Workshop at SUNY Buffalo; the English Department and the Americanist Speakers and Colloquium Series at the University of Wisconson-Madison; and the American Literature Reading Group, the English and Spanish departments, and the McNeil Center for Early American Studies at Penn. Earlier versions of sections from various chapters in this book have appeared in the volumes *Hemispheric American Studies* and the *Blackwell Companion to American Literary Studies* and in the journals *ALH, Clio,* and *PMLA*.

This project owes more than I can say to the generosity of colleagues and friends at other universities. Caroline Levander and Bob Levine got the project off the ground as my editors for an essay that turned out to be the seed of the larger book. I had never had the benefit of working so closely with editors at such an early stage of drafting an essay, and I learned the joys of collaborative work because of them. As my series editor, Caroline saw this entire book through from beginning to end, and from matters practical to theoretical—from insisting that I stop my hand-wringing, hang up the phone, and write a proposal, to helping me see the larger stakes of my interests. Throughout my writing, Susan Gillman has inspired me with her work on adaptation and translation; she gave me more than one frame for my project simply by sharing her brilliance and enthusiasm. Kirsten Gruesz has been a scholarly model and an irreplaceable interlocutor along the way. And Ralph Bauer, who also helped guide my first book into being, read the entire manuscript and shared the benefit of his erudition, skepticism, and support. I also owe special thanks to Guillaume Aubert, Allison Bigelow, Michael Elliott, Roland Greene, Matthew Pratt Gutterl, James Horn, Gordon Hutner, Bianca Premo, José David Saldívar, Ramón Saldívar, Tatiana Seijas, Eric Slaughter, Fredrika Teute, Jennifer Harford Vargas, Tim Watson, and Lisa Voigt for reading and responding to parts of various chapters with extraordinary care, and to Sarah Krakoff and Jacki Rand, who taught me things I needed to know long before I knew I would write this book.

Here at UVA, I can't name all the graduate students who have shaped this project over the last years by accompanying me during seminars as I discovered new texts with them and tested my earliest hypotheses; they will, I hope, remember some of these discussions. But I must especially thank Jenny Braun, Alexandra Harmon, Lindsay Van Tine, and Maria Windell for reading drafts, helping with research, and sharing their own expertise. My colleagues in English, American Studies, and around the university have also been a great source of support to me since my arrival here in 2005, and I want to thank my chairs in particular: Gordon Braden, Jahan Ramazani, and Cynthia Wall. A number of my colleagues generously read and helped me to revise different portions of my book, or were important interlocutors at various points; they include Lawrie Balfour, Alison Booth, Sylvia Chong, Steve Cushman, Rita Felski, Cori Field, Lisa Goff, Bonnie Gordon, Jennifer Greeson, Susan Fraiman, Grace Hale, Janet Horne, Eric Lott, Deborah McDowell, Jerry McGann, Emily Ogden, Vicki Olwell, Caroline Rody, Marlon Ross, Sandhya Shukla, and Jennifer Wicke. The UVA Department of Spanish, Italian and Portuguese has also been a great help; for their questions, insights, and encouragement, I am grateful especially to David Gies, Mané Lagos, Ricardo Padrón, Gustavo Pellón, Fernando Operé, and Randolph Pope. Ruth Hill left UVA for the Spanish and Portuguese department at Vanderbilt, but she was an early reader and supporter as I started this project, and I learn from her every time we talk. For all of these colleagues' sustained guidance, criticism, and support, and most of all for their friendship, I am so thankful.

And I thank my beloved family: my parents and in-laws for their abiding emotional support, for their constant logistical help, and for being wonderful grandparents; my mother, especially, for her love of languages and multiple meanings, and for her painstaking help on my translations from Spanish; Campbell and Malcolm, for loving to hear stories and asking hard questions about them, and for every time they stopped kicking the ball indoors when it was about to hit my laptop; and finally Bruce Holsinger, for reading every word with love and honesty, and for sustaining me in every possible way.

{ A NOTE ON TRANSLATION }

This is a book about translators and motivated mistranslations, and for that reason alone I have tried to be as clear as possible about my own use of translations and translating practices throughout these pages. For the most part, I have provided my own translations even when there is a standard, published translation of the original. In some cases, I have followed this policy because of a translator's actual invention of words and phrases that do not exist in the original Spanish. In others, however, I have followed it because the existing translation smoothens out what is rough and obscure in the original, thereby overclarifying what was never clear to begin with. Where I have made my own choice to clarify, I have offered my inferred referents in brackets so that readers will know the words are mine, and are in that sense conjectural. These are, to use Lawrence Venuti's term, highly *foreignizing* translations, both in the sense that they do not generally attempt to assimilate either words or syntax into language that is more familiar and less laborious to parse, and in the sense that they do not attempt to domesticate the strangeness of texts that were sometimes written under constrained circumstances. In all cases, I have directed readers to both the originals and the published translations and, where relevant, have discussed certain translational choices in the main text or the notes.

The Unsettlement of America

Prologue

In 1561, a Spanish ship sails into the coastal waters of what is now the Chesapeake Bay and takes on board an Algonquian-speaking Indian who will soon be christened Don Luis de Velasco. He is named after his honorific godfather, the viceroy of New Spain, and over the ensuing decade, Don Luis, as the Spaniards call him, becomes a transatlantic traveler and assimilated bilingual, residing in Spain, Cuba, the Floridas, and Mexico City. He receives a classical education, acquires literacy, and holds a royal allowance. He also begins to suggest to various Spanish colonial officials and religious leaders the project of returning to his own country—Ajacán—to help convert its inhabitants and settle the land. The stories that Don Luis tells about the abundance of Ajacán are appealing to his Spanish interlocutors, and in 1570 he departs Cuba and sails up the Atlantic coast to his homeland with a group of Jesuits, who are charged with forming a colony. Upon their arrival, Don Luis acts as a translator between the Natives and the settlers; he informs the Jesuits that the people of Ajacán are delighted by this turn of events and are indeed imploring the Spaniards to stay. Yet when the ship's pilot returns eighteen months later to deliver supplies, the settlement at Ajacán has disappeared—it is a Spanish "Lost Colony," a harbinger of England's mysteriously abandoned Roanoke settlement of the 1580s. Unlike the Lost Colony of Roanoke, however, the Spanish settlement in Ajacán yields a survivor and witness, a young woodsman who accompanied the Jesuits and who tells the story of the colony's demise. The Jesuits were murdered, he claims, by their own translator, the cosmopolitan Don Luis de Velasco.

Taking the story of Don Luis as both its point of departure and its critical provocation, *The Unsettlement of America* has several aims. First, I hope to bring broader attention to Don Luis himself—as an early modern indigenous subject of the sixteenth-century Atlantic world who traveled far and wide and experienced nearly a decade of Western civilization before acting decisively against European settlement. While historians have long been aware of the failed settlement at Ajacán (often casting it as a fleeting Spanish counterpart to the later, ostensibly permanent Jamestown), this book attends specifically to the interpretive and knowledge-producing roles played by Don Luis as a translator acting not only in Native-European contact zones but in a complex arena of inter-indigenous transmission of information about the hemisphere.

At the same time, this book argues for the conceptual and literary significance of *unsettlement*, a term enlisted here in multiple, interrelated ways. Unsettlement signifies in its literal sense as the thwarting or destroying of settlement along with the active attempt to discourage future European colonization—a heuristic term for understanding a wide range of texts related to settler colonialism, including those that recount Don Luis's decade-long sojourn as a transatlantic traveler and colonial translator. As one of this project's keywords, "unsettlement" crystallizes several conceptual points that distinguish it from a number of related terms more commonly used. The term "resistance," in particular, broadly encompasses any kind of action against an imperial or colonizing agent, undertaken by anyone in almost any context, and for a host of reasons, ranging from struggle on behalf of a collective to the leveraging of personal power or advantage within a structure of dominance: resistance is so broad and ubiquitous that it almost implies a certain futility. By contrast, the project of unsettlement as explored in these pages is undertaken by an indigenous subject and involves the concrete attempt to annihilate or otherwise put an end to a European colony, or to forestall or eliminate a future colonial project. As a term, *unsettlement* signals not merely the contingency and noninevitability but the glaring incompleteness of the history of the New World as we currently know and write it.

The term *settlement*—against which, of course, the concept of unsettlement is semantically derived and defined—has traditionally been used in the historiography of the Anglo-American colonies, and it has always functioned as more than just another word for colonialism: it has from its earliest usages connoted a specifically *English* and particularly Protestant style of colonialism that is in contrast to its (always implied, sometimes explicit) Spanish foil: *conquest*. Settlement, that is, has always posited itself as inherently superior to and less violent than conquest; as both term and concept, it is in some sense built upon the premise of English (and, later, U.S.) predominance in the hemisphere. The heuristic of *un*settlement works against that premise, and against the foundational opposition of settlement and conquest. Indeed, the frame of unsettlement should help to clarify not only the ideological work that such terms do but what we can learn from the interplay of the different scholarly traditions that have embraced or questioned them.

Unsettlement thus highlights what can often be obscured in the historical differentiation between settlement and conquest, English and Spanish, the United States and (Latin) America, by exposing something very simple that indigenous people in the Americas seem to have understood before European settlers did: that colonial settlement—by whatever name we call it—always threatens even when it does not achieve the unsettlement (the removal, the attempted genocide) of the people who were already there. Thomas Harriot's sixteenth-century Native interlocutors told him this directly, surprising and taking him aback with the violence they both saw and foresaw in the English, whom Harriot characterizes largely as chaste and gentle. Mystified by their view, Harriot includes it within a general discussion of the purported Native belief in English superiority, most of which sounds a familiar note of colonial projection—though not this statement: "Some would likewise seem to prophesie that there were more of our generation yet to come, to kill theirs and take their places." Many scholars take their cue from Harriot and cast this pronouncement as remarkably prescient, an uncanny foretelling of an unknown future. But as paraphrased from the Native speakers, it is actually far more descriptive and empiricist, a conclusion drawn from observation of "that which was already done." The predicted killing and usurpation are not unfortunate by-products, in this view of settlement, but are in fact what "some thought the purpose was." As a statement about the ideological concept of settlement, these words could not be more literal, and they bring to the foreground one of the central and flawed premises of settler colonialism: the idea that the Americas were inhabited but not settled by indigenous peoples prior to the arrival of Europeans. The concept of *unsettlement* helps to expose what European colonial projects sought to achieve and simultaneously disavow through a powerful verb: to settle (or, in Spanish, *poblar*, to populate).

But the term *unsettlement* also functions in this book as an implied argument for the unsettling of *mind* implied by the earliest usages of the word "unsettle" that appeared (not coincidentally, I think) in the years following the first major attempts at English colonization in the Americas. To unsettle in these years is to confound, to change a fixed opinion or view, to leave in a state of uncertainty: to "unsettle . . . and disquiet [the] mind"; to "unsettle and discontent the minde," to "perplexe or unsettle the Reader." Though these usages refer most often to matters of religious dispute, the origins of the term cannot easily be separated from the issues of land and priority that were emerging alongside settler colonialism in the New World. One of the earliest instances of the term occurs in a 1608 tragedy about the division of territory, when the Earl of Kent observes the mental unraveling of King Lear: "his wits begin to unsettle."

By the following year, when the chaplain Robert Johnson wrote *Nova Britannia*, his sermon promoting the Virginia Company, the link between the term "unsettle" and the endeavor "to Plant and settle English Colonies" was explicit—and it related directly to the contest for New World empire between England and Spain. England had rights in the Americas, Johnson claimed, precisely because it had respected *Spanish* land claims in the Americas: "we so passed by their dwellings, that in seating our selves, wee sought not to *unsetle* them" (my emphasis). Johnson's case for the English right to settle "another countrie, farre distant and remote from [Spanish] habitations"—Virginia—is thus premised upon this refusal to "unsettle" prior Spanish colonial claims, in accordance with what is known as the doctrine of first discovery: as he puts it, "we now intend to ground vpon [a] Discouerie and actuall possession, taken [via the Roanoke colony] in the name and right of *Queene Elizabeth*, in *Anno* 1584." The problem with basing a settlement claim upon the lost colony of Roanoke was, of course, the failure of "actuall possession," as Johnson clearly understood, when he noted nervously that "it is true indeede (as some may obiect) [it] is now aboue twentie yeeres agoe since these things were done, and yet euer since in al this time, we neuer sawe or heard of any good that hath come from thence." Actual possession, Johnson suggests here, matters less than priority—than "those beginnings" at Roanoke which *would*, had history unfolded differently, have constituted "a most royall addition to the Crowne of England." By this logic, then, the Spanish settlement at Ajacán, which preceded Roanoke by well over a decade, legally unsettled—and continues to unsettle—the English claim on the land patented as "Virginia."

Drawing upon this historical convergence of conceptual, legal, and literal forms of unsettlement, this book argues for the kinds of counterfactual and reparative practices of reading the historical past that emerge once we achieve critical distance on the assumed inevitability of European settlement—and on the institutions and legacies of conquest itself: the processes of conversion and assimilation in the sixteenth century; the development of American Indian law out of the doctrine of first discovery in the nineteenth; and the assumption of English rather than Spanish colonial priority at the ostensible site of U.S. national origin in the quadricentennial celebrations of Jamestown in 2007, among others. *The Unsettlement of America* recovers this vexed hemispheric history from within the extraordinary narrative afterlife of Don Luis, embodied in a wide array of diplomatic, religious, historical, epistolary, and literary writings from the middle of the sixteenth century to the middle of the twentieth. This diverse archive emerges as the story of Ajacán is transmitted across discrete languages, histories, and cultures, from Mexico and Peru to the ports of Spain and the legal milieu of Philip II's royal court in Madrid; from the coastal Floridas and Havana to the future Virginia; from U.S. territorial expansion in the nineteenth century to the hemispheric ironies shaping the era of the Good Neighbor Policy. In tracing the elusive story of Ajacán as it unfolds from the colonial era across the centuries, this book posits Don Luis as a kind of *un*founding father, and in doing so speculates on the implications of the broader, transhistorical afterlife of the story for the present concerns of the Americanist field.

One of my assumptions here is that our prevailing literary and historical narratives of the Americas will be enriched by a more nuanced and capacious understanding of the practices and politics of translation, one that resists the understandable scholarly tendency to apprehend translation in the early modern era largely as a tool of empire, a dutiful metonymy of *translatio imperii*. Setting aside this assumption is a first step toward recovering the particular history of American unsettlement embodied in the story of Don Luis, for it helps to clarify a much larger historiographical tendency to privilege supposed instances of "successful" translation—translation that ostensibly yields information accurately to its target audience—at the expense of those instances in which translation seemingly fails. As a result, early Native interpreters such as Pocahontas, Squanto, and Sacajawea have endured as embodiments of felicitous translation, while the story of Don Luis—which hinges on the translator's overt performance of interpretive rupture rather than mediation—has been not only largely unremembered but at times actively forgotten, even, as I show here, willfully erased from historical memory. Even in the field of translation studies itself, where the lines between successful and failed translations have been usefully called into question, scholars often proceed as if the most significant insights of contemporary translation theory simply do not apply to the history of indigenous interpreters in the colonial Americas—as if the role of hermeneutic subject were the privilege of lettered translators only, and therefore not to be occupied by the interpreter between speaking subjects. This book works from a different premise, arguing for the crucial role of what I will call *motivated mistranslation* in the shaping of hemispheric encounter, and proposing it as the default condition of all translation in the colonial American world and in many of the subsequent literary and historical writings that have sought to represent it.

I am by training and inclination a literary scholar rather than a historian, and several careful, historically-minded readers of earlier drafts of this project have helped me see the potential pitfalls attending my particular modes of interpreting in this book. First, I have been cautioned against taking a somewhat utopian view of what I cast here as the inter-indigenous transmission of knowledge across disparate parts of the hemisphere, particularly given the insights of recent work in Native history that has labored to show how early indigenous polities were just as likely to exploit their relations with Europeans in order to expand their sovereignty over other Native groups as they were to engage in direct opposition to colonization. The Tlaxcalans in Mexico offer a famous case in point, but examples abound in the English colonial world during the seventeenth and eighteenth centuries as well. Second, I have been warned against treating the indigenous translators in this book anachronistically, as self-determining individual subjects of modernity rather than products of their early cultural and historical moments. While I understand this skepticism on both fronts, I also believe that it is to some extent symptomatic of more than just a clash of disciplinary protocols and my own persistence in pushing sources and my interpretations of them in often speculative directions. There is a long scholarly tradition, however equitable today in allotting significance and agency, of viewing Native historical subjects as products of culture rather than producers of knowledge, while tacitly granting that the European historical subject can be both at once. That my own readings swing heavily in the other direction, privileging knowledge over culture, is certainly true. I hope that they are also in some measure salutary—even if they demand, as they surely will, their own correctives in the future.

American literary history needs the story of Don Luis de Velasco, and not only because his itinerant Atlantic career enacts the field's self-avowed commitments to transnationalism and multilingualism. As an early modern, Algonquian-speaking interpreter who traveled from what is now Virginia to Spain, Mexico, Cuba, and the Floridas, making at least four transoceanic and numerous shorter voyages, Don Luis offers a useful provocation to the literary-historiographical and pedagogical renovations announced by both the transatlantic and the hemispheric approaches current in the field. In particular, if Don Luis's career as a traveler and translator speaks to the ongoing transnational turn in American studies, his story and its imaginative afterlife can be most richly understood only by engaging the most significant critical insights of recent Native American studies, particularly that field's emphasis on the outernational and cosmopolitan dimensions of Native history and literature. Don Luis's story illuminates the stakes of this global indigenous history, contributing to an emergent critical perspective in important and often self-reflexive ways.

Both the story and its enduring transmission between Europe and the Americas evoke the largely unwritten history of what Jace Weaver has called the "Red Atlantic," a framework that pushes us to view the indigenous interpretive work studied here as a central component of transatlantic exchange rather than a marginal strand within a field still currently defined primarily by British-American and European-African encounters. The microhistory that radiates outward from the story of Don Luis and its transmission far exceeds the Atlantic world, however, for it extends from Peru to today's Virginia, and from Cordova, Spain to the Southwest of what is now the United States. Because the material of the story is inherently comparative, crossing languages and discrete colonial and national formations, it invites a carefully reparative mode of reading the past, whereby details from one historical account are imported across space and time to fill in the absences of another, bringing into view what has been silenced or omitted in the written record, while asking us to imagine and speculate about alternative historical outcomes.

Situated within this critical framework, the story of Don Luis invites the American literary field to address certain dilemmas attending its own recent turn to the transnational. Don Luis himself provides a salutary corrective in the wake of this turn, an indigenous subject wholly unlike the celebrated border dwellers and hybrid culture heroes populating many anthologies. He unsettles and confounds what is arguably the field's most enduring critical inheritance—the theoretical encumbrance of multiculturalism—precisely because his story so forcefully resists assimilation as a cultural contribution to the ever richer and more varied narrative of "America." Such a narrative to some extent implicitly structured my own first book, *Transamerican Literary Relations and the Nineteenth-Century Public Sphere*, with its focus on the unacknowledged cultural desires and anxieties that defined a transamerican literary milieu involving multiple languages and national affiliations during a period of fluctuating U.S. borders in the mid-nineteenth century. In this book, by contrast, I focus on a range of periods that precede and postdate the rise of U.S. literary nationalism across the *longue durée* of settler colonialism, and I am concerned with what the telling and retelling of a particular narrative of colonial unsettlement can reveal about both the longer continuities of hemispheric history across space and time and the current limitations of scholarly practice. For the story of Don Luis virtually allegorizes the ethnohistorical imperative to recognize the mutually constituting nature of imperial "discovery" by shifting the focus of inquiry toward the *knowledge*, rather than the (multi)culture, of those whom Europe sought to colonize in the Americas. The history of indigenous knowledge that resides within the disparate records of Don Luis's story concerns in part the conceptual origins of the so-called New World during the long sixteenth century; this body of knowledge constitutes an indigenous apprehension of the American hemisphere as a geopolitical entity—and crucially, it emerges not only from Native-European encounter but from inter-indigenous exchanges which, as we shall see, occurred in the Floridas, Mexico, and Cuba as well as in the understudied contact zones created by Native travelers and knowledge producers in metropolitan Spain. That Don Luis was not the only indigenous interlocutor with a compelling interest in shaping the European-authored written record to suit his immediate and long-term aims is part of the point here; indeed, his transatlantic and hemispheric trajectory might be understood to constitute an early modern adumbration of those modes of indigenous exchange and transmission that would later form a transnational foundation for modern Indian letters.

While assembling the narrative of Don Luis itself from disparate and contradictory sources, this book attempts to excavate from the written record traces of the complex and intricate indigenous intellectual labor embodied by this sixteenth-century Native translator and grappled with by those who have passed on and puzzled over his story, from an elite Inca historian writing in seventeenth-century Spain to an Anglo-American novelist descended from a Jamestown settler and writing in twentieth-century Virginia. I have tried to tread with care upon the contested terrain of Don Luis's world, mindful throughout of the persistent fantasy of authenticity in scholarly encounters with indigenous history and culture. I do not purport to have access to a putatively original indigenous identity, nor do I wish to celebrate Don Luis as a singular, heroic figure of Native agency and cultural resistance. I am interested instead in the discernible traces of Don Luis's acquisition and transmission of knowledge—in both transatlantic and hemispheric as well as Native-European and inter-indigenous contexts—and in how this circuit of knowledge transmission in turn came to shape historical outcomes as well as the historical record itself. Ultimately, *The Unsettlement of America* suggests how the story of Don Luis may unsettle our own contemporary modes of knowledge production, and shows what we can learn from the demands that his story makes upon the interpretive processes that guide us.

Part I of this book, "The Methods and the Story," explores the early colonial context in which the story of Don Luis initially emerges. Chapter 1, "Mistranslation and Unsettlement," outlines the book's key concepts by sketching out a history of American unsettlement that finds its origins story in La Navidad, the first European colony in the New World. Drawing upon examples ranging from Columbus's *Diario* to the captivity of John Smith to the speculative figure I am calling "Hispanophone Squanto," this chapter proposes an alternative historical narrative centered around instances of failed settlements, lost colonies, disappeared colonists, abandoned colonial efforts as well as willfully false and other kinds of failed translations. I aim here to develop a kind of reparative critical approach to the material explored in the ensuing chapters—an approach that seeks to construct imaginative or speculative possibilities rather than merely to expose or destabilize an ideological position. This critical reparation requires supplementing the hermeneutics of suspicion and moving beyond a new historicist conception of translation limited to its purview as the distorting projection of the colonizer onto the words of the colonized by focusing as well upon the occluded history of indigenous knowledge production that becomes visible when we reframe scenes of imperial translation as scenes of strategic mistranslation—scenes that underwrite a long history of American unsettlement.

With this critical framework in mind, Chapter 2 turns to the book's exemplum of unsettlement, "An Unfounding Father: The Story of Don Luis," introducing the transatlantic and hemispheric dimensions of his itinerant career as recorded in a series of Spanish letters, voyage logs, and *relaciones* from the sixteenth and seventeenth centuries. This chapter proposes a provisional model of early modern indigenous authorship embedded within the earliest accounts of Don Luis's role as a translator. By formally distinguishing the varied narrators within the primary documents that first record his story, I try to recover Don Luis's authorial work in creating his own compelling narrative, persuasive enough in its own moment that it ultimately restored him to his homeland and allowed him to shape the outcome of events there. These early accounts of Don Luis's story foreground the geopolitics of knowledge in the sixteenth-century Americas, shedding light not upon the nature of indigenous identity or cultural inheritance but upon what and how Don Luis knew, and how this form of subaltern knowledge shaped historical events while wrestling with the very colonial idiom embedding and seeking to control it.

The sixteenth-century accounts of Don Luis sought to transform his story of unsettlement into a fixed narrative of Indian barbarism and Catholic martyrdom. Yet once the story of Don Luis appeared in print, initially in Pedro de Ribadeneyra's *Life of Father Francis Borgia* (Madrid, 1592), it also achieved an afterlife no longer circumscribed by either Spanish colonialism or Jesuit hagiography. Part II of this book, "The Afterlives of Don Luis," explores two instances of the sixteenth-century translator's subsequent reappearance in the literary history of the Americas. Chapter 3 pursues the mystery of Don Luis's uncanny appearance at the end of *La Florida del Inca* (Lisbon, 1605), by the mestizo Peruvian historiographer El Inca Garcilaso de la Vega—an appearance that has proved a conundrum for Garcilaso scholars because Don Luis's strange and violent story provides a counterintuitive conclusion to the text's magisterial account of the 1539 Hernando de Soto expedition in La Florida. As I argue here, however, this odd interpolation of Don Luis becomes discernible once we recognize how Garcilaso has rewritten his source text: by casting the destruction of the Ajacán settlement as an act not of volatile barbarity but of premeditated and even pre-articulated response to what Don Luis has learned about Spanish conquest elsewhere in the hemisphere. Garcilaso's prehistory of Don Luis provides the interpretive key, in fact, to the revisionist critical mode that defines *La Florida del Inca* as a larger work, particularly its engagement with two central texts of Spanish colonialism in the New World, Bartolomé de las Casas's *Brevísima relación de la destrucción de las Indias* (1552) and the *Relación* of Álvar Núñez Cabeza de Vaca (1542), which el Inca recasts in an analytic spirit that we might call the sensibility of unsettlement. Garcilaso's critical lens upon the *Relación*, in particular, offers a productive frame for American literary studies—a field in which Cabeza de Vaca has become increasingly canonical over the last two decades, to judge from our anthologies. Cabeza de Vaca's narrative, and Garcilaso's rewriting of it under the sign of unsettlement, together suggest that the field's alleged triumph over American exceptionalism has been in part a mere reconfiguration. This sense of *Americas* exceptionalism has important bearing on how we define the epistemological sophistication, the ethical credentials, and the continued modernity of our scholarly work.

Chapter 4, "Don Luis in La Florida," explores the world of Spanish-Calusa encounter in the sixteenth-century Floridas, both before and after Don Luis traveled there while making his way back to his homeland in Ajacán. The chapter begins with the little-known account of a former captive of the Calusa Indians, Hernando de Escalante Fontaneda, who served as a translator for Pedro Menéndez de Avilés during the same period when Don Luis was also in the Floridas with the Adelantado. The ambiguous account of this strange interpreter—a Creole man who came of age among the Calusa Indians and had lived with them most of his life at the time of its writing—has received little attention from literary scholars, largely because of its violent and explicitly anti-Indian pronouncements. Yet Fontaneda's account embodies a complex, juridical engagement with Spanish conquest that results in what I define as a narrative mode of unsettlement: a trenchant critique of Spanish colonial discourse and its attendant laws that works doggedly toward the goal of thwarting settlement—precisely, that is, toward discouraging future Spanish attempts to colonize La Florida. At the same time, exploring Don Luis's role in the inter-indigenous circuit of narrative transmission and human migration connecting the Calusa Indians and colonial Cuba, the chapter proposes an early modern hemispheric indigenous consciousness—a deeply *political* understanding of the threat to indigenous sovereignty throughout the hemisphere that left the Calusa with a growing conceptual map of New World colonialism, which ultimately enabled them to unsettle the entire South Floridian coast. The final section of the chapter turns to a firsthand, early seventeenth-century travel narrative in which Don Luis reappears in the Floridas alive and well years *after* his destruction of the colony in Ajacán. Written by the Carmelite friar and man of letters, Andrés de San Miguel, *Relación de los trabajos* presents a baroque chapter in the afterlife of Don Luis, one that resuscitates the translator from the death grip of the historical past, assigns him autonomous powers of movement and relocation, from Ajacán to a site near Havana, and gives him a powerful written afterlife: engaged in a new strand of history, leading a group of Floridian Indians, Don Luis sunders the early modern topos of interpretive transparency with a particularly unsettling form of *desengaño* or disillusion.

After his destruction of the Ajacán colony, then, the story of Don Luis traveled far and wide, allowing the translator to live on in La Florida as a figure for Native dissidence across time and space. During the sixteenth and seventeenth centuries, the story exemplified unsettlement: the thwarting of a potential Spanish occupation of Don Luis's homeland, the insurgent possibilities of translation, the inter-indigenous transmission of knowledge from throughout the Americas and across the Atlantic, and the threat of indigenous revolt against European empire on a hemispheric scale. The narrative did not make its way into the English language, however, until the middle decades of the nineteenth century, when it would become abundantly clear that Don Luis's story had the potential to unsettle the national U.S. historical plotline in a variety of ways.

Part III of this book, "The Translation of Don Luis: From the Treaty of Guadalupe Hidalgo to the Good Neighbor Policy," examines the U.S. after-life of Don Luis during two significant historical moments of hemispheric relations. Chapter 5, "The Politics of Unsettlement in the Nineteenth Century," explores what happened to the story of the Spanish colony at Ajacán when it was unearthed, transmitted, and unsuccessfully suppressed during the era of U.S. expansionism—precisely when the legal basis for expansion was largely defined by the history of colonial settlement and the so-called rights of first discovery. The chapter focuses particularly on the work of Robert Greenhow, a lawyer, translator, and historian working for the U.S. State Department in the 1840s, and the remarkable steps he took to suppress the documentation of the sixteenth-century Spanish settlement that he found in the writings of the eighteenth-century Spanish historian, Andrés González de Barcia. No one was in a better position than Greenhow to understand that the post-Mexican War era was not an ideal time to go muddying the jurisdictional waters of "First Discovery" by announcing Spanish priority in what became the state of Virginia, the putative birth-place of the nation. Greenhow committed a scholarly act of suppression, entered into the official U.S. historical record over a century after the publication of González de Barcia's history—and in doing so, I argue, he was closing up legal loopholes, actively obscuring the historical evidence of a Spanish settlement that preceded the English on Virginia soil. The trajectory of Greenhow's scholarly career—which includes his duplicitous political use of Edgar Allan Poe's unfinished novel *The Journal of Julius Rodman*—brings to the foreground the geopolitical stakes of the story of Don Luis at a particular moment when U.S.-indigenous and international relations dramatically converged with the U.S. Supreme Court case of *Johnson v. M'Intosh* and its reconfiguration of the early modern doctrine of discovery. Don Luis's reappearance in two later nineteenth-century texts—William Cullen Bryant's *A Popular History of the United States* and Alice Fletcher's *Indian Education and Civilization,* the official, congressional report that underwrote the Dawes Act of 1887—recasts the Ajacán narrative as Anglo-America's primal, counterfactual, nationalist fantasy: the origination of a Spanish-American United States that might have prevailed. The chapter concludes by exploring the work of two contemporaneous Omaha translators, Susette La Flesche Tibbles and her half-brother Francis La Flesche, who knew Fletcher and her work, who witnessed the massive expropriation of indigenous lands before and after the passage of the Dawes Act, and who responded to the series of Native erasures at the heart of nineteenth-century historical thought. Tibbles's writing undertook a pointed analysis of the relationship between settler colonialism and the Dawes allotment agenda, while La Flesche began a series of anthropological studies that emphasized the epistemological limits of the project of ethnology, and particularly its problematic dependence upon translation. Tracing a history of Western misapprehension of indigenous religious philosophy from the era of colonial missionaries through the emergence of anthropology as a discipline, Francis La Flesche worked ultimately to create a scholarly legacy for future indigenous intellectuals by producing anthropology specifically as a means of Native knowledge production.

Turning from the Dawes Act of the nineteenth century to the context of the U.S. South and U.S.-Latin American relations in the twentieth, Chapter 6 explores two literary works about English versus Spanish colonial priority produced during the era of Franklin D. Roosevelt's Good Neighbor Policy: Paul Green's symphonic drama, *The Lost Colony*, first staged in 1937; and a 1942 novel that I suggest responded sharply to Green's play, James Branch Cabell's *The First Gentleman of America*—a now little-known work that features Don Luis as its protagonist. Both texts take up the colonial history venerated by Greenhow, and both rewrite historical instances of unsettlement as foundational stories of "America," or U.S. national emergence from the perspective of the U.S. South. Both emerge from a historical tradition in crisis, marked by the logical impasse of conflicting state, regional, and national self-representations, when the meaning of the U.S. South was defined by its new, uncanny twin: the hemispheric South to which the former slaveholding states had once looked longingly as a source of extended power, but with which they were now inextricably intertwined by the Great Depression, a legacy of military occupation, and the hotly contested idea of a shared Western Hemisphere history. As this final chapter shows, *The Lost Colony* articulates colonial Roanoke as the antithesis of Virginia, as the true (North Carolinian) colonial origin of the U.S. nation, and, finally, as the tragic site of a Spanish atrocity that sharply differentiates the histories of the English and Spanish Americas and the U.S. South from its hemispheric counterpart. Cabell's *The First Gentleman of America*, published within weeks of the U.S. entrance into World War II in late 1941, enacts a broad investigation and rebuttal of the "Western Hemisphere Idea" itself. For Cabell stages his recovery and retelling of Don Luis's story as an ironic encroachment of the hemispheric South upon the historical consciousness of the U.S. "Old South," whereby twentieth-century Virginians are asked to come to terms with their hispanophone, indigenous forebear—and to celebrate his act of unsettlement as a triumph over the Spanish, a victory that left "America" free, after settlement by the English, to become Anglo- rather than Latin America.

This final iteration of the story of Don Luis de Velasco appeared just two years after the first English-language publication of Ernest Renan's now-classic essay "What is a Nation?" in 1939. "Forgetting," Renan famously wrote, "is an essential factor in the creation of a nation and it is for this reason that the progress of historical studies often poses a threat to nationality." Perhaps this explains why, in both Cabell's meticulously researched historical novel and his later writings about colonial history, he argues explicitly that the story he tells must be forgotten for the sake of U.S. national coherence, and he slyly predicts (and arguably ensures) what he calls the "Flight into Oblivion" of his historical protagonist, Don Luis. *The Unsettlement of America* aims to understand this history of forgetting on multiple levels—historical, narrative, and disciplinary—and to bring back from "oblivion" and across hundreds of years of mistranslation this extraordinary Native interpreter from the sixteenth century. As I suggest in the epilogue, the story of Don Luis de Velasco brings the early modern Native hemisphere into critical relation with our contemporary transnational one—and in doing so ultimately unsettles the foundations of U.S. territoriality itself.

{ PART I }

The Methods and the Story

Mistranslation and Unsettlement

On October 14, on the island that he has just named San Salvador, Columbus kidnaps a group of seven Taíno Indians to serve as translators. For Columbus, this abduction is an act of significant forethought, registering his intention that these captives "inquire and inform . . . about things in these parts"—a first step toward the subjugation of all the inhabitants of San Salvador, who might one day be "taken to Castile or held captive" on the island if Ferdinand and Isabella see fit to order it so.[1] The taking of these indigenous translators in 1492 has been no less momentous for contemporary scholarship, perhaps especially in early modern English and American literary studies: in the year of the Columbian Quincentenary, Stephen Greenblatt memorably called it "the primal crime in the New World . . . committed in the interest of language"; Eric Cheyfitz concurs that "translation was, and still is, the central act of European colonization and imperialism in the Americas."[2] The concept of translation as an imperial instrument was as commonplace in Columbus's day—when the fifteenth-century Castilian grammarian Antonio de Nebrija famously observed that "Language has always been the companion of empire"—as it is in our own.[3] The controversial thesis of Tzvetan Todorov's *The Conquest of America* proceeded directly from Nebrija's famous dictum, and while Todorov's argument regarding the inferiority of indigenous modes of communication has been almost universally repudiated, his assumptions about the imperial reach of translation have continued to limit our thinking in important ways.[4]

The first two chapters in Part I of this book each address this critical inheritance in different ways. Chapter 2 will introduce the book's central figure, Don Luis, who deployed translation to lay the groundwork for an act of unsettlement that would shape the history of North America for decades to come. The current chapter, on the other hand, returns to the scene of Columbus's primal linguistic crime to consider its role within an alternative origins story.[5] How we frame and comprehend this canonical episode has obvious bearing on how we write the early American literary past, for Columbus's writings inaugurate the Western record of a now largely anonymous body of Native translators engaged in the acquisition and inter-indigenous dissemination of diplomatic knowledge and political expertise regarding the hemisphere and the early Atlantic world. The network of intellectual production and transmission adumbrated by these Native translators has been easy to overlook precisely because of the continued critical perception that *The Unsettlement of America* aims, in part, to call into question: the understanding of translation in the colonial American context solely as an imperial tool.[6] If Columbus violates the "rhetorical sovereignty" of the Native captives, to use Scott Lyons's term, denying "the inherent right and ability of peoples to determine their own communicative needs and desires in the pursuit of self-determination," much contemporary scholarship unwittingly repeats that denial by misrecognizing these captives' use of translation to engage in acts of political diplomacy on behalf of a self-determining people—and thereby to set "at least some of the terms of the debate."[7] Our dominant scholarly narratives of colonial settlement in the early Americas are intimately tied to this critical misrecognition. Working against it is a first step toward recovering the history of American unsettlement that is the subject of this book, for it throws into relief a pattern of memorializing instances of supposedly "successful" translation—in which translation purportedly yields knowledge or information with accuracy—while tacitly forgetting or marginalizing those instances in which translation explicitly fails.

The distinction between successful and failed projects of translation is, of course, an artificial and unstable one—as demonstrated by a venerable genealogy of translation studies, running from Walter Benjamin through the contemporary work of Susan Bassnett, Lawrence Venuti, Emily Apter, Edwin Gentzler, and others.[8] Yet even in the field of translation studies—a field until recently nearly invisible to American literary history, as Kirsten Silva Gruesz has observed—there is an unfortunate tendency to bracket out the important insights of contemporary translation theory when attending to the history of indigenous interpreters in the colonial Americas, as if the role of hermeneutic subject were somehow naturally restricted to the translator of texts and not available to the speaking interpreter.[9] The Spanish term for "interpreter" in the context of the colonial Americas was less often the masculine *intérprete* than the feminine *lengua*, which implied this very restriction of hermeneutic agency, reducing the intellectual work of the indigenous translator to the synecdochal, corporeal, and implicitly gendered role of the tongue. "La lengua," Hernán Cortés notoriously wrote of his interpreter Malintzin or La Malinche, "es una india desta tierra" ("the tongue . . . is a female Indian of this land").[10] This was all Cortés had to say about the multilingual woman who translated Nahua into Mayan and, later, his own Castilian language, making it possible for him to communicate with a complex Aztec bureaucracy. Contemporary scholarship can often be similarly reductive. When indigenous interpreters in the colonial American context become the object of analysis, the critical focus of translation studies seems to narrow rapidly, reducing these translators either to victims of "historically specifiable acts of translative violence" or to romanticized facilitators of Native-European harmony.[11] The latter formulation is a particular staple of the proleptic U.S. storyline, emphasizing as it does "the country's debt to Amerindian translators and interpreters"—a debt exemplified by the story of Squanto who, as one translation theorist puts it, though "initially the victim of a British kidnapping, seemed to forgive the horror of his abduction [and] helped to negotiate a treaty between the Pilgrims and the Massasoit Indians, which led to over fifty years of peaceful coexistence."[12] So powerful is the colonial American model of "successful" translation, in other words, that it reasserts itself even in the scholarly realm that has been most dedicated to dismantling the concept of the transparently faithful or accurate translation in the literate and literary contexts.

In this chapter, I approach the colonial American literary past by recovering the evidence of what I am calling "motivated mistranslation" rather than assuming the default of either its "successful"—or even merely misunderstood—counterpart.[13] The resultant readings evince a range of conceptual frames for approaching the story of Don Luis (told at length in Chapter 2), and for the difficult and complex project of apprehending the unsettlement of America—including what we might take to be the origins story of this alternative history, which I elaborate in the chapter's first section by offering a speculative reading grounded not in Columbus's own narrow construal of translation as an instrument of (European) empire but instead in a series of motivated mistranslations actively dispatched by that collective of indigenous interpreters he regarded as his to control. This framework of motivated mistranslation, I argue, helps in making a decisive shift in focus from the particular cultural perspectives of disparate Native groups in specific places and times to broader questions about the production and circulation of Native knowledge in this era.

The second section turns to a range of indigenous translators to explore what the discourse of translational mastery hides, beginning with John Smith's invention of Pocahontas as a figure of interpretive fidelity and a simultaneous narrative distraction from the unspoken story of his own flight from the English to the Indians. The third section explores one of Smith's textual predecessors, the Spanish captive Juan Ortiz, as portrayed by the anonymous sixteenth-century Portuguese officer known as the Fidalgo d'Elvas or Gentleman of Elvas and the contemporaneous Peruvian mestizo historian El Inca Garcilaso de la Vega. Comparing their two accounts clarifies the distinction between autonomous and heteronomous systems of translation while bringing to the foreground the network of indigenous translators that the discourse of translational mastery, as inaugurated by Columbus, attempts to occlude. The final section reconsiders the pedagogical story of Squanto and the Pilgrims in light of the chapter's larger focus on mistranslation and unsettlement. Attending here to the Iberian dimensions of this indigenous translator's career, I introduce the speculative historical figure of "hispanophone Squanto"—a subject who disrupts the Pilgrim story of translative fidelity to the English while providing an interpretive frame for the book's subsequent chapters.

Columbus and La Navidad: A Parable of Unsettlement

Any reading of Columbus's writings must begin by acknowledging their vastly mediated nature. As Margarita Zamora has shown, Columbus's letters concerning his first voyage are most likely "distillations" that he made from his own *diario* or logbook, "that is, products of Columbus reading himself."[14] Moreover, Columbus's original *diario* is long lost; what survives today comes to us through verbatim passages recorded in a biography written by Hernando Colón, Columbus's son, and in a paraphrase, which also includes some direct quotations, written by the Dominican friar Bartolomé de las Casas, who owned a copy of Columbus's original.[15] Neither of these purveyors of Columbus could be called neutral. Hernando, as Zamora reminds us, likely "ransacked" the *diario* for those passages that would help to consolidate the most heroic possible version of his father's experiences in the Americas.[16] Las Casas, meanwhile, sought to subordinate the "mercantilistic and imperialistic" elements of Columbus's original text to its self-conscious "idealistic and poetic" elements, transforming it into a "coherent Christian discourse" through a paraphrase that might more properly be termed an interpretive revision (62).

These issues of mediation have long raised questions about methodology that attend all interpretations of colonial sources but that are especially perplexing in the case of Columbus. After all, Columbus—by his own account, in the highly mediated version of that account that we now have— continually controls the flow of information to his own shipmates, and certainly follows this practice as well when it comes to what he chooses to record and not to record in the *diario* and his letters. How, then, are contemporary scholars to make inferences about the past given that we have only mediated access to what Columbus actually wrote about his experiences—and given that Columbus's writing, behind this veil of mediation, was also a highly self-aware performance intended for the Catholic monarchs and ultimately wider publication? While I can of course claim no more privileged access than anyone else to what happened during Columbus's first voyage—and even less to the historical intentions of Columbus's Native guides and interpreters—I would suggest that the opacity of the Columbian textual legacy may, in the case of the reading that I advance here, be evidence of plausibility rather than an interpretive limitation. This reading diametrically opposes the explicit interests of all the parties who had a direct authorial hand in shaping the record we have of the first voyage: Columbus, Las Casas, and Hernando Colón all had different but overlapping rhetorical agendas in their writing, none of which draw support from what I will argue is the basic subtext of unsettlement that underwrites the extant citations and redactions of the original logbook—and yet, as I hope to show, that subtext is there *despite* the overwhelmingly manufactured story told in the existing record.

For even through the opacity of its layers and the interests of those who have shaped our record of it, Columbus's logbook reveals something rather startling: that quite soon after he has committed the foundational kidnapping of the seven Taíno Indians, it is the abducted interpreters-in-the-making who are themselves directing the supposed voyage of discovery. Indeed, when Columbus is unsure in what direction to proceed, he turns to his indigenous captives, who purportedly tell him, "by signs that there were so very many [islands] that they were numberless. And they named by their names more than a hundred."[17] If Columbus's ability to understand the captives must necessarily be viewed with skepticism, it is nevertheless also clear that these captive translators present him from the beginning with an overwhelming stream of information that proves singularly unhelpful, even to the extent of obstructing the voyage's further progress. And when Columbus finally sails to Santa María de la Concepción, he does so specifically because, as the *Diario* records it, "these men that I have had taken . . . kept telling me that there they wear very large bracelets of gold" (79). Whether or not he has understood the words of his translators, Columbus has followed the signed indications of their directions, and continues to do so throughout the remainder of the voyage.

Even so, by the time of their arrival at Santa María, Columbus loses some confidence in his interpreters: "I well believe that all they were saying [of gold bracelets] was a ruse in order to flee" (79). Already, then, the possibility of motivated misinformation on the interpreters' part haunts the larger project of translation for which the seven captives have been detained. Columbus himself can envision only a very limited horizon of possibilities for evaluating the information supplied by his interpreters: they are lying, he reasons, simply because they are seeking to escape. The logic here is clearly retroactive, for while the ship anchors off Santa María, two of the San Salvadoran translators jump overboard and make their way ashore. Yet the successful flight of these two interpreters is followed by several events that not only belie Columbus's logic but also call into question the unidirectionality of imperial translation itself. After the San Salvadoran translators have escaped on the island of Santa María, where they have presumably communicated their experience in captivity, a new Native interlocutor draws alongside the ship in a canoe. Columbus understands the event as another capture and decides to use the opportunity of this unplanned abduction to stage a release that will win the Spaniards good favor with the Amerindians (81). It never seems to occur to him that this purported captive might have a tactical motive of his own—*raison d'État*—for being on the ship. Columbus plies him with gifts, sends him back ashore, watches as he reunites with the Natives of Santa María, and then imputes to the former captive a point of view that he believes himself to have generated and manipulated:

> He considered it a great marvel, and indeed it seemed to him that we were good people and that the other man who had fled had done us some harm and that for this we were taking him with us. And the reason that I behaved in this way toward him, ordering him set free and giving him the things mentioned, was in order that they would hold us in this esteem, so that . . . the natives will receive [us] well. And everything that I gave him was not worth four *maravedís*. (80–83)

So satisfied is Columbus with his dissimulation, and with what he imagines to be his control of an unequal exchange, that both he and his future readers lose sight of the obvious: Columbus's Native interlocutors share his desire to create a diplomatic impression, to manipulate cross-cultural perception in order to shape the course of future political events.

En route to the next island, Fernandina, Columbus's ship is approached again by a lone canoe. This time a Native mediary virtually offers himself as a potential translator: "He came up to the ship and I had him enter, which was what he asked" (85). By this point, the initial European act of kidnapping has become something else entirely: a diplomatic engagement initiated by an indigenous agent who has his own politico-linguistic interests. Columbus nevertheless clings to the unidirectional model of statecraft, outlining a plan to carry this new voyager to Fernandina and "give him all of his belongings in order that, through good reports of us . . . the natives will give us of all that they may have" (85). Even when Columbus observes that his new interlocutor is carrying two Spanish *blancas*—"because of which I recognized that he was coming from . . . San Salvador" (85)—his powers of induction still do not extend to their logical conclusion: the mediary has been shadowing the movement of the ship, traveling with a foreign currency, and has reasons of his own for boarding the vessel.

Columbus cannot see this, and neither can much contemporary scholarship: both suffer from what Craig Womack notes are peculiar "forms of myopia that undermine sociopolitical sovereignty."[18] But once we recognize every small engagement of these Native interlocutors as a political act of diplomacy premised on self-determination, key details in Columbus's story begin to appear in a different light. Consider an earlier scene from the voyage as Columbus explores eastern San Salvador. Coasting along the shore, the ship is hailed by large groups of San Salvadoran Natives, who come down to the beach calling and offering water and food to the famished voyagers. Columbus, however, soon becomes "afraid, seeing a big stone reef that encircled that island all around" (75); the waters near this part of San Salvador are treacherous for porting. But more dangerous to Columbus is his failure to recognize that the Indians' gesturing, their communication of apparent hospitality in summoning the Spaniards toward the reef, may require more than a literal interpretation. Before he has even encountered their words, Columbus has already failed to imagine that the diplomacy of the San Salvadorans, like all international diplomacy involving a potentially dangerous opponent, deploys the appearance of social niceties to effect underlying strategy. As the voyage continues, Columbus's inability to conceive of a Native interest in manipulating the flow of information—to apprehend the multidirectionality of diplomacy that underlies all translation in this milieu—will continually distort his view of what is actually occurring as the voyage pursues an ultimately fruitless itinerary in search of gold, back and forth from Cuba to Hispaniola, "according to the indications that these Indians that I have give me" (109).

Nowhere is this more apparent than during the occasion of Columbus's founding of La Navidad, the first European settlement in the Americas. The precise location of this settlement remains unknown, though archeologists continue to search for it in Haiti, near the northern coast where one of Columbus's ships was wrecked in December 1492, catalyzing his decision to build a fort using the remains of the vessel. The *Diario* blames the wreck on a disobedient steersman who left the helm to a ship boy against the Admiral's express orders, with disastrous consequences. But later in the logbook Columbus inadvertently suggests a different explanation for the wreck when he introduces Guacanagarí, the "king" of that part of the island, "who on [the previous] Saturday had sent to invite and beg [Columbus] to come with the ships to his harbor" (279). In this version of events, Columbus appears to have been deliberately approaching the island—and to have been responding to Guacanagarí's summons. Whether or not this "king," like the hospitality-proffering Natives of San Salvador, deliberately gave directions that guided the vessel onto the reef, the *Diario* registers a hint of reproach toward Guacanagarí simply by recording his fervent invitation.

Columbus understood the founding of La Navidad to be no less momentous than the kidnapping of the first seven Taíno translators. As Columbus's son, Hernando Colón, explains in his biography of his father, it seemed to the Admiral

that God had permitted [the shipwreck] to happen that he might make a settlement there and leave the Christians who traded and gained information about the country and its inhabitants, learning their language and making conversation with that village, so that when he returned there from Spain with reinforcements, he would have someone to guide him in all that was required for the settling and subjugation of the land.[19]

On his return to Spain from the West Indies, Columbus made careful notations about the location of La Navidad—and not only for his own convenience. The notes had a symbolic purpose and were meant for a wider audience; as Hernando put it, "The Admiral judged it appropriate to mention these landmarks in order to make known the location of the first settlement and Christian land that was founded in this Western world."[20] In his own famous letter from the first voyage, dated February 15, 1493, Columbus announced with fanfare, "In this [island of] Hispaniola, I have taken possession of a large town which is most conveniently situated for the goldfields . . . and have built a fort there."[21] It is perhaps his most profound act of colonial nomination during an entire voyage based on this linguistic process: "I have named this town Villa de Navidad."[22]

Despite the prestige Columbus invested in this site, few university students today could readily identify La Navidad as the first European settlement in the Americas: one that, in Hernando's words, included a fortress along with "thirty-nine men, with many trading goods and provisions, arms and artillery, with the ship's boat, and carpenters, caulkers, and with all the rest necessary for comfortably making a settlement, namely, a physician, a tailor, a gunner, and other such persons."[23] Students often know the names of Columbus's ships—the *Santa María*, the *Pinta*, and the *Niña*—but in my experience they have rarely heard of the "first settlement " and Christian town, the earliest American colony, the original "lettered city" of the imperial imagination, to use Ángel Rama's phrase.

Why? Because La Navidad was gone when Columbus returned in 1493. In the account of Diego Álvarez Chanca, a physician on the second voyage, First Discovery becomes Southern Gothic as the ship arrives at Hispaniola.[24] The Spaniards find two corpses near the bank of the river, and two more bodies upstream, and their ship is followed by a canoe of Amerindians who row away at their approach. Columbus orders the lombards (or smoothbore cannons) to be fired in hope of summoning the Spaniards, but "they never responded."[25] The next day, Columbus searches the land and finds the fort "burned and destroyed."[26] Only now will Columbus and his men accept what they have already been told by one of their captive indigenous interpreters, now a seasoned transatlantic voyager who has the information through his own channels of transmission: that the settlers at La Navidad are "all . . . dead," destroyed by those whom Columbus had earlier pronounced "the most timorous people in the world."[27] Their translator in chains, now fluent in Spanish, has known the violent ending for some unspecified stretch of time, perhaps even since the founding of La Navidad—but so unsettling is this outcome of the first American settlement that, as Chanca puts it, "we had not believed it."[28]

With this unnamed transatlantic interpreter as its initial narrator, the demise of La Navidad offers a kind of origins story for the unsettlement of America, one of many such episodes consigned to relative oblivion by the history of those privileged, "successful" settlements that tend to organize our narratives of early (and especially North) American literary history: Jamestown, Plymouth, Massachusetts Bay, Rhode Island, and paradoxically even (as we shall see in Chapter 6) the so-called Lost Colony of Roanoke. To elaborate unsettlement in its fullest implications, however, requires a reparative approach to a written colonial archive that we think we already know.[29] For the exclusionary historical disposition of this archive is itself a powerful lens onto what Diana Taylor has called the "repertoire" of subaltern history, suggesting that the occluded history of indigenous knowledge production will become more visible when we reconsider scenes of imperial translation as moments of strategic and motivated mistranslation underwriting a *longue durée* of American unsettlement. In approaching this long history, I am less interested in establishing change and continuity over time than in the possibilities of what Susan Gillman calls reading "adaptively": recognizing both "the incommensurability of languages" as they are translated across and within national borders and the "simultaneously present" quality of the disparate historical and political contexts each iteration carries with it. Such an approach eschews what is merely the "putative neutrality of comparison as a method," as Russ Castronovo and Gillman note, in favor of asking how mistranslation itself might help us to envision the "radical temporality" inherent in narratives of unsettlement as they are told and retold across times and places, as well as the mutually constituting relationship of provisionality and contingency that Robert Levine observes between the past and the present.[30]

For all of these reasons, we need to reimagine the role of indigenous interpreters—and the early American literary history in which they are recorded—within the "translation zone," to borrow Emily Apter's phrase, where translation and mistranslation alike become "means of repositioning the subject in the world and in history."[31] Such a focus will necessarily bring transatlantic and hemispheric approaches into dialectical relation, rather than privileging one by occluding the other.[32] At the same time, putting unsettlement at the front and center of such a reconstellated literary history speaks as well to the recent emphasis in Native American studies on the "outernational" or global dimensions of Indian history and culture, in which U.S. literary history becomes a relatively short-lived part of a "longer and larger continental history that is by definition predominately Native American."[33] Mistranslation and unsettlement formed vital parts of the history of the "Red Atlantic," as Jace Weaver has termed it—a space formed by the movement of "Native ideas, resources, and peoples themselves travel[ing] the Atlantic with regularity and [becoming] among the most basic defining components of Atlantic cultural exchange"—and thus also contribute to both what Robert Warrior has aptly termed "Native intellectual trade routes," and what Sean Kicummah Teuton has called the "international imaginary" produced by "indigenous cosmopolitanism."[34] Such perspectives clarify the extent to which Columbus's interpreters—those who escaped, those who remained in chains, those who survived the voyage to Spain and back—participated in a process of transatlantic discovery and exchange that was not simply Native-European but inter-indigenous, as the translators and would-be translators traveled from island to island, and from the Americas to the European contact zones created by their arrival in Spain. From the moment they were directing the course of Columbus's voyage off Hispaniola, these translators were both forming and participating in an inter-indigenous and hemispheric network of knowledge production whose contours and implications even such compromised texts as the *Diario* may help us discern.

Treasonous Translators, Interpretive Infidelity, and the Unsettling Captivity of John Smith

It has been said that oblivion is the fate of the translator, who, in most accounts, must play second fiddle, whether to critics and literary authors or to the agents of foreign policy.[35] But if the long-held critical tendency to view translation as a second-order form of aesthetic and political work often consigns the figure of the translator to obscurity, our early American literary and historical narratives have been shaped, as I have been suggesting, by the equally pervasive problem of remembering and privileging ostensibly "successful" translation at the expense of those episodes during which motivated mistranslation shapes the historical outcome of events. In the early American field, our histories have tended to focus primarily upon the translational labor of indigenous figures such as Pocahontas, who served as her father's emissary between the Powhatan people and the settlers in Jamestown, and whose marriage to John Rolfe secured a diplomatic peace between the Indians and the English; or her New England counterpart, Squanto, the Patuxet Indian who served as a translator and diplomat between the Wampanoags and the Pilgrims, and who became the future Native hero of what is now the national Thanksgiving story; or Sacajewea, the Shoshone "interpretess" who accompanied Lewis and Clark across thousands of miles, brokering peace with the Indians during their dangerous journey to the Pacific. The prominence of female interpreters and the implied role of gender in the Anglophone myth of successful translation are as clearly discernible as is the feminine status of the Spanish term *lengua*. Indeed, the historiographical privileging of the feminized and ostensibly successful work of translation occurs in the wider, hemispheric American context as well: colonial Mexican history offers a central if often vilified place to Malintzín or La Malinche, Cortés's Nahua translator and the mother of his child, without whose translative services, some have argued, he could not have conquered Mexico. But it does not always bother to remember Melchorejo and Julianillo, the two male Mayan interpreters who apparently obstructed the Spaniards' attempts at communication during the Juan de Grijalba expedition until one of them died and the other managed to run away.[36]

Similarly, while the Pocahontas, Squanto, and Sacajawea stories have endured in the American imagination, re-emerging with particular clarity in certain historical moments—the Pocahontas story achieved unprecedented popularity just after the Civil War, for example—countless other indigenous interpreters have been forgotten.[37] These are the "treasonous translators," to adapt the old but still provocative Italian adage, whose plotlines of *traduttore, traditore* tend to go nowhere in most historical narratives because they disturb the unspoken premise of successful translation that has been indispensable in shoring up the evidentiary claims of national history and its central, foregone conclusion: the putatively inevitable settlement of America. Their names remain, like La Navidad, far less familiar, if remembered at all.

Francisco de Chicora, for example, was the baptismal name given to a Native man who was kidnapped from his southeastern homeland in what are now the Carolinas during the mid-sixteenth century and brought to Hispaniola, where he learned Spanish and practiced Christianity. He traveled to Spain and gave extended testimony about the Catawba Indians to the great Italian chronicler of the New World, Peter Martyr, and he entranced the Spanish court with a detailed account of his place of origin and its mineral riches and agricultural abundance. Francisco de Chicora's narrative would endure across generations of Spaniards eager to find wealth to the north of Mexico; it also enabled him to accompany Lucas Vázquez de Allyón, the Auditor of Santo Domingo, as the translator for a major colonial venture back to his homeland in 1526, which led to the founding of San Miguel de Gualdape, the first European settlement in what is now the United States— and another forgotten place. Allyón brought with him 600 Spanish colonists and a large supply of African labor—one that predated the fateful arrival of slaves in Jamestown by almost a century. Like La Navidad, however, the settlement was doomed—at the first landfall, Francisco de Chicora's translational work ended before it began when he fled back to the Catawba Natives. As a translator, he disappears at this point from the Spanish historical record, but the ensuing failure of the colony within three months marks his abiding if unspoken place there: the Catawba staged a collective project of unsettlement at San Miguel de Gualdape, and the enslaved Africans soon seized their own freedom and fled, like the translator Francisco de Chicora before them, to the interior.[38]

Decades later, the Roanoke Indian known as Wanchese offered his translational services to the English when they attempted to create their first New World
colony in present-day North Carolina. Wanchese traveled to London in the
late sixteenth century, helped Thomas Harriot learn the Algonquian language,
returned with 100 English colonists in 1586, and quickly upended the project of
imperial translation he had appeared to be sustaining while abroad; taking with
him the newfound knowledge of the colonizers gained in their metropolis, he
abandoned the colony and began waging strategic attacks against it. His com-
patriot Manteo stayed on with the English as an apparently faithful interpreter
and guide, but as with all translation—and mistranslation—only the translator
knows where his or her true fidelity lies. Roanoke, too, followed the way of La
Navidad, becoming the first English story of unsettlement.[39]

Early in the next century, Epenow, a Nauset Indian from Massachusetts,
also became a translator after learning English in London. His captivity had
begun in 1611 when he was abducted by an English slave trader, Captain
Edward Harlow, along with twenty-nine other Nauset Natives, off what is now
Martha's Vineyard. Harlow had hoped to sell his prisoners as slaves in Spain,
but they wound up in London instead, where Epenow met a Native captive
from Maine, Assacumet, who had been seized in 1605, and who spoke a language in the same Eastern Algonquian linguistic family. Epenow began to
learn English from Assacumet, which pleased the London promoters of colonization with whom they had both been placed; as the English colonial en-
trepreneur Sir Ferdinando Gorges noted in *A Briefe Narration of the Original
Undertakings of the Advancement of Plantations into the Parts of America*
(1622), Epenow could soon speak to his audience, bidding them "Welcome!
Welcome!" when he was circulated throughout the city as a New World
human curiosity—a source of cheap wonder later glossed by Shakespeare
in *The Tempest* and *Henry VIII*.[40] But Epenow and Assacumet were generating more than the linguistic skills needed to enhance the colonial spectacle for which they were recruited. They were simultaneously participating
in an emergent network of indigenous knowledge production, and quickly
apprehending the specific discursive context within which they could shape
the course of future events: the language of mineral wealth. When Epenow
described the presence of a goldmine in what is now Martha's Vineyard, and
proposed his own linguistic services to support an expedition there, he transformed himself from a slave and a human exhibit into an interpreter and diplomatic agent. Gorges agreed to sponsor the translator's voyage home in 1614.
Epenow's first interpretive act was to arrange his own escape under a cover
of arrows launched by the Wampanoags—and this was only his preliminary
step in the larger project of thwarting English settlement in the surrounding
Massachusetts islands over the next decades.[41]

If we take Melchorejo and Julianillo, Francisco de Chicora, and Wanchese,
Assacumet and Epenow, not as exceptional figures of *traduttore, traditore* but

as our assumed model for such interpreters' use of motivated mistranslation in colonial diplomatic contexts—in which, even when captive or otherwise coerced, indigenous translators may be simultaneously working on behalf of self-determining peoples—then even the most familiar stories of settlement begin to disclose a counternarrative hinging precisely upon unsettlement. Consider the celebrated story of Pocahontas's rescue of John Smith, which he dramatically recounts in the third book of the *Generall Historie* (1624), and which deploys the paradigm of "successful" translation to occlude and distort in a variety of ways. Skeptical readers since at least the nineteenth century have considered the episode an invention, not least because of its complete absence from the first and therefore presumably less constructed account that Smith wrote of his captivity in *A True Relation* (1609); some contemporary anthropologists have sought to validate but recast the rescue scene as a Powhatan intercultural adoption ceremony, misunderstood and thus misrepresented by Smith himself.[42] But perhaps a better way of understanding the disparity between Smith's two accounts of his experience with the Powhatan Indians is to recognize the emergence of transparent translation in the later text as the master signifier of Smith's self-transformation, through the story of his captivity, into an ideal colonizer—one who, while writing from London, hopes very much for a future assignment in Virginia. Pocahontas's rescue of Smith does not merely anoint him as the chivalric hero of his own story; it also performs the narrative sleight of hand that distracts from the unsettling problem at his story's heart—his flight from the English to the Indians—by reconsolidating his story as a captivity narrative.

The potential European trajectory toward indigeneity was indeed more unsettling to the colonial *narrative* project than either the explicit or implied indigenous thwarting of settlement. After all, there were many English runaways from Jamestown—and they were not only fleeing the colony, but actively *seeking* life among the Indians. As George Percy noted in *A Trewe Relacyon* (1612), "To eate many our men this starveinge Tyme did Runn Away unto the Salvages whome we never heard of after"—and, like Smith, they were vilified in their absence: "dyvrs . . . men beinge Idile and not willeinge to take paynes did Runne Away unto the Indyans many of them beinge taken ageine [the Governor] in A moste severe mannor cawsed to be executed."[43] The phenomenon of English settlers who chose and sought life among the Indians presents a radically alternate plotline within the story of Anglo-American colonization, one that is never fully acknowledged or fleshed out in colonial writings themselves—or for that matter in most of our histories of the period.[44] But it is a plotline that nevertheless reappears periodically in the literature before its unsettling implications are glossed over or quickly contained. In Smith's foundational narrative of Indian captivity, it is Pocahontas who achieves the suppression of this plotline—first introduced in Smith's 1608 *A True Relation of Such Occurrences and accidents of noate as hath happened in Virginia*—by embodying subsequently, in his 1624 *Generall Historie of Virginia, New England, and the Summer Isles,* a figure of successful translation.

Indeed, Smith's first account of his capture—written in 1608 after his return from living with the Powhatan Indians—tells a story almost nonsensical for an experienced military leader: a captain who has canoed miles away from Jamestown suddenly leaving his band of men behind and venturing off alone with his Indian guide "to see the nature of the soile," and not to be heard from again for six weeks. Even his own account of his ensuing Indian "captivity" cannot conceal what is essentially the story of a very hungry man securing food for himself in a new home: as Smith explains of his first days as a prisoner, "a quarter of Venison and some ten pound of bread I had for supper, what was left I reserved for me and sent with me to my lodging. Each morning 3 women presented me with 3 great platters of fine bread, more venison than ten men could devour I had." No wonder that when Smith, perhaps newly robust, appears six weeks later, one day suddenly back in Jamestown and handing off guns to Powhatan's "trusty servant" in an act that might easily be construed by the English as treason, he was greeted with suspicion by many, including the President, who vowed "the next day to have put him to death," like any other runaway.[45]

But by the time Smith writes *The Generall Historie*, published in 1624, he has significantly changed what was initially a rather weak and suspicious story. Indeed, the episode of Pocahontas's rescue provides the narrative hinge between Smith's supposed captivity and his otherwise inexplicable freedom—marking his transformed status from prisoner into new purveyor of valuable cross-cultural knowledge, and therefore ideal colonial leader. Pocahontas herself becomes the central figure for the trajectory of successful translation that Smith will oversee in his new role: whether as her father's emissary, when she brings to Smith "every foure or five days" an utterly transparent message of goodwill from the Powhatan leader—"much provision, that saved many of their lives"—or when, as the king's "dearest jewell," she comes to Smith on "a darke night . . . through the irksome woods," with "the teares running down her cheeks," to betray her father by disclosing the Powhatan plot to destroy Jamestown. The purported content of one message can thus cancel out another; what matters most is the transparency of the translation that Smith has single-handedly secured, which obscures the narrative thread of willing captivity at the heart of his first account.[46]

Perhaps Smith's greatest invention in the *Generall Historie*, then, is not the rescue itself but the process of successful translation that he claims through Pocahontas as an alibi for his own unsettling rejection of the English colony—at least until Powhatan apparently decided to send his English visitor back to Jamestown. This narrative of interpretive fidelity ultimately endows Smith with the translative authority to offer his readers, at the end of Book Two, a glossary of Indian terms "Because many do desire to know the manner of their Language."[47] Though Smith learned what he knew of that language during what was arguably his abandonment of Jamestown for an Indian life, here he offers up the Powhatans' Algonquian words to English readers as one of Virginia's many plentiful resources—and himself as the exemplary purveyor of this new commodity of knowledge.[48] Yet for all his pretense to interpretive mastery, Smith never forgot the originary story of American un-settlement—the demise of La Navidad—that persistently undermines both his own writing and future scholars' claims of imperial translation: as he reminds his readers later in the *Generall Historie*, "Columbus, upon his re-turn from the West-Indies into Spaine, having left his people with the Indies, in peace and promise of good usage amongst them, at his returne backe found not one of them living, but all treacherously slaine by the Salvages."[49]

Autonomous Translation and the Story of Juan Ortiz

Smith's 1624 account of his captivity and rescue is itself, as numerous scholars have observed, a likely translation of sorts—for it bears significant resemblance to the tale of another New World captive who was suppos-edly rescued by an Indian princess: the story of Juan Ortiz, who traveled to Florida as part of the doomed Pánfilo de Narváez expedition in 1527, and who lived among the Indians for a decade until he was discovered by soldiers from the Hernando de Soto expedition of 1539.[50] According to the early sources that tell his story, Ortiz was a captive of the Indian leader known as Ucita and was on the brink of execution by fire when, in a dra-matic turn of the plot, the cacique's daughter intervened on his behalf and persuaded her father to hold the Spaniard as a captive instead of killing him (see Figure 1.1).[51] Later, when Ucita again decided to have Ortiz put to death, the noble daughter apprised him of the danger and, so the story goes, arranged for his escape to a nearby *cacique* who treated him kindly until his recovery by Soto's forces.

Smith—always obsessed with the history of Spanish colonization—prob-ably knew the story of Ortiz's captivity and rescue from a 1557 account authored quasi-anonymously by the Fidalgo de Elvas—or the Gentleman of Elvas, a Portuguese officer who accompanied the Soto expedition—which was later translated into English and published by Richard Hakluyt in 1609.[52] In Hakluyt's version of the Gentleman of Elvas's account, Ortiz becomes an indispensable in-terpreter for Soto after his return to life among Spaniards; indeed, in this version of his story, translation plays the pivotal role upon which the success or failure of an imperial venture turns. So crucial is Ortiz's interpretive role that his death in Chapter 28 leaves Soto literally unable to proceed in his travels: "without an interpretour, hee feared to enter farre into the land, where he might be lost" (89). In his absence, the Spaniards turn to a Native interpreter, "a youth that was

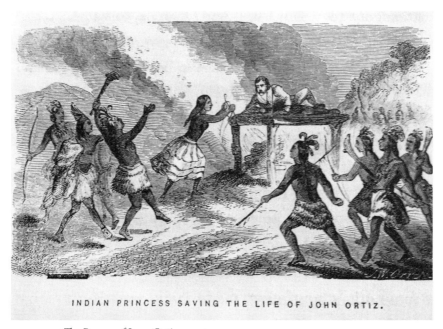

INDIAN PRINCESS SAVING THE LIFE OF JOHN ORTIZ.

FIGURE 1.1 *The Rescue of Juan Ortiz*

Source: From Lambert A. Wilmer's *The life, travels and adventures of Ferdinand de Soto, discoverer of the Mississippi* (Philadelphia: J. T. Lloyd, 1859). Photograph courtesy of State Archives of Florida.

taken in Cutifachiqui did serue for Interpretour, which had by that time learned somewhat of the Christians language"—but with little success:

> The death of Iohn Ortiz was so great a mischeife for the discouering inward, or going out of the land, that to learne of the Indians, that which in foure words hee declared, they needed a whole day with the youth: and most commonly hee vnderstood quite contrarie that which was asked him: whereby it often happened that the way that they went one day, and sometimes two or three daies, they turned backe, and went astray through the wood here and there. (89)

In the terms of translation studies scholar Michael Cronin, the Soto expedition has had to forego an autonomous system of interpreting—where "colonizers [depend upon] their own subjects [to understand] the language or languages of the colonized"—in favor of a heteronomous system, which involves capturing or otherwise employing indigenous interpreters who then learn the imperial language.[53] The results in this case are easy to gauge: imperial translation devolves abruptly into either non-comprehension or deliberate sabotage or, perhaps most likely of all, the latter masked as the former. Whatever the case, the loss of Ortiz means the virtual termination of the venture because, as Hakluyt's Gentleman of Elvas puts it, "by land they could not goe for want of an Interpretour" (108).

But even *before* Ortiz's death, the system of autonomous translation—and, more significantly, the narrative of transparent or successful translation for which Ortiz seems to stand—is insistently dogged by certain interpretive instabilities and failures. In Chapter 20, for example, when Soto is about to carry out the execution of several of his own men who have offended by stealing from Indians, Juan Ortiz intervenes at the request of several senior Spanish officers. He does so, however, not by speaking out against the death sentence but by strategically *mis*translating the testimony of a group of Indians who arrive to lodge a complaint against the condemned men:

> Iohn Ortiz . . . changed their words, and told the Gouernor, that the Cacique said, he had notice how his Lordship held those Christians in prison for his sake and that they were in no fault, neither had they done him any wrong, and that if he would do him any fauour, he should set them free. And he told the Indians; That the Gouernor said, he had them in prison, and that he would punish them in such sort, that they should bee an example to others. Hereupon the Gouernor commanded the prisoners to be loosed. (65)

Though Ortiz is merely following orders in this passage, he is nevertheless also knowingly deceiving—*traduttore, traditore*—both Soto and the complainant group of Indians, and in doing so he thereby raises the possibility of future interpretive betrayals.

More destabilizing than this possibility, however, is the lack of linguistic authority that Ortiz exhibits in key portions of Hakluyt's version of the account. After his escape from Ucita, for instance, Ortiz finds himself again imperiled in the town of the new *cacique*, Mococo, because the languages of the two towns are different, and so the Spaniard "could not tell them who hee was, nor how hee came thither, nor was able to answer anything for himself" (24). The account emphasizes that Ortiz's lack of ability to cross from one indigenous language to the other is not merely an impediment to communication but "so great [a] danger" that it nearly brings his death: when the Indians "vnderstood him not," they "began to compasse him to shoote at him" (24). Ortiz is reduced to hiding in a grove of trees and crying out nonsensically that he is "a Christian, and that he was fled from Vcita"; he is saved in the end only by "an Indian that could speake the language and vnderstood him; and pacified the rest; who told them what hee said" (25).

When the Spaniards recover Ortiz after ten years among the Indians, then, they have not really thereby achieved an autonomous system of interpretation. As the Hakluyt version of the Gentleman of Elvas's account continually makes clear, the Spaniard Ortiz is but one participant in a larger web of primarily inter-indigenous translation without which he would be unable to interpret anything during most of his journey with Soto. Thus, when the Spaniards are leaving the town of Patosa and they discover that they have been betrayed by an Indian youth who had promised to lead them to a new province but who has led them astray, the account notes that Soto cannot dispense with the false guide because, as Hakluyt's Gentleman of Elvas puts its simply, "there was neuer another whom Iohn Ortiz did understand" (41). Ortiz's system of translation is fully heteronomous; without his own indigenous translator, he can neither convey nor comprehend.

Writing decades after the Gentleman of Elvas, the Peruvian mestizo historian El Inca Garcilaso de la Vega also told the story of Juan Ortiz in his 1605 account of the Soto expedition, *La Florida del Inca* (a text I discuss at length in Chapter 3).[54] Where Hakluyt's Gentleman of Elvas strains but ultimately fails to sustain Juan Ortiz's central role in its narrative of successful translation, El Inca Garcilaso appears from the outset to undermine and even to mock the premise of transparent interpretation. In Garcilaso's telling, when Soto and his company first arrive in Florida, they immediately misunderstand an Indian who is trying to tell them about Juan Ortiz's existence in a nearby town because of his "poor pronunciation, added to the worse understanding of the good interpreters who were declaring what he desired to say."[55] But establishing the defective nature of interpretive understanding in this instance is less the point than is the propensity of the Spaniards to believe in the transparency of translation every bit as much as Columbus—and like the Discoverer, to hear in the Indians' words what they want them to say: "As those listening took for principal aim to go in search of gold [*oro*], hearing the Indian [interpreter] say Orotiz, without looking for other declarations understood that plainly he said that in his land there was much *oro*," or gold.[56] The Spaniards themselves ensure the failure of translation here—and, as Lisa Voigt notes, that is part of the Inca's point: failure is built into the psychic machinery of colonial translation.[57]

Like the Gentleman of Elvas, but to an even greater extent, Garcilaso emphasizes the inter-indigenous translational web upon which Ortiz depends entirely. Early on, Garcilaso mentions "four other interpreters" who are traveling with the expedition, and he sometimes refers to a "group of interpreters," "among which was Juan Ortiz"—but as the journey continues so does the growth of the translative chain. "It is to be noted," Garcilaso writes in Book 4, that

> when the Governor arrived at Chicaca, because of the great variety of languages there were, corresponding to the many provinces he had passed through, that almost each one had its language different from another, ten and twelve and fourteen interpreters were necessary in order to speak to the Cacique and the Indians of those provinces: and the messages were passed from Juan Ortiz to the last of the interpreters, who were placed as conduits, in order to receive, and to give the messages to the other, as they were being interpreted from one to another. With this wearisome labor the

Adelantado asked for and received the account of the things that of all that
great land he needed to be informed. (Book 4, Chapter III, 229v).

While the last sentence would seem to declare a process of successful translation, culminating in Soto's reception of the correct information about which
he has asked, the preceding part of the passage unavoidably calls into question the accuracy of the transmitted contents by stressing the multiple sites
of interpretation—ambiguously computed here as "ten and twelve and fourteen"—and thus the possible transformations of the intended messages. El
Inca contrasts the "wearisome labor" of this unstable process, moreover, with
the very different translation system that springs up among the indigenous
captives of the Spaniards:

> This labor was lacking in those particular male and female Indians taken,
> whichever province they were from, by ours for their service: because within
> two months of having communication with the Spaniards they understood
> what their masters said to them in the Castilian language, and they in the
> same language could make themselves understood, that which was oblig-
> atory and most common. And at six months of knowing Spaniards they
> served as interpreters for other new Indians. All showed this ability in the
> language, and for anything whatsoever that they took to be very good, all
> those of this great kingdom of Florida. (Book 4, Chapter III, 229v)

It is not entirely clear why these captive translators, even after they have acquired Spanish, are able to communicate directly with "new Indians" without
means of a translative chain corresponding to the "great variety of languages"
throughout Florida. Yet Garcilaso leaves little room for doubt as to which interpretive system is superior. The final line of the passage, with its sweeping
claim about "all" the Indians of Florida, implies what was probably obvious
to Garcilaso as a multilingual, mestizo historian: that such indigenous interpretive skills were used intermittently and strategically—when it was "[taken]
to be very good," for example—but not necessarily otherwise.[58]

Garcilaso mocks the assumption of successful translation most explicitly,
however, in a much-cited passage from the *Comentarios reales*, his celebrated
history of his home country, first published in 1609. In an extended account
of the origin of the Spanish name for Peru, Garcilaso offers what Zamora
calls his imaginative "reenactment of the first verbal encounter" between
Spaniards and Indians on an early exploratory voyage off the Pacific coast.[59]
Arriving in the new territory, the Spaniards capture an Indian who is fishing
in a river and ask him the name of the land in Castilian and signs:

> The Indian, by the gesticulations and movements of the hands and face [the
> Spaniards] were making at him (as if to a mute) understood that they were
> asking him [something] but did not understand what they were asking,
> and to what he understood [the question to be], he responded quickly

(before they did him some harm) and named his own name, saying Berú, and added another and said Pelú. He meant to say: If you're asking me my name, I'm called Berú; and if you're asking me where I was, I'm saying that I was in the river. . . . The Christians understood according to their desire, imagining that the Indian had understood them and had responded purposefully, as if he and they had been speaking in castilian, and since that time, which was the year 1515 or 16, they have called that richest and grand empire Perú, corrupting both names, as the Spaniards corrupt almost all the words that they take from the language of the Indians of that land. . . . [60]

Garcilaso's basic argument here, as Zamora notes, is that "the Europeans are incompetent interpreters of the language of the Indians."[61] But the account also registers an implied point in its representation of the perspective of the captive Indian, whose purported second response to the Spaniards answers a hardly plausible question—one to which, as he surely understands, the men who have just seized him already know the answer: "if you're asking me where I was . . . I was in the river." To answer a question that he knows has not been asked hints subtly at a form of what Doris Sommer might call a "featherbed resistance" (a forthcoming pose that is not forthcoming) in the Native informant's response to the interrogation—one that belies Garcilaso's insistence that the Quechua-speaking man is telling the Spaniards what he thought they wanted to know, and indeed belies even the premise that "he did not understand what they were asking."[62] The story of the "first" linguistic encounter, after all, is often based on a myth of mutual incomprehension—as in, for example, the apocryphal story of the origin of the name "Canada" as a French deformation of Natives trying to say in Spanish "aca, nada"—there's "nothing here"—to discourage further European interest.[63]

But if "aca, nada" emplots the irony of a diametrically opposed perspective on "discovery," Garcilaso's account has the additional effect of ironizing the Western ethnographic quest for primitive linguistic origins in which he is himself purportedly engaged in this discussion of the word "Peru." For, as his account reminds us, the anthropological investigation itself entails a "denial of coevalness" by failing to see both the potential priority of discovery on the part of the Native interlocutor (the Quechua-speaking man may know enough already about these putatively discovering Spaniards to thwart their line of questioning) and how the very interaction with the Other *in the present* comes to falsely shape the European account of the past.[64] To put it another way, a part of what the Spaniards misrecognize in Garcilaso's scene is the temporality of translation. One of the key ways in which the discourse of Western Discovery first began to protect its own temporal fortress, its own self-modernity, was by masking the often disturbing and ambivalent presence of the translator, as though there were no fissure or gap between the multiplicity of meanings in one language and those in another—while also denying the possibility that the indigenous objects of purported discovery have already constituted themselves as the discoverers.

Hispanophone Squanto

A decade after Garcilaso published the *Comentarios,* the Pilgrims arrived at Plymouth in 1620, ready to engage in what William Bradford called the "discovery of this place" (66). Like any project of discovery, theirs too was upheld by a temporal fortress—but one that experienced an odd affront during their first weeks on land when the very first Native person they encountered turned out to speak English. James Clifford calls this uncanny moment "the Squanto effect," the dislocating experience of arriving in the New World—or at any place ostensibly beyond modernity—only to discover there a Native interlocutor who not only speaks English but already knows, indeed has already discovered, the purported discoverers.[65] But this by no means unusual phenomenon should more properly be called—at least in the Anglophone context—the "Samoset affect." For Samoset is the name of the *first* Indian the Pilgrims met after their arrival in Plymouth—before they met Squanto—and he too already spoke English. It is worth noting that before the Pilgrims met Samoset, they had only glimpsed the Indians of Plymouth who, as Bradford puts it, "came skulking about them, and would sometimes show themselves aloof off, but when any approached near them, they would run away" (79). By the time he wrote *Of Plymouth Plantation*, between 1630 and 1647, Bradford appears to have read these actions as a kind of cowardice, but they also communicate something straightforward in his text: a clear Native refusal of encounter in the absence of a translator. When a translator becomes available, the nature of the communication swiftly changes: "About the 16th of March," writes Bradford, "a certain Indian came boldly amongst them, and spoke to them in broken English, which they could well understand but marveled at it" (79).

The conjunction in the last clause—*but*—is at first perplexing, as it would seem to suggest that the Pilgrims' marveling at Samoset's use of English is unexpected in light of their comprehension of his language—rather than connected to it: as in "they could well understand [*and*] marveled at it." Yet buried in this single conjunction is the story of colonial translation writ large; what it suggests is that the representation of translation that the discourse of Western Discovery has always depended upon has here been momentarily disrupted by Samoset's linguistic performance. Indeed, as Cheyfitz has argued incisively, Western Discovery organized itself since at least Columbus around the "fiction" that the Discoverer will indeed "well understand" the purported Native object of discovery via a practice of translation that is represented as instantaneous and utterly transparent—but most certainly not because the Native interlocutor already speaks the European tongue. The marvel here is not, in other words, that the English "could well understand" Samoset but that Samoset *already* communicates in their language. The Discoverer's representation of translation produces an effect of imperial comprehension—an omniscient point of view that narrates the European-Native encounter—which prepares for the first part of the clause (they could well understand Samoset) but not the second (but they marveled at it—at the fact that he spoke to them in their language). What the "Samoset effect" disturbs, then, is the representation of translation, which empties out the temporality of translation's multidirectional processes, rendering invisible both the initial incommensurability of its interlocutors and the crucial remainder of this incommensurability, which includes both the untranslatable and—most crucial for this study—the possibility of motivated mistranslation.

As Bradford continues to describe the encounter with Samoset, he strains to resume control over the representation of translation that has been disrupted:

> At length they understood by discourse with him, that he was not of these parts, but belonged to the eastern parts where some English ships came to fish, with whom he was acquainted and could name sundry of them by their names, amongst whom he had got his language. He became profitable to them in acquainting them with many things concerning the state of the country in the east parts where he lived, which was afterwards profitable unto them; as also of the people here, of their names, number, and strength, of their situation and distance from this place, and who was chief amongst them. His name was Samoset. He told them also of another Indian whose name was Squanto, a native of this place, who had been in England and could speak better English than himself. (79–80)

What registers most clearly in this passage is Bradford's futile rhetorical struggle to contain the "marvel" of Samoset's "discourse"—which is in no small part his acquisition of English prior to the arrival of the Pilgrims. After clarifying that this English-speaking Native man is out of place—neither indigenous to Plymouth nor indeed "of these parts"—Bradford attempts to recast Samoset's cross-cultural understanding as "profitable" not to the agent of knowledge, Samoset himself, but to the objects of his knowledge—the "sundry" English he "could name." Indeed, Bradford repeats his claim that Samoset was "profitable unto" the prior English arrivals as if to forecast his value to the Pilgrims as a source of knowledge "concerning the state of the country" and, more worrisome, its people—their "names, number . . . strength . . . situation and distance" from the new settlement. Yet compacted into this passage lies a certain narrative reversal that Bradford's account seems unable to control. For Bradford—always a great accountant of information—cannot seem to specify or elaborate upon *any* of these "many things" that Samoset supposedly imparts; instead, we learn only that Samoset brings them Squanto, who has foreign-language skills that surpass his own—and who, having "been in England," already possesses the precise information about the English that the English desire of the Indians.

Squanto's own translative disruption of the Pilgrim story deserves far more scrutiny than it has thus far attracted. As a pedagogical Indian, Squanto, like Pocahontas, has always stood for the transparency and empty time of translation. As Bradford puts it, Squanto "continued with the English . . . and never left them until he died"; he existed on their temporal plane, circumscribed in his role as "their interpreter," and thus "a special instrument of God for their good beyond their expectation" (81). No surprise, then, that today's pedagogical Squanto is an exemplary figure of Anglo-American encounter, symbolizing the wholesome agricultural exchange between English and Indians, the cross-cultural fruits for which we give thanksgiving as a multicultural, and yet (still) ostensibly Anglo-American nation.[66] Yet both these narratives—Bradford's as much as our own national-pedagogical one—elide what Bradford himself also recognized as the essential ambiguity of Squanto's role as a translator, one who "sought his own ends and played his own game," as he famously put it in *Of Plymouth Plantation*, pursuing an agenda that mystified the English settlers in Massachusetts and has since then intrigued subsequent historians.[67] Our national-pedagogical storyline depends as well upon the successful containment of Clifford's "Squanto effect," the unsettling narrative revelation that Squanto always already speaks English, in the sense that he speaks it prior to the Pilgrims' arrival and the instantiation of "American" history, indeed that he has already lived in the metropolis itself, in London. But the most significant erasure upon which the national-pedagogical Squanto depends is of a crucial third term in the transatlantic purview of the translator's geopolitical understanding: the third term of Spain.

Before he was in England, before he spoke English, and long before he came with Samoset to meet the Pilgrims, Squanto had lived in Spain for as many as three years.[68] How do we begin to account for this little-discussed Iberian dimension of the translator's career, to which Bradford makes brief allusion in his first description of Squanto?

> He was a native of this place, and scarce any left alive besides himself. He was carried away with divers others by one Hunt . . . who thought to sell them for slaves in Spain. But he got away for England and was entertained by a merchant in London, and employed to Newfoundland and other parts, and lastly brought hither to these parts by one Mr. Dermer, a gentleman employed by Sir Ferdinando Gorges and others for discovery and other designs in these parts. (81)

Bradford's account deftly encloses Squanto's time in Spain within a narrative trajectory running from the Native's bereft and isolated indigeneity— "scarce any left alive besides himself": a "Last of the Mohicans" story *avant la lettre*—to his productive and fulsome English affiliation. What happens before Squanto's arrival into this English world—starting with the pivotal 1614 event of his abduction from America—is told in abbreviated form and mapped neatly onto a simple moral geography: there is a single villain, "one Hunt," who carries away his "divers other" Indian victims to the malign region of enslavement known as "Spain," which is diametrically opposed to the destination of Squanto's mysterious escape, "England," where he is "entertained," gainfully "employed," and ultimately "brought hither" in a colonial project of "discovery and other designs" implicitly unlike its Spanish counterpart.

It is not surprising to discern here a hint of the Black Legend—the historiographic demonization of Spanish colonial atrocities as a foil for the supposed moderation and temperance of English colonial practices—shaping Bradford's moral opposition of Spain and England.[69] But it is worth noting that this persistent opposition still shapes even contemporary historical narratives of the early modern transatlantic world, in which we find "thousands of American natives labor[ing] in Spain" and "hundreds perish[ing] en route," while in merry England, on the other hand, "many" of such kidnapped Natives "remained," as one historian recently put it, "voluntarily, for months or years . . . befriended by prominent Englishmen and accorded respectful hearings by government officials—even, at least once, by the House of Commons."[70] This is not to dispute the disparate historical trajectories of Spanish and English colonization but, rather, to observe how the legacy of the Black Legend's moral oppositions can produce vastly one-sided conclusions about Native point of view and vested interests. Squanto constitutes a powerful case in point, as I have suggested: contemporary historical accounts continuously assume that he bore "no lasting resentment" for his abduction and therefore sought to aid the English in colonization.[71] A number of recent textbooks venture so far into the realm of moral geography as to assert that Squanto was redeemed from slavery in the dark of Spain by an English rescuer, "freed by an Englishman who took him to London," or "ransomed by a sympathetic Englishman."[72]

But there is in fact no record of how Squanto "got away for England," as Bradford vaguely put it—and both the lack of any would-be rescuer's self-promoting account and Bradford's own grammatical attribution of agency suggest strongly that Squanto found a way to England on his own. By supplying the pedagogical Squanto story with a "sympathetic" English rescuer, such contemporary accounts conveniently counterbalance the villainous Englishman who abducted Squanto in the first place, Thomas Hunt: "a worthlesse fellow of our Nation," as Gorges referred to him, "more savagelike than . . . the poore innocent creatures" he kidnapped (209). As Gorges's characterization makes clear, Hunt—as an Englishman engaged in the transatlantic trade in Native slaves—presents an embarrassing problem for the long-standing narrative opposition of English and Spanish colonial practice.

Perhaps this is why even contemporary historical narratives appear to cast Hunt as a single agent gone rogue, as if he alone managed to induce some twenty-seven Massachusetts Natives onto his ship, and to convey them without incident to Malaga, Spain, where he began to sell them off as slaves. In fact, Hunt was a master of ship serving on an English exploratory mission in the region under the supervision of none other than John Smith—seven years after Smith's ambiguous "captivity" with the Powhatan Indians near Jamestown. When Smith returned to England, so the story goes, he left Hunt in charge of completing a fishing expedition, after which Hunt was supposed to take his wares to Spain for trade. Most histories today suggest that what Hunt did after Smith's departure—the abduction of nearly thirty Natives for intended sale into slavery—was against Smith's wishes and against protocol; certainly Smith distanced himself from Hunt's actions on the grounds that Hunt had "abused the Salvages where hee came, and betrayed twenty seven of these poore innocent soules, which he sould in Spaine for slaves," incurring the Indians' "hate against our Nation."[73] Yet Smith's real problem with the Hunt kidnapping seems to have been that it made his own "proceedings[,] to be so much the more difficult"—and Smith's personal moral agenda when it came to the matter of Native slavery was less than consistent. By the time he wrote the *Generall Historie*, he was indeed looking to "the Spaniards" and "how they got the West Indies, and forced the treacherous and rebellious Infidels to do all manner of drudgery work and slavery for them," as an example of "how to suppresse" the Indians, which the English should follow rather than model themselves against— and as a relatively uncontroversial example, as Smith observes, "so often related and approved, I omit it here." Thomas Hunt was not, in other words, the aberrant, Hispanicized English exception that he often appears to be in our historical accounts.

But if the national-pedagogical Squanto depends upon and reinforces the legacy of the Black Legend, how might the historical subject who was brought to Spain but sidestepped his intended fate as a slave reorient our understanding of the history in which he appears—and of the process of colonial translation in which he famously participated? To fully apprehend the larger implications of Squanto's experiences at this juncture of his transatlantic career—about which we know so frustratingly little—requires both the associative and the imaginative flexibilities of intellectual and speculative history, respectively. Most of what we know about what Squanto experienced in Spain comes down to a few bare facts recorded in Gorges's *A briefe Relation*. After Hunt arrived in Malaga, he began to sell off his human cargo into slavery—"as many as he could get money for" (210)—but Squanto escaped this particular form of servitude when a group of Spanish priests interceded and took the remaining captives, Squanto included, into the custody of the Catholic Church. As Gorges explains,

But when it was understood from whence they were brought, the Friers of those parts tooke the rest from them, and kept them to be instructed in the Christian Faith; and so disappointed this unworthy fellow of the hopes of gaine he conceived to make by this new and divellish project. (210)

Despite its brevity, this account suggests several possible elements shaping Squanto's situation and subsequent experiences in Spain. First, we learn here that the Spanish buyers and traders in the slave market in which some of Squanto's fellow captives were sold were not initially aware of these Indians' geographical origin, and it is apparently the new knowledge of this origin that catalyzes the intercession of the priests. It seems likely that their northern origin—from the place the English were calling New England—constituted proof to the priests and perhaps others that these captives were not legally suitable for enslavement in Spain, which had by then passed numerous laws forbidding the enslavement of Indians outside the context of what they called "just war."[74] No aggression leveled by the blasphemous Protestant English upon the Native inhabitants of the Americas could be considered a "just war" in early seventeenth-century Spain; thus, the revelation of "whence they were brought" would enable the Spanish priests, by law, simply to remand Squanto and the other Indian captives from their custody under Hunt. Such a contextual speculation finds textual support, moreover, in the apparent fact that no money changed hands between the priests and Hunt, the latter "disappointed" in his "hopes of gaine."

Second, we learn here that Squanto and the other captives were intended for a particular educational trajectory, "to be instructed in the Christian Faith"—a specifically Catholic tutelage, undertaken by priests, which would by necessity require the acquisition of some Spanish and possibly Latin as well. To attend to this linguistic trajectory in its fullest implications is in some sense to recognize an emergent historical figure—hispanophone Squanto, we might call him—who precedes the always already English-speaking figure celebrated in fourth-grade classrooms at Thanksgiving, and who calls into question what we thought we knew about him. To recognize hispanophone Squanto is not just to acknowledge that Squanto's experiences in the Spanish language constitute another translative layer within his interpretive role vis-à-vis the English and the Native groups of seventeenth-century New England, though this is certainly important. To recognize hispanophone Squanto is also to take account of the sequencing and the sum of the languages he spoke, from the Algonquian dialects of the varied Massachusetts polities in which he lived to the bartering French he almost certainly learned when interacting with Samuel de Champlain's successors on fur-trading missions to the devotional Spanish of the religious orders where he was taken by the priests in Malaga to the entrepreneurial English of the colonial investors with whom he interacted once he arrived in London.[75] We should probably add to this list the polyglot pidgin of sailors in the Atlantic world, for when Squanto "got away to England," as Bradford puts it, he surely did so on a ship, and most likely—once we dispense with the fanciful British rescuer—did so by acting as one of the ship's crew, as he would most certainly not have gone in the company of his religious tutors (Catholic priests hardly being welcome on English soil in these years).[76]

However he got to England, Squanto's arrival there provided the means for his eventual return to his homeland via another English voyage of discovery. In this sense, his "getting away for England" evinces the geopolitical understanding that he appears to have developed as "hispanophone Squanto"; once there, he understood enough about European, inter-imperial rivalry to know what to say about mineral wealth to induce his English hosts to sponsor another voyage to New England. To construct a speculative history of hispanophone Squanto is thus to reconsider his translative work for the Pilgrims by conceiving of him not only as a former captive of Englishmen—one who, to repeat my earlier and skeptical citation of translation theory, "seemed to forgive" his abduction—but also as a former student of Spanish priests, one who might be newly understood within a particular intellectual genealogy. For the Malaga priests who objected to the sale of Squanto and the other New England Indians in Spain were able to do so as a result of a specific philosophical foundation elaborated by the Dominican friar Antonio de Montesinos, who preached against indigenous enslavement in the early sixteenth century on the island of Hispaniola, and later by his famous convert, Bartolomé de Las Casas. Entering the Dominican order after hearing Montesino's sermon, Las Casas came to be known as the "Defender of the Indians" when he protested the brutal treatment of indigenous Americans, arguing in the famous Valladolid "debate" for their natural rights against the Aristotelian theologian Juan Ginés de Sepúlveda, who posited the Indians as natural slaves.[77] Squanto's escape from the fate of slavery in Malaga was predicated, in other words, on a tradition of human rights, articulated in that debate, which came to shape subsequent Spanish colonial law if not actual practice.

Even more to the point, hispanophone Squanto had lived in a part of Europe where Amerindian slaves from Mexico and Central and South America were a common sight, far more common than their northern counterparts in England, where Jamestown's Pocahontas had arrived just before Squanto made his way there.[78] But unlike Pocahontas, Squanto arrived in London from a Spanish port city that witnessed the influx of Amerindian slaves from throughout the hemisphere; hispanophone Squanto was already *worldly*, in the exilic, political sense of that term, and he would have known far more about Spanish colonization in the Americas than the provincial Pilgrims for whom he later translated.[79] The early English effort at colonization in Plymouth must have seemed fragile by contrast, its future outcome hardly inevitable—and yet the figure of hispanophone Squanto could have held no illusions about what this unremarkable English planting might one day mean: Las Casas had called it the "devastation" or "destruction" of America, and Squanto would have seen the human refuse of its process with his own eyes while in the slave market of Malaga, Spain.[80]

Read in this light, Squanto's translational services for the English may be understood somewhat differently: not as a form of forgiveness for his prior capture, and not—it goes almost without saying—as an effort at cross-cultural hospitality. Acknowledging the Spanish dimensions of Squanto's career, we may even wish to resist what I think of as one of the most persuasive historical interpretations of his translational labor for the Pilgrims: as the only available employment left for the so-called last of his kind—for a politically isolated figure who sought individual power where he could, and who had enmities with rival indigenous groups.[81] The conceptual figure of hispanophone Squanto invites us to imagine another scenario altogether—of high-stakes indigenous diplomacy, conducted on a small New England field, but with a transatlantic and hemispheric perspective upon the potential consequences at hand.[82] In this milieu, almost nothing that the Pilgrims believe about Squanto can be taken at face value—including the purported death threat made against him by the sachem Massasoit, which supposedly bound Squanto to the English forever for his own safety—for all the information they have comes to them through translated scenes of resolution or conflict with the Indians that often sound peculiarly as though they have been staged as a means of shaping English views of the situation at hand. To state the obvious: what they know about their translator depends always upon Squanto's own translations, or those of another indigenous interpreter.

Even the famous scene of his death in *Of Plymouth Plantation*—in which the Catholic-educated Squanto, as if he did not understand monotheism, "desir[ed] the Governor to pray for him that he might go to the Englishmen's God in Heaven; and bequeathed sundry of his things to sundry of his English friends as remembrances of his love" (114)—may be read in this context as a dark parable of colonial translation. Bleeding at the nose, Squanto understood from this "symptom of death" that he would succumb to his illness (114). He had also seen enough of the spread of infectious disease throughout his life to understand its basic pattern; earlier, to Bradford's disapproval, Squanto had described the plague as a weapon to be sent by the English "amongst whom they would" of the Indians.[83] In his final hour, Squanto spoke the familiar language of a deathbed conversion. It was perhaps a second scene of conversion for a translator likely baptized as a Catholic, and one that drew the English close to him and ensured that his possessions would be passed on to his "English friends" rather than buried in the ground where—as the Roanoke Indians had earlier described disease patterns to colonist Thomas Harriot—the "invisible bullets" that brought on illness could do no harm.[84] In passing on these possessions, perhaps Squanto was making an interpreter's final effort at a significant transmission—and a final act of unsettlement: an act deliberately mistranslated for the English, who then naively recorded it as a dying Indian's final gesture of submission to a superior English God. Indeed, behind the English interpretation of events, which has been handed down to future readers as "American" literary history, stands the unsettling figure of hispanophone Squanto—the translator and thus also the actual source of narrative governance: the hidden authorial hand, the true teller of the tale.

An Unfounding Father

THE STORY OF DON LUIS

Within the broad translation zone of the Red Atlantic, then—a zone embracing countless anonymous and little-known Native interpreters, from Columbus's abducted translators to hispanophone Squanto—it is indigenous *knowledge*, rather than culture, that the history of unsettlement brings to the fore, tempering the logic of multiculturalism, and particularly the ever-present idiom of authenticity in scholarly encounters with Indian history. In some sense, as the previous chapter tried to show, multiculturalism and new historicism are flip sides of a single, highly durable coin: on one side we see the powerful, self-authenticating technology of European literacy, and on the other an abundance of Native cultural perspectives to be subsumed by a contested but still unified "American" literature.[1] Instead, by recognizing what Walter Mignolo calls the "double process of translation" by which indigenous epistemologies both appropriate and transform rather than simply resist their colonial counterparts, we might look for the Native conceptual origins of the so-called New World in the early modern Americas: for the discernible traces of the acquisition and transmission of knowledge—in transatlantic and hemispheric, Native-European and inter-indigenous contexts—and the means by which this circuit of knowledge transmission in turn came to shape historical outcomes and the historical record itself.[2]

This shift in focus from culture to knowledge in turn allows for an obvious but crucial recognition that we have still not fully absorbed: that the catastrophe of New World encounter introduced changed, adaptive, and improvisational modes of understanding that exceeded and altered cultural expectations and assumptions among Native peoples as surely as it did among Europeans. It did so arguably earliest of all among indigenous interpreters, who were the first to achieve bilingual fluency and the new ways and means of knowing that accompanied it. Thus, when we encounter their acts of interpretive infidelity in European texts, we must not dismiss them as crude

colonial stereotypes of "Indian mendacity," glitches in the imperial translative machine, nor (worse) as the antics of trickster figures best understood
within a supposedly original cultural frame of reference. To do so is to ignore
the evidence of a vast indigenous history of knowledge production and transmission to which we have only the most limited access—but nevertheless a
responsibility to try to discern.

This chapter assembles the complex trajectory of Don Luis's itinerant career from a range of sources: a series of Jesuit letters and *relaciones* from the
sixteenth and early seventeenth centuries; the writings of the Spanish adelantado of Florida, Pedro Menéndez de Avilés, and his brother-in-law, Gonzalo
Solís de Merás, along with other colonial officials; as well as a variety of documents attesting in various ways to the details of Don Luis's life among the
Spaniards and his travels around the Atlantic world. Many of these sources
have allowed historians of the colonial Americas in recent years to tell a richer
and fuller story about the circumstances surrounding the Spanish Jesuit settlement in what would become English Virginia, while anthropologists and
ethnohistorians have widened our understanding of the various southeastern
Native cultural contexts from which the man known to the Spanish as Don
Luis emerged, and to which he ultimately returned.[3] My own focus in this
chapter is on Don Luis's participation in transatlantic and hemispheric networks of indigenous knowledge production, and as such I read the sources for
the ways his story inflects diverse discursive resources in the New World that
he was both encountering during his travels and decisively changing with his
act of unsettlement. The chapter argues finally for a mode of reading that may
allow us to discern a provisional model of early modern indigenous authorship recorded within the earliest accounts of Don Luis's role as a translator.
We need to keep in mind the deceptively simple historical fact that Don Luis's
authorial agency in creating his own compelling narrative was persuasive
enough in its own moment that it finally restored him to his homeland and
allowed him to influence profoundly the outcome of events there. As I read
them here, in other words, the early accounts telling Don Luis's story are most
important not for what they might tell us about the nature of his cultural
identity but for their indications of the particular kinds of knowledge Don
Luis was able to generate and transmit through his own narrative acts, shaping historical events while also contesting and transforming the very colonial
idioms in which his narration is recorded.

How Paquiquineo Became Don Luis

From the recorded European perspective, the story of Don Luis begins in the
summer of 1561, when a Spanish ship called the *Santa Catalina* sailed into the
Bahía de Santa María, now known as the Chesapeake Bay.[4] The ship had been

exploring the coastline of the land the Spaniards called La Florida, a dimensionless expanse of territory stretching indefinitely northward from New Spain (today's Mexico).[5] As an initial setting, La Florida was, to the story's European characters, little known and unconquered: both promising and deadly. It had, by the early 1560s, brought only staggering losses to those Spaniards who ventured there after Juan Ponce de León became the first European officially to discover it in 1513. Ponce de León himself did not survive La Florida long enough to do more than name it; an early victim of the first attempt to colonize, he was shot with a poison arrow by Calusa Indians in 1521. The Pánfilo de Narváez expedition of 1527 and the Hernando de Soto expedition of 1539 fared no better; these ventures were spectacularly botched, as were the smaller attempted settlements of San Miguel de Gualdape in 1526 and Santa María de Filipino in 1559.[6] But in 1561 King Philip II of Spain still held hope of seeing a successful colony established north of Mexico, and many of those working in his service still believed in the narrative devised by the Native translator Francisco de Chicora (discussed in the previous chapter) of a land overflowing with treasure and abundant agriculture. The story told by Francisco de Chicora exerted a powerful narrative influence over its initial European audience, and was then perpetuated by later Spanish narrators interested in promoting colonization efforts—which is why, despite the unpromising history of sixteenth-century Floridian settlement, the *Santa Catalina* was coasting the Atlantic seaboard when it was hit by a storm and sought shelter in the Bahía de Santa María.[7] The Spaniards aboard the ship called the land *Ajacán*—as they heard (or thought they heard) it named by two Algonquian-speaking Indians whom the crew took on board.[8] Later, the land would also be referred to simply as Don Luis's homeland, *la tierra de Don Luis*.[9]

As in most early American stories of this kind, the two Natives who came aboard the ship supposedly did so willingly—though how precisely the Spaniards defined willingness or how, in the absence of any translator, these young men conveyed willingness is not clear. Indeed, as Camilla Townsend has shown, it is more than likely that they conveyed the opposite.[10] The Spaniards apparently perceived one of the two Indian voyagers (or captives) to be a person of important rank; the other they quickly cast as his servant and thus a minor figure in the unfolding drama. Predictably, then, of this culture-crossing pair, only the presumed social superior became a central character in the story; Spain's House of Trade records his indigenous name as Paquiquineo.[11] His presumed servant remains unnamed, largely disappearing from the story's new European setting once the *Santa Catalina* arrived back in Seville, where the factor (or agent) of the voyage, Antonio Velázquez, made the decision that of the two Ajacán Indians only Paquiquineo, the "principal person," would accompany him to King Philip's court in Madrid.[12]

Velázquez evidently apprehended Paquiquineo's potential role in a familiar story—an exotic arrival turned favored royal subject—and accordingly requested and received an allowance for suitable clothing for the "naked" Ajacán Native.[13] Over the next five months, Paquiquineo stayed at the king's court, where he appears to have caught Philip's attention and earned his esteem. Juan de la Carrera, a Jesuit priest who knew Paquiquineo ten years later, observed that he had been "educated at the court of king Philip II and had received from him many favors"; another priest noted that even by 1570, when Paquiquineo was living in Cuba, the Native traveler was sponsored directly by the royal court: "our King in Spain had ordered him an allowance and clothed him; and [the Native] knew so much that he confessed and received communion."[14] All accounts agree that Paquiquineo was "muy ladino" (both highly fluent and very crafty) and that he became, at some point over the course of his transatlantic education, "muy discreto en sus razones" (very ingenious in his argumentation; very subtle in his reasons): a not only proficient but highly effective speaker of Spanish, able to convince and persuade a variety of powerful interlocutors.[15]

As in the story of Francisco de Chicora, Paquiquineo's emergent bilingualism—his widely noted rhetorical agility in the Spanish language—is central to understanding one of the surprising outcomes of this story: how he was able eventually to return to Ajacán despite the considerable odds against it. Many Spaniards on both sides of the Atlantic were losing interest in La Florida by the time Paquiquineo got to Philip's court; each attempt at Floridian colonization had by then yielded nothing but disaster. As the seasoned conquistador Ángel de Villafañe explained in a 1562 report to the king, there was in the whole of La Florida simply "no land where settlement can be made."[16] Yet after meeting with Paquiquineo and hearing his story, King Philip decided that same year to send him back to Ajacán, despite all warnings that Florida was a losing proposition. Paquiquineo was to travel with the Admiral Pedro Menéndez de Avilés, who had recently commanded the great *Armada de la Carrera*, a Spanish treasure fleet sailing from Mexico and the Caribbean back to Spain in 1560, along with two Dominican friars, who were charged with undertaking a conversion effort in Ajacán, and supplied with trade goods with which to entice the Ajacán Natives toward a new religion. The king also wanted Menéndez to obtain an accurate latitude reading for the Bahía de Santa María, so that other ships could undertake a subsequent colonization effort.[17] The precise nature of Paquiquineo's rhetorical influence upon Philip II's mandate is unknown—but its ultimate significance, like that of the story Chicora told, is clear. Paquiquineo was, despite La Florida's waning reputation as a colonial prospect, on his way home in 1562.

What new knowledge was Paquiquineo acquiring during the course of his early travels? By 1562, he had seen Spain, and briefly Portugal, where the *Santa Catalina* stopped en route to Seville and Madrid, but no part of the Americas other than his own homeland in Ajacán. He had thus not yet witnessed the large-scale violence of New World conquest—on the order of Mexico, Peru,

Cuba, or Hispaniola—at first hand. Perhaps he had heard the names of these places and even understood something of their significance from listening to Spaniards during his time in Madrid. What is far more significant, however, is the compelling hemispheric body of knowledge regarding the state of post-conquest, indigenous New Spain, as seen from the perspective of two Natives from Mexico—a body of knowledge to which Paquiquineo had direct, documented access. For when Paquiquineo and his companion had first been taken aboard the *Santa Catalina* in 1561, they were introduced not only to Spaniards but to two indigenous Mexicans who had been brought along specifically as interpreters, and who shared the transatlantic voyage to Spain with Paquiquineo and his unnamed companion from Ajacán. One of these indigenous men, recorded under the name Alonso de Aguirre, learned to speak Algonquian with Paquiquineo over the course of their long trip across the Atlantic and their five-week voyage between Portugal and Seville. There is no record, of course, of what the two Ajacán Indians and the two indigenous Mexicans discussed during their time together, but some transmission of information and understanding indisputably took place. For when Alonso de Aguirre learned of King Philip's plan to send Paquiquineo back to his unconquered homeland, he petitioned for the right to accompany the Algonquian-speaking Indian back to Ajacán as well, declaring that he, though from New Spain, was now fluent in Paquiquineo's language and, remarkably, "devoted" to him.[18]

The historical record confirms that Aguirre's petition to stay with Paquiquineo and travel to Ajacán was granted, but it yields nothing, once again, about the nature of their communications with each other. What did it look like, this emergent and dialogically constituted understanding of the state of the pre- and post-conquest indigenous Americas, which these four Native travelers from disparate parts of the hemisphere were surely and probably urgently engaged in producing when they spoke to each other in a language that the Spaniards could not understand? Whatever its specific substance, this new understanding would have been further elaborated on their second transatlantic voyage, this time back to the New World. And perhaps we can glean, however distantly and indirectly, some sense of this inter-indigenous production of knowledge from the strange details surrounding what turned out to be the unexpected failure of this 1562 voyage back to Ajacán.

The ship stopped first in New Spain, where Paquiquineo and his Algonquian-speaking companion were taken to Mexico City to prepare for the new settlement in Ajacán. Soon after their arrival, however, Paquiquineo and his companion were both taken gravely ill—too ill to continue on the next leg of the voyage. Together with Aguirre, they were supposed to have served as guides for the Dominicans as they sailed up the coast of La Florida to find the correct entrance into the Bahía de Santa María; afterward, they were to have acted as translators between the Spaniards and the Ajacán Natives during the founding of the new settlement. But when Paquiquineo and his companion were taken ill in Mexico City, the ship that was bound for La Florida left without them, and the proposed trip to find Ajacán was indefinitely thwarted. In Mexico City, meanwhile, Paquiquineo and his Algonquian-speaking companion declared that they were dying, going so far as to request emergency baptismal rites. As Fray Pedro de Feria, the head of the Dominican Order in Mexico City, later observed in a letter to King Philip, the ailing young men "arrived at such a point that it was not thought they would escape death": "For that reason, having learned of their desire to be baptized, as they had asked for it more than once, they were given the sacrament of baptism."[19] After they were christened on their deathbeds in Mexico, the two Ajacán Natives both proceeded to make miraculous recoveries; as Fray Feria puts it in the next sentence of his letter, "Our lord was moved to give them back their health" (31).

What might this fleeting and partial story suggest? The detail of the "devoted" relationship between Paquiquineo and Aguirre, who became fluent in his companion's language, indicates that two indigenous subjects from very different parts of the Americas had a strong interest in communicating with each other—and in a tongue other than Spanish. For unspecified reasons, they had an interest in remaining together, and thus presumably in establishing a circuit of knowledge exchange that included their respective companions from Ajacán and New Spain. Moreover, the detail of the sudden and simultaneous illnesses that prevented the return expedition to Ajacán—followed by equally sudden recoveries once the ship had sailed without its indigenous guides—suggests perhaps even the possibility of a feigned double affliction designed to manipulate the course of events: intended to *precipitate* the failed outcome of the proposed voyage to Paquiquineo's homeland. Perhaps, in other words, after they could communicate with each other in a tongue unknown to the Spaniards, the Ajacán and Mexican Natives collectively developed their ideas about the violent subjugation of the indigenous people of New Spain, on the one hand, and the unconquered status of Ajacán, on the other—and then acted accordingly to thwart a Spanish return to Paquiquineo's homeland at that time. Finally, the detail of the two Ajacán Indians' repeated requests for baptism reveals the surprising fact that they had not participated in any conversion while in Spain, where it was surely offered to them and apparently refused. Why would they change their minds after traveling from Spain to Mexico, and inland to Mexico City, seeing first-hand enslaved Indians all around them along the way? Perhaps they were both truly taken ill, both truly wanted conversion to the faith of the Spaniards in the face of death, and both made immediate recoveries after receiving baptism. But it is also possible that the extended encounter with Aguirre and his Mexican companion shaped Paquiquineo's understanding of the legal consequences of conversion. For Paquiquineo's situation as an indigenous captive and would-be interpreter changed significantly with his embrace of

Christianity—a fact that he may have understood when calling for a deathbed baptism "more than once" before making his miraculous recovery.

With baptism, Paquiquineo became Don Luis de Velasco: he was named after the Viceroy of New Spain himself, who had first ordered the voyage of the *Santa Catalina* and who now acted, according to the priest Carrera, as Don Luis's baptismal sponsor and his "godfather" (LL 131). But once baptized, Don Luis de Velasco, along with his companion from Ajacán, attained a different status under Spanish colonial and religious law, which held that indigenous converts could not be returned without religious supervision to their homelands, where they might apostatize, leaving them in a worse spiritual state than if they had never been baptized.[20] Fray Feria, writing to King Philip soon after the baptism, in February 1563, explained the theological and logistical problem that these miraculous deathbed recoveries now presented: "It is believed that your desire to return them to their land depended on their being pagans, as they were when they left you" (32). In their newly baptized state, however, the two Ajacán Indians were "now Christians and members of the church," and, as Feria warned, "if they were returned to their land alone and without ministers who could keep them from straying from the faith and from Christian law, and if they were to return to their rites and idolatries and thus lose their souls, their baptism would have caused them to be damned" (32). The baptisms thus placed new and unexpected responsibilities upon the Dominicans who had performed them; they could not in good conscience turn over Don Luis and his companion to a conquest of Ajacán that lacked appropriate religious organization. To do so would be "a great inhumanity, and even a grave offense against our Lord" (32).

We must also bear in mind here that, in receiving baptism, the two Ajacán Indians entered a new juridical space in which religious and civil-military interests were frequently at odds. Dated February 13, 1563, Feria's letter to King Philip from Mexico City reveals that there was soon a face-off of sorts between the Archbishop of New Spain and Menéndez de Avilés regarding the fate of Don Luis and his companion. Once the Ajacán Natives had made their miraculous recovery, the Dominicans who oversaw their baptisms kept them in the Convent of Santo Domingo for religious instruction until another ship could be outfitted—at which point Menéndez, still under the king's orders, sought to redraft the two men into service as translators and guides in a new expedition to colonize Don Luis's homeland. When the Dominicans—who saw the expedition as an unprecedented missionary opportunity—requested the right to accompany Menéndez on the conquest of Ajacán, he refused them and "denied the departure of the religious" (32). The Archbishop in turn appealed to Catholic law and "ordered Pedro Menéndez not to return the Indians to their homelands since no ministers would go with them" (32).

By requesting and receiving baptism, in other words, Don Luis and his companion effectively ensured their protection under Dominican auspices;

they were no longer to be remanded into service as interpreters in any civil-military conquest of Ajacán that did not include what the Dominicans deemed to be sufficient religious supervision.[21] At the same time, Don Luis and his companion gained new rights as Christianized Indians under Dominican protection. They were quite suddenly "at full liberty to go to Spain," Feria tells King Philip in his letter, and they were "encouraged to do so" (32). But with their new status as converts, the Ajacán Indians demurred, choosing instead to remain with the Dominicans in Mexico City: "they said that if they were not going to return to their land, they preferred to stay here than to go all the way to Spain" (32). Feria's indirect report of this point of view establishes more than a preference on the part of Don Luis and his companion, however; the demurral in the face of "encourage[ment]" otherwise, which introduces a subtle conflict in which the two Ajacán Natives prevailed, suggests that Don Luis and his companion understood the specific legal consequences of conversion—and indeed may even have understood them before the onset of what may have been manufactured illnesses. If so, it was likely Aguirre and the other indigenous Mexican interlocutor (who drops out of the written re-cord at this point) who first transmitted knowledge of the politico-religious landscape of New Spain, apprising Don Luis and his Ajacán companion that with a sudden conversion they could thwart or at least defer an intended mil-itary conquest of their homeland—and that with conversion the two Ajacán Natives would be "at full liberty" to choose to remain in Mexico despite being encouraged to return to Spain. This is a speculative scenario, to be sure, but it is one that explains some of the more dubious or coincidental aspects of the record: the repeated requests for baptism after it was refused in Spain; the simultaneous and miraculous recoveries of the Ajacán Indians; and the later rhetorical power that Don Luis acquired and used to such great effect.

Not surprisingly, Feria understands what has transpired during the conver-sion of the two Ajacán Natives not as the thwarting of a military expedition but as a religious triumph. "Thus they remained here," he writes, "treated like sons and taught the things of our faith," and they "are still among us, who take care to teach them the doctrine and all that is appropriate" (32). The Viceroy of New Spain himself, Feria explains, "takes a special interest in them and over-sees their good treatment" (32). With conversion, then, Don Luis and his com-panion achieved both a means of furthering their geopolitical understanding of the culture of conquest and a site of relative refuge within which to do so.

Rhetorical Instrumentality and the Failed Expedition of 1566

But if Don Luis had by now twice thwarted Menéndez's projected conquest of Ajacán, Fray Feria's letter also makes clear that this indigenous traveler and future interpreter had not lost interest in returning to his homeland. Indeed,

Feria's account shows that Don Luis had by then begun himself to shape the public discourse about Ajacán by characterizing its resources and by suggesting to the Dominicans the project of converting its inhabitants through his own interpretive labor. By now a highly assimilated bilingual and a cosmopolitan indigenous traveler to Portugal, Seville, Madrid, and Mexico City, Don Luis presented a singularly persuasive figure, and Feria is duly impressed not only by "the fine presence and capacity of this Indian" but by "what he tells us of his land" (32). Feria does not offer Philip much specificity in the letter—particularly absent are details of the kinds of mineral riches that might attract strong civil-military interest—but he does remind the king that a Dominican mission in Ajacán would "augment your territories" (33). It is clear, moreover, that Don Luis has emphasized the remunerative potential of his homeland in at least one other way, for Feria notes that "it is well populated with peaceful people" (32). In this projected colonial context, robust population is not merely a sign of divine favor, the mark of the *locus amoenus*, but also a new and untapped source of labor—particularly if the population promises to be easily subdued, as Feria clearly believes: "Those people are peaceful, and it is believed that they would be even more so if this Indian were to go there and give an account of what he has seen and the benefits he has received."[22] Already, then, Don Luis has become indispensable to the project Feria envisions, so much so that the Dominicans believe "that our lord has arranged all of this business and sent this Indian so that he may be the means of saving all of that land"—and of pacifying its human resources (32).

Feria's letter bears the traces of Don Luis's rhetorical instrumentality, then, but it also offers some insight into why the Dominican colonial interest in Ajacán was not the one to which Don Luis ultimately attached himself. For even as Feria extolled the virtues of his divinely appointed interpreter in the projected mission to Ajacán's "peaceful" inhabitants, Feria still envisioned a military accompaniment to this religious conquest: "No more than forty or fifty men would have to go with the religious, in one ship," he explains to King Philip, "which would be able to pacify the people there" (33). A religious mission accompanied by military "pacification" would likely not have been, from Don Luis's point of view, very different from the expedition that he and his companion had narrowly avoided when they became ill and sought final-hour conversions. After all, by this point the two Algonquian-speaking Natives would no longer have had to rely on the testimony of Aguirre to understand what the colonization of Ajacán would mean for its indigenous inhabitants: they had seen firsthand what New World colonialism looked like fifty years after the Conquest of Mexico; they had by then witnessed themselves the mass enslavement of Indians throughout New Spain.[23] That Menéndez had similar plans for Ajacán was clear to anyone paying attention; over the next few years he wrote to King Philip repeatedly of his plans to colonize in the Bahía de Santa María and referred to the "thousand slave licenses" he had requested in order to build an unassailable bulwark against possible French competition throughout La Florida.[24] Thus, however much Don Luis initially promoted Dominican interest in his homeland through his enticing descriptions of it, Feria's eventual plan to return the two Natives there accompanied by forty or fifty Spanish soldiers bent on "pacify[ing] the people" would surely have been more than unwelcome to the would-be Ajacán guide and translator. This may well illuminate what happened next: the oddly ambiguous failure in 1566 of a military-reinforced Dominican mission sent by Menéndez to settle Don Luis's homeland.

Menéndez had by then been endowed with the official right to conquer and govern all of La Florida; named adelantado in 1565, he founded St. Augustine the same year, establishing what is now the oldest continuously-occupied European settlement in the current United States. It is not entirely clear when Don Luis left Mexico and joined Menéndez for the expedition to colonize Ajacán, but it was almost certainly not until 1566 since, as of mid-December 1565, Menéndez referred to him in a letter to King Philip as "the Indian Velasco . . . who is in New Spain."[25] Menéndez's correspondence also confirms that Don Luis had continued over the years to encourage Spanish interest in Ajacán with his particular descriptions of it. As before, Menéndez was still concerned with garnering forces to forestall possible French encroachment in that area—"or else," as he warned Philip, "they will go to the Bay of Santa María which is 100 leagues north of Santa Elena where the Indian Velasco is from" (177). But by late 1565, when he mentions Don Luis by name, Menéndez was also invested in finding Ajacán for more specific reasons likely promulgated by "the Indian Velasco" himself: "to benefit from the mines" there and to find its nearby water passage to the Orient, "an anchorage . . . which is 80 leagues inward from the Bay of Santa María" and adjacent to "another arm of the sea which goes in the direction of China, and comes out in the Southern Sea."[26] Menéndez is both unequivocal about the accuracy of his information and reticent about his source: "and this is absolutely certain," he tells King Philip of the passage to China, "although nobody has ever gone this way to the Southern Sea" (178). Yet Menéndez apparently trusts his informant's descriptions of Ajacán enough to speak confidently to Philip about the "settlement I shall found in the Bay of Santa María.[27]

Like the earlier expedition, however, Menéndez's projected voyage to Ajacán in 1566 would fail. Over the course of that year, Don Luis left Mexico and traveled with the adelantado back and forth from Havana to the recently founded St. Augustine to Santa Elena, the colonial island-outpost off present-day South Carolina. In the process, Don Luis must have witnessed the decimated indigenous population of colonial Cuba; he would also have been able to observe, by contrast to Mexico and Cuba, the relative fragility of Spanish colonial settlement throughout La Florida during this decade, when French and Spanish forces threatened to obliterate each other's prospects.[28]

And, most important of all, Don Luis would likely have conversed at length with indigenous inhabitants from these new parts of the Americas, particularly the hispanophone Calusa interpreters who were also traveling with Menéndez between Havana and La Florida during these months (as I discuss in Chapter 4). By the time Menéndez finally decided that August to send out the expedition to the Bahía de Santa María, Don Luis had multiple sources of empirical and indirect evidence by which to understand that a return to his homeland under these particular circumstances, accompanied by military force, would likely mean devastation for Ajacán.

The expedition began straightforwardly enough. According to an August 1 document, Menéndez instructed his appointed captain for the voyage to the Bahía de Santa María with utter confidence in the guide and translator: "I send Don Luis, Indian, to his country, which according to him is between the 36th and 39th degree along the shore, and all the people of that territory are his friends and the vassals of his three brothers."[29] Possessed of both the precise geographical coordinates and the ostensible allegiance of the Indians via Don Luis's familial and diplomatic ties, Menéndez sees fit to delegate only a small military force—"from 12 to 15 soldiers"—with two Dominican friars. He emphasizes his interpreter's promise of loyalty: "the said Don Luis says that he will treat [the friars and soldiers] as companions and friends, and all the Indians in those parts will become Christians" (551). Despite Menéndez's high hopes, however, the subsequent voyage did not go as planned. Official depositions signed by the expedition's notary public record an August 14 landfall at 37 30'—"which according to Don Luis was in his territory"—but before the ship could dispatch its boat "a contrary wind [lasting four full days] arose which forced them to weigh anchor with all speed and put out to sea."[30] Ten days later the ship entered another river at 36°; the notary public explains in the next deposition that "since the Indian Don Luis claimed that his territory extended from the 36th to the 39th degree along the coast, the said pilot . . . took the ship inside the river."[31] From one entry to the next, the notary's continued emphasis on the fact that these landings hinge entirely on Don Luis's geographical testimony suggests strongly that the Spaniards' confidence in what their Indian guide tells them may be waning. Nevertheless, the next day, on August 25, the notary records that the captain and soldiers have gone through the motions of ritual discovery, making their way to shore, walking through the land, cutting branches to make and plant a cross, and then naming the river after the Apostle San Bartolomé; in doing so, they "seize and take possession of the said land and harbor" for King Philip and officially notarize the event.[32] Yet the signs of imminent failure are already here, for Don Luis drops out of the notary's record at precisely this moment of purported territorial acquisition. Nowhere does the August 25 deposition mention the translator, his "country," or any human presence on the land.

The next deposition, from mid-October, is written from Spain, where the ship has arrived after failing to proceed to the "country of Don Luis." The pilot is being sent to the royal court with all the documentation from the thwarted voyage; the two friars are on their way there as well, "and are taking with them the Indian Don Luis."[33] But there are nagging questions even before the story is told. If the expeditionary ship was able to make it within the vicinity of Don Luis's homeland, as claimed in the earlier deposition, and was then able to cross the Atlantic to Spain, why could it not have continued to search for Ajacán? What has happened to account for the failure of the expedition?

According to Gonzalo Solís de Merás—Menéndez's brother-in-law, who accompanied the adelantado throughout La Florida and thus witnessed the embarkation of the 1566 expedition—the circumstances of the failed settlement were in fact quite suspicious. In Solís de Merás's fascinating telling of the misadventure—the *Memorial* of Pedro Menéndez de Avilés, composed in 1567—Menéndez sent the Dominicans and the soldiers to Ajacán along "with an Indian, a brother of the cacique of that country, whom for 6 years the Adelantado had brought with him": "he was very fluent and of a very good understanding, and a good Christian; he was called Don Luis de Velasco."[34] If there is a treasonous translator lurking within the "good Christian" who was guiding the 1566 voyage—and "with [whose] help" and upon whose protection (*"con su favor"*) the Spaniards depended "to colonize that land and try to make the Indians Christians" (258)—Solís de Merás never says so. But his account of the failed 1566 settlement is an oddly conflictive one, placing the blame for what happened on the Dominicans even as it also bears the traces of Don Luis's rhetorical influence:

> The friars were from Peru and New Spain, a very luxuriant country [*tierra muy viciosa*]: they had experienced some hunger in Florida, and toil and danger. It seemed to them they could not bear such a bad life; in secret they stirred up [*alteraron*] some of the soldiers, which required little effort to accomplish, and stirred up the pilot; and in agreement, taking testimonies that with the storm they could not go there [to Ajacán], they came to Seville, defaming the country and speaking ill of the King and the Adelantado, because they wanted to settle and conquer it. (258)

This not entirely persuasive account condenses a number of salient elements relating to the thwarted expedition. First, the account introduces the comparative, hemispheric stakes of the endeavor: the overabundant, spoiling life in Peru and Mexico (implied by the term *viciosa*), which is opposed to the deprivation of Florida, explains the supposed distaste of the friars for their new assignment. Ajacán is not a desirable place to colonize because, like all of Florida, it purportedly offers a bad or difficult life (*tan mala vida*). Second, Solís de Merás makes clear his belief that the 1566 failure to locate and settle Ajacán was not accidental but planned; not a storm but a secret conspiracy accounts for the inability of the ship to reach the Bahía de Santa María. Third, the account implicitly undermines the official, colonial practice of "taking testimonies" from the participants in expedition and conquest; the alleged falsification of the friars, soldiers, and pilot calls into question the authority of all colonial accounts, firsthand and otherwise, including the one that Solís de Merás has himself produced. Finally, and most significant, Solís de Merás's version of events suggests a lasting outcome that would have a profound impact on the future of Ajacán: its reputation as a viable colonial site has suffered alongside the reputations of those who would attempt to "settle and conquer" it—a remarkable achievement from the point of view of anyone who hoped for Ajacán to remain permanently unsettled.

It is difficult not to intuit the role of the translator—the source of the prior accounts of mines and a passage to China—at the center of this discourse on the dismal prospects offered by Ajacán. This was not, after all, the first time that Don Luis had come close to but in the end bypassed his intended role as a participant in the conquest of his homeland. Like his deathbed conversion and recovery in 1562, the failed expedition of 1566 also suggests odd, unusual circumstances—and, perhaps more important, both instances thwarted the efforts of the Spaniards to return to and colonize Ajacán. That Don Luis wanted to return to the Bahía de Santa María is clear from numerous accounts, beginning with that of Fray Feria. But he was only willing to return there, it appears, under particular circumstances that precluded military pacification and thus the settlement and conquering of his homeland.

Don Luis's *Negocio*: Jesuit Spiritual Conquest and the 1570 Settlement of Ajacán

By 1570, Don Luis was coming close to achieving exactly those circumstances. He had by then made his way from Spain back to the New World, this time to Havana.[35] Carrera, who met Don Luis at this time, later recorded the shadowy details of the translator's second appearance in Cuba. His retrospective account, included in his official *relación* from 1600, offers a fleeting but suggestive portrait of Don Luis from this period:

> . . . There arrived in Havana an Indian native of *la Florida*, who called himself don Luis de Velasco, who as a principal person and having been educated in Mexico by the friars of Saint Dominic, and baptized there at the hand of the viceroy don Luis de Velasco, who was, as I believe, his godfather, he [the viceroy] gave him his name. This [Indian Don Luis] had been educated at the court of King Philip II and had received from him many favors: finally, the King sent him back to his country, where he said he was a great chief [*gran señor*], with some Dominican friars, who brought him

again [across the Atlantic], I don't know why, and finding himself tossed aside by the friars, he came to discuss this plan [*este negocio*] with the admiral, Pedro Menéndez; whom, based on what the indian told him of the grandeurs of his country, and on the news that the Admiral already had previously about there being by this land another sea and another navigation of great importance for the discovery of great kingdoms such as Tartary and others bordering it, the Adelantado listened to the indian, and discussed it with Father Baptista, who was at that time with the Admiral in Havana, where all this was occurring. The two reached an agreement easily, and without further discussion, the Father understanding that God had offered him [in the person of this Indian Don Luis], as he had to Father master Francis Xavier, another Paul of the Holy Faith, and another greater Japan, and of more importance . . . (LL 123)

An entirely cosmopolitan Native traveler, Don Luis was by now known as both the godson of the Mexican viceroy and a worldly and important subject in his own right. He had seen four transatlantic crossings, had been to Spain twice, and had been educated both by Dominicans in Mexico and by royal tutors in King Philip's court. In Cuba, where he now presented himself as "tossed aside" by the Dominicans, Don Luis was still living under the authority of Menéndez, governor of the island and adelantado of La Florida. And if Don Luis had earlier played a role in thwarting the 1566 expedition to Ajacán, he now apparently formulated an undertaking more specifically of his own design. Moreover, he successfully persuaded Menéndez of "this plan" ('*este negocio*') by again describing the "grandeurs" of Ajacán and confirming its water passage, via "another sea," to the Orient. While Carrera does not specify the parameters of the plan here, he does make clear that its origin is with Don Luis, and that Menéndez both "listened to the Indian" and presented his plan to a priest, Father Juan Baptista de Segura, the appointed vice provincial of the Jesuit order in Florida. Father Segura, too, is persuaded of Don Luis's plan; he envisions Don Luis becoming a great Christian translator in an imperial project to rival the Portuguese Overseas Empire in Asia.

The latter part of Carrera's description makes clear that part of what made Don Luis's *negocio* so compelling to Father Segura was its engagement with the discourse of pacification.[36] Unlike the Dominicans, the Jesuits had begun religious missionary activity in the New World only in 1549, with the arrival of the first missionaries in Brazil. A relatively new order, founded a mere ten years earlier, in 1539 by Ignatius Loyola, a former warrior turned priest, the Jesuit Company (as its name suggests) envisioned itself as a body of spiritual soldiers particularly suited to the "peaceful conquest" that was by the mid-sixteenth century mandated by Spanish imperial policy.[37] By the late 1560s, a number of Jesuit leaders were thus especially drawn to a new theory of spiritual conquest, initiated by the Dominicans, which held that soldiers and secular colonists were not only unnecessary but in fact detrimental to the success of religious missions in the Americas and the lasting conversion of the indigenous inhabitants there. As Pope Pius V put the matter bluntly in a 1569 letter to Menéndez, "there is nothing more important for the conversion of these idolatrous Indians than to make every effort to keep them from being scandalized by the vices and bad habits of those who voyage from Europe to those lands. This is the keystone of the arch of this holy undertaking and in it is contained the very essence of your pious aim."[38] In the years directly after the failed 1566 Dominican expedition to colonize Ajacán, in other words, the Jesuits were particularly open to the premise that military accompaniment threatened the potential success of their missionary work—and this suited them well, apparently, to the *negocio* that Don Luis presented to Menéndez.

The basic parameters of this *negocio*—of Don Luis's proposed mission to Ajacán in 1570—are easily discerned in Carrera's account of the mission, for Segura shared with the Jesuit Brother "all the designs and plans and hopes for this journey" (LL 123). While Segura agreed upon the plan presented to him by Menéndez—without "further discussion"—Carrera claims to have found the *negocio* troubling from the start. Writing with the clarity of hindsight, Carrera casts Segura's willingness to undertake the plan as evidence of "a holy and sincere Christian heart," but also woefully dangerous: "I pointed out the difficulty in the execution [of the plan]," Carrera recalls: "I begged and ardently entreated him to better consider it and to talk with all the Fathers there, and in accordance with this to see what would be most beneficial" (LL 123–24). But Segura was apparently too fully convinced to consider altering the basic premise of Don Luis's *negocio*—which was, in Carrera's stark description, "to go to parts so remote and cut off, and to relinquish all, trusting in an indian, without protection of soldiers . . ." (LL 124). Thus, in the new concept of the soldier-less spiritual conquest—an ostensibly purer mission that would prevent anyone from giving "a bad example to the Indians," as Carrera put it (LL 124)—Don Luis found a *negocio*, a plan, a set of suitable circumstances for his return to Ajacán in 1570. That August, he set out with a small group of Spaniards intent on forming a tiny Jesuit colony: Segura and a second Jesuit priest, Luis de Quirós; three Jesuit brothers, Gabriel Gómez, Sancho Zaballos, and Pedro Mingot de Linares; three lay catechists of the order, Cristóbol Redondo, Gabriel de Solís, and Juan Baptista Méndez; and a Spanish Creole boy, Alonso de Olmos, born and raised in the Americas, who was to serve as the expedition's woodsman. They traveled from the outpost at Santa Elena back up the Atlantic coast, but this time without any military accompaniment—and this time Don Luis successfully located and arrived in the Bahía de Santa María. The Jesuit settlers set to work laying the groundwork for a Spanish attempt at full-scale colonization of the area: they chose an inland site, constructed lodging, built a small chapel, and discussed theology with the Indians, Don Luis acting as their interpreter. Their ship remained in port for the next two days before setting to sea with a letter to the royal treasurer of Cuba and former governor of Havana, Juan de Hinistrosa, documenting the arrival and progress of the colonists. The letter is signed by Father Segura and his assistant Father Luis de Quirós, but its true author is arguably Don Luis himself, who needed to tell a particular kind of story to achieve an ambitious end: the long-term unsettlement of Ajacán.

Epistolary Theory and the Record of Indigenous Authorship: The Quirós and Segura Letter

Dated September 12, the Quirós and Segura letter is the single surviving document written by a firsthand participant in the 1570 settlement. Penned just after the arrival of the settlers in Ajacán, thirty-one days after their departure from Santa Elena, the missive is not especially long and at first glance says little of interest about Don Luis or his homeland. But the formal and generic dimensions of the letter and its specific narrative idiosyncrasies reveal a compelling alternative history that belies its studied neutrality. Even its dual authorship, entirely conventional, announces from the outset a certain problem of narrative absence that structures the entire letter:

> ILLUSTRIOUS LORD,
>
> The grace of the Holy Spirit be always in the soul of Your Grace, Amen. As Father Vice-Provincial has no chance to write to Your Grace, concerned over the hurry needed in dispatching the pilot in returning to this land, he ordered me to write you this in his name, giving account of our journey and the rest.
>
> Having been delayed in arriving near here much more than we had expected by those difficulties which Your Grace will understand usually occur in the discovery of new lands, and [by] the discomforts of the weather, as the pilot will narrate to Your Grace more at length . . . we arrived here where we unloaded the gear yesterday. . . . (LL 85)

Acting as both autonomous author and subservient scribe, Quirós offers the account that will follow in Segura's name only, and as a mere preliminary to the oral but more substantial account of the pilot. The necessity of the pilot's swift return, moreover, stands as the primary reason offered for the absence of Segura's firsthand and written account: Segura is anxious to have the pilot reach Havana as soon as possible, where "*mas largamente dara cuenta*," where he will "narrate at more length" (LL 85). The statement not only suggests the pilot's assumed corroboration of Quirós's written account of events—"*as the pilot will narrate*"—but also highlights the discrepancy between Quirós's account and the future account to be offered by the pilot. The oral account will be longer and will presumably contain details missing from the written version—perhaps, the syntax of the last sentence suggests, details related to the unnamed "difficulties which Your Grace will understand usually occur in the discovery of new lands." The latter phrase announces its reliance on the particular knowledge and apprehension of its specific reader, Hinistrosa, and his ability to "understand" or infer the nature of adversities that Quirós has chosen to signal but quite self-consciously not to specify in the written and thereby enduring version of events. The reader knows only that these exigencies attend the colonial project: that they are "usual" is somewhat qualified, even undermined, by their nevertheless unforeseen occurrence—they have caused a delay in arrival at Ajacán, "much more" of a delay than was expected.

To speculate about what Quirós is leaving out of his letter when he refers Hinistrosa to the oral account of the pilot requires us to consider the kinds of details that Quirós *does* choose to offer in writing, particularly when he describes the early disappointment of the arrival in Ajacán:

> We find the land of Don Luis to be very different than we thought, not because he was at fault in giving his account of it, but because our Lord has chastised it with six years of barrenness and death, which has caused it to be left very depopulated compared to what it used to be, and because the deaths have been many, and [many] also those who have drifted to other lands to provide for their hunger, there remain but few of the people, whose leaders say that they wish to die where their fathers died, although already they have no maize, and have not found wild fruit, which they usually eat, neither roots nor anything else to eat, except for a very small amount obtained with great labor [because of the] already parched soil, and for this reason the Indians have had nothing more than good will to offer us, nor to those who came in the ship and certainly these Indians of don luis have shown good will in the way that they could, it seems to them that Don Luis has risen from the dead, and that he comes from heaven, and since all of those who have stayed are his relatives, they are greatly consoled in him and they have regained their strength and hope that God wants to help them and they say that they want to be like don Luis begging us to stay in this land with them, and the cacique, brother of Don Luis, having a very sick three-year-old son who was seven or eight leagues from here, and it appearing to him that he is already close to death he has requested that they go to baptize him, for which it seemed to the Vice Provincial to send last night [*a(yer) noche*] one of ours to baptize him for being already so close to death. (LL 85–86)

The details of this passage from Quirós's account have provided a number of historians with seemingly straightforward data about the situation in Ajacán, specifically evidence that the land had suffered terrible food shortage and depopulation when the Spanish arrived, and that the Indians were initially quite receptive to their visitors and would-be colonizers. Daniel Richter notes that "the paradise [Don Luis] described had, unbeknown to him, endured 'six years of famine and death'," and he concludes that the Indians' "begging [the Jesuits] to remain" may well have been because they wanted "prestige goods" the Spaniards were bearing, such as their chalices. Karen Kupperman similarly apprehends in the Jesuit letter a direct line to the Indians' point of view: "Devastating drought had sown despair among the Americans," yet the mission's possibilities "seemed hopeful," she writes; the Natives "believed Don Luis had returned from the dead to help them," but he "told his people that he had come only to lead them spiritually."[39]

But literary considerations yield a very different history when we pause to consider how the Jesuits in the early modern period actually regarded their own letter-writing process. Ignatius Loyola outlined that process quite specifically in a 1542 letter, directed and sent in multiple copies to all Jesuits in the order, and referring to the importance of Jesuits' upholding epistolary genre requirements for the success of the order's larger project.[40] "I recall having frequently told you and, when you were away, having often written," chides Loyola, to write letters which "can be shown to others; that is, to anyone at all" (62). Yet Loyola has apparently had frequent cause to withhold some missives because of their inferior epistolary quality:

> We dare not show some letters to friendly eyes who wish to see them, because of their lack of order and the irrelevant items they contain. Now, these friends are aware that we have letters from this one and that one, and they feel offended if we refuse to let them see these letters; thus we cause more disedification than edification. Everyone seems to have failed in this regard, and so a copy of this letter is being sent to all. (62)

Loyola's missive outlines two major criteria for the epistolary project: "see to it that your letter writing be directed [1] to the greater service of His Divine Goodness"; and (2) to "the greater advantage of our neighbor" (62)—in other words, the greater advantage of the letter's specific recipient, usually a superior, and by extension, the larger order itself. Loyola then offers more specific instructions about what appropriate Jesuit letters should include: "put down what each one is doing regarding preaching, hearing confessions, giving the Exercises, and other spiritual activities, as God makes use of each for the greater edification of our hearers and readers" (62). But he cautions his readers about what to exclude from their letters as well: "if the soil you are working be unproductive and there be little to write about, put down briefly something about health, your dealings with others, or such matters. Do not include irrelevant details but leave them for separate sheets . . ." (62).

The ensuing instructions do not clarify what such "irrelevant details" might be, but in the context of what he calls "unproductive" soil—perhaps especially that of the New World being advertised as an Eden, needing only a bit of tending for the happy conversion of its inhabitants—it seems clear that Loyola is instructing the Jesuits not to include in public letters details that might hint at anything less than shining success in their work. To avoid such problems in ordering and selection of details, Loyola suggests an elaborate editing process that "helps keep [one] from making mistakes": write the letter once "putting down what will be edifying," then "reread and correct it, keeping in mind that everyone is going to read it" (62–63). Then write it out "a second time, or have someone else do it, for whatever appears in writing needs closer scrutiny than what is merely spoken; the written word remains as a perpetual witness that cannot be changed or explained away as is easily done with speech" (63). And "in case your memory fails," Loyola concludes, "keep this letter or a digest of it before you when you write . . . ." (64).

Read alongside Loyola's theory of the epistolary arts, and his exacting genre specifications, the Quirós and Segura letter appears far from historically transparent in its descriptive work. If the Jesuits find "the land of Don Luis to be very different than we thought," then—true to Loyola's instructions—they are careful here to avoid the mistake of presenting its spiritual soil as "unproductive": the Natives immediately "hope that God wants to help them" and are, remarkably, "begging us to stay in this land with them." But the next sentence's abrupt shift to the sick child and Father Vice Provincial sending "one of ours to baptize him" recalls Loyola's injunction to avoid "irrelevant details" suggesting "unproductive soil" by instead writing "briefly something about health, your dealings with others [and] what each is doing regarding . . . hearing confessions . . . and other spiritual activities." Read in light of Loyola's Jesuit *ars dictaminis*, then, this brief passage suggests a fraught relation between the spoken and the unspoken, whereby the presence of certain subjects or modes—that of health, say, or extreme brevity—may in fact illuminate the untold subject of the larger discussion.

At the same time, the Quirós and Segura letter has included an explicit reference to a narrative outside the text of this particular missive: Don Luis's "account of [Ajacán]." Like the promised account of the pilot, this narrative too is oral and unrecorded. Unlike the pilot's account, however, this narrative has already been created and circulated at the time of Quirós's writing, which in turn sheds an oblique light on its content despite our lack of direct access to its oral medium. For Quirós's reference to its very existence speaks clearly in this passage to the disappointed expectations of the Spanish upon arrival to a land "very different" than hoped for. The Jesuits' insistence that Don Luis is not "at fault" in having offered an apparently very different narrative of Ajacán in fact brings that exact possibility to the foreground. Precisely what kind of "account" had Don Luis offered the Jesuits when he urged a mission in Ajacán? Here again an attention to generic conventions seems crucial in limning the signifying force of this missing narrative: for the Spanish term the Jesuits use is "relación," the equivalent of "account" in English, but in the sixteenth century also a specific genre that proliferated within and was particularly suited to New World contexts. While New World Spanish writers such as Hernán Cortés, Álvar Núñez Cabeza de Vaca, and Bartolomé de Las Casas, for example, all explicitly situate their works within the genre of the *relación*, it is also, as colonial Latin Americanists have shown, a notably "humble" genre, "rooted in feudalism," one that "ordinary people could avail themselves of," "familiar even to the less-educated" because of its pragmatism: a *relación* makes a case, seeks a specific end, and encodes the "dynamics of petition" in its address to superiors who sat in judgment of it.[41] Though we do not have access to the oral text of Don Luis's own *relación* describing and urging colonization of Ajacán, the intertextual relation suggested by certain details in the Jesuit letter strongly indicate that it made its case for Jesuit settlement through particular topoi that would, in fact, have been familiar to Don Luis from both his religious education in Mexico and his contact with various priests and soldiers in Spain, Cuba, and Florida: the topoi of El Dorado and the abundant Eden, for example, the paradisiacal place of endless riches and innocent Indians, whose natural meekness and goodness render them ideal subjects of conversion, and whose natural generosity empties material conquest of its violence. More broadly, after all, it was precisely Las Casas's claim that Spanish atrocities had destroyed the indigenous Eden of the Caribbean and New Spain that led the Jesuits to the doctrine of peaceful conversion, and that had, in 1570, brought the Jesuits to Ajacán without military accompaniment of any kind that might corrupt their spiritual work in the Edenic place that Don Luis appears to have described.

If what the Jesuits find in Ajacán differs starkly from what they believed they would find, Quirós and Segura nevertheless struggle to avoid passing a negative judgment in their letter upon Don Luis's *relación*. They do not find "falta" (lack, error, or personal fault) in his account, and so they must explain the narrative discrepancy yielding their disappointed expectations through the logic of divine discipline: in rhetorical terms, what they perceive is the *locus desertus*, the site of depopulation, and the *locus morbus*, site of disease and death—a human landscape marked by God's disfavor ("Our Lord has chastised it").[42] And yet even the Jesuits' observation of scarcity and depopulation, which many historians have taken largely at face value, might be characterized as a perception rather than a fact, if we keep in mind that much of the information they report in their letter is of course contingent upon the mediation of Don Luis himself, the only bilingual Spanish-Algonquian translator available for communication with the Ajacán Indians. Indeed, recent work on disease ecology in the Native southeast, which suggests that only after English colonization did Columbian Exchange diseases have more than a limited effect, would seem to validate the possibility that Don Luis transmits a false narrative of depopulation to the Jesuits.[43] Perhaps not surprisingly, then, another firsthand Jesuit account of the Ajacán Indians, written less than two years later, describes the state of Ajacán rather differently than does the Quirós and Segura letter: "What I have seen in this land is that there are more people here than in any of the other lands I have seen until now along the discovered coast [of La Florida]" (LL 106). Having lived and worked as a missionary in the Florida outposts of Tacobago, Guale, and Orista, this priest of the order made several comparative observations about Don Luis's homeland that would seem to contradict Quirós's description: "It seems to me that [the natives here] live more settled (*más de assiento*) than in other parts where I have been. . . . There are fewer inconveniences and inconsistencies [here] than in other parts where I have been. . . . [and] it appears to me that there are *more people* and [that] this land is *more populated* with natives than the others where I have been."[44]

Thus, if we comprehend the historical event of Don Luis's translative mediation between the Jesuits and the Indians as precisely a *literary* feature of the text that records this event, we can better understand the implicit but powerful narrative tension throughout the letter of Quirós and Segura: a tension between the explicit narrator, here Quirós, and the implied narrator, Don Luis, who tells the Jesuits much of the story that Quirós will narrate. This tension registers most obviously in Don Luis's insistent presentation of himself to the Jesuits through the putative perspectives and emotions of the Natives: phrases like "it seems to them" signal his own characterizations of indigenous frames of mind that he in turn narrates for the Jesuit writers in familiarly European frames of reference. Avowing that he appears to the Natives as "risen from the dead," as if "he comes from heaven"—a figuration that at once recalls the resurrection of Christ and the legendary (and apocryphal) Aztec identification of Cortés as the god Quetzalcoatl, returning from afar—Don Luis draws upon a trope of apotheosis that was by then already a recurring staple of Spanish colonial discourse.[45] Next detailing a Christian scene of deathbed conversion that mirrors his own in Mexico City, Don Luis directs the Jesuits' attention to a child—hidden from view of the settlers and named only as the young son of the "cacique, brother of Don Luis"—and the occasion of a potential last-minute salvation before an imminent demise.[46] Quirós clearly presents all this information as evidence of a general ripeness for conversion; yet it is equally, indeed *more,* plausible to read Don Luis's configuration as a motivated adaptation of colonial and Christian tropes to a new situation, one in which he himself, rather than the Jesuit Fathers, has now assumed some portion of narrative control.

Don Luis's interpretive role in mediating Ajacán and its inhabitants for the Jesuits achieved two obvious but important effects. On the one hand, it served to convince the Jesuit leaders to continue their mission and to send on its way their ship, which was certainly outfitted with weapons that the spiritual colonists did not have after its departure. Had Don Luis waited to arrive on land and then merely run away, leaving the Jesuits to return to Santa Elena or Cuba without him, he would have risked an aggressive response toward his homeland from the captain and sailors. Perhaps more important, he would have given up his own authority as an interpreter and thus the crucial opportunity to shape the narrative that would be transmitted via letter to prospective colonizers of Ajacán. Don Luis's first narrative goal in interpreting Ajacán for the Jesuits was thus to convince them to stay, despite the seeming lack of indigenous subjects who appear to be available for conversion. According to Don Luis's account as transmitted by Quirós, late March and early April will bring many tribes to Ajacán for planting season and a search for food, providing them with a "great willingness for the Holy Gospel" (LL 86). Don Luis's central character in this interpretive narrative is appropriately the *cacique* himself who "has sought this very thing especially with great solicitude": the preaching of the Holy Gospel to arriving tribes (LL 86). As Quirós notes, "Therefore, it has seemed best to Father to risk remaining" (LL 86).

On the other hand, however, no one in Santa Elena, Cuba, or Spain reading Quirós's letter from a utilitarian point of view could be encouraged by its details, supplied by the translator, of famine and death, fruitless labor, parched soil, wandering Indians, and hunger. Most daunting (if least climatologically accurate) is Don Luis's narrative of Ajacán's extreme weather: "the great snows found in this land" prevent the Indians from hunting for their already meager source of food, the "roots by which they usually sustain themselves."[47] The indigenous characters of Don Luis's account heighten the effect of its doomed setting, all avowing that they "are so famished, that [they] all believe they will perish of hunger and cold this winter" (LL 86).

Indeed, taken as a whole, the Quirós and Segura letter appears to provide a virtual advertisement *against* further colonial endeavor anywhere near Ajacán, despite Quirós's often strained attempts to frame in positive terms the translated accounts offered by Don Luis. Grasping at the possibility of a long sought-after northwest passage—an opportunity to perform "service to Our Lord and His Majesty" with "an entrance into the mountains and to China" (LL 86)—Quirós focuses the final part of his portion of the letter on the one piece of translated news that is neutral:

> The information that until now was possible to have about the inland region is what some Indians whom we met farther down this river [gave]. They informed us that three or four days' journey from here was the mountain, and two days [*las dos dellas*] one goes on a river and after the mountain another day's journey or two one can see another sea. (LL 87)

But the "information" proffered here is not really new and adds little or nothing to what the Spanish would already know before gathering this confusing testimony from "some Indians": there are mountains to cross, and travel inland by river will be necessary. The promise that crossing the mountains will allow a view of "another sea" is diminished by the vagueness about this body of water. Even Quirós knows that his acquisition of knowledge from the Indians will be of little value on the transatlantic market of information. "If anything else can be known with more certainty and clarity, we will get it," he promises, before closing with a description of the settlers' dire situation as a means of apology: "Thus there has not been opportunity to get more information" (LL 87).

The uncertain and unsettling nature of the information that the Spaniards are receiving from the Indians via Don Luis thus underwrites much of the letter. In Segura's brief section of the missive, after confirming that he has "ordered Father Quirós to give a long account to you of everything," he addresses a mysterious non sequitur to Hinistrosa, a firm refusal to what was apparently a request to find and bring back another indigenous youth to send to the Indian school in Havana for a colonial education and a future career as a translator: "In no way does it seem suitable to me to send a boy there, someone [taken] from these Indians, as the pilot will explain, and other reasons [cosas]" (LL 87–88). At the same time, Segura also outlines an odd chain of transmission of information about getting to Ajacán, one that makes little sense given that Hinistrosa has never traveled there: I am "writing to His Majesty [King Philip]," Segura writes, that "Your Grace will send on to His Majesty clear news and information of the route for coming to Axacam [sic]" (LL 87). Why Segura will not include this information in his own letter to King Philip becomes clearer, however, in light of a strange warning made by Quirós that any subsequent supply ship must follow a different route into the mainland of Ajacán. "It is not convenient to enter by the river as we did," Quirós cautions darkly, "for we did not have as good information from the Indians concerning where best we should have entered" (LL 86). The Jesuits, it seems, do not know exactly *where* they are in Ajacán—"As to the information about . . . the route along which [any subsequent] pilot should be directed," Quirós notes, "[the current] pilot will give it"—and they do not trust the indigenous guidance they have received thus far (LL 86).

The possibility of such intentional misguidance appears again in the final section of the letter, a postscript in which Quirós explains the technique by which new Spanish ships may find the settlers. It is clear from what he says here that the Jesuits cannot avoid relying upon the Indians for knowledge of arriving ships so far from the settlement to which Don Luis has directed them. But the Jesuits appear no longer to trust the people "begging [them] to remain" in Ajacán, for they are attempting to reduce their role from guides to messengers, re-exerting some of the narrative control they have lost to Don Luis through the technology and transmission of writing. "From the time it is understood that the frigate is to come with the help requested," Quirós writes:

> An Indian or two will be sent with a letter to the mouth of the arm of the sea, where any ship coming must pass; they will make a large smoke cloud by day and a fire at night, and more than this, when the ship arrives the

people there will have your sealed letter and they will not give it until [the sailors] give another one like it, which will be as a sign that those who come are friendly and are those who bring the message. Your Grace take heed of this sign or inform whoever comes about it, the letter will carry notification about the way which must be followed in entering and *will serve as a guide.* (LL 88)

The plan for ensuring proper recognition between newcomer Spaniards and the Indians watching for them thus depends upon a series of exchanged signals, proceeding from the nonverbal smoke clouds and fires to the equally nonverbal mimesis of the two letters—the Indians will have one and will expect to see "another one like it."[48] Entirely circumventing the need for any process of translation, the system next incorporates the use of these letters as verbal texts whose contents are inaccessible to the Indians—*cartas guardadas*—both by virtue of their "sealed" and their *written* form. That the Jesuits will rely on the Indians as letter-bearing proxies is perhaps unavoidable given the inland site of their settlement. But inscription, according to their new plan, will now substitute for the usual indigenous guide: the letter and not the Indians will transmit the necessary information and lead the newcomers to the settlement.[49]

The Jesuit narrators themselves, in other words, have perceived the subversive possibilities of translation to which they are subject in Ajacán. Quirós's postscript notes almost defensively that their interpreter "does well as was hoped, and is most obedient regarding that which Father orders him to do, with much respect for Father, as also for the rest of us here" (LL 88). On the other hand, relations with the Natives have already deteriorated in the few days since their arrival:

before the Indians whom we met on the way would give to us from their poverty what they had; after, as [the Indians] saw that these [men] had brought I don't know what trinkets for the ears etc. of corn, they would bring the ears and other food and would ask that [the men] give them something and they would give it, [the Indians] arguing that this is how it was done with the others, and since Father had forbidden that anyone do this, so that they would not become accustomed to it and then afterwards want to trade [for food], [the Indians] returned with it. (LL 88)

Despite their "most obedient" interpreter, then, the Jesuits are losing confidence in their understanding of the Native point of view and the meaning of their interactions. The letter conjectures that this problem with the Indians must be "Due to an error . . . made by whom on the ship I don't know . . . some trade of food was made, [and] it was seen later [in] the inconvenience that followed" (LL 88). But Quirós's external narrative of some seaman's "error" in trading with the Indians for food is underwritten by the trace of a more motivated form of communication—a trace that resides in the striking absence of any explanation from their interpreter of the Natives' new economic position. If the indigenous point of view is left pointedly untold here, the Natives' choice to barter rather than "give . . . from their poverty" is clear enough, for it leaves the Jesuits entirely without sustenance, and in a situation grown increasingly dire. There runs throughout the entire letter, in other words, a deforming tension between Don Luis's supporting interpretive role in the narrative of conversion and redemption that the Jesuits seek to inscribe and his central and wholly autonomous role as an internal narrator of a story that is shaping the outcome of events themselves: the hidden authorial hand behind both the letter of Quirós and Segura and the ultimately failed ending of their colony.

The Lost Colony of Ajacán and the Letter of Juan Rogel

The letter of Quirós and Segura received no answer until the spring of 1572, when a ship under the direction of the original pilot returned to the Bahía de Santa María carrying supplies for the tiny Spanish settlement. Though the pilot knew his way back to the original site of disembarkation, there was no "Indian or two" waiting with a sealed letter bearing directions. Instead, the pilot and his crew saw a group of Ajacán Natives on the coast whose strange performance—one writer would later term it a "stratagem" (*ardid* [LL 117])—suggested to them a sinister situation: several of the Indians donned Jesuit habits and walked back and forth while the rest of the group called out to the ship that "there were the Fathers [and] to come [ashore]."[50] Alarmed by the sight of the Indians dressed as priests, the Spanish crew quickly decided to return to Cuba. Before doing so, however, they were able to capture and take with them two Native hostages, one of whom jumped overboard while at sea. The other was brought to Havana, where he eventually conveyed the news that the Cuban colonial authorities and Jesuits most feared: the settlers in Ajacán had apparently been killed by their own translator, the Christian convert and godson of the Mexican viceroy, "el don Luisillo": young Don Luis himself (LL 117).

Yet the captive also informed his interrogators that one member of the lost colony of Ajacán had been spared: a young boy named Alonso de Olmos.[51] Alonso was the Creole son of a Santa Elena settler and had served in the mission as a woodsman; despite his youth, he represented a possible source of information about what had happened to the settlement in Don Luis's homeland. When Menéndez learned that his second attempt at a colony in Ajacán had been destroyed, and that his long-time interpreter had betrayed him, he determined to accompany the next voyage there himself; in August 1572—it had been almost two years since Quirós and Segura wrote their letter about the beginning of the Jesuit settlement—Menéndez arrived in Ajacán in search of Alonso and the truth about the demise of his colony. He also directed his soldiers to capture Don Luis and to seek ample retribution for the deaths of the other colonists, which they did through the capture and mass execution of numerous Ajacán Natives. Don Luis was never found. But Alonso was soon brought forth, and he had a profoundly unsettling story for Menéndez and the Spaniards who had come to rescue him. In telling it—and this is a crucial point for all that will follow—Alonso became the sole eyewitness to the events in Ajacán over the previous year and the sole source of information about what happened between Don Luis and the Jesuits.

The first and most immediate record of Alonso's recovery and his oral account of what happened between Don Luis and the Jesuit colonists was written by Father Juan Rogel, a priest who had served in Santa Elena and Havana, and who had known Segura and the other missionaries as well as Don Luis before they sailed to Ajacán in 1570. In August 1572, Rogel accompanied Menéndez and his soldiers—along with the Indian captured by the pilot who had failed to find the settlers earlier that spring—back to Ajacán to find Alonso and to confirm the fatal outcome of the settlement. In an August 28 letter to Francis Borgia, who was by then the Superior General of the Jesuit Society in Spain, Rogel provided an account of the trip written directly from the Bahía de Santa María, penned just after the return of Alonso to the Spaniards:

> Arriving at this bay, the Governor gave order that we go and search for little Alonso, who is the boy who came with Father Baptista, of whom we had news that he had not been murdered, from one of the Indians of these parts that the pilot captured, when he went the second time, and we brought him [the Indian] in chains in our company . . . It seemed [best] to me to go [inland] carrying the imprisoned Indian in my company, in order to be translator for us. The order the Governor gave to the pilot of this frigate was to try to take the principal chief of that shore, uncle of Don Luis, [along] with his principal people . . . and in taking them, to ask that they give us the boy and that later we would release them: and so it occurred to the letter . . . (LL 103)

If Rogel's focus in the account is upon the triumph of Alonso's recovery from the Indians, it is also upon the precision to-the-letter with which it has been achieved: by means of ostensibly transparent communication with the Ajacán Natives. As the account continues, the Indians' discourse emerges with perfect clarity: "they said that a principal chief had the boy, who was two days journey from there, and was near this port," explains Rogel, and "they asked us for time to send for him and bring him. We gave them the time they asked for. . . ." (LL 104). As if unmediated, this smooth exchange across languages serves as a fitting prelude to the wholeness and utter certainty of the first-hand Spanish account that the Menéndez mission hopes to achieve: "It is a marvelous thing," as Rogel puts it later in the letter, "in how short a time the governor learned what had happened there by means of the boy" (LL 104).

Yet Rogel's text also undermines its own fiction of transparent understanding, as the foregoing passage suggests. For a new translator has entered the story of Ajacán: picked up, as was Don Luis, by a Spanish vessel, this interpreter by contrast is an "imprisoned native," "brought . . . in chains." In stressing the state of Spanish security from this interpreter's flight or retribution, Rogel's repetition of the image also figures the violence and instability of translation in the colonial context. "[T]o ask that they give us the boy" requires both the interpretive will of their chained translator—a hostage to the Spanish for about four months by this point—and the "taking" of new Indians, whose release is contingent first upon successful communication and then upon compliance with the requested transaction. The Indians eventually produce Alonso, of course, but not until the Spanish have "killed some Indians who were trying to shoot arrows at us and wounded a soldier," and then fought off another "ambush of many canoes loaded with archers ready to attack the vessel . . . concealed so that no one was seen except the two who steered and told us that they brought us oysters" (LL 104). Finally, Menéndez orders "a blast from the arquebuses into a pile of Indians who were crowded on the riverbank," and "lots [are] killed" in the battle over Alonso: for, apparently, "the chief who had the boy . . . did not want to let him be brought to our ship" (LL 104). Marked at every turn by bloodshed, the "marvelous" translational process by which Alonso was eventually "sent . . . to this port with two Indians" proves to be anything but smooth or transparent (LL 104).

Moreover, Alonso's role, once he is returned to the Spanish, also proves more problematic than Rogel is willing to acknowledge. As figured in the priest's letter, Alonso supplements and provides a kind of double for Don Luis's role as an internal narrator in the Quirós and Segura letter—and, as we shall see, Alonso's internal narration registers a similarly deforming tension between the Jesuit and indigenous points of view:

> I will now give Your Paternity account of how came the death of Ours who were here, according to what this boy reports. He says that later [after] arriving here Don Luis abandoned [the Jesuits], because he did not sleep in their house more than two nights, nor was he in the village where the Fathers made their settlement, more than five days, and [then] he went off to live with a brother of his who lived a day and a half away from where Ours were; and Father master Baptista [Segura] having sent a novice Brother two times to call [on him], [Don Luis] refused to come [back] and Ours remained in great suffering, for they had no one by whom they could make themselves understood to the Indians. (LL 104–05)

Rogel begins by foregrounding the dependence of his own status as a narrator upon the narration provided by Alonso: the ensuing story can only be told according to "what this boy reports." Drawing upon familiar religious and colonial tropes, this internal narration figures Don Luis's gradual physical movement away from the Jesuits in correspondence with his return to Native heathendom: from the two nights of intimacy in the same sleeping hut to his five days in the Christian space of the Jesuit village and finally to the journey away, where he lives with the Indians, Don Luis's apostasy signifies both spatially and temporally—just as his spiritual transformation, from agent of Christian conversion to murderous savage, is both corporeal and discursive. Alonso's internal narrative thus privileges the Jesuits' loss of their translator as a source of "great suffering" even over the problem of starvation: "no tenían con quien poderse entender con los indios" (LL 105)—a phrase that evokes, in this particular context, the Jesuits' central problem as that of making themselves understood rather than that of understanding.

But the Ajacán Natives understand the Jesuits far better than vice versa, as Alonso suggests in the strange, internal narration of Rogel's letter:

> And as [Father Baptista] sent twice for [Don Luis] and he did not come, he decided to send Father Quirós and Brother Gabriel de Solís and Brother Juan Baptista to the village of the cacique which is near where Don Luis then was, so that they could bring him with them, and barter for maize on the way. And the Sunday after the feast of the Purification, Don Luis went to the three [Jesuits] who were returning home with other Indians, and Don Luis shot an arrow through the heart of Father Quirós: and there murdered the three who were coming to call on him. And later he went to the village where the Fathers were, in peace and with great dissimulation with many other Indians, and murdered the five who were left there; and the same Don Luis was he who gave the first wounds with one of the machetes they [had] sent to trade with the Indians, and he had just murdered Father Maestro Baptista with an axe, and later those [Indians] who came with him finished off murdering the rest. . . . And later they distributed all the clothing among Don Luis and his two brothers who participated in murdering [the Jesuits]. . . . After having murdered the others, [Alonso] says that [Don Luis] left the vestments and books and the rest that he had closed up in coffers; and after Don Luis returned they all took their share [*hizieron su repartimiento*]; and a brother of Don Luis, [Alonso] said, is going about wearing the vestments for saying Mass and the altar cloths; and the silver chalice, this captured cacique told me, Don Luis gave to a principal cacique who is in the interior; and the paten [was given] to one of these Indians that [we have] captured; and some of the [holy] images were tossed aside . . . (LL 105–07)

In this murky account of the colony's violent demise, narrated by a Creole boy who has lived for two years among the Ajacán Indians, but filtered through Rogel's letter to his Jesuit superior, we can nevertheless see clearly how little understanding the Jesuits have of Don Luis's actions and his refusals to return to their village, and how great their dependence upon him for mere survival in trading for maize. Other aspects of the account, however, remain more mysterious. While the larger letter follows some colonial conventions, in this unsettling portion structured by Alonso's account, Don Luis and his comrades are hardly the unthinking and brutal but easily intimidated savages that many early European texts specialized in constructing. According to Alonso's internal narration, for example, the Indians have chosen a particular holy day—"the Sunday after the feast of the Purification"—to mark with Don Luis's final apostasy. They enact the murders not impulsively but "in peace and dissimulation," and with an evident unity of agreement and purpose. Alonso emphasizes, moreover, that Don Luis quite specifically destroys his former masters with their own tools of colonial enterprise, when he is himself the one who inflicts the first wounds "with one of those machetes they sent to trade with the Indians." After the murders are completed, Alonso explains, the Indians distribute and make use of the rest of the Jesuits' belongings: going around clothed in the Mass vestments and altar cloths; giving away clearly functional items such as a silver chalice and a paten; and finally throwing away some of the less useful images of Christian worship (algunas imágines . . . las hechó por la calle).[52] These appear, in other words, to be carefully discerning and partially symbolic acts of resistance to the religious colonialism represented by the Jesuits' belongings—which are strikingly apportioned here among the Indians in a *repartimiento*, a strange and ironic restaging of the colonial labor division that apportioned Indian slaves to Spanish colonists.

In telling the story of Don Luis's betrayal, as told by Alonso, Rogel's letter strains to contain the story's inherently unsettling qualities by framing the alleged crime against the Jesuits within a narrative of religious *castigo*, the divine punishment or chastisement for mortal sin, in this case administered by the colonial hand of Menéndez himself (LL 106). "The country remains very frightened from this chastisement the Governor inflicts," Rogel notes with evident satisfaction, "for before [the Indians] said they were able to kill the Spaniards without [their] offering resistance": "But, as they have seen the opposite of what [they saw] in the Fathers, they tremble, and this chastisement has resounded greatly throughout all the land, and if this [further] chastisement is done, it will be even more famous" (LL 106).

Not only have the Spanish achieved retribution for the deaths of the Jesuits, Rogel insists, but the *castigo* itself has achieved terrifying narrative prominence among the Indians. Those who know the tale of Menéndez's chastisement are fearful; the story is already *sonado*—famous—and promises to become more so if, in further chastisement, Menéndez kills the rest of the Indian hostages who are being held until Don Luis and his two brothers are brought forward. The captured cacique has "promised," Rogel explains, "that he would bring them within five days" (LL 106). But Rogel's triumphal account of Indian shock and awe before the Spanish *castigo* falters when he admits that the Spaniards are in fact still waiting (*este término estamos esperando*)—perhaps not even so much for Don Luis to be remanded as for the allotted time to run out (LL 106). The Spanish are quite unlikely, as Rogel already seems to know, to achieve the extradition of their fugitive by the Indians.

Toward the end of the letter, Rogel's account returns to Alonso's internal narration and offers up a mysterious episode that appears to contain the Ajacán Indians' acts of unsettlement within a Catholic framework of meaning. In a kind of structural reversal that strains to provide closure to the tale, there remains unscathed in Ajacán "a large crucifix in a chest": "some Indians told this boy [Alonso] that they do not dare approach that chest, because three Indians who wanted to see what was in it, died there later; and so they say that they keep it closed and protected" (LL 107). The narrative implication attached to this event is both heavy and ambiguous. There is, on the one hand, what appears from the Catholic point of view to be the corrupted trinity of the "three Indians," who are destroyed by the powers attributed to the sacramental chest—or perhaps by their curiosity to see inside its Pandora's box of Christian mystery. On the other hand, the purported consequences of the event—which is, after all, not witnessed by Alonso but, according to his own internal account, transmitted from "some Indians"—present some curious contradictions: the Indians "do not dare approach" the chest but they nevertheless possess or have it (*la tienen*); they keep it closed, and it is also guarded (*guardada*), as if to prevent others from opening it. The Indians have, moreover, destroyed the remaining purveyors of Christian doctrine: "About the books," Rogel concludes without fanfare or flourish, "[Alonso] said that they told him that [after] removing the clasps, [the Indians] threw them on the ground (*en la calle*) and tore them all up" (LL 107). If the death of the three Indians who wished to see inside the crucifix-laden chest registers, from the Jesuit author's point of view, a symbolic punishment visited upon the heathens and evidencing divine triumph, the Natives' obliteration of the devotional texts suggests a powerful response to a more literal source of danger: the religious ideology of the Spaniards who wish to colonize Ajacán. This final detail apparently proves too stark to reframe within triumphal terms, for Rogel announces in the final paragraph of his letter, "And as nothing else occurs to me to write, I stop . . ." (LL 107).

Don Luis, *Estragado*: The *Relación* of Juan Rogel

By the time Rogel composed his official *relación* of the story of Don Luis and the Jesuit settlement, nearly four decades later, between 1607 and 1611, he had indeed found something more to write—and new ways of telling his tale in order to elide, and effectively to compensate for, the problems of translation marking his first account as well as the letter of Quirós and Segura. Unlike his 1572 letter to Borgia, Rogel's *relación*, written at Borgia's request and clearly intended for a wider audience, does not assume the reader's prior knowledge of Don Luis. Rogel sketches his background before introducing the events in Ajacán:

> . . . And [Menéndez] returned from Spain, where he had run across a Christian Indian, a native of Florida, who, some Dominican friars passing through there, brought him to Mexico and there he received baptism, Don Luis de Velasco, father of the present viceroy, being his godfather. And thus the Indian was called Don Luis, the son of a petty chief [*un caciquillo*] of la Florida. (LL 115)

The central indigenous figure of the narrative thus enters the story this time through mere happenstance, introduced straightforwardly by the designation of his Indian identity, his religious status, and his country of origin. His arrival in Mexico is somewhat vaguer, attributed to some unnamed friars of another order who passed through his country at an unspecified time. But the striking nature of the ensuing baptism of this character under the direction of a figure of unmistakably high status—"the father of the present viceroy" of all New Spain—is clear-cut. And there is no mistaking the biting social irony introduced by the outcome of this event, which allows an Indian of questionable status—the son not of a *cacique* but a *caciquillo*, a diminutive lord, a petty chieftain—to take not only the name but the title of a prominent colonial official (LL 115).

But what begins as an irony of seemingly arbitrary events—brought by friars to Mexico, the Indian becomes "Don Luis" because of his baptismal sponsor—evolves over the next lines of the relation into a dimension of *character*, when Rogel describes this newly named Indian figure as "*muy ladino*" (LL 115). Rogel justifies and elaborates this ambivalent, foreshadowing descriptor by remarking that Menéndez "delivered [Don Luis] to Father Baptista [Segura] in Havana because he was spreading the word (*publicava*) that he was the son of a great *cacique*, and as such, our King in Spain had ordered him to be given an allowance and dressed him" (LL 115).

Rogel thus evinces a quite specific kind of character—distinct from the cryptically obedient and helpful Don Luis who inexplicably kills his Christian fellows and religious masters. There is nothing mysterious or particularly frightening about this new version of the translator. He may not be who he says he is, and he knows how to make a minor profit from his lies, but he *is*—from the narrative's vantage point, anyway—what he *appears* to be: a boastful charlatan. The distinction between the narrative's vantage point and that of its characters is crucial to the relation's symbolic meaning and effect. Where the narrative casts a figure who "spread the word" of his exaggerated status—and the verb *publicar* here evinces the very overlap of oral and written forms of narrative within which Don Luis's authorship survives—its character "Father Baptista" (Juan Baptista de Segura) mistakenly takes Don Luis at face value and believes he will not only remain loyal to the Spanish Jesuits but will afford "the help which Saint Paul [found] in Timothy" (LL 115). The allusion to the two biblical travelers and missionaries allows Rogel to characterize Segura as naïve and perhaps also grandiose—to consider himself a latter-day Paul—as well as to foreshadow the violence awaiting at Ajacán, where the Jesuits (rather than Don Luis) will in fact share a fate similar to that of Timothy, who was beaten and stoned to death by angry pagans for trying to preach conversion to them.

At the same time, Rogel's relation introduces a specific narrative thread concerning the previously unexplained motive for Don Luis's actions, which settles some of the questions raised in his original letter. The problem with Don Luis, Rogel contends, was adultery:

> On entering the province of Ajacán, Don Luis soon became corrupt [*maleó*] and left the Fathers, succumbing to women [*entregándose a mugeres*], leaving the Fathers and Brothers alone . . . Father [Segura] . . . sent Father Quirós to where [Don Luis] was to beg him to come, [but] the ill-fated [Don Luis] had become wholly corrupted [*estragado*] . . . (LL 115–16)

Modern historians, from Lewis and Loomie on, have often reproduced this narrative of sexual apostasy, and without qualification, though it only entered the record decades after the events—and was entirely absent in Rogel's on-the-spot 1572 letter detailing Alonso's account of what happened.[53] Yet the introduction into the narrative of Don Luis's adultery—or polygamy as Carrera described it: Don Luis "gave himself over with more abandon and with free rein [*sin rienda*] to all kinds of sins, marrying many women in pagan mode"—conveniently occludes other possible motivations for his destruction of the Spanish settlement, eliding a knowledge-based rationale with an ostensibly impulsive one, both cultural and physical (LL 126). In other words, the suggestions of a reasoned act of unsettlement marking Rogel's 1572 letter—the destruction of the books and Christian images, for example—are written over by a more familiar narrative: Don Luis's mortal sins with Indian women have left him *estragado*—corrupted, destroyed, ruined beyond redemption. Where before Don Luis destroyed the Jesuits with their own tools—"one of those machetes they sent to trade with the Indians"—now he degenerates into a primitive savage, "armed with clubs and poles" (LL 116). His very speech has become violence in this version—"to raise his club and to greet [Father Segura] were both the same thing, in such a way that giving his greetings [to Father Segura], he took his life"—a metaphorical figure for treasonous translation that will be reproduced in other Jesuit versions of the story.[54] The role of translation, too, has been eliminated entirely: the chained *lengua* from his

1572 letter plays no part in the recovery of Alonso, and is instead "kept in prison near Havana," though he will not "reveal the truth" (LL 117). In the absence of any explanation about their means of communication with the Indians, it becomes impossible in this version of the story for Rogel to say how and under what circumstances Alonso is returned to the Spanish. But when he inexplicably reenters the narrative, Alonso takes on the role of the missing translator—serving not as synecdochal indigenous *lengua* but as full-fledged *intérprete*, or interpreter—in a singularly one-way act of translation: he baptizes and catechizes the captured Indians, after which the Spaniards "hanged them from the ship where the Adelantado went, suspending them from the mast (*las entenas*)" (LL 117). The subversive possibilities of translation neatly contained, the narrative ends with the story of the closed chest and the fatal crucifix within. Now more detailed and rhythmic, the new version of the tale features each of the three Indians approaching the chest individually and meeting their fates sequentially rather than at once. It is no longer merely a punitive event but *un milagro*—and it fulfills a specific generic function: the required miracle attending any narrative of martyrdom designed to achieve canonization for its subjects.[55] Rogel's *relación* thus rewrites the unsettlement of Ajacán at the heart of his 1572 letter, domesticating Alonso's shattering story as the basis of potential Jesuit sainthood.

The Fictive and Visual Don Luis

Later Jesuit writers went on to retell the story inherited from Rogel, and in doing so they were forced to grapple with an unsettling problem of genre: how does one tell a conversion story in which the central figure of redemption apparently recants? As these later Jesuit relations move in time from the event itself, the writers begin to introduce increasingly self-conscious literary qualities and more pronouncedly fictive modes of characterization alongside more heavily allegorical meanings. Don Luis has no longer apostatized; he is inherently evil, a "*mal indio*," biding his time until he can become "*señor*," master over the fathers who are ostensibly leading him; he is "a blood-thirsty wolf [emerged from] sheep's clothing," and "another Judas" whose actions are elaborated through exegesis of specific biblical passages.[56] The fathers are tortured in elaborate ways before they are killed, the killings themselves embellished with competing forms of symbolism. In one version, Don Luis steals the clothing of Father Quirós after killing him, and then dresses as a priest before launching the attack on Father Segura and the others.[57] In another, he approaches the Jesuits the day before "the feast so solemn of our Lady of Candelaria" and requests hatchets to distribute among the Natives as "he wished to go with all the Indians to cut wood in order to construct a church for the Virgin"; with Segura kneeling at the altar, Don Luis—in a symbolic desecration of the chapel—"came and gave him a great blow to the head with the machete."[58] But this religious allegory finds a secular, colonial frame in the figure of Menéndez de Avilés—"*otro Alexandro*," as the Santa Elena colonist and official Bartolomé Martínez called him—who, according to some versions of the story, first encountered the young Don Luis in Ajacán and brought him to Spain to meet the king, and who later returned to lead the punitive mission (LL 148). "Another Alexander," Menéndez both begins and ends the story, and lends it epic flourishes of conquest and adventure through his early arrival among the Indians whom he "regale[s] with food and clothing," and of military prowess and victory, through his later retribution for the deaths of the fathers (LL 148).

By the mid-seventeenth century, the story of Don Luis found its way into visual representation as well when Matthias Tanner, a Jesuit professor of theology and philosophy writing in Prague, incorporated it into his massive 1675 history of Jesuit martyrs around the world, *Societas Jesu usque ad sanguinis et vitae profusionem militans*.[59] The illustrations that accompany Tanner's account, engraved by the German artist Melchior Küsel, include two images adapted from events in Ajacán—one of which offers a memorable portrayal of Don Luis himself.

The image (see Figure 2.1) is often reproduced in current historical accounts, and it easy to see why. The illustration captures not only the action of the killing, set dramatically against a swirling sky and wind-blown tree—a stark physical landscape that parallels a starker human one—but also the story's elusive oppositional figure, the always opaque Don Luis, who appears here in fleshy detail. Though the caption omits his name—citing instead Father Juan Baptista de Segura, Brothers Gabriel Gómez, Pedro Mingot de Linares, and Sancho Zaballos, and lay catechist Cristóbol Redondo, who were "in Florida for their faith in Christ slaughtered"—the visual figure of Don Luis in fact overshadows all of the Jesuits.[60] Küsel's engraving proposes a villain considerably larger than his Spanish victims, four of whom lie slain on the ground, while the frail and kneeling figure of Segura awaits the hatchet poised above. More pronounced than Don Luis's proportional size, though, are the muscular contours of his nearly naked body, prominently displayed as a contrast to the fine-featured and fully clothed victim. Before undertaking the killing of the Jesuits, we are meant to understand, Don Luis has shed his European attire and reverted to what the artist envisions as his original dress; his blank eyes, ill-proportioned limbs, large and heavy features all contribute to the illustration's larger story of degeneration into savagery, made familiar by a number of the later Jesuit narratives. The weapon that Don Luis wields in this depiction is in fact not the primitive club of such accounts; it is one of the hatchets brought by the Jesuits themselves, an instrument of colonial settlement now turned against them. Yet the most significant detail in the illustration lies in the artist's subtle deviation from Tanner and his

P. Ioañes Bapt: de Segura, Gabriel Gomez, Petrus de Linarez Sancti, Sauelli, Christoph: Rotundi, Hisp: S.I. in Florida. pro Christi fide trucidati A. 1571. 8. Feb.
C. Screta del.   Melch. Küsell f.

FIGURE 2.1 *Don Luis and the Martyring of the Jesuits*

Source: From Matthias Tanner, *Societas Jesu usque ad sanguinis et vitae profusionem militans* (1675). Photograph courtesy of Albert and Shirley Small Special Collections Library, University of Virginia.

sources. Where Tanner follows his predecessors in describing the large group of "Caciquem" or Indian caciques who attack the Jesuits, Küsel has presented a single figure in this depiction: there is no collective with whom—and on whose behalf—Don Luis acts in his murders of the Spaniards. The engraving thus reduces a shared military act of unsettlement to a barbaric instance of individual violence.

Less well known than the "Martyrdom of Juan Baptista Segura," as the image is sometimes titled, is the earlier Küsel engraving to appear in Tanner's account of the failed Ajacán settlement. This illustration (see Figure 2.2) depicts the "barbarous killing for their faith in Christ," as the caption puts it, of the priest Luis de Quirós and two of the lay catechists, Gabriel de Solís and Juan Baptista Méndez.[61]

In this depiction, Don Luis has been eliminated from the engraving's subject matter, but he remains nevertheless the absent center that disturbs from without. Only the priest and the two lay catechists are visible in the scene, while their killer is hidden from the viewer, who must reconcile the illustration with Tanner's text. Is Don Luis too despicable to be shown or not important enough to detract from the spectacle of the dying Jesuits? The engraving seems to sidestep the question by highlighting quite different literary dimensions of the narrative, tethering the story of Don Luis to a recognizable Western aesthetic tradition while also apparently acknowledging its ultimate incongruence with that tradition. The landscape of Ajacán is remarkably detailed and immediately evokes the weird foreignness of the setting; the twisting branches and lush plant life threaten to overwhelm the scene's human figures, who are themselves awkwardly at odds with one another. The left-hand figure is the youngest and thus, contrary to the caption's ordering, is probably not Quirós but one of the less important catechists, either Solís or Méndez. Impaled by two arrows, he holds his arms out wide, in prayer and resignation to his fate. His eyes are cast back at something or someone, perhaps the killer whom he once trusted, but the expression on his face is impassive and gentle. There is no distress here, only the innocence and acceptance of a handsome youth (he is by far the most visually appealing of the three figures) pierced to death by arrows: a sixteenth-century Spanish Saint Sebastian in the New World. But this particular Sebastian's heroic poise cannot fully evoke the triumphant aesthetic achievement of Christian discourse for which it traditionally doubles. The left-hand catechist is already a colonial ghost: half obscured by the substantial bulk of the middle figure, he floats disembodied and wraith-like above his two companions. They too have been shot with arrows for their faith, but they devolve markedly within the very tradition they should rightfully inhabit. The middle figure fails to rise to the centrality of his positioning; his face wholly hidden from view, he clutches his head rather than bear his exquisite suffering with the impassive dignity of a true Catholic martyr. The right-hand figure—bearded and older,

FIGURE 2.2 *The Martyring of Priest Luis de Quirós, Gabriel de Solís, and Juan Baptista Méndez*

Source: From Matthias Tanner, *Societas Jesu usque Ad sanguinis et vitae profusionem militans* (1675). Photograph courtesy of Albert and Shirley Small Special Collections Library, University of Virginia.

probably the priest Quirós—similarly fails to assimilate to the scene's iconography: arms spread less in heroic acceptance than as if he were staggering, he twists his head back awkwardly to look with dismay not at the viewer, nor the killer, nor the heavens, but at his own corporeal wounds. His right-hand sleeve hangs empty and meaningless in the foreground, reminding the viewer that the story of Don Luis cannot be told smoothly even when its problematic antagonist is removed from the scene of narration—as he is in Tanner's Latin version of the story, which has "Ludovico" (Don Luis) "flee[ing] far into the interior, stricken by penitence, looking to expiate his tremendous guilt and grief, wandering through the mountains to the desert regions (*per montes ad loca deserta*), to waste away" (451).

'*En este me he engañado*', or, What Happened to Alonso?

Küsel's illustrations of events at Ajacán raise a question of viewership that the written accounts do not: who saw what happened there? From whose point of view does the artist engrave? The answer, of course, is the "adolescentem Alphonsum," as Tanner calls him (449), the young boy Alonso—upon whom *all* future versions of the story of Ajacán depend. This is why Menéndez "plerosque comprehendit" ('understood much'), as Tanner puts it, after "seizing the captive Alonso" (450); without him, there would be no more story to tell than there is of the lost colony of Roanoke.

Carrera, who was stationed at Santa Elena and had outfitted the Ajacán expedition before its debarkation in 1570, was, like Rogel, also present for the Spanish recovery of Alonso. Carrera had accompanied Rogel and Menéndez on the mission to seek Alonso in 1572, and like Rogel, who understood Alonso's return as *una cosa maravillosa*, "a marvelous thing," Carrera too sees the boy's salvation as a miraculous work of God (LL 104). But Carrera put a more specific name to the importance of Alonso's recovery, and framed his re-entry among the Spanish within a specific legal context: "It pleased Our Lord that this boy who was called Alonso de Olmos remained alive, for from his mouth, as an eyewitness"—*como testigo de vista*—"we should learn all these things" (LL 128). As Carrera well understands, Alonso's status as *testigo de vista*—as the eyewitness who gives his testimony to the authors of the Jesuit *relaciones*, who then relate that testimony directly "from his mouth" to the written page—is crucial both to the genre itself and to its legal standing. The presence of a *testigo de vista* and the written *relación* that his testimony enables together make possible a range of goals and potential outcomes: from the justification of the mission and its disastrous outcome to continued funding from the religious order and the Spanish Crown to the possible canonization of the slain fathers as martyrs of the faith. But the *testigo de vista* is also a guarantor of meaning not only under the law but in a more general narrative sense as well: for without Alonso's testimony, there is no ending, no closure, no structure within which the story of Don Luis and the Jesuits can emerge. Indeed, if, as Roberto González Echevarría has shown, the legal rhetoric of the *relación* as a genre "ensur[es] the enfranchisement of the author and lends credence to his form," it is also true, in the case of the Ajacán archive, that the legal form of the *relación* itself lays bare the fundamental narrative problems inherent in colonial accounts of European-indigenous encounter in the New World: the violence and instability of translation—emblematized, as we have seen, by the figure of the chained Native interpreter—alongside the impossibility of meaning in the absence of translation.[62] In the absence of Don Luis, then, Alonso must fill his role as both translator and internal narrator of the story of Ajacán—but without reproducing its treasonous ending.

The Jesuit and other official colonial relations of Ajacán refuse to acknowledge the strangely twinned roles of Don Luis and Alonso as the bilingual interpreters and cross-cultural internal narrators upon whom their collective narrative depends. But the structural similarity of the two figures pulses anxiously through the story of Alonso's recovery, as told here, for example, by Martínez:

> . . . [A]s [Alonso] got the news that there were ships on the coast, he stole away from the cacique. . . . and at night, marking [the place on the coast], he fled to the ships. He arrived at the beach at daybreak [*este día*] . . . [and] swam across [to the boat] . . . Since he came naked and browned by the sun, no one recognized him, and they understood him to be an Indian. He cast his eyes about the ship and saw his father . . . and recognizing him, threw himself at his feet, kissing them and saying: This [,] this is my father; because, as for five years he was not speaking our language, suddenly he could not manage to speak, and [also because of] the great happiness he had in finding himself in the protection of [*en poder de*] the Christians.[63]

If Alonso is unrecognizable to the Spanish after living among the Indians for almost two years—stretched by this account into five, as if to better account for the consequences—the slippage between European and Indian, Christian and heathen, is neatly contained by the narrative frame of the passage, which establishes his fervent desire to return to the Spanish through his flight in the dark of night and his daybreak swim to the ships, a rebaptism into his former identity, "in the protection of the Christians," as he emerges, naked and reborn, from the sea, and utters the words that establish his paternity as a Christian and a Spanish subject: "This is my father!" Yet the concluding sentence of this natal scene undermines the representation of Alonso's filial pronouncement with its recognition that the boy can no longer speak—"de repente no acertava a hablar"—or rather, that his language is no longer "*nuestra lengua*," no longer primarily Spanish, but Algonquian.

As we have already seen, however, Alonso never made such a breathtaking escape from the Indians: Rogel's first letter describing the recovery, written on the spot in August 1572, right there on the waters of the Bahía de Santa María, makes it clear that Menéndez had to drive a hard bargain with the Ajacán Natives over Alonso, and not until the Spanish took hostages and killed them was the boy brought to the ship. Most accounts also suggest that because of his youth, and possibly also his lay status, the Natives of Ajacán protected Alonso, and he was adopted into the family of an Ajacán leader, where he lived until the arrival of Menéndez's punitive expedition. Rogel's first account in the 1572 letter accordingly emphasizes the boy's linguistic utility for the Jesuits' future colonial ambitions:

> . . . and so we keep this boy, good translator, who has almost forgotten Spanish, raised in the Company he conforms to our way of life, and now after having left captivity, asking him if he wished to go with his father [who also is here] or with us, he said that he only wanted to go with us. And in order to make him retain the language and not forget it, I am in doubt whether to bring with me an Indian boy, who has come along with [Alonso], disowning his parents and country in order to come with him, [and] so that he practices the language in the meantime until Your Paternity or Father Provincial direct otherwise. (LL 106)

Here again, the repetitive exchange of young boys groomed to translate for the Spanish bears obvious structural similarities to the initial story of Don Luis. As Don Luis did, Alonso is now separating both from his adoptive indigenous father, the leader who, in Rogel's own words earlier in the letter, "would cherish him and hold him as a son," and from his birth father, who has also accompanied the punitive expedition (LL 105). And as Don Luis did, Alonso chooses here to follow the Jesuits. Most remarkably, a young "Indian boy" in the company of Alonso—perhaps an adoptive brother—may be "disowning his parents and home" in order to facilitate Alonso's growth as an interpreter for future settlements in Ajacán.

But by the time Rogel writes his second account, between 1607 and 1611, his cross-cultural internal narrator and future interpreter has nearly dropped out of the story, retained only in a few lines as a minor source of information: "This was revealed by a boy . . . . his name was Alonso, and because of his young age the Indians did not kill him or because God ordered it so" (LL 116). Why has the figure of Alonso been diminished rather than embellished in the second and more elaborate of Rogel's accounts—especially given that he was, after all, the sole *testigo de vista*, the sole Spanish-speaking eyewitness source of information about the Jesuits' fate, and thus the *single* source for all of the ensuing accounts of the Jesuit mission in Virginia—including *all* our contemporary historical accounts of this episode of Spanish colonial history?

This discrepancy surrounding Alonso points to others. Rogel's 1572 letter, for example, alleges that Don Luis hopes to kill Alonso, thereby destroying the single Spanish-speaking witness of his murder of the Jesuits, yet by the time Martínez writes his relation, another story has emerged, in which Alonso plays a different role. The Creole boy is "grande amigo del Don Luis" ['great friends with Don Luis'] in this account, and so Father Segura chooses him specifically to go and persuade the renegade to return to the Spanish, but he supposedly loses his way and wanders into the village of another chief, and thus avoids the fate of the Spanish settlers (LL 151). Similarly, where Rogel's 1572 letter as well as the relations of Carrera and Martínez highlight Alonso's stalwart Christian identity and his fervent wish to "die with Christians [rather] than live alone with Indians," "among infidels and barbarians" (LL 105, 128), the first printed version of the story, in Pedro de Ribadeneyra's *Vida del Padre Francisco de Borja* (Life of Father Francis Borgia, 1592), discussed in Chapter 3, suggests that Alonso was spared by the Ajacán Natives for precisely the opposite reason: "because . . . they knew he had not come to preach and to prohibit them from the worship of their idols" (LL 144).

The contradictions swirling around the figure of Alonso take on even more significance in light of a brief and remarkably self-conscious note recorded in the margin of Ribedeynera's text, which discusses Alonso but leaves him unnamed: "Este mancebo se dezia Alonso de Olmos, y no se hallo al martirio, como él contó" ('The youth was named Alonso de Olmos, and he was not present at the martyrdom, as he recounts' [LL 147]). The correction thus supplies missing information—Alonso's name—even as it calls into question the meaning of Alonso's account of all that has occurred: for, "not present at the martyrdom," he no longer retains the status of *testigo de vista*. The final clause of the marginal note, moreover, raises the question of veracity in a more pointed way. With its ambiguous pronoun—*él*—the clause suggests simultaneously that either the writer of the story "recounts" erroneously that Alonso was there at the martyrdom or, more ominously, that Alonso himself is the one who "recounts," falsely, that he was present, when in fact he was not.

This peculiar marginal correction was probably penned by Martínez, who included Ribadeynera's account with his own relation, "Martirio de los padres y hermanos de la Compañía de Jesus que martirizaron los Indios de Jacán, Tierra de la Florida" ("The Martyrdom of the Fathers and Brothers of the Jesuit Society Who Were Martyred by the Indians of Jacán, [in the] Land of Florida"), written in Potosí, Bolivia, in 1610.[64] Yet Martínez's version of Alonso's role in the story suggests not so much erroneousness on the part of Ribadeynera but—even as Martínez denies the very possibility—mendacity on the part of Alonso, the would-be *testigo de vista*:

> What I have told is what was being said in the fort of Santa Elena, [at] the
> time that I was there (which was, as I said, eight years), about the death of

the b[lessed] Fathers and Brothers of the Company of Jesus, they martyred in Ajacán, and what the aforementioned Alonso recounted many times, who was for four years a soldier in Santa Elena, after he escaped; and he was believed, for being virtuous, the son of honorable parents and good Christians. Only in the cruelties that he has recounted, which are understood to be much greater than those that were recorded [*escrito*] , could it be to differ in anything from what happened; because really, as I have said, there was not a single person to be found at the martyrdom of the said Fathers and Brothers; because no Christian who saw it escaped; and what has been said is for having heard it from the mouths of the Indians, who are liars and hide their abominations and treacheries. (LL 154)

What Martínez attempts to achieve in this passage is the authentication of his *own* relation of the martyrdom—what he has therein "dicho tengo . . . de la muerte de los B. Padres y Hermanos"—through a series of fairly obvious rhetorical strategies: declaring his narrative to be common knowledge ("lo que se platicava"); marking his own repetition of information ("como tengo dicho"); declaring both his personal reception of the tale and Alonso's reiteration of it "muchas vezes"; and, finally, asserting the veracity of Alonso's account by endorsing his personal virtue and appealing to the authority of his family's reputation as upright and Christian. But Martínez's anxious acknowledgement of a narrative discrepancy surrounding the deaths of the Jesuits—"podría ser diferenciar en algo"—works against his own process of self-authentication. The ambiguous syntax of his qualification regarding "las crueldades que se [h]an contado" muddies the question of both speaker and intention: was Alonso, in his reiteration of the tale, the originator of the later accounts "que se entiende fueron mucho mayores que las que se [h]an escrito," or did a more complex chain of transmission magnify the "crueldades" as the narrative "se platicava," passing across everyone's lips? Either source of the discrepancy calls the authority of Martínez's own relation into question, causing him to retreat, again, to repetition, declaring that "verdaderamente . . . no se halló ninguna persona al martirio de los dichos Padres y Hermanos." His declaration of this absence necessitates yet a further qualification in the ensuing line, where he specifies that the absence is a legal rather than a literal one: "ningún *cristiano*" was present, and thus there is indeed "no one" to serve as *testigo de vista*. The final line of the passage effectively rescinds the first one, for it categorizes his own relation, what he himself has "told . . . about the death of the b[lessed] Fathers and Brothers," as unsubstantiated— as groundless as any other narrative about the Jesuits' demise—precisely because anything said was first heard from the Indians, "que son mentirosos," and perhaps also, he suggests, the narrators of a particular story about "maldades y traiciones," a tale that they "hide." And it is a tale, as we shall see in subsequent chapters, that will ultimately circulate far and wide in the

Atlantic world and beyond, to the profound unsettlement of many listeners and readers.

Yet Martínez's characterization of the Indians as liars, however much it conforms to prevailing colonial stereotypes, rings here as a kind of denial, a displacement onto the "boca de los indios" of the inconsistency, discrepancy, and potential mendacity that he suspects in Alonso himself, the known internal narrator of the tale of the Jesuits' deaths—a suspicion that Martínez registers in his marginal note about Alonso ("he was not present at the martyrdom, as he recounts") and that shadows his strange description of Alonso's death earlier in the relation:

> [He] was killed later, in the town of Orista, with 21 soldiers . . . (truly miserable and wretched, it would have been much better to have died [as a] glorious martyr with his companions), going on a trade for pearls, [among] the most savage Indians there are in Florida, and they tortured them as recounted [*y hizieron dellos las crueldades referidas*]. (LL 153)

Martínez's observation that Alonso died seeking worldly treasure ("a un rescate de perlas") rather than the salvation of souls effectively pronounces a judgment on his character; it reads as an assessment of Alonso rather than of an arbitrary but "truly miserable and wretched" event: indeed, *it would have been much better* had Alonso not survived Ajacán at all. Why this dark hint about Alonso's death? And why the change in his status as exemplary Christian and holy witness to the martyrdom of the slain Jesuits, the figure of whom Carrera wrote that "It pleased the Lord to keep [him] alive . . . as an eyewitness," "como testigo de vista"?

A possible clue lies in a cryptic note scrawled in the margin of Rogel's first text from August 1572 alongside his description of Alonso's satisfaction in being returned to the Spanish Jesuits. "En esto me [h]e engañado, porque se [h]a estragado mucho despues que [h]a viv[i]do solo entre indios, ni quiere estar con nosotros, no conviene," writes Rogel: 'In this I was mistaken, for he was much corrupted after living alone among Indians, he does not want to be with us, it doesn't suit him'—or, more ominously, if we don't assume a tacit "le" before "conviene": "he is not suitable."⁶⁵ Rogel apparently found this later commentary upon Alonso significant enough, in other words, that he returned to his original text in order to inscribe a marginal gloss critiquing his own internal narrator as both deceptive—for *engañado* can also mean "deceived"—and, like Don Luis, *estragado*, corrupted and utterly destroyed. Alonso's remarkable transculturalism—the fact of his having "liv[ed] alone among Indians"—thus subverts Rogel's narrative confidence in documenting the outcome and the larger meaning of the mission: a seemingly insurmountable problem given that Alonso's internal narration bears sole responsibility for transmitting the failed outcome of the Jesuit mission in Ajacán.

This single inscription throws the entirety of the collective, colonial Spanish narrative into doubt—as well as the historical narrative we now have available in contemporary scholarship—opening the possibility for a new story altogether, one apprehended in reading, quite literally, from the margins, and suggestive of an emphatically different point of view on the part of the bilingual and bicultural Alonso. The untold story suggested in this marginal note forms a compelling counternarrative to the official colonial story the Jesuits themselves wanted to tell: a counternarrative of adoption, kinship, and identification with the Natives, and a story of feigned allegiance to the Spanish—"I was deceived," says Rogel—that parallels the more consuming story of Don Luis's false conversion and his violent act of unsettlement.

At the same time, as this chapter has tried to show, the figures of Don Luis and Alonso insistently foreground the geopolitics of knowledge in the sixteenth-century Americas rather than the nature of indigenous identity or cultural inheritance: the Ajacán documents do not allow us to speculate responsibly about who Don Luis and Alonso were, but they do shed light upon what and how these two figures knew, and how this knowledge shaped both historical outcomes and subsequent writers' responses. Don Luis and Alonso both might be understood to represent and enact the production of what Walter Mignolo has termed "border gnosis," or the subaltern critical thought that emerges in response to the discursive violence of imperialism—a "fractured enunciation," as Mignolo envisions it, "embedded in indigenous experiences and genealogies of thought" and existing in tense dialogue with the very colonial idiom seeking either to control or suppress it.[66] To recognize the intricate internal narrations of Don Luis and Alonso is thus to find in the Ajacán archive more than another, predictably unreliable colonial narrative; it is to discern both subjects operating with a complex, multivalent, and powerfully active understanding of the idioms and conventions of colonial discourse. And as Rogel's bewildered marginal commentary on Alonso's corruption and unsuitability reveals, the bicultural, hybridized frameworks of knowledge within which Don Luis and Alonso acted and narrated in the sixteenth century cannot be fully excavated or transparently understood from inside the perspective of Western modernity, or through its forms of knowledge alone. In this sense, the story of Don Luis and Alonso serves as a kind of gloss on the field of transnational American Studies—largely written from inside the United States, and usually in English—and its own responsibility to consider and make self-conscious the geopolitics of knowledge delimiting the work that we do. This is not, of course, a sufficient critical endpoint for the field—but neither is it a rote posturing of monolingual culpability and the institutional privileging of English. It is instead a first step toward recognizing and trying to give audience to perspectives and forms of knowledge formed beyond the scholarships of Western epistemology, produced at the margins of the modern Western world, and lying, in this particular case, in the literal margins of the written account of what happened in sixteenth-century Ajacán. To open up the category of knowledge in our own work means recognizing our failure to see beyond the historical process as defined from the perspectives of our various disciplines—and recognizing that when we unknowingly or willfully assimilate the margins to the narratives we already know, we are left—like Rogel—"*engañado*": mistaken and, perhaps, deceived.

PART II

The Afterlives of Don Luis

El Inca Garcilaso De La Vega and the
Political Don Luis

THE HEMISPHERIC EPISTEMOLOGY
OF *LA FLORIDA DEL INCA*

The story of Don Luis de Velasco emerges from its first inscriptions in the six-teenth century as a narrative of extraordinary ambivalence indelibly marked with the powerful, distortive effects of unsettlement: a story of thwarted co-lonial endeavor and treasonous translation unsuccessfully masked as trium-phal Christian martyrdom. It is a story about the indigenous production of knowledge in the context of early modern European warfare in the Americas: of the inter-indigenous transmission of hemispheric history; of subversive in-ternal narration, a translator's wresting of narrative control from the text's very writers; and, ultimately, of a mode of indigenous "authorship" of the European-written historical record itself.

This chapter begins to piece together the equally complicated trajectory of Don Luis's afterlife once his story reached print. My central focus here is the remarkable adaptation of Don Luis's story in 1605 by the Golden-Age Peruvian writer El Inca Garcilaso de le Vega in *La Florida del Inca*. Garcilaso's interpolation of Don Luis into his magisterial history of the Hernando de Soto expedition of 1539 provides the interpretive key, as I hope to show here, to the revisionist critical mode that defines *La Florida del Inca* as a larger work. This revisionism crystallizes Garcilaso's engagement with two central texts of Spanish colonialism in the New World, Bartolomé de las Casas's *Brevísima relación de la destrucción de las Indias* (1552) and the *Relación de Álvar Núñez Cabeza de Vaca* (1542), which El Inca subversively recasts in an analytic spirit that we might call the sensibility of unsettlement.

Garcilaso's critical lens upon the *Relación*, in particular, offers a produc-tive frame for American literary studies—a field in which Cabeza de Vaca, a sixteenth-century Spaniard who was wrecked off the coast of Florida during the failed expedition of Pánfilo de Narváez in 1527, has (to judge from our anthologies) become increasingly canonical over the last two decades. Yet Cabeza de Vaca's mounting prominence in the field augurs the very critical perils that the story of Don Luis, particularly as elaborated by Garcilaso, allegorizes and in some sense warns against. Approaching the narrative of Cabeza de Vaca from this vantage point, the last section of the chapter explores its anticipation of a theoretical dilemma that organizes the American literary field, particularly in its hemispheric dimension: an abiding structure of Western literary primitivism that continues to shape our (mis)readings, including a critical romanticization of the captivity genre that occludes its most radical possibilities; a scholarly mystification of translational mastery that elides the role of the interpreter and the ever-present possibility of mistranslation; and the almost inevitable academic enlistment of those foundational points of exclusion that guide what we can and cannot see, what we remember and forget. In this sense, Cabeza de Vaca's narrative, and Garcilaso's rewriting of it under the sign of unsettlement, together shed new light on the extent to which the field's alleged triumph over American exceptionalism has been a mere reconfiguration. The result—what I propose below as *Americas* exceptionalism— is central to how we continue to define the epistemological sophistication, the ethical credentials, and the continued modernity of our scholarly work through gestures of inclusive exclusion. The story of Don Luis thus stands behind another of this book's central aims: to locate our own field of inquiry within a *longue durée* of colonial encounters, a centuries-long history defined by the circulation, exchange, and withholding of knowledge—and by the deliberate and inadvertent transmissions of doubt and error—pertaining to the hemisphere and its history, from the colonial moment through the present.

Pedro de Ribadeneyra and the Emergence of Don Luis as a Political Figure

The first printed account of Don Luis's destruction of the Spanish settlement at Ajacán emerged, appropriately enough, in the work of a translator, the distinguished and prolific Spanish Jesuit priest, Pedro de Ribadeneyra.[1] Widely known for his translation of Augustine's *Confessions* and his biography of Ignatius Loyola, Ribadeneyra included an account of the failed Jesuit mission in Ajacán when he produced, late in his life, a biography of Loyola's successor, Francis Borgia, who had sponsored the sixteenth-century missions along the coast of La Florida. Ribadeneyra's *Vida del Padre Francisco de Borja*, first published in Madrid in 1592 (and then again in 1594 and 1605), brought the story of the Jesuit martyrdom into print as one small anecdote in its larger project of disseminating and celebrating an account of the religious works overseen by Borgia.[2] But once the story of Don Luis made its way into print circulation, it achieved an afterlife no longer circumscribed by Jesuit hagiography.

The crux of Ribadeneyra's account lies clearly in the inscription and preservation of the individual names of the martyred fathers and brothers. "There
they died for the spreading of our holy faith," he writes, "I have set down their
names here to keep the memory of these aforementioned Religious, for in
zeal for souls they poured out their blood with such steadfastness and joy"
(LL 144). Ribadeneyra does not bother to record the site of the mission by
the name Ajacán, labeling it quite generally as *la Florida*, somewhere in the
interior—"*la tierra adentro*" (LL 143). The point for him is that the Jesuit settlers traveled into known danger, "far distant from the sea and any human
protection," a "half-deserted place," "inhabited by naked savages" (143). Yet
Ribadeneyra also proves in this account to be quite true to his reputation as
the inaugurator of a modern, rigorously objective hagiography, in which he
assumes the role not of a participant or subjective eyewitness but of a disinterested narrator, one who relies on extensive documentation and the psychological and historical insights of scholarly remove.[3] Ribadeneyra's version of
the story, like all the accounts before it, points to Alonso de Olmos's knowledge of what transpired:

> All this a Spanish youth, whom the Fathers had brought along with them,
> saw and described; whom, because he was a boy and they knew he had not
> come to preach and take away from them the worship of their idols, they
> left off killing; and he was a captive among them for some years, until the
> Lord freed him from such a savage and fierce tribe and he told what has
> been related [here]. (LL 144)

Though Ribadeneyra does not cite Alonso by name, his account documents
its own crucial source as both eyewitness testimony and firsthand narrative—
"*vio y notó,*" "seen and described"—while efficiently summarizing and elaborating on the reasons for his survival: youth and a lay status ensuring the
sanctity of Native worship, "*la adoración de sus ídolos.*" On the ambiguous
means of Alonso's return to the Spanish, Ribadeneyra hedges his bets by
assigning all agency, unproblematically, to "*el Señor,*" the Lord.

When Ribadeneyra brings forth his central indigenous character, he maintains his rhetorical stance of objective remove. Unlike Carrera, for example—
who foregrounds his own sense of foreboding when he describes meeting Don
Luis, and claims to have seen all along that "*no le tratava verdad,*" 'he didn't
deal in the truth' (LL 124)—Ribadeneyra introduces the translator briefly and
neutrally but, nevertheless, with a faltering narrative tell:

> With [the Jesuits] went a *cacique* or important lord from that same land of
> Florida—whom the adelantado Pedro Menéndez de Avilés had brought to
> Spain, and having been taught in the ways of our sanctified religion, re-
> ceived with the greatest shows of happiness the water of the sanctified bap-
> tism and was called Don Luis—because it was thought that an important

person, with many relatives, familiar with that land, could help Ours in converting his subjects and friends, as he had promised.[4]

Ribadeneyra's narrative perspective is largely omniscient, filtered only faintly through the Spanish point of view—"*se juzgó*"—and the dramatic irony of what is implied to have been a false conversion. Yet this seemingly objective perspective is nevertheless, as we have seen in the previous chapter, to a great extent shaped by information most likely provided by Don Luis himself: his important status, his large familial network, his knowledge of the projected colonial territory. The final subordinate clause—*como él lo prometía*—both confirms Don Luis's role in the production of the whole Ajacán project and strikes an uncertain note back upon the layered clauses justifying the decision to bring him along, and without any military support. As Ribadeneyra notes, the Jesuits "boldly entered into the interior led by Don Luis, without permitting any Spanish soldier to accompany them, though many volunteered" (LL 143). Whether or not Don Luis played a part in the decision to exclude soldiers from the mission, Ribadeneyra does not say, but its effect is unambiguous: ". . . Don Luis and his relatives and friends fell upon the said Fathers and took their lives. And at dawn of the next day, they fell upon the rest [of the Jesuits], and without speaking a word to them, with Don Luis as captain and guide" (LL 144).

If the outcome of the Jesuits' failure to bring along soldiers to Ajacán is clear, the murky problem of how to explain Don Luis's actions, given his supposed conversion, lingers throughout the narrative genealogy of Jesuit writings carrying the story. Ribadeneyra addresses this problem with a characteristic degree of objective logic, offering two opposing conjectures: Don Luis betrayed the Jesuits, he speculates, "either because [he] had apostatized and returned to idolatry, and found himself confused, or because he had already been conspiring and weaving this wickedness" (144). Don Luis's alleged killing of the Jesuits resulted, in other words, either from the confusion of his failing conversion, his apostasy to Native ways—or there was never a conversion to begin with, and it was only staged as the means to *la maldad*, the wicked end. From this perspective, it is the concept not of a failed but of a *faked* conversion that most ominously expands the conditions of possibility that frame Don Luis's betrayal to include such factors as premeditation and a series of reasoned and carefully organized actions. Unlike the immediate and reflexive habit of lying that Spanish colonial discourse often attributes to the Indians, and that presents little perceived threat since it is assumed as normative and therefore both predictable and legible, the possibility of *long-term* deception on the part of Don Luis—engaged here by Ribadeneyra—destabilizes the foundations of the discourse itself, which from its very origins had always presumed both its own control over, and the transparency of, all communication across languages, as well as the ultimate manipulability of the Indians, whether "lying" or not, that this translational model supposedly ensured.

For Ribadeneyra to cast Don Luis as a potential figure of *engaño*, of pre-meditated deceit, is in effect to relocate him from the discourse of Spanish colonization—and the bifurcated logic of what became known as the Valladolid debate over the efficacy of Indian conversion and the ensuing question of Indian rights—to an entirely different discursive terrain, that of international politics and its attendant figures of geopolitical knowledge and *raison d'état*: rhetorical and ethical flexibility, strategic maneuvering, diplomatic improvisation—and outright mendacity, under the sign not of innate habit but of contingent power.[5] Indeed, for Ribadeneyra to figure the possibility of Don Luis as having "already been," from the beginning, "conspiring and weaving" his desired political end—the failure of Spanish settlement in Ajacán—is to condemn him not as a Sepulvadean Indian barbarian fit only for slavery (the colonialist antithesis of Las Casas's pure and innocent figure) but as a Machiavellian agent of the state, a political diplomat machinating in the service of national interest, who in effect explodes the sixteenth-century primitivist binaries of both sides of the Valladolid debate. Within three years, Ribadeneyra would in fact publish his famous anti-Machiavellian treatise, *Tratado de la religión y virtudes que deve tener el príncipe cristiano, para governar y conserver sus estados* (Madrid, 1595), in which he sought to refute Machiavellianism on its own terms by arguing that matters of national interest and security are in fact better served by adherence to "true" Christianity (which ensures divine protection)—and that Christianity made more effective military leaders than any idolatrous philosophy of *raison d'état*.[6] The figure of Don Luis—both an idolater and, considered in the *longue durée* of the Spanish failure to colonize the mid-Atlantic region of La Florida, a stunningly effective military leader—would of course substantially challenge this line of argument. And perhaps Ribadeneyra had both Don Luis and the instability of imperial translation in mind when he struggled in this treatise to theorize a political philosophy reconciling Christianity with the pragmatism of national interest: "this reason of state is not unitary, but dual: one [kind is] false and apparent, the other solid and true; one deceitful and diabolical, the other certain and divine."[7]

It is this unspeakable concept of Don Luis as a political figure, I believe, that accounts for the repeated insistence of the Jesuit narrators upon his silence during and after the massacre. Despite a general consensus that Don Luis was among the Spanish a "great talker," indeed a teller of highly effective tales, the Jesuits are remarkably consistent in representing the absence of his speech in relation to the overthrow of the settlement. Like his Jesuit predecessors, Ribadeneyra stresses Don Luis's wordlessness during the killings—which he and his "relatives and friends" commit "sin hablarles palabra," without speaking a word to them. Moreover, the absence of Don Luis's direct speech in the Jesuit accounts stands in marked contrast to what we hear from the Spanish characters, who articulate their responses to the events in both direct and indirect reported speech—as when, for example, in Carrera's letter, Father Quirós "turned to Don Luis and asked him [*dixole*] what was this, what they wanted to do and why they were killing them" (127). The Jesuit characters sometimes seize monological control even of their own deaths—as when, again in Carrera's letter, Father Baptista speaks "with much joy at seeing him: 'You are very welcome, Don Luis'" (127). Representing Don Luis's response to such questions and pronouncements made by the Spanish characters in the narrative, the Jesuit writers persistently elide his speech both with and *as* violence: "Raising his club and giving his greeting were all one," begins Rogel's grim chiasmatic metalepsis: "in such a way that in wishing [Father Segura] well, he took his life" (116). Or in Carrera's more straightforward metaphor: "[H]is responses were arrow shots" (127). Don Luis's mute violence serves as both substitute for and preclusion of speech—and thus preclusion of any possible articulation of the meaning of events from his imagined point of view. It is as if Ribadeneyra along with the Jesuit authors before him has grasped the powerful, shaping political agency of Don Luis's narration, which subtends the failure of the mission and the deaths of the settlers from its very inception: far more than his actions, that is to say, Don Luis's speech has become unthinkable. But all this would change once the story of Don Luis was transmitted by print, allowing him to be reborn into new textual genealogies. The afterlife of his story begins with the Peruvian mestizo historiographer El Inca Garcilaso de la Vega, who would give to Don Luis what the Jesuit narrators could not bring themselves to imagine or represent: words.

Garcilaso's Desolate Americas: Don Luis in Cordova, Spain

The sixth edition of *The Norton Anthology of American Literature,* issued in 2003, informs students and instructors that El Inca Garcilaso de la Vega "might well be seen as the first distinctively American writer" (70). The pronouncement is tentative but significant in the anthological world, where the designation of priority—of firstness—is laden with undefined historical value. Yet by the seventh edition, the entry on this earliest of "distinctly American" authors had disappeared, and seemingly for good. Each edition must cull carefully from the one before it to make room for new voices in an ever-expanding canon that is dedicated in large part to increasing ethnic diversity; and El Inca, despite his name, did not make the cut.

The son of a Spanish conquistador father and a royal Incan mother, Garcilaso was born in 1539, in Cuzco, Peru, baptized as Gómez Suárez de Figueroa. Descended of the ruling elite on *both* sides of his parentage, he grew up in the immediate aftermath of Francisco Pizarro's conquest of Peru and saw firsthand both its legacy of violence and its equally violent (and entirely related) failures of translation: the monolingual disengagement of the

Spanish conquerors from the project of learning to speak the languages of the conquered. His was, as Doris Sommer notes, "a personal history of impossible translations between mother tongue and fatherland"; the failure of translation would thus be a central theme in his later work as a historian writing about conquest in the Americas and the often opaque encounter of Spaniards and indigenous Americans.[8]

In Cuzco, young Gómez Suárez de Figueroa was raised in the house of his father, Sebastián Garcilaso de la Vega y Vargas, a military captain who was highly favored by both Pizarro brothers and who had received, for services rendered, a large *encomienda*, a specific number of indigenous persons legally compelled to offer their tribute in labor and wealth. Also living in the house for a time was Gómez Suárez de Figueroa's mother, Isabel Chimpu Ocllo, an Inca noblewoman, cousin of the last emperor, Atahualpa, who had famously showed his contempt for the conqueror's religion by tossing a breviary on the ground after being asked to swear fealty to Christianity.[9] Chimpu Ocllo was, according to the custom of the day, not legally married to the aristocratic Spanish father of her child. Moreover, how they communicated is unclear, for neither spoke the other's language. But Gómez Suárez de Figueroa spoke both their languages: he was educated both by colonial tutors (including a canon of the Cuzco cathedral, who taught him Latin) and by his mother's Indian relatives, who taught him in the classical traditions of indigenous Peru, including the notational system of the quipu. Yet even as the aristocratic mestizo child was acquiring the canonical stories of Native Peruvian history from Chimpu Ocllo's family, he was also watching his military father put down Indian rebellions throughout Peru and fight against the Spanish Crown's imposition of the New Laws, which sought to outlaw indigenous slavery.[10]

This violently contradictory bicultural home of Gómez Suárez de Figueroa changed forever in 1551, however, when his father took a legitimate Spanish wife—and his mother was married off to a Spaniard of lesser rank, a merchant. (The story of Doña Marina, the so-called mother of mestizo Mexico, who was also passed on to a Spanish husband after Cortés lost interest, comes to mind here.) Gómez Suárez de Figueroa continued to live with his father, who acknowledged him in his will as a "natural" (illegitimate) but nevertheless recognized son. Upon his father's death, when Gómez Suárez de Figueroa was twenty years old, he left Cuzco for Spain, probably because the trip was clearly specified by the terms of the paternal will—but perhaps also, some scholars have speculated, because Philip II apprehended potential subversive influence in a budding mestizo intellectual and summoned him away from the volatile landscape of Peru, where the Inca lords were that same year petitioning the King to put a stop to the *encomienda* system.[11]

Because he was descended from the ruling class as much on his mother's Inca side as on his conquistador father's, it is easy to see why Gómez Suárez de Figueroa would have understood himself to be doubly noble, doubly elite, when he first arrived in early modern Spain in 1561. He made his way soon thereafter to Philip's royal court to petition—unsuccessfully as it turned out—for what he argued was money owed to his father's estate and, like a true *hidalgo*, he entered Spanish military service and went to fight the Moors in Andalucía. His attempts to secure the rights to his father's spoils of conquest, gained in the subjugation of his mother's people, along with his participation in Spain's wars of Islamic extirpation, powerfully exemplify the complex subject position occupied by mestizos in early modern Spanish America and, under different pressures, in Spain itself. So too does the fact that Gómez Suárez de Figueroa, a few years after his arrival in Spain, changed his name to reflect his unsanctioned paternity, becoming Garcilaso de la Vega. The new appellation instantly associated him with a venerable Spanish family of aristocratic warriors and writers, including the famous soldier-poet who had more or less inaugurated the Renaissance in Spain and happened to share the same name. Indeed, it is not hard to understand why, in the land of the Inquisition and the *reconquista*, where the discourse of *pureza de sangre* or purity of blood raged all around him, a Peruvian mestizo would make this dramatic change to his identifying moniker.[12] The new subject position he announced with this name was far removed, to say the least, from the situations faced by the vast majority of indigenous peoples in those parts of the Americas beset by conquests.

Yet Garcilaso's experiences in Spain also gave him a new vantage from which to view his own subject position as well as the history in which it was produced—perhaps especially after 1563, when Garcilaso applied to return to the land of his birth and was apparently thwarted, thus facing permanent exile.[13] At the same time, while his repeated claims upon his father's estate were denied over the years, his visits to the court exposed him to travelers arriving to see the king from throughout the Americas (including even, perhaps, Don Luis, as I will discuss below). What precisely Garcilaso came to believe as a result of the court's rejection, his lifelong exile, and the new knowledge he was gaining about both the Iberian world and the broader history of the hemisphere is hard to gauge, though it is clear that he felt bitter disappointment at what he regarded as his personal marginalization. It is also clear that out of this ideological vortex he emerged as an author—and when he did so, he chose to refashion his identity yet again, this time insistently adding *El Inca* to the name that had before asserted only his paternity, and proclaiming "*soy indio*" (I am an Indian), as he began his career as a translator and historian.[14] To announce himself not merely as *El Inca*, scion of ruling overlords, but as *indio,* the broad, all-encompassing Spanish term for the indigenous inhabitants of the Americas that in effect denied their status as *gente de razón* or people of reason, was a bold gesture indeed. As a repeating motif in Garcilaso's work, this identification places the author, at least in part, "outside European discourse," as José Rabasa has argued.[15] "*Soy indio*" also signals an emergent consciousness of a hemispheric, indigenous point of view regarding the larger context of the American hemisphere—a point of view that is never fully articulated but that necessarily exceeds his elite subject position as a mestizo Inca of noble descent.

El Inca Garcilaso de la Vega is most famous for his two-part history of his mother's people and their vanquishing by his father's, the *Comentarios reales de los Incas,* published in Lisbon in 1609. It was this masterpiece, which paid homage to both sides of his own elite lineage, that earned him his long-standing reputation as one of Spain's most notable prose writers of the Golden Age and as the originary man of letters in *las Américas*, the first truly (Latin) American writer.[16] And it is this work that has in turn generated much of the venerable tradition of Garcilaso scholarship, from the foundational but still little-discussed studies of José Durand to today's José Antonio Mazzotti and Margarita Zamora.[17] But El Inca wrote another American history as well, which he undertook simultaneously with the writing of the *Comentarios* and which was also published in Lisbon, four years earlier: *La Florida del Inca* (*The Inca's Florida* [1605]). Though it was at least eighteen years in the making and took a similarly epic approach to its subject, *La Florida* has always been outsized by the celebrated *Comentarios*, as Raquel Chang-Rodríguez has shown, and remains a relatively marginal text despite the enduring significance of its canonical author.[18]

This is certainly due in large part to the very different subject matter of the two histories, and to the unequal authorial relation to each. The *Comentarios* is not only a work about Garcilaso's homeland, the country of his upbringing until the age of twenty, but also a historiographic endeavor authorized by the author's personal knowledge and experience as the childhood recipient of oral Incan history passed down from his relatives not long after the onslaught of Spanish colonization. It is also the history of a "successful" conquest, one that is ostensibly deemed necessary by the historian himself for its Christianizing mission. *La Florida del Inca*, on the other hand, recounts a history of failed conquest: the Soto expedition from its embarkation in Andalucía, Spain through its demise on the banks of the Mississippi River, after which the surviving expeditioners reached Mexico with less than half their original forces. Moreover, El Inca never set foot in Florida or visited any other part of North America, and he could not so straightforwardly draw upon his own experiences to authorize his history. Certainly, Garcilaso had personal connections to some of the participants in the expedition, through whom he could corroborate his history; and, perhaps more important, the geographical swath of the still unconquered Floridas offered a lesser-known and highly relevant historical subject to Spanish readers at the turn of the sixteenth century. Nevertheless, that he chose to write about a monumentally disastrous expedition, of which he himself had observed nothing, continues to beg questions—about his point of view, his interest in the history of the wider hemisphere beyond Peru, and his authorial motivations. Ultimately, as I will argue here, *La Florida del Inca* develops a kind of hemispheric epistemology crystallized within the story of Don Luis, one that is generated through unsettling rewritings of prior colonial texts and the foregrounding of translational problems.

Garcilaso's retelling of the story of Don Luis is brief but takes a place of utmost prominence, occurring in the final pages of the last chapter of the sixth and final book of *La Florida*.[19] Titled "Of the number of Christians, secular and religious, who in Florida died before the year 1568," the chapter has proved mysterious to Garcilaso scholars on a number of grounds.[20] In the first place, there is the seemingly small matter of El Inca's incongruous numerating of the chapters in this book, as observed in a footnote by John and Jeanette Varner, the translators of the definitive English version, *The Fabulous De Soto Story: The Florida of the Inca* (1980): "The edition of 1605 includes twenty-two chapters in Book 6," the Varners note, "while *stating* that there are only twenty-one" (my emphasis): "Contiene veynte y un capitulos."[21] The Varners accordingly rewrite the statement—"[The book] contains twenty-two chapters"—in their edition of Garcilaso's introduction to the sixth book. "Such an obvious mistake," they argue, "we have felt it wise to correct in our translation" (637). Yet El Inca announces quite clearly in the *tabla* of the book's contents that the final chapter will address not the subject of Christian martyrdoms in Florida before 1568 but "the wanderings and hardships of Gómez Arias and Diego Maldonado," two explorers from the Soto mission. Indeed, the intention to finish *La Florida* with this chapter is unmistakable in light of the final words of the tabla entry's last sentence: "*with which the history ends*"—a subordinate clause that renders the entire statement harder to explain away as a superficial "mistake" than the one that immediately follows, and which the Varners correct: the book "contains twenty-one chapters."[22] Their small translational correction, unnoted and unmarked where it actually occurs in the text—relegated to a footnote some seventy pages later—recasts as an "obvious mistake" what is perhaps more likely the trace of a change in Garcilaso's authorial plans: a change that occurred late in the writing of his history, sometime after he composed the introduction to the sixth and final book, which was originally intended to end with the chapter on Arias and Maldonado.

At the thematic level as well, the twenty-second chapter presents a puzzle. Garcilaso's own explanation initially seems clear enough: having "given extensive notice of the death of Governor Hernando de Soto," and of various "principal cavaliers" and "numerous other noble and valiant soldiers," the historian feels it to be "a contemptible thing not to commemorate the priests, clerics, and religious" who accompanied the soldiers to Florida and died with them—their memorialization is only fair: "it is right that they not remain in oblivion."[23] Yet in the preface to his volume, Garcilaso hints at a temptation—one he claims to have resisted—"to incite and to persuade with the recounting of this history," manipulating his Spanish readers toward the ostensible goal of acquiring "the land [of La Florida] for the augmentation of Our Holy Catholic Faith": "to deceive with fables and fictions those who in such an undertaking might wish to invest their estates and lives" in further colonial projects in La Florida. He names not commemoration but *evangelism*—and, by logical extension, the future Spanish acquisition of La Florida—as his primary goal in writing: "no other end has motivated me than the desire that the Christian religion extend itself over this land so long and wide."[24] If we take him at his word—by no means a given—then we can only judge it a colossal strategic error (an "obvious mistake" that far exceeds any incorrect numeration of his chapters) for Garcilaso to have chosen to finish his epic history of the Soto expedition with an account of the many *failures* to establish the Christian religion among the indigenous Floridians, and with descriptions of the violent Christian martyrdoms inflicted by the "infidels."[25] In particular, the story of the Jesuits in Ajacán, with which he ends both the chapter and the entire work, seems particularly unsuited to advertise for—indeed strikes the *coup de grace* against—future missionary or colonial endeavors.[26]

After carefully generating a list of secular Christians who have died in Florida, noting that the total "exceeds fourteen hundred," Garcilaso turns to "the priests and the religious" to foreground a specific historiographical problem (348). The information relating to priests and other religious is far more limited than that referring to commanders and nobles, he repeatedly points out. The best historical information relates to the Soto expedition, but even this finally comprises a narrative of gaps and losses when it comes to its religious participants: the record "did not retain their names"; "I did not find out from what land [they] came or the names of [the] companions" (348–49). In the case of accounts of the Ponce de León, Vásquez de Allyón, and Narváez expeditions, the lack of documentation concerning the religious participants is drastic: there is simply no record of the religious (*no* [*h*]*ay memoria*), "as if they did not go" (348).

In this context of historical erasure and lack, Garcilaso's single citation of a source in this chapter is thus particularly striking—and it tells us something about why Garcilaso changed the original plan of his sixth book to add a final chapter on Christian deaths in La Florida: "Of which [incident] Father Maestro Pedro de Riba de Neyra also writes."[27] The specific incident that he attributes here to Ribadeneyra is, of course, the murder of the Jesuits by Don Luis. What the reference suggests, I would argue, is that it was the story of Don Luis specifically that inspired Garcilaso to deviate from his initial organization and draft a final chapter devised precisely to include that story. Sometime after completing his introduction to the sixth book of *La Florida*, in other words, Garcilaso came across Ribadeneyra's *Life of Borgia* and was sufficiently moved by or taken with the account of Don Luis therein that he deviated from his original plan for the sixth book and added a final chapter to his nearly completed manuscript, in which he discussed the destruction of the Jesuit settlement.

To appreciate the fullest range of interpretive possibilities opened up by the mysterious and violent end of *La Florida*, we need access to the larger story of Don Luis that is intertwined with the events that occur when the Spanish Jesuits attempt to settle in sixteenth-century Ajacán. The Varners seem not to have been familiar with this story, for in their English translation they have misread Garcilaso's mention of Don Luis as a reference to the priest Luis de Quirós, and cast him as the Spanish victim rather than the Native perpetrator of the violence that ensues—an understandable mistranslation given the ambiguous syntax of this particular sentence in Garcilaso's original text, which will be quoted later—but one that has rendered invisible the richest context in which the strange ending of *La Florida* may be glossed. Indeed, once we understand that the martyrdom story that Garcilaso tells at the end of *La Florida* is that of Ajacán, and that the central indigenous character in question is in fact Don Luis, we have a much more pointed sense of how the ending of his text, and indeed the history as a whole, signifies across a hemispheric history of unsettlement.

For Garcilaso doesn't simply retell the event as he found it told in Ribadeneyra, his source text. Working instead by a supplemental logic, Garcilaso appears to address primarily what is missing in his own self-identified source, filling in its gaps rather than repeating its central details. Indeed, where Ribadeneyra's narrative drives toward the martyrdom as its central, climactic event and ends by memorializing the individual martyred Jesuits by name, Garcilaso's version of the story offers the names of the Jesuits at the beginning of his account, in an almost perfunctory manner:

> In the year five hundred and sixty-eight eight religious of the same company, two priests and six brothers, went to Florida. He who went as their superior was called Bautista de Segura, native of Toledo, and the other priest called himself Luis de Quirós, native of Xerez de la Frontera, the country of the six brothers I did not find out, whose names are as follows: Juan Bautista Méndez, Gabriel de Solís, Antonio de Zavallos, Christóval de Redondo, Gabriel Gómez, and Pedro de Linares, who took in their company an Indian, [a] lord of vassals, [a] native of Florida. (349v)

There is no encomium, as in Ribadeneyra, to the courage of the Jesuits or their willingness to sacrifice themselves. Garcilaso eliminates both the specific description of the mission's principal figure, Segura—who had been, in Ribadeneyra's words, "very beloved by Father Francis in Spain for his great virtues and religious life" (LL 144)—and his Christian (first) name: Juan. Moreover, the syntax of the second statement in this passage seems almost deliberately convoluted: the ritual naming of the martyred fathers is subordinated grammatically to the loss of information—the birthplaces that El Inca "did not find out"—and, most important, to the Jesuits' central indigenous interlocutor, whom Garcilaso introduces in the final clause of his sentence. Significantly, Garcilaso introduces Don Luis as the grammatical object of Jesuit action, rather than a subject in his own right, depriving him accordingly of a name even as he specifies his noble rank and place of birth. But Garcilaso also pauses his narration at the first mention of this Native figure—punctuating a desire or need for particular clarity that is noticeably absent when it comes to the slain Jesuits—and devotes a new sentence to a subject entirely unaddressed by Ribadeneyra:

> How he came to Spain it will be well for us to give an account. It is thus that the Adelantado Pedro Meléndez went to la Florida three times from the year 1563, until the year 1568 in order to rid that coast of certain French corsairs, that were trying to settle and populate there. During the second of these voyages he brought seven Floridian Indians, who came with great friendliness, dressed in the same manner that we have said they go about in their land carrying their bows and arrows of the very excellent kind that they make for their greater adornment and finery. The Indians who were being taken to Madrid so that his majesty *Rey don Phelipe* could see them, passed through one of the outlying hamlets of Cordova. (349v)

Neither here nor elsewhere in the text does Garcilaso explain *why* "it will be well," '*sera bien*,' to tell the story of Don Luis's journey to Spain—a story noticeably absent from his source text (which notes only that "the Adelantado Pero Meléndez [*sic*] de Avilés had brought [him] from [Florida] to Spain" [LL 143]). Perhaps *bien* signifies here in the general sense of fine or appropriate, but the length of this seeming digression, as well as its absence in Ribadeneyra's version, suggests that there may be another, more motivated rationale for the inclusion; perhaps "*sera bien*," in Garcilaso's estimation, for specific reasons rather than vague ones. The context of endless and futile inter-imperial rivalry—Menéndez's multiple trips to Florida, years apart, to hunt for French colonies to uproot—does not lend a promising sense to the project of Spanish settlement there, again undermining Garcilaso's purported aim. Similarly, while the text emphasizes that the Indians whom Menéndez takes come with him not only willingly but enthusiastically, it also makes clear that their primary function is spectacular: to be seen in their natural state by the sovereign, King Philip. This state, moreover, is one of armament: their apparent sense of "adornment and finery" is constituted by their weapons.

At the same time, the use of the plural first person in the first and sixth lines of this passage, as elsewhere in *La Florida*, ambiguously suggests both a self-referential formality—the pause that foregrounds the narrating process itself before the narrative proper ensues—and the presence of another, different narrative voice: Garcilaso's purported informant for the entire history offered in his volume. Garcilaso is notoriously silent in *La Florida* as to the identity of his informant, whom he calls his "author"—*mi autor*—except to identify him as an alleged survivor of the Soto expedition, and thus a purported eyewitness to much of what El Inca narrates in the history as a whole. Though scholars of *La Florida* now generally agree that this informant was likely to have been the *hidalgo* Gonzalo Silvestre, an aging veteran of the Soto expedition, Garcilaso's unnamed *autor* is of course also, to some extent, his own construction—both conveniently present and conspicuously absent at particular moments in his narration—and a long-standing narrative topos (one thinks of Chaucer's fictional Lollius, "myn auctor," his purported source for *Troilus and Criseyde*).[28] Thus, when Garcilaso announces that "it will be well for us to give an account," he foreshadows the imminent arrival of his narrative informant not in the witnessing sidelines, where he has remained throughout most of the history, but on the scene of action itself:

> The author who gave me the relation of this history and who lived in that town, knowing that Indians from la Florida were passing through, rushed to the countryside to see them and asked them from what province they were? And so that they would see that he had been in that Kingdom he asked them if they were from Vitachuco, or from Apalache, or from Mauvila, or from Chicaça, or from other provinces where they had great battles? (349v–50)

With this passage, then, Garcilaso has added a new scene to the story as told in Ribadeneyra, one that takes place in Cordova, Spain long before Don Luis returns to La Florida and his homeland in Ajacán. Curiously, Garcilaso now adds a bit of distance here between himself and the informant by no longer using the intimate possessive: *mi autor* has become simply "the author." And Garcilaso also finds it necessary to remind readers, at this late stage of his volume, that "the author" is the source of his history, he "who gave . . . the relation"—the term *relación* evoking, as with the Jesuit relations, not just the giving of an account but the quasi-judicial making of a case, the pragmatic seeking of an end, and the receiving of judgment.[29] In the context of this particular scene, Garcilaso's informant indeed has a case to make. Depicted here as hastening with some urgency, literally jumping to meet the Floridian Indians, this Spanish veteran of the Soto expedition uses his geographical and historical knowledge—ticking off the battle sites of Vitachuco, Apalache, Mauvila, Chicaça—to prove his transatlantic experience, "that he had been in that Kingdom." The end he seeks, as the two question marks in the passage make clear, is information. What follows next is an ambiguous scene of unambiguous foreshadowing—made all the more astonishing by the dark revisionist twist that it gives to Garcilaso's source text in Ribadeneyra:

> The Indians seeing that that Spaniard was among those who had gone with the Governor Hernando de Soto, looked at him with evil eyes and said

to him: Leaving those provinces in such a desolate state as you left them, you all want us to give you news of them? and they did not want to reply to him more and speaking to each other, they said (according to what the interpreter who was accompanying them said) it would be of greater gain for us each to give him an arrow wound than the information he asks of us [;] saying this (to make understood the desire they had to shoot at him and the dexterity with which they would shoot) two of them shot arrows high into the air with so much force that they were lost from sight. Recounting this to me, my author told me that he feared they would shoot at him as those Indians are crazy and daring principally in the case of weapons and valor. (350)

In this shattering scene of recognition, the Indians understand and receive Garcilaso's informant, just as the soldier intended in making his case, as someone "who had been in that Kingdom." What they recognize, however, is not their mutual knowledge of a land across the Atlantic and the "great battles" undertaken there but instead their interlocutor's status as a Soto veteran and would-be conqueror, a pillager of indigenous provinces, and part of a collective that seeks information about the New World. As Garcilaso stages this scene, then, Don Luis (here with his fellow Indians) knows long before returning to Ajacán that he would choose battle with the Spanish colonizers over any disclosure of information to them: in other words, that a mere parry for news from La Florida is, in this hemispheric point of view from which Garcilaso writes, a practical equivalent to military aggression in Ajacán. Crucially, the words that Garcilaso gives to Don Luis and his fellow Indians in this passage are not lies or false promises but an all too meaningful question: in the space of a single sentence, Garcilaso endows them with a fully articulated point of view, and an interpretive lens through which to read the future silence of the Indians, and in particular that of Don Luis.

The strategy of the Indians is paradoxically both to decline to speak another word and to clarify, through an interpreter and then with gestures, their message of refusal and retribution. This message is delivered with such intensity that Garcilaso's informant (again troped metafictionally as *mi autor*) fears for his life—a startling reversal of the presumed power dynamic, given that the "author" is in Spain and the Indians are in captivity. When the Indians instead shoot into the air, the arrows that disappear from view underscore not only the physical power of these indigenous figures but their opacity: the informant may see them in the moment as "crazy and daring," "locos y atrevidos," but the reader, to the contrary, sees that the Indians know how to keep their knowledge—and, when desired, their intentions—invisible to their captors. Rewriting his source text, Garcilaso thus introduces an entirely new episode, one that retroactively casts the murder of the Ajacán Jesuits as an act not of volatile barbarity but of premeditated and even pre-articulated retribution for the "desolate" state of La Florida after Soto's expedition.

As Garcilaso recounts the rest of the story and ends both Book 6 and the larger history itself, this scene subtly but unmistakably changes the most salient meaning of what ensues:

> Those seven Indians were baptized there, and six died in a short time. The one who remained was a lord of vassals[;] he requested permission to return to his land, he made great promises, that he would act as a good Christian in the conversion of his vassals to the Catholic faith, and of the rest of the Indians in all that Kingdom. For this reason, the religious admitted him into their company, understanding that he was going to help them, as he had promised[;] in this way they went to La Florida, and they entered the land many leagues inward, they passed through great swamps and marshes, they did not want to bring soldiers in order not to give a bad example to [*escandalízar*] the Indians with weapons . . . (350)

All details of the story must now be read, of course, in light of the words of the Indians themselves: from their baptism in Spain to the request of the single survivor, Don Luis, to return to his homeland, to the "great promises" he makes about converting the Indians of that land. In Garcilaso's telling, that is, it is Don Luis, rather than the Jesuits or other Spaniards, who first has the idea of returning to Ajacán—and the idea is clearly linked, via the words of the Indians, to his knowledge of the "desolate" outcome of Spanish colonialism elsewhere in La Florida, from Vitacucho to Chicaça. Moreover, Garcilaso significantly rewrites the Indians that Ribadeneyra had inscribed under the sign of primitivism ("*salvajes desnudos*" in a land "far away from . . . any human protection"), casting them instead as vassals of the lord Don Luis, inhabiting a "Kingdom" rather than an uncivilized land. Even the desire of the Jesuit priests to travel without soldiers so as not to give a bad example to the Indians, '*escandalizar los Indíos*,' now reads not only as misguided, but as a misguided *trope*, a Las Casas-esque noble savagism, in light of the Indians' own words about the aftermath of Spanish colonialism in La Florida. It is the desolate state of La Florida, Garcilaso suggests, that explains Don Luis's actions once they arrive in Ajacán:

> When the Cacique had them in his land, where it appeared to him to be safe enough for killing them, he told them to wait for him there, that he was going four or five leagues ahead to prepare the Indians of that province so that with joy and friendship they would hear the Christian doctrine, that he would return within eight days. (350–350v)

In another instance of pointed reflexivity, the "lord of vassals" has now become a "*cacique*," the indigenous term abruptly unsettling the prior European frame of reference. Moreover, the elaboration of the various steps of Don Luis's calculation—leading the Jesuits into his own territory, even as they believe *he* is following *them* on a mission of conversion; waiting until he has found a place "safe enough for killing them" before leaving them alone, content in the belief that he is off somewhere predisposing a new group of Indians to Christianity, further suggests the cacique's ability not just to dissimulate but to manipulate the Jesuits' own discourse against them. Thus, with the phrase "to prepare the Indians," '*disponer los Indíos*'—which evokes the sense not only of preparation but stipulation, decree, doctrine—Don Luis casts himself (in Garcilaso's telling) as a figure for John the Baptist, who went "preaching in the wilderness": as Isaiah figured him, "The voice of one crying in the wilderness . . . Prepare ye the way of the Lord, make his paths straight" (Matthew 3:1–3). Of course, even the literal "paths" down which Don Luis has led the Jesuits have been not "straight" but, as Garcilaso ironically notes, marked by "swamps and marshes." Don Luis seeks, quite precisely, "to prepare the Indians" in their response to the arrival of Christianity—but in quite a different way than the Jesuits expect:

> The religious waited for him fifteen days, and when they saw that he was not returning they sent to him Father Luys de Quiros, and one of the brothers to the village where he had said he was going. The don Luys, with many others of his [people], seeing [the religious] in front of themselves, as a traitor apostate, without speaking a word to them killed them with great rage and cruelty, and before the other religious could learn about the death of their companions, and flee to some other of the nearby provinces to save themselves[;] they fell upon them the following day with great force and fury, as if they were a squadron of armed soldiers, which hearing the noise of the Indians, and seeing the weapons they carried in their hands they fell to their knees to receive the death that they would give them for practicing the faith of Christ our Lord. (350v)

This passage marks Garcilaso's first and only mention of his "cacique" by name: "el Don Luys." Yet with the naming of Don Luis, the syntax grows almost correspondingly distorted in the passage's second sentence—producing an ambiguity which, in combination with the confusingly similar name of the priest whom Father Segura sends to confront the apostate ("Luys de Quiros"), apparently led the Varners to conflate the two figures named Luis, despite the clarity with which Garcilaso's cited source text identifies Don Luis by name. The Varner translation of the ending of *La Florida* thus posits Don Luis as the Spanish priest and victim of an unnamed cacique: "But here the Cacique with many of his people, on seeing Don Luis and his companion before him, as a traitor apostate and without uttering a word, slew them both with great rage and cruelty" (642). An understandable error in this context, their mistake nevertheless produces another, modern-day erasure of Don Luis from the definitive English translation of *La Florida* and the larger literary-historical record. It also empties this confusing passage of a great deal of its narrative power by eclipsing the revelation of Don Luis's name (which, as we shall see in the next chapter, held enduring significance even for seventeenth-century Spanish readers and writers), for only with the revelation of his name is it clear that the central figure in the passage is not Luis de Quirós, the victim, but in fact the Cacique Don Luis, his murderer. Indeed, shifting our focus from the victim and martyr to the perpetrator of unsettlement, we notice details that would not otherwise seem significant: that in the Garcilaso version of the story, Don Luis has told the Jesuits where he is going and how to get there, for example, and that he and his fellow Indians ("many others of his") are apparently waiting for the Jesuits' approach—"seeing them in front of themselves"—as if they had laid a trap for their pursuers.

As in the prior Jesuit texts, the Indians kill the Jesuits "without speaking a word to them." But here, the substitution of violence for language carries a quite different valence than it did in the Jesuit writings, where it signaled the Indians' lack of language and thus humanity. For Garcilaso—the author who has at the outset announced his authority in this text as his Indianness: "*porque soy indio*"—has already given Don Luis and the other Indians the relevant words and allowed them to claim a meaning for their actions in Ajacán: the "state of desolation" in which the Spanish left La Florida. And though Garcilaso, like the prior Jesuit writers, charges the Indians with "rage and cruelty" in their killing of the passive Jesuits who fall "to their knees to receive the death that they would give them," his account offers a small but significant variation on Ribadeynera. Where Ribadeneyra says of the Jesuit deaths simply, "[They] died for the spreading of our Holy Faith" (LL 144), Garcilaso puts grammatical emphasis on the agency of the Indians, citing "the death that they would give [the priests] for practicing the faith of Christ our Lord." The outcome is the same in both versions, of course, as is the religious martyrdom of the Fathers. But Garcilaso's seemingly minor rewording also pointedly suggests that Don Luis and the Indians choose to kill the priests *because* they are practicing Christianity—and because, in other words, they understand the project of religious conversion to be coextensive with, rather than separate from, colonial violence and conquest: thus the Indians, in Garcilaso's words, "fell upon them with great impetus and fury, as if they were a squadron of armed soldiers." The analogy is incomplete but wholly subversive: Garcilaso stops just short of contending that the conversion project is itself akin to military aggression upon the Indians.

The subsequent description of the Indians' clearly blasphemous behavior marks another significant departure from Garcilaso's source text—as well as another instance in which the Varner translation empties Garcilaso's text of its most potentially unsettling possibilities. While the Varners have done the contemporary reader the favor of breaking down and clarifying Garcilaso's long sentences, their reduction of his contorted prose into neat independent clauses effectively alters the emphasis of meaning—or lack of emphasis—in the original. The Varner translation, for example, creates separate paragraphs between the Indians' killing of the Jesuits and their subsequent treatment of the victims' belongings and then marks the transition between the two paragraphs with a compound sentence that subordinates the actions of the Indians to a second independent clause announcing the apotheosis of the Fathers: "At that the infidels struck them most cruelly, and they as devout religious departed this present life to enjoy that of eternity." The following paragraph neatly turns to the next event in a clearly marked sequence: "The Indians, after having killed these men, opened a chest in which they had carried books of the Holy Scripture, breviaries, books, and sacred vestments for saying mass. . . ." (642). Yet Garcilaso's original account of events is far less easily parsed and, more important, makes meaning through a different pattern of emphases:

> The infidels gave them death most cruelly such that they terminated the present life as good religious to enjoy eternity, the Indians having put them to death opened a chest, that was filled with books of the Holy Scripture, with breviaries and missals and vestments, for saying mass, each one took from the vestments the one he preferred and put it on as he pleased, ridiculing and scorning that majesty, and richness, taking it as poor and vile, three of the Indians, while the others went about jumping and dancing dressed up in the vestments they had put on, took out a crucifix that had been in the chest, and they were staring at it [when] they fell down dead suddenly. The rest casting the vestments they had worn on the ground all fled, of this also writes the father maestro Pedro Riba de Neyra. (350v–1)

Unlike the Varner translation, which highlights the Jesuits' arrival in eternity by positing it as the hinge between two distinctly marked paragraphs, Garcilaso's original text in fact makes the opposite gesture, grammatically subordinating the martyrs' ascent by sandwiching *la eterna* between the Indians' actions: the "giv[ing]" of death "most cruelly" to the Jesuits and their again "having put them to death" and then opening the chest. The Indians and not the Jesuits are the grammatical subject of this sentence, and their killing of the priests becomes the source of both the repetition and the redundance that mark and stylize Garcilaso's prose in this passage. In Garcilaso's account of both the killing of the Jesuits and the Indians' subsequent treatment of their belongings, all of the actions inhabit the same unbroken grammatical flow of time in a single sentence, evoking a sense of violence and confusion that has been utterly excised from the sequential clarity of the English version. Moreover, Garcilaso's account differs strikingly here with that of his source text, which stages the deaths of the three Indians who open the Jesuits' chest as the triumph of a Christian miracle over the possibility—but not the actuality—of blasphemous desecration: Ribadaneyra unambiguously insists that the Indians are so amazed and astonished by the sudden deaths of the offending Indians that they run away "without touching anything they had taken" (LL 144). Garcilaso, however, stages an elaborate desecration—replete with mockery, vile and base treatment, jumping, and dancing—that occurs prior to the sudden deaths of the Indians. These deaths punctuate the ending of the chaotic scene and the sentence that narrates it, but there is no marvelous wonder or amazement to mark the moment as a triumphal miracle. Instead, Garcilaso's Indians enact a further violation upon the religious articles, casting the vestments on the ground—and here again, the style is marked by repetition and redundance. What comes across in Garcilaso's telling is not so much divine retribution, as in Ribadeneyra, but unpunished escape: "they all fled" (350v). The entire episode of triumphal miracle is thus deflated in Garcilaso's version, tacked on casually with his citation of his source: "of this also writes the father maestro Pedro Riba de Neyra."

Drawing the six-book tome of *La Florida del Inca* to its conclusion, Garcilaso brings the story of Don Luis to an end with a final paragraph that embeds another dense set of rewritings and, ultimately, a hemispheric gloss on the Spanish colonial project:

> So these eighteen priests, ten of whom represent the four orders we have named, the eight clerics, and the six brothers of the Holy Fellowship, in all twenty-four, are those who before the year fifteen hundred and sixty-eight died in La Florida for practicing the Holy Gospel, excepting the fourteen hundred secular Spaniards who in four journeys went to that land, whose blood I hope to God is crying out and pleading not for vengeance like that of Abel but for mercy like that of Christ our Lord, so that these Gentiles may come into the knowledge of His Eternal Majesty under the obedience of Our Mother the Holy Roman Church, and such it is to believe and to hope that the land which has so many times been watered with so much blood of Christians may yield fruit in proportion to the irrigation of this Catholic blood that has been poured upon it.
>
> May glory and honor be given to God Our Lord, the Father, Son and Holy Ghost, Three persons and only one true God. Amen.
>
> The End. (351)

Stepping back from the failed settlement in Ajacán, the final passage of *La Florida* returns to the more general subject of the larger chapter as outlined in its title—"The number of Christians, both secular and religious, who died in Florida before the year 1568"—and summarizes in almost belabored fashion the mathematical process by which its findings have been adduced, painstakingly detailing the numbers (eighteen, ten, eight, six, twenty-four, fourteen hundred) and the representative categories (priests, orders, clerics, brothers, secular Spaniards). But this calculation of deaths is also in an important sense a record of failure, and Garcilaso makes the ambivalence of these martyrdoms clear in voicing their two potential opposing meanings, and the two attendant possible outcomes: vengeance and mercy. While Rabasa and Voigt among other scholars have seen in this passage Garcilaso's endorsement of a "discourse of tolerance"—a call for nonviolence in the face of colonialism's violent binarisms of Spanish-Indian, Christian-heathen—his very hope for Christ's mercy finds meaning only in the context of the other possibility: revenge.[30] Significantly, moreover, Garcilaso does not posit his fervent preference for mercy in relation to Spanish *response* to the offending Indians—although that context is certainly a logical one—but rather figures it through the speaking voice of the martyrs' blood, which he cannot apparently hear or interpret with certainty. He thus hopes—perhaps even expects, if we presume the other meaning of *esperar*—that this blood speaks for mercy rather than vengeance: but by definition he cannot be sure. Even the biblical opposition he draws upon here is ambivalent: for if the Epistle to the Hebrews casts Jesus as "the mediator of a new covenant" and argues that Christ's "sprinkled blood . . . speaks a better word than the blood of Abel," this revelation rests upon a long biblical tradition of aligning Abel's blood *with* the blood of Jesus in a typological lineage of martyrdom, as in the Gospel of Matthew's reference to all "the righteous blood shed upon the earth, from the blood of righteous Abel unto the blood of Zacharias" (Matthew 23:35).

If the blood of the slain Spaniards can thus speak simultaneously as the blood of both Jesus *and* Abel, then Don Luis and the other offending Indians stand in silently here for the biblical Cain—a widespread figuration in early modern European colonial discourse, as Garcilaso would certainly have known.[31] The construction of Amerindians as descendants of the originary, fratricidal nontillers of the earth, and thus the moral inferior to the land-cultivating Europeans, enabled what Ben Kiernan calls "a new agrarian vision" interwoven with an emergent racism that "helped fuel early modern Europe's enclosures, land clearances, and colonial expansion"—a discourse of agriculture and blood that ultimately gave rise to the history of Western genocide reaching across the centuries (5). Garcilaso too envisions a kind of agricultural-hematological project in this final passage, but he shifts the larger meaning of the project away from an argument for the rights of tillers to the land they farm, and instead toward a metaphorical harvest produced from the "irrigation of . . . Catholic blood": the proportional fruit of Christian knowledge. In this context, the mark of Cain takes on a different biblical significance: to cast Don Luis and his fellow Indians implicitly as the murderous Cain in this final passage of *La Florida* would also assign them a special divinely-ordained protection, since God promises vengeance on any who see the mark of Cain and then kill him: " 'If anyone slays Cain, vengeance shall be taken on him sevenfold.' And the Lord put a mark on Cain, lest any who came upon him should kill him."[32] In this sense, Garcilaso's "blood crying out and pleading not for vengeance like

Abel but for mercy like Christ" returns to and retropes the biblical "voice . . . crying in the wilderness" (Isaiah 40:3)—and in so doing powerfully warns against both Spanish vengeance upon and Spanish mistreatment of the Indians. Indeed, in this final passage Garcilaso is echoing the famous 1511 sermon of Antonio de Montesinos, the Dominican friar whose fiery words Las Casas later memorialized, and who pronounced his Spanish audience on the island of Hispaniola to be living "in mortal sin" as a result of colonialism and its "detestable wars on . . . people who lived mildly and peacefully in their own lands." "I am the voice of one crying in the wilderness," Montesinos told his listeners. "In order to make your sins known to you I have mounted this pulpit, I who am the voice of Christ in the wilderness of this island . . ."[33] At the end of his volume, then, Garcilaso positions the story of Don Luis within a wider hemispheric history—one in which the Christian martyrs are perhaps less important than the discouraging case they make, in religious as well as pragmatic terms, for future attempts at colonizing North America.

But the layered meanings embedded in the ending of Garcilaso's *La Florida* do not fully explain his elaboration of a Don Luis episode in Spain that was not in his source text in Ribadeneyra. Where did this episode in Cordova come from? Perhaps it is true that El Inca's anonymous informant met Don Luis in Cordova, just as Garcilaso writes in *La Florida*. Yet it is also possible to speculate that Garcilaso himself crossed paths with Don Luis, who arrived in Spain and King Philip's court for the first time in 1561, the same year in fact that Garcilaso arrived there from Peru. Some historians believe that King Philip had remanded Garcilaso to Spain and permanently exiled him there because he feared the elite mestizo's allegiances and potential influence among the conquered Incas.[34] Whether or not this is true, one can imagine that Garcilaso—despite his usual eagerness to legitimate and authorize his writing with firsthand evidence—would not likely be forthcoming about meeting Don Luis himself, if in fact he did so, given the latter's status as a murderous apostate by the time he appeared in Ribadeneyra's history. To admit to having met Don Luis during either of his trips to Spain would have been to open himself to dangerous suspicion—a problem that El Inca did not face when conversing with the aging conquistador Francisco Pizarro, for example, or the famous defender of indigenous rights, Bartolomé de las Casas, both of whom he also met in King Philip's court.[35] Moreover, if Garcilaso also met Don Luis in Spain, he would likely have met him in the company of several other indigenous inhabitants from the New World, including Aguirre and their companions from Ajacán and Mexico, respectively—a scenario which of course mirrors the one El Inca describes in *La Florida*, where Don Luis is traveling with a group of Indians.

It is a speculation, to be sure, but if Garcilaso and Don Luis indeed met at Philip's court when they both arrived in Madrid, then they too would have had a mutual interest in sharing information from their respective parts of the hemisphere, Ajacán and Cuzco, Peru. For Garcilaso knew well and first-hand the ways in which the monolingual shortsightedness of the Spanish had visited tragic historical consequences upon the Incas, and he possessed a cross-cultural and bilingual understanding analogous to that which Don Luis was rapidly developing in 1561, and had already achieved by 1566.[36] Whatever the case, we can say with certainty that Garcilaso was drawn to the cross-cultural and translational mediations presented in Don Luis's story by the following decade, when he added a final chapter to the already completed text of *La Florida* that included Don Luis's destruction of the Jesuit settlement in Ajacán.

In telling the story, Garcilaso ostensibly condemns the apostasy of Don Luis and celebrates the martyrdom of the Jesuits—following his source text in Ribadaneyra, but also of course adding the foreshadowing scene in Spain with the other Indians. In this sense, Garcilaso adumbrates a kind of tension between his story's explicitly condemnatory point of view and its ambiguous signification as a narrative sequence of supposed historical events. But what is finally most striking about Garcilaso's version of the Don Luis story is the fact that, in a seemingly inscrutable revision of his source text, Garcilaso chooses to omit Alonso de Olmos from the story entirely—and at the expense of the story's credibility: for without Alonso, as we have seen, there is no witness to tell the story of what happened in Ajacán. This absence is all the more glaring in a text so manifestly concerned with complex processes of historical authentication and the status of *testigo de vista* almost everywhere else in the work (especially when including Alonso would involve one of Garcilaso's favorite figures: the European captive).[37] Instead, thwarting the Western historiographical impulse to establish sources of information, forms of corroboration and verification, and means of external evaluation, Garcilaso's story floats unmoored from these modes of knowledge and becomes instead epigraphical (though its brief summation of Don Luis's story concludes rather than begins the larger work): it reprises its more general theme—the violent indigenous unsettlement of religious conversion and imperial acquisition—by dangerous but unspecified association rather than explicit statement or logical analogy. Almost two centuries later, Spanish colonial authorities famously would ban Garcilaso's *Comentarios* due to a suspected association between his texts and indigenous revolt during the Tupac Amaru II rebellion in 1780.[38] That Garcilaso's other, more famous text was accused of advocating indigenous violence suggests perhaps not only that Spanish and Creole readers interpreted it so in the case of this particular work but that, more generally, his writing—including *La Florida*—may have also signified within an indigenous genealogy of thought, even if we now have access only to the eighteenth-century Spanish and Creole reading of what that signification was.[39]

"The present high price of negroes in that place": Garcilaso's Las Casas

With his ending to *La Florida del Inca*, Garcilaso thus inscribes a pre-history for Don Luis, rewriting his source text in Ribadaneyra to lend this indigenous figure political consciousness, interiority, and, however briefly and fictively, a historical voice. Revising the narrative of Don Luis's return to Indian barbarism, Garcilaso offers instead a figure of unsettlement, motivated to thwart New World colonialism through the powerful work of treasonous translation. At the same time, Garcilaso signals with the story of Don Luis a model through which we may read the larger text of *La Florida* itself—a text which performs its own treasonous translations, its own revisionary subversions of colonial discourse. For once we see the contours of the new story of Don Luis that Garcilaso makes possible, other narrative threads and critical trajectories begin to emerge from some of the most opaque and troubling passages in the larger history.

In the first book of *La Florida*, for example, there is an extraordinary passage in the twelfth chapter, which narrates the passing of Soto and his men through Cuba on their way to begin the expedition to La Florida. Garcilaso's headnote to this chapter flags the significance of the passage by contrast with the otherwise rather mundane main subject matter at hand. The first part of the headnote declares a forthcoming record of "The supplies that the Governor provided in Santiago de Cuba," while the second announces, rather more promisingly, "One notable occurrence concerning the natives of those islands" (20). The notable circumstance, as it turns out, is entirely unrelated to the matter of supplies for the Soto expedition, but as so often with Garcilaso, the digression turns out to be more important than the main narrative trajectory, describing not the historical moment of Soto's visit but a Cuba of the future, of Garcilaso's own moment in composing *La Florida*:

> . . . this land [of Cuba] was prosperous and rich [in those days], and very populated with Indians, of which a little later almost all [of them] hanged themselves: the cause was, that as all that region of ugly land is very hot and humid, the native people in it had become soft, and lazy, and [good] for little work, and as for the great fertility and fruits, that the land of theirs had, they had no necessity of working much in order to sow, and reap, that however little maize that they planted, they gathered yearly more than that which they needed for the sustenance of natural life, that they did not aspire to any other thing as they did not recognize gold for riches, nor value it[;] they thought it was wrong to take [gold] from the streams and [from] the face of the earth where it grew; and as little the trouble the Spanish gave them about it, [the Indians] felt it excessively: and as also the devil would

incite for his own part, and with people so simple, depraved, and idle[,] he could do what he wished: it happened that in order not to mine for gold, which in this island is good and abundant, they hung themselves in such a manner and with such haste that there were one day at dawn fifty houses of that same town full of Indians hung with their wives and children that there hardly remained any living[;] it was the saddest thing in the world to see them hanging from the trees like thrushes when they are snared in bonds: and no remedies that the Spaniards tried and enacted to prevent [the suicides] were enough. In this abominable plague the natives of the island consumed themselves, and [on] their neighboring islands, so that today there is almost none. From this event arose the high price of negroes in that place today, in order to bring them to all parts of the Indies to work in the mines. (20v–21)

The passage exemplifies a typically Garcilasoan digressive tactic in which a forceful critique is lodged within a seemingly irrelevant tangent. Both shocking and insistently opaque, this tangent offers a strange account of the destruction of Cuba's indigenous population that appears to condemn the "depraved and idle" Indians for their own demise without holding the Spaniards accountable for any part in the tragedy of the Indian decimation. As Raquel Chang-Rodríguez notes, the characterization of the Indians as '*viciosos*' is especially "troubling," though the "graphic and desolate image [of the Tainos 'suspended from the trees like thrushes when they are snared'] points to and amplifies the impact of the conquest"—which Garcilaso will refer to later in the chapter as the "the conquest of the Indians."[40] But a closer examination suggests that this ambivalent passage is in fact less about the destruction of Cuba's Indians than it is about colonial discourse itself, about its illogical workings, its ideological blind spots, the mechanisms sustaining its self-delusion. Garcilaso first signals this metacritical dimension of the tangent in the overly abrupt transition from the plenitude of the Cuban past (prosperous, rich, and with a large Indian population) to the post-genocidal state of its present, and the implausibility of the assigned causality: "the natives of the island consumed themselves." The explanation calls upon the familiar tropes of the abundant New World Eden, where the soil bears fruit without human labor, and its resultant "soft and lazy" Indians—but here again, a familiar discourse turns in upon itself with the admission that these Indians do in fact sow corn, and apparently with enough efficiency to ensure that "they gathered yearly more than that which they needed for the sustenance of natural life." The law of Galatians thus works in the Indians' favor, it seems, and Garcilaso's reference to their surplus of harvest introduces into the passage an economic dimension that troubles its ostensibly Christian perspective on the behavior of the Indians: if Garcilaso avers that *el demonio* lies behind their refusal to work, he also concludes that, like everyone else, the devil too acts "for his own part" ('*por su parte*'). If the subsistence agriculture of the Indians produces a surplus of food, in other words, they have no material motivation to enter into the Spanish economic system; the problem is less that they are "simple, depraved, and idle" than that gold has a different meaning in their economy: they do not "recognize [it] for riches."

But it is in his repeated references to the Indian suicides by hanging that we find the specific object of Garcilaso's embedded critique, for the "abominable plague" he describes comes directly from the *Brevísima relación* of Las Casas, who famously documented the horrors of Spanish mistreatment of the Caribbean Indians: in Cuba, Las Casas wrote,

> After the Indians . . . were cast into the same servitude and calamity as those of Hispaniola, seeing all of themselves and their people die and perish without any help for it, some began to flee into the wilderness, others to hang themselves in desperation and lack of hope, and husbands and wives to hang themselves together, and with them hang their children. And because of the cruelties of one most tyrannous Spaniard . . . more than two hundred Indians hanged themselves. An infinite number died in this manner.[41]

As Garcilaso was well aware, to invoke the Indian suicides described by Las Casas was also of course to remind his seventeenth-century readers of the Spanish atrocities described in the *Brevísima relación* and other Las Casas writings. Whether these readers believed or approved of Las Casas's writings would not have been the point; the mere reference to the Indian hangings confirms the irony of Garcilaso's pointed understatement regarding indigenous enslavement: "and as little the trouble the Spanish gave them about it, [the Indians] felt it excessively"—that is, their enforced labor in the mines for gold. At the same time, the assertion that "no remedies that the Spaniards tried and enacted to prevent [the suicides] were enough" again recalls Las Casas, who published precisely such a list of "remedies," laid out in his 1516 *Memorial de remedios para las Indias*.[42] Garcilaso does not need to say why he deems these efforts insufficient—that "today there is almost [no Indian left]" is after all evidence in itself—but his dismissive allusion to the *remedios* suggests again that it is Las Casas's discourse in particular that he seeks to ironize here. Most commonly celebrated as the protector of the Indians, Las Casas nevertheless kept the economic and political needs of Spain fully in mind when crafting his *remedios*; the entire text of *Memorial* may even be read, as Daniel Castro has argued, as "little more than a primer for the acculturation and successful exploitation of the Indians" (71). The economic self-interest underpinning Las Casas's moral stance was clearly not lost on Garcilaso, who pointedly ends the digression by announcing the crude financial upshot of the Indian decimation: "the high price of negroes in that place today." Like the references to *Brevísima relación* and *Memorial*, this final observation—that Spaniards confronted the labor shortage caused by the decimation of the indigenous population by "bring[ing Negroes] to all parts of the Indies to work in the mines"—also of course evokes Las Casas, who would by the eighteenth century be widely (if falsely) denounced for having single-handedly prompted the introduction of African slavery in the West Indies in his efforts to save the Indians.[43]

That this passage should reveal subtle but disparaging references to Las Casas is hardly surprising given Garcilaso's well-known antipathy for the Spanish priest, clearly spelled out in the *Comentarios*.[44] The importance of the passage lies instead in its mode of critique. Quite unlike the direct assaults on Las Casas through the words of others in the *Comentarios*, the mode of this passage, as with Garcilaso's treatment of the story of Don Luis, is distinctly revisionist, allowing the author to register an oblique point of view (often counter to the text's explicit or stated perspective) in the slippage between his sources, their original contexts, and his own use of them. This point of view may in turn ask us to rethink some of the conclusions of the best scholarship on Garcilaso, which has sometimes assigned Garcilaso's distaste for Las Casas solely to his own elite self-interest. As Adorno argues, for example, "Garcilaso had a particular loathing for the Dominican because of his career-long opposition to encomienda," which angered Garcilaso on behalf of his *encomendero* father, who had once disagreed with Las Casas's campaign against "the sale of the rights in perpetuity to Spanish holders of Peruvian encomiendas" (94). But by the time Garcilaso wrote *La Florida* and the *Comentarios*, his father was not only dead but had long since abandoned his mother for a legitimate marriage to a Spanish woman; the lost rights of Spanish *encomenderos* may have been a far less urgent problem for the exiled mestizo author than were the larger implications of conquest throughout the American hemisphere as he wrote his histories of Peru and Florida. Garcilaso's adaptation of Las Casas in *La Florida* suggests, I would argue, a less personal and more analytical antipathy for the priest who described the devastation of the Indies and then proposed *remedios*, including the importation of African labor. The real force of Garcilaso's critique in this passage lies not in his condemnation of the "abominable" suicide of the Indians of Cuba but in a revisionist performance that masterfully exposes the double-sidedness of colonial discourse as it emerged in the so-called debates at Valladolid: how it has, on the one hand, like the Spanish theologian Juan Ginés de Sepúlveda, characterized the Indians as "vicious and slothful," while, on the other, like Las Casas, declared their Edenic innocence and yet sought to exploit them under the guise of protection. Sepúlveda and Las Casas, Garcilaso in effect suggests, were part and parcel of the same imperial worldview.

Cabeza de Vaca and Captivity (Un)redeemed:
The Case of Lope de Oviedo

In *La Florida*, then, Garcilaso draws upon Las Casas's *Brevisima relación* to undermine his own stated position while also exposing in the Defender of the Indies an imperial double standard. This satirical mode stretches beyond mere humanist skepticism, however; it is a form of critical unsettlement that sunders the foundations of the colonial project it appears to support—and it registers even more profoundly in *La Florida* when it comes to what is perhaps Garcilaso's most vexed relationship with a prior text: the *Relación de Álvar Núñez Cabeza de Vaca*.[45] Cabeza de Vaca figures prominently if silently in the pages of *La Florida*, where Garcilaso summons him in order to rewrite the ubiquitous colonial figure of the captive redeemed—and thereby to call into question the model of successful translation and transparent cross-cultural communication upon which the *Relación* and the colonial project more generally depend.[46] But to see Garcilaso's act of revision in this fuller context requires a reexamination of Cabeza de Vaca himself—and of the famous captivity narrative that purveyed his myth far and wide while suppressing the story of another captive, the author's double and scapegoat: Lope de Oviedo.

Over a decade before Hernando de Soto famously crossed the Mississippi River, Cabeza de Vaca was wrecked off the coast of Florida during the failed expedition of Pánfilo de Narváez in 1527, after which he traveled for eight years across present-day Alabama, Mississippi, Louisiana, Texas, Arizona, and New Mexico, living among different coastal and inland indigenous groups, before he and three fellow castaways made a stunning reappearance in Nueva Galicia (north-central Mexico) to the surprise of the Spanish forces newly stationed there. But if the broad outline of this remarkable story is now well known, few readers of Cabeza de Vaca's account will recall the name of Lope de Oviedo, a castaway from the same expedition who also survived the initial attempt led by Narváez to explore inland Florida—and who, like the author, also wound up living among a coastal group of Floridian Natives. Unlike Cabeza de Vaca, Lope de Oviedo never produced a written account of his experiences, nor was he ever "delivered" from his indigenous life or restored to his Spanish compatriots. In fact, we know little to nothing about him. Lope de Oviedo makes only a few brief appearances in Cabeza de Vaca's account before he abruptly disappears from the text, and even among specialists his marginal role in this much-studied narrative has attracted little or no attention.

Yet Lope de Oviedo provides the account with its most crucial narrative alibi while also embodying the story that Cabeza de Vaca sought most anxiously not to tell: the story of a man's indigenous acculturation in the New World and his subsequent choice not to return to life among Spaniards. As a minor figure in the *Relación*, Lope de Oviedo provides Cabeza de Vaca's narrative with an indispensable justification for the narrator's own delay in returning to his European life. But Lope de Oviedo's *story*, which is never explicitly told within the narrative and yet reverberates through it, compellingly undermines the narrator's most emphatic claims about what he called his "sad and wretched captivity" in North America.[47] Like John Smith's first account of his captivity, Cabeza de Vaca's narrative is the repository for a story that he only partially tells, a story that never achieves form within the larger *Relación*. What Cabeza de Vaca's narrative offers in lieu of the story it cannot tell is an epic elaboration of its own authorial protagonist as a suffering hero returned from the primitive wilderness to protest a civilization that he now finds flawed. This more "literary" Cabeza de Vaca emerges in part through the narrative's suppression of a living person and historical agent— that is, through the story's elision of Lope de Oviedo as the marginal figure of a narrative tangent.[48]

First published in 1542, and addressed to King Charles I of Spain (Charles V of the Holy Roman Empire), Cabeza de Vaca's *Relación* presents a firsthand account of the main events comprising the failed expedition in Florida led by Pánfilo de Narváez: the departure from San Lúcar de Barrameda, Spain, with 300 men, and with Cabeza de Vaca serving as their crown treasurer; the intervening stops in Hispaniola, Cuba, and Trinidad; sea voyages and storms; an abortive attempt to enter Florida on horseback after leaving the ships behind; and, finally, the experience of what the narrator terms a captivity among the indigenous peoples of Florida and later northern Mexico before he and three fellow castaways arrive in Nueva Galicia. Crucial to the failed outcome of the expedition is Narváez's self-interested abdication of authority in the worst moment of crisis, when the Spaniards on shore are attempting to return to their ships on precarious rafts. The problem, as the narrative stages it, is a conflict between cowardly selfishness (as enacted by Narváez, who flees in the best equipped raft) and an honorable collectivism (as embodied by Cabeza de Vaca, who attends to the sick and wounded after his own raft is left behind). The narrator insists so straightforwardly upon this conflict between cowardice and honor, individualism and corporatism, that it is easy to overlook an arguably more telling conflict that slips into the narrative at this moment before quickly receding.

Just after Narváez's abdication of leadership, the group left behind is stranded without a raft, "naked as the day [they] were born," and weak from cold and hunger. Cabeza de Vaca, having chased down a group of coastal Natives—and having, he avows, "made them understand through gestures how a raft had sunk on us and three members of our company drowned"— now proposes a possible course of action: "I asked the Christians and said that, if it seemed acceptable to them, I would ask those Indians to take us to their houses" (98–101). The attempt to solicit group approval here suggests the gravity of the proposition—as does the response it elicits: "And some of them who had been in New Spain replied that we should not even speak of it" (100–01). In the ensuing lines, Cabeza de Vaca both undermines and strategically reframes the intensity of this refusal by noting that his companions' reaction derives, erroneously, from the soldiers' experiences in New Spain during the conquest of Mexico and their consequent belief that "if [the Indians] took us to their houses, they would sacrifice us to their idols." This gesture toward the misguided nature of their fears effectively directs attention away from the fact that his proposal has marked a discursive limit of sorts, arriving at or implying what cannot be said. Cabeza de Vaca ultimately abandons the pretense of consensus and concedes that he "did not heed their words, but rather beseeched the Indians to take us to their houses"—a request in which the Natives apparently "showed that they took great pleasure" (100–01). Given the vehemence of the Spaniards' objection, the disagreement proves oddly fleeting within the larger account. Indeed, the narrative moves quickly past it precisely because the moment speaks elliptically but unmistakably to the most difficult problem within Cabeza de Vaca's narrative: how to explain not just the fact but also, far more problematically, the apparent *choice* of his entrée into Native life—how to tell the story of what is essentially a requested captivity.

The ensuing narrative repeatedly describes without specifying a kind of consensual bondage. After the Indians are "beseeched" to do so, they convey the Spaniards into ostensible imprisonment: "close to nightfall . . . they took us, and by their carrying us by clutching us tightly and making great haste, we went to their houses . . . so rapidly that they almost did not let our feet touch the ground" (100–01). From this point on, the narrative works assiduously to explain not only what the experience of life among the Indians was like but also—less directly yet far more urgently—why Cabeza de Vaca found it necessary to remain among the Indians as long as he did. A telling moment occurs when another group of stranded Narváez explorers, led by Andrés Dorantes and Alonso del Castillo, arrives in Cabeza de Vaca's village, precipitating a scene of distraught recognition—a scene that oddly parallels and presages the famous moment of *mis*recognition, which occurs at the end of the account and precipitates Cabeza de Vaca's permanent return to his Spanish identity. In this early scene, Dorantes and Castillo appear to have no trouble recognizing Cabeza de Vaca and the Spaniards with him, but they are disturbed by what they perceive: "Upon encountering us, they received great fright to see us in the condition we were in" (102–03). Yet by this point in their requested captivity, Cabeza de Vaca and his fellow *cautivos* have, by his own account, been well fed and "treated . . . so well" that they are far less uncomfortable than before they entered into supposed bondage. Thus, their visible "condition"—which gives Dorantes and Castillo "great sorrow," particularly their nakedness, because they have "no clothing other than what they were wearing" to offer them—must have been marked not by their lack of physical well-being but by the signs, instead, of an incipient assimilation.[49] Once we begin to see the narrative's oblique gestures toward this incipience—which remains unarticulated because the narrator himself "should not," or cannot, "even speak of it"—other signs of ambivalence emerge. No sooner has Cabeza de Vaca "agreed . . . to go forward [to] the land of Christians" with the combined groups of Spaniards than he has also convinced them to stay, having "decided to do what necessity dictated, which was to spend the winter there" (104–05). Indeed, the entire middle portion of the account seems to revolve around this tension between leaving and remaining: between traveling along the Gulf coast to the intended destination at the Pánuco settlement in New Spain and residing in Florida with the Natives.

Not surprisingly, then, the account grows tense and muddled when Dorantes and Castillo finally take the initiative in unifying the fourteen castaways, "gather[ing] together all the Christians who were somewhat dispersed," to travel together along the coast toward Pánuco (116–17). The narrative's palpable challenge here is the production of a coherent rationale, for Cabeza de Vaca, rather than going with Dorantes and Castillo, lingers on with the group whom he now calls "my Indians":

> As I have said, I was on the other side, on the mainland, where my Indians had taken me and where a great sickness had befallen me, such that if any other thing were to give me hope of survival, that illness alone sufficed to deprive me of it altogether. And when the Christians found this out, they gave to an Indian [a] cloak of sable skins . . . so that he would cross over to where I was to see me. And thus twelve of them came. . . .
>
> After they had crossed, the Indians who held me informed me of it, and of how Jerónimo de Alaniz and Lope de Oviedo had remained on the island. My sickness prevented me from following them, nor did I see them. I had to remain with these same Indians from the island for more than a year, and because of the great labors they forced me to perform and the bad treatment they gave me, I resolved to flee from them and go to those who live in the forests and on the mainland. (116–19)

In a passage whose most salient feature is its overdetermination, Cabeza de Vaca articulates a range of contradictory reasons for not joining the Dorantes and Castillo group: he is separated by distance from the group, he is too ill to travel with them, the illness has left him with too little hope of survival to care about leaving, he doesn't know the group is leaving until the Indians inform him of it, and, once again, his illness prevents him—*and* he never saw the departing Spaniards in the first place. Interspersed within this frantic litany of the multiple, individually sufficient, and collectively self-cancelling causes of his remaining is the significant information that the group has tried unsuccessfully to bring Cabeza de Vaca back into the fold by sending an Indian messenger. As the narrator puts it somewhat paradoxically, Cabeza de Vaca "had to remain" until he "resolved to flee"—not to the Spaniards, however, but to another group of Indians.

Recounting his circumstances after the departure of the Dorantes and Castillo group, Cabeza de Vaca next offers a vivid description of his own evolving role as a merchant within the indigenous groups among which he lives and travels, gathering extensive knowledge as he trades. On the one hand, this occupation confers an obvious narrative advantage, endowing the *Relación* with a value that may be offered to King Charles I in lieu of any material wealth brought back to Spain: it becomes evidence of his superior knowledge, as he puts it in his opening address to the king, of precisely the sort of "information [that is] not trivial for those who in your name might go to conquer those lands."[50] But Cabeza de Vaca's role as a merchant also serves him well in the temporal moment of the narrative: "because practicing it, I had the freedom to go wherever I wanted, and I was not constrained in any way nor enslaved, and wherever I went they treated me well and gave me food out of want for my wares, and most importantly because doing that, I was able to seek out the way by which I would go forward" (120–21).

If this passage establishes the freedom of the protagonist, which in turn enables the production of the narrative's knowledge value, it also presents an unsettling generic problem for the larger story of captivity. Cabeza de Vaca clearly understands this on some level, for he qualifies this description of his unlimited personal liberty and protection from the problem of hunger during his life among the Indians via a single but telling phrase—"most importantly" ('*lo más principal*' 120)—that suggests that leaving his indigenous life is his first priority. It is a priority—"to seek out the way by which I could go forward"—that nevertheless finds only the vaguest articulation even in this retrospective telling of his story. As the narrator concedes within a few sentences, "The time that I spent in this land, alone among [the Natives] and as naked as they, was nearly six years" (122–23).

This bald statement breaks abruptly into the narrative almost as if someone outside the text—for example, an official recording a legal declaration—had just posed the question directly: how long *did* you remain there? And, of course, Cabeza de Vaca presumably *was* asked exactly that question when he gave his sworn testimony, along with Dorantes and Castillo, for the Joint Report prepared in Mexico City in 1536 upon his return to life among Spaniards—six years before the initial publication of the *Relación*.[51] He was also almost certainly asked a related question during the production of this now-lost report—a question of potentially shattering implications—for he explicitly answers it in the next and perhaps most ambiguous section of the *Relación*:

> The reason I stayed so long was to take with me a Christian who was on the
> island, named Lope de Oviedo. His companion, de Alaniz, who had stayed

with him when Alonso del Castillo and Andrés Dorantes left with all the others, had since died. And in order to take him out of there, I crossed over to the island every year and begged that we go, in the best manner that we could, in search of Christians. And every year he kept me from going, saying that we would go the following year. In the end I took him. And I carried him across the inlet and four rivers that are along the coast, because he did not know how to swim. And thus we went forward with some Indians. . . . (122–23)

The scenario oddly mirrors the earlier description of Cabeza de Vaca's failure to leave with the Castillo-Dorantes party, with the narrator now taking the part of the traveling group and crossing over between island and mainland to urge a departure. What remains ambiguous in the passage—precisely when one would expect the clarity presumably associated with long-standing disagreement and cajoling—is exactly why Lope de Oviedo wants to remain among the Indians and why Cabeza de Vaca agrees to wait for him. To add to the confusion, given that the castaway in question is an expeditionary of lesser rank (whom Cabeza de Vaca has previously commanded as a superior), the narrative's assertion that Lope de Oviedo repeatedly "kept [him] from going" appears downright dubious. On the other hand, Lope de Oviedo provides the narrative with precisely the scapegoat that is required for explaining why its protagonist "stayed so long."

By the time Cabeza de Vaca reunites with Dorantes, Castillo, and Estevanico—the only three survivors of the party that had earlier left him behind—Lope de Oviedo is no longer there to corroborate (or deny) the story that we now have. As Cabeza de Vaca tells it, after he has taken the subordinate expeditionary with him—whether by persuasion or force he does not say—the entourage encounters a new group of hostile Indians from whom they hear frightening tales and receive "slaps and blows" as well as threats:

And fearing this, Lope de Oviedo, my companion, said that he wanted to go back with some women of those Indians with whom we had crossed the inlet. . . . I entreated him repeatedly not to do it, and I pointed out many things, but I was unable to detain him by any means. And thus he returned and I remained alone with those Indians. (124–25)

Lope de Oviedo's purported cowardice, like his inability to swim, allows the narrative to showcase the narrator's bravery as it earlier established his selflessness—while also providing a convenient cover for Cabeza de Vaca's extended stay among the Indians. But Lope de Oviedo is also a kind of doppelganger, and when he departs the *Relación*, he acts out the narrative trajectory that Cabeza de Vaca must anxiously abjure: a return to the Indian life that they had *both* manifestly resisted leaving.

Lope de Oviedo's untold story thus shadows the conclusion of Cabeza de Vaca's narrative, and his eventual return to the Spaniards, on multiple levels. Whether it is the protagonist or his marginal double who truly achieves deliverance from the "sad and wretched . . . captivity" is left open to debate given that the final pages of the *Relación* explicitly call into question the meaning of freedom. As the narrator observes with painful irony, "[I]t is evident how much men's thoughts deceive them, for we went to [the Spaniards] seeking liberty, and when we thought we had it, it turned out to be so much to the contrary" (252–53). In the most general sense, the remark suggests the extent to which Cabeza de Vaca's New World experiences have brought into sharp relief the deceptive, culturally relative nature of liberty. Specifically, however, this remark points to the active suspicion under which Cabeza de Vaca's return was held by the Spaniards who encountered him in Nueva Galicia: the ostensibly *returning* castaways are treated, in fact, as a threat to Spanish security, "sent . . . off under the guard of an *alcalde*" and "remove[d . . .] from conversation with the Indians" with whom they had been traveling (252–53). Cabeza de Vaca casts this turn of events as an outrageous consequence of the Spaniards' greedy plot to continue enslaving Indians, a plot that was, at the time he produced the *Relación*, illegal under Spanish imperial policy—and that therefore presents a conveniently unsanctioned foil against which to position his own credentials as the best potential representative of royal Spanish interests, the most effective "pacifier" (rather than enslaver) of the Indians.

At the same time, the narrator's purported outrage at the intended enslavement of Indians—an outlawed but nevertheless ubiquitous Spanish practice that could hardly have surprised him—provides the account with another digressive alibi, this time for the threatening figure that the Spaniards clearly understood Cabeza de Vaca to embody—and also, perhaps, with a kind of narrative mystification of the enduring problem of his journey: why he and his three fellow castaways chose to leave the coastline once they had nearly reached their intended destination in Pánuco, forging ahead into the unknown interior of North America where they had no reason to believe they would ever find Spaniards. Perhaps Cabeza de Vaca persuaded the other three that a return to Spanish life was either impossible or no longer desirable; or perhaps the four collectively reached that conclusion based upon the experiences they had while traveling across the land accompanied by a large group of Indians. Whatever the case, in casting its protagonist as a kind of conscientious objector who suffers for his principles of pacification, the narrative subtly draws our attention away from the very possibility that the Spaniards in Nueva Galicia seem to have had in mind when they put Cabeza de Vaca under guard and separated him from the indigenous group with which he traveled: that he and his three companions were not necessarily attempting to *return* to the Spaniards when they encountered them, quite by chance, in northern Mexico.[52]

The primary narrative work of the *Relación* may be precisely this performance of distraction, a virtuosic shifting of the reader's attention away from the obvious—away from the story that his account has been almost but not quite telling all along. The *Relación* achieves its distractive performance and accomplishes a now-celebrated feat of self-mythologizing—one that would not only exonerate him from apparent suspicions of treasonous behavior but would in fact earn him a future colonial posting as governor of the Río de la Plata colony in South America—by presenting a foundational story of Western modernity: the enduring plot of "going native." This narrative trajectory is *not*, to be clear, Lope de Oviedo's, for the narrative structure of Western literary primitivism demands the narrator's positioning within civilization as its mode of contrast, its production of a return with a difference. It is thus Cabeza de Vaca's manifestly changed identity—perceived by Spaniards and Indians alike—that differentiates him from, and consolidates the narrative's suppression of, Lope de Oviedo, who merely remains in his life among the Indians with nothing to show for it. Unlike Lope de Oviedo, Cabeza de Vaca performs toward the end of the *Relación* upon a stage designed to showcase his post-captivity difference as the manifest sign of his superiority over the Spaniards who have arrested and detained him. Rather than state the protagonist's emergent superiority outright, the narrative slyly ventriloquizes it through the speech of the Indians of Nueva Galicia, whom the Spaniards are underhandedly seeking to coerce:

> The Christians [in Nueva Galicia] . . . made their interpreter tell [the Indians] that we were of the same people as they . . . and that we were a people of ill fortune and no worth, and that they were lords of the land whom the Indians were to serve and obey. But of all this the Indians were only superficially or not at all convinced of what they told them. Rather, some talked with others among themselves, saying that the Christians were lying, because we came from where the sun rose, and they from where it set; and that we cured the sick, and that they killed those who were well; and that we came naked and barefoot, and they went about dressed and on horses with lances; and that we did not covet anything but rather, everything they gave us we later returned and remained with nothing, and that the others had no objective but to steal everything that they found. . . . Finally, it was not possible to convince the Indians that we were the same as the other Christians. (250–51)

The last seven lines of the passage are probably the narrative's most famous.[53] As many readers have observed, Cabeza de Vaca's use of the first-person plural pronoun has dramatically shifted by this point in the narrative, marking what seems to be almost a categorical separation from the Spaniards or "Christians." In a series of antithetical parallelisms emphasized with anaphora and asyndeton, this highly rhetorical speech pronounces Cabeza de Vaca's divinely ordained transformation: a Jesus-like man who hails naked and barefoot from the East, cures the sick, gives from his poverty—and, crucially, a man with whom the Indians identify and to whom they look as a spiritual leader. In the "sad and wretched" duration of his captivity, the narrative argues, Cabeza de Vaca has achieved profoundly Christian results. But the scene also achieves a secular payoff through the narrative's larger structure of primitivism: its endowment of the protagonist with the marks of his surpassing modernity vis-à-vis not only the narrative's guileless and loyal Indians but also the Nueva Galicia Spaniards who mistrust Cabeza de Vaca—and with whose testimony he is essentially in competition as a writer. The moment in which the narrative establishes Cabeza de Vaca's experience of having gone native—registered in the Indians' refusal to recognize his Spanishness, or even the potential imperial similitude between him and the "other Christians"—is central to the process of the protagonist's subject formation: Cabeza de Vaca emerges as a modern man defined specifically by his commitment to the royal law against robbing and mistreating the Indians and by a cross-cultural understanding that is not only more capacious and humane as a result of his primitivism but also, to the Indians as much as to readers, utterly transparent. By contrast, the narrative captures the failed modernity of the Nueva Galicia Spaniards in their inability to translate themselves and their point of view successfully to the Indians—as well as in the coercive and opaque nature of the translation process itself.

It is at this key point in the narrative that Cabeza de Vaca directly addresses the problem of failed translation for the first time. Up to this point, the narrative has featured numerous episodes of translation, scenes of communication between Spaniards and Indians, all of which have unfolded smoothly whether via words or gestures, and many of which foreground Cabeza de Vaca's own cross-cultural prowess and ability to produce transparent communication of meaning. Here, however, the Nueva Galicia Spaniards have "made their interpreter" present their case, and still the Indians believe that "the Christians were lying." In the ensuing pages, Cabeza de Vaca's narrative begins to make unprecedented concessions regarding the strains and burdens of translation, the possibility of its failure, and his own limited place within a larger translational chain involving multiple languages and interpreters. He and his fellow returning castaways now find themselves, at times, less than persuasive in their interpretive roles, such as when he admits, "We had great difficulty convincing the Indians to return to their homes and secure themselves and sow their maize" (248–49). Similarly, when Melchor Díaz, the *alcalde mayor*, asks Cabeza de Vaca to help with recalcitrant Indians by "hav[ing] them called together and order[ing] them on behalf of God and Your Majesty to come and settle the plain and work the land," the narrative emphasizes the protagonist's indispensability in bringing success to the conquest but nevertheless concedes a significant problem: "To us this seemed very difficult to put into effect, because we did not bring any Indian of ours or any of those who usually accompanied us and were skilled in these matters" (254–55). The skills in question are, of course, those of translation; lacking an indigenous interpreter, Cabeza de Vaca apparently worries about his ability to deliver on the implied promise of controlling the Indians.

Such difficulties of communication, however, are quickly resolved into a scene of seamless understanding and powerful transmission by means of another translative chain. Here again the narrative acknowledges the mediation of Native interpreters—but recasts this mediation as a mystifying effect of Cabeza de Vaca's own authority, made manifest when the Indians held captive by the Spaniards first learn about him: "these Indians had been with the Christians when we first arrived to them, and they saw the [600 Indians] who accompanied us and learned from them about the great authority and influence that through all those lands we had possessed and exercised, and the wonders that we had worked and the sick people we had cured" (254–57).

Cabeza de Vaca's reputation, in other words, precedes him: by merely arriving on the scene, this redeemed captive (and pretender to future colonial authority) introduces a model of successful, transparent, and utterly persuasive communication with the Indians. The series of interpreters acting on Cabeza de Vaca's behalf proceed to address all the Indians and explain Christian theology in some detail before pronouncing the terms of the Spaniards' demands. The Indian masses, who have heretofore been avoiding the Spaniards, remarkably respond "that they understood everything very well and . . . that thus they would do it as we commanded it" (258–61). By his own account, moreover, Cabeza de Vaca uses these powers of communication to "secure" the 600 indigenous people with whom he has been traveling as well as those he meets in Nueva Galicia—assuring them all of their safety among the Spaniards (260–61).

And though he glosses neatly over it in the concluding story of his victimization by those he casts as greedy conquistador villains who cannot understand or make themselves understood to the Natives, Cabeza de Vaca's cross-cultural prowess is—by the internal logic of his own account—the precise means by which these Indians are betrayed into slavery. In the end, then, Cabeza de Vaca's fiction of mutual comprehension is as self-serving and deadly as the monolingual logic of the *requerimiento* that he reads before his Indian audience, the infamous declaration of Spanish sovereignty and authority (discussed in greater detail in Chapter 4). The violent hallmark of its political mode is a linguistic performance of "inclusive exclusion," that "seizing of the outside," as Agamben defines it in his writing on sovereignty, from which the law defines the "sphere of its application" (104–05). Only those Indians who understand the language of the *requerimiento* can consent to conversion, and thus achieve, like all Christian Spaniards, the ostensible guarantee of legal status as "subjects and vassals" of the Crown, "free without servitude," with all the "privileges, and exemptions, and . . . benefits" entailed therein ("Requerimiento"). Those Indians who do not understand Spanish and do not consent to their subordination to the Crown and Church, on the other hand, are also included in sovereignty's embrace, but precisely via their exclusion as subjects: they become slaves.

The Failure of Imperial Translation: Garcilaso's Cabeza de Vaca

None of these contradictions surrounding the nature of colonial translation were lost on Garcilaso. And for him, the self-aggrandizing account produced by Cabeza de Vaca after his dramatic recovery provided an opportunity for a parodic recasting of what is now a favorite captivity narrative in early American literature, an exemplary prototype—whether Chicano, southwestern, hybrid, or hemispheric—against which the entire Anglo-American tradition may be unflatteringly measured.[54] To be sure, Garcilaso's overt stance toward the famous ex-captive appears utterly respectful, almost as if he were paying homage to an acknowledged superior.[55] Indeed, he invokes Cabeza de Vaca or his account on five separate occasions in *La Florida*, and goes out of his way to cite scrupulously from his text, noting not only specific observations from his source but often the chapters in which they occur. Yet even in those passages where Garcilaso cites Cabeza de Vaca by name and praises him, there is always a strand of critical irony underpinning the commentary, beginning with his first reference to the ex-captive early in *La Florida*. In Chapter 3 of Book 1, where Garcilaso enumerates the many failed expeditions in Florida before Soto's attempt, he cites the dramatic reversal of fortune visited upon the author of the *Relación,* or *Naufragios*:

> . . . Pámphilo de Narváez went to Florida in the year 1557 [*sic*], where he along with all the Spaniards that he carried was lost so miserably, as in his *Naufragios* recounts Álvar Núñez Cabeza de Vaca, who went with him as treasurer of the Royal Purse. [Cabeza de Vaca] escaped with three other Spaniards and a negro, and God Our Lord having shown them such mercy, that they went so far as to perform miracles in his name, with which they earned such a reputation and trust from the Indians, that they worshipped them as gods[;] [Cabeza de Vaca and his companions] did not want to stay among [the Indians], rather as soon as they were able they left that land in all haste, and they came to Spain to solicit new governorships and having obtained them, things happened in such a way that they ended up sadly, as recounts this same Álvar Núñez Cabeza de Vaca, who died in Valladolid having come in chains from Río de la Plata where he went as governor. (5)

Contrary to its first sentence, this passage is not really about the Narváez expedition or its failure or even three unnamed Spaniards and "a negro" who also escaped being "lost so miserably." These merely provide a pretext for the real subject of Garcilaso's interest: a bureaucrat, the "treasurer of the Royal Purse," and the *Relación* that made his name famous. Garcilaso mentions Cabeza de Vaca's name twice within the space of the short passage, elaborating it in full to frame the beginning and end of his commentary, and even flagging his final mention as "this same Álvar Núñez Cabeza de Vaca" lest the reader lose the thread before El Inca delivers his dark punch line via a reference to Río de la Plata—where, in a painful irony for the most part lost on American literary history, Cabeza de Vaca was ultimately arrested under allegations of (among other things) mistreatment of the Indians.[56] At the same time, if Garcilaso quite predictably attributes Cabeza de Vaca's performance of healing miracles to the agency of "God Our Lord," he also subtly undermines the associated divinity of the healers themselves by pointing out that they were not contented to continue this work "in his name"—"to stay among [the Indians]." Instead, he emphasizes, they abandoned their ostensibly sacred project "in all haste" in order to solicit the distinctly worldly rewards of "new governorships." Their very desires seem linked to the sad end that awaits them in Garcilaso's next clause, which circles in on its specific object of scrutiny by repeating Cabeza de Vaca's full name and attributing the information of this end to him—quite illogically, it turns out, when the end in question appears to be his own death in Valladolid. In the space of his short introduction of the *Relación* (or *Naufragios*), Garcilaso thus manages to evoke the potentially blasphemous dimensions of Cabeza de Vaca's role among the Indians: once "worshipped as [a] god," this fallen idol will end by returning "in chains" from the New World.

Even Garcilaso's most positive commentary on Cabeza de Vaca—which occurs in the second chapter of Book 5, where he describes the prevalence of wooden crosses among the Floridian Indians who had "received news of the benefits and marvels that Álvar Núñez Cabeza de Vaca . . . had performed by virtue of Jesus Christ Our Lord" (261)—is oddly offset by the story that immediately precedes it: the tale of the Lope de Oviedo-like figure of Diego de Guzmán. When this Spaniard accompanying the Soto expedition goes missing, Soto believes him to have been killed by the Indians and is just preparing to take vengeance upon a group of indigenous captives when one of them makes the remarkable suggestion that Diego de Guzmán is not a victim at all but a "treason[ous] . . . Spaniard who denied his own people (negó a los suyos) without our having forced him to do so or even known of his going" (259v). This indigenous captive furthermore proposes that Soto might gain proof that Diego de Guzmán is indeed alive and well by requesting written communication from him via the Indians who are accused of killing him: "for by his handwriting, since we ourselves do not know how to write, it may be seen that he is living" (259). The Spaniards do as suggested and receive their proof of Diego de Guzmán's betrayal: an insolent charcoal scrawl of his name with no further message. The incident calls into question the colonial mystification of literacy: far from being awed or tricked by the technology of writing, Garcilaso's Indians themselves suggest a written message to bear out the truth of their own statement—even as it reminds readers that not every Spanish castaway is a captive hoping to be recovered from Native life.

Thus, when Garcilaso turns immediately after this commentary to the subject of Cabeza de Vaca, the story of Diego de Guzmán still echoes, perhaps even reminding readers of the strangely willing nature of the ex-captive's captivity. Whatever the case, however, Garcilaso makes a point of calling Cabeza de Vaca's account into question in more explicit ways throughout *La Florida*, particularly in Chapter 4 of Book 2 where he deems it suitable "not to move forward without touching upon what Álvar Núñez Cabeza de Vaca writes in his *Comentarios*" since it is "all contrary to what we are writing" (96v–97). The material in question hardly seems worth pausing to quibble over, concerning as it does Cabeza de Vaca's unfavorable descriptions of the physical geography of the province of Apalache, which El Inca himself acknowledges is in part "very bad" though in part "very good" (96v). Yet Garcilaso uses the occasion to enumerate seeming problems in Cabeza de Vaca's testimony and then to emphasize precisely by denying it that his own history "contradicts that of this cavalier" (97v). Primary among the problems in Cabeza de Vaca's account, El Inca charges, is his reliance on Native testimony: "it is to be warned that a great part of the relación that Álvar Núñez writes of that land is what the Indians gave him; as he himself says, those Castilians did not see it" (97). There is no *testigo de vista* in the cavalier's account, in other words, for there was no "possibility for [him or other Spaniards] to tread upon it and see it with their own eyes" (97). But if sight and subjection (*hollarla*) go hand in hand for the Spanish expeditioners, the narration of the Indians proves more powerful than either in Garcilaso's telling: for "the Indians," he states, "would have spoken badly rather than favorably of their land in order to discredit it, so that the Spaniards would lose their desire to go there " (97). The indigenous production of a false, colonial discourse does the primary work of unsettlement, Garcilaso suggests, undermining the authority of Cabeza de Vaca's *Relación* while also contributing subtly to the ultimate failure of the Soto expedition.

But Garcilaso's most profound critique of the *Relación* is registered in his rewriting of the story of Juan Ortiz, which offers a trajectory of captivity and translation that parallels Cabeza de Vaca's.[57] Like Cabeza de Vaca, Juan Ortiz was connected to the Narváez expedition and, as we saw in Chapter 1, experienced an Indian captivity; he was sent from Cuba on a rescue mission to look for the missing Narváez and his men and was taken captive in 1528. Over a decade later, when Soto and his men arrived in Florida in 1539, they stumbled upon Ortiz alive and well after eleven years of living among the Florida Indians near Tampa Bay. Like Cabeza de Vaca, then, Ortiz too shared the distinction of a purported redemption, of return from his Indian captivity, and like his fellow captive redeemed, he too offered his translative services to future Spanish expeditions—in this case, the very expedition that had recovered him. He became Soto's interpreter.

As Lisa Voigt has observed, the Juan Ortiz story "gains paradigmatic importance in *La Florida del Inca*": unlike the other known accounts of the Soto expedition, which consistently mention but do not stress the role played by Ortiz, Garcilaso's version elaborates the episode of Ortiz's captivity and recovery in great detail, investing it with narrative structure and emplotment. In Voigt's view, Garcilaso's interest lies in showing how the "transformative power of captivity" can be "positive" rather than "dehumanizing"—in "emphasiz[ing] the captive's potential role as a mediator who, like [Garcilaso] himself, can identify with both of the cultures in contact." In this reading, Garcilaso identifies with and valorizes Ortiz for the bilingual mediative abilities that are the happy by-product of captivity: "the emergence of a hybrid result of intercultural contact" that allows him to engage in a simultaneously diplomatic and narrative process (107). I would argue, however, that Garcilaso's story of Juan Ortiz is less an endorsement of or a plea for intercultural understanding than it is a parodic staging of treasonous mistranslation, including his own. Specifically, El Inca identifies Ortiz not with himself (or with his own figurative captivity in exile in Spain) but with that other famous Floridian captive, Cabeza de Vaca—whose *Relación* Garcilaso rewrites under the sign of dark comedy.

Garcilaso's story of Juan Ortiz follows the basic narrative trajectory of Cabeza de Vaca's captivity, from tortuous beginnings to a confrontation with death to a felicitous state of empowerment that precedes recovery. In the *Relación*, Cabeza de Vaca enters his captivity "like the figure of death itself" (86) and there endures "the great labors [the Indians] forced [him] to perform," his "fingers so worn that when a reed touched them it caused them to bleed" (96). The Indians give Cabeza de Vaca and his companions "slaps and blows . . . and [throw] mudballs at [them], and each day [place] arrows at [their] hearts saying that they wanted to kill [them] as they had killed [their] other companions" (99). Likewise, in Garcilaso's *La Florida*, Juan Ortiz, "more dead than alive" among his captors, must perform "ceaseless labor," sports "blisters . . . like halves of oranges . . . [with] much blood [running] from them," and suffers "daily torture," "such cruel blows, slaps and lashes each and every day" (30–31). Moreover, if in the *Relación* Cabeza de Vaca estimates that "no hardship endured in the world equals this one" (109), he soon enough finds that his curative powers gain him great respect among the Indians, particularly after he allegedly heals "one who had been dead [who] had arisen revived and walked about and eaten and spoken" (118). Similarly, in *La Florida* Juan Ortiz too must confront the realm of death in the series of trials he endures during captivity: he is sent to a graveyard "to guard by day and night the dead bodies" in their "sepulchers" (31). Entering this world of shades, Ortiz too performs a resuscitation of sorts, saving himself precisely by finding "a better life with the dead [*los muertos*] than with the living" (32). While guarding the sepulchers, Ortiz kills a scavenging lion; and, like Cabeza de Vaca in the *Relación*, in doing so he achieves a miracle among the dead, which in turn garners him the adulation of the Natives: "because in that land in general they take it as a miraculous event [*cofa de milagro*] for a man to kill a lion, and with great veneration and respect they treat [the man] who manages to kill it" (33).

Juan Ortiz's adulation is short-lived, however, and the faint irony which pervades Garcilaso's account of his heroism reflects pointedly back upon the dramatic heroics in the prior account of Cabeza de Vaca—who not coincidentally has been widely credited with the first European sighting of a North American mountain lion or cougar. "And though it is true that the lions of Florida, Mexico, and Peru are not so large or so fierce as those of Africa," winks Garcilaso, after praising Juan Ortiz: "after all they are lions and the name is enough, and even though the common proverb says, that they are not so fierce as they are painted: those who have found themselves near [lions] say that they are much more fierce than the sketched ones . . ." (33). This odd but telling passage directs its critique in more than one direction: both at the hyperbolic language of New World accounts, in which the very naming of flora and fauna invents as much as it represents America ("the name is enough" to create its own reality), and, with his wry understatement about the distinction between live and painted lions, at the skepticism of those European readers who would challenge New World hyperbole from afar, without true proximity to what they judge.

In telling the story of Juan Ortiz, however, Garcilaso calls into question not only the rhetorical style but the founding assumptions of Cabeza de Vaca's narrative. For the story of Ortiz's capture returns Garcilaso's own narrative to the historical moment of the Narváez expedition, as narrated by Cabeza de Vaca, which El Inca revisits from a very different point of view that in turn overlays his account of Soto more generally. Thus, when he recounts the initial arrival of Soto and his men in Florida at the outset of Book 2, Chapter 1, Garcilaso begins by describing the enraged reaction of the cacique Hirrihigua, Ortiz's first captor. As Garcilaso tells it, Soto attempts to communicate with Hirrihigua by sending him

> endearments, gifts, and promises . . . via the Indians[,] his vassals, whom [the Spaniards] had taken . . . [But Hirrihigua] emphatically refused to come out in peace, nor listen to any [messages] sent to him[;] rather he became angry with whomever carried them to him, saying that since they knew how offended and hurt he was by that [Spanish] nation, they should not bring their messages: that if it were [the Spaniards'] heads, those he

would receive with great pleasure, but that their words, and [their] names he did not want to hear. (29)

Soto—like Cabeza de Vaca—clearly assumes the model of transparent cross-cultural understanding in this initial encounter with the Indians: having captured some Indians, the Spaniards instruct them to carry a beneficent message to their leader. Unsurprisingly, the leader never materializes and the messengers never return. But in Garcilaso's gloss of the encounter, this assumption of translational transparency becomes the vehicle for its own hilarious undercutting: for Garcilaso both assumes its existence and deploys it to restage precisely the kind of scene of Spanish diplomatic prowess that Cabeza de Vaca promoted in his own narrative. Instead of stating explicitly that Soto's message of "endearments . . . and promises" is either misunderstood or thoroughly compromised (not least by the Spaniards' initial capturing of the messengers), Garcilaso represents Hirrihigua's lack of response as a sign of comprehension: as both a deliberate refusal of engagement with the Spanish and an exercise of dominion over the very interpreters "whom [the Spaniards] had taken" and sought to control. The entire episode becomes the occasion not of Spanish ambassadorial authority but for Hirrihigua's flourish of rhetorical irony in the last sentence of the passage—a flourish that precisely anticipates the paradoxical message of Don Luis and his fellow Indians in Spain: both to refuse to speak another word and to promise retribution.

In a similarly paradoxical gesture, Garcilaso frames his version of the ensuing Juan Ortiz story as both tangential and central: ". . . although we are somewhat stretching out [the story]," he concedes, "we will not be leaving [behind] the intention[;] on the contrary [the digression] will contribute much to our history" (29v). What is the "intention," this *propósito* of the story, and what specific value is adduced in telling it? As Voigt notes, Garcilaso makes a point of waiting until much later in the narrative to tell us why Hirrihigua holds a particular fury for the Spanish: Narváez and his men cut off the cacique's nose and threw his mother to wild dogs. Thus, in her astute reading, Garcilaso's larger point is to "locate the origin of discord between Spaniards and Indians in Spanish treachery, while making Native hostility the ostensible focus of the narrative" (110). But while Spanish cruelty is certainly part of what comes across in his telling, I would reiterate here that Garcilaso's interest is always to some extent a meta-narrative one as well, as suggested in particular by the scene which directly follows his announcement of the so-called digression. Here, Garcilaso describes the method of Juan Ortiz's capture, which occurs when a Spanish vessel arrives in Florida seeking Narváez sometime after the Spaniards' harsh treatment of Hirrihigua:

> . . . as the Cacique learned that [the ship] was one of those of Narváez, and that it was searching for [Narváez's men], he wished to catch all those who came inland in order to burn them alive, and to reassure them, he

pretended to be a friend of Pánfilo de Narváez, and he sent to them to say that as their captain had been there, and had left an order as to what the ship should do if it should arrive in that port[;] and in order to persuade them to believe him, he showed from the land two or three sheets of white paper and other old letters, which from the former friendship of the Spaniards, or however it may have been, he had been able to have, and had kept very guardedly. (29)

As in the scene of Soto's arrival, here again we find the assumption of transparent communication across languages, as Hirrihigua sends word of Narváez to the Spanish to lure them in. But unlike Soto who (in Garcilaso's account) presumed he could master the encounter simply by articulating his position through captured interpreters, Hirrihigua assumes no such continuity of meaning: as a purposeful deception, his stated message is intended to reassure them but not to communicate a true point of view. Most significantly, the cacique attempts to consolidate this duplicitous verbal maneuver through the production of texts: the sheets of white paper and "old letters" that he has guarded very carefully until the appropriate time. The ruse not only inverts the old dynamic of mystification via literacy so common to early modern colonial discourse—in which the technology of European writing elicits submissive awe from the Native oral culture—but also quite literally models a technique of textual appropriation, of repurposing Spanish writing against the Spaniards themselves by situating it in an alternative context. Hirrihigua's trick may fail, but—unlike Soto—he accomplishes his larger purpose with his next maneuver, through which he captures Juan Ortiz. That his revisionary act of textual appropriation might be said to parallel Garcilaso's own is clear in the final line of the chapter, in which the Spaniards, having lost Juan Ortiz and three other men, "find themselves *burlados*"—*burlesqued* by the Indian *caballeros* or "cavaliers" ("the name . . . seems inappropriate," Garcilaso says) in a parodic twist worthy of Cervantes.[58]

Garcilaso's story of Juan Ortiz thus offers up what we might call a Don Quixotian version of Cabeza de Vaca—a perspective which may help to account for the narrative's more disturbing moments of hilarity in the most inappropriate of places, as when Hirrihigua's rage is fueled not only when he remembers his mother's gruesome death but "when he went to blow [his nose] and did not find his nostrils," as if the innocent Juan Ortiz "himself had cut them off" (33). Like Cabeza de Vaca, Ortiz is unrecognizable to the Spanish when he finally reunites with them, but Garcilaso stages the scene of anti-agnorisis as partly comedic: unlike the other accounts of Ortiz's dramatic first words to the Spanish, Garcilaso's version presents Ortiz as a buffoon, unable to identify himself except by shouting the name of his home—Sevilla—which he mispronounces as "Xibilla," just before he is seized by Alvaro Nieto "with one arm" and put "across the haunches of his horse as if [he had been] a child" (39v). And while Cabeza de Vaca describes himself in the *Relación* as "unable to wear . . . for many days" after his return to the Spanish the clothes given him by the governor (169), Garcilaso contends in *La Florida* that the governor in Florida immediately "gave [Juan Ortiz] a suit of black velvet": but since he had for so long "gone naked he could not bear it . . . he wore only a shirt, some linen pants, a cap, and some shoes, and . . . he went about thus for more than twenty days until little by little he became accustomed to being dressed" (40v). Here again, the discrepancy between Ortiz's nakedness and the suit of black velvet (unmentioned in the other accounts) registers an oddly humorous note that recasts the refrain of vulnerable nakedness that structures Cabeza de Vaca's account.

Juan Ortiz thus becomes the butt of Garcilaso's ironic, revisionist relation to Cabeza de Vaca's text. Aligning them through various shared details, Garcilaso offers a figure who undercuts the self-mythology of Cabeza de Vaca's narrative, especially the latter's claim to the special knowledge and abilities gained through captivity and transmitted through narrative. For in Garcilaso's staging of post-captivity return, the ex-captive's trajectory suggests the opposite. Ortiz, in El Inca's version of the story, narrates little to nothing anywhere in the episode—after all, "he had forgotten [even so much as how] to pronounce the name of his own land," and is directly quoted only once: when he calls out in a loud voice, "Xibilla, Xibilla, [trying] to say Sevilla, Sevilla" (39v). Moreover, in contrast to Juan Ortiz's garbled and halting attempt at speech, Garcilaso presents us with the long, eloquent discourses of Mucozo, the benevolent cacique who takes in Ortiz and protects him from Hirrihigua. When Soto attempts to thank Mucozo for saving Ortiz and returning him to the Spanish, the cacique responds with an elaborate speech that almost exceeds its status as indirect quotation with its rhetorical effect of immediacy:

> . . . that what he had done for Juan Ortiz, he had done for his own respect, because [Ortiz] having gone to him to commend himself to [Mucozo] in his need, and to seek aid of himself and his house, by the law of his people he was obligated to do that which he had done for [Ortiz]. . . . and that his having sent [Ortiz] to his lordship [Soto], had been more for his [Mucozo's] interest and benefit than for serving his lordship, since it had been [done] in order that [Ortiz] in the role of advocate and mediator, through his intercession and merits, would attain favor and grace: so that in his [Mucozo's] land no harm would be done. And so neither the one nor the other action did his lordship have to thank nor receive as a favor: but that he [Mucozo] was pleased, however it had come to be, of having happened to do something of which his lordship, and these cavaliers, and all the Spanish nation, whose fond servant he was, had been thankful and shown themselves to have received satisfaction. He begged his lordship that with the same approval he

would receive him into his [lordship's] service, under whose protection and shelter his person and house, and state, recognizing for principal lord the Emperor and King of Spain, and secondarily his Lordship as his captain general, and Governor of this Kingdom, that were this favor granted him, he would hold himself more advantageously rewarded than had been the merit of his service, done in the interest of Juan Ortiz, or for having freely returned him, an act that his lordship had so much esteemed: about which he said that he esteemed and held in greater value seeing himself as that day he saw himself, favored and honored by his lordship and all these cavaliers, as any good he had done in all his life: and that he publicly promises to make every effort from then on to do similar acts in service of the Spaniards: since those had turned out so well for him.[59]

The surface point of Mucozo's speech is clear enough; he eloquently pledges his fealty to both Soto and the Spanish, recognizing the Emperor and King of Spain as his sovereign. But in the next lines, Garcilaso calls Mucozo a "prudent courtier" (*discreto cortesano*), a comparison that suggests the proper milieu through which to interpret the passage on its own terms: the humanist universe of *Il Cortegiano*, which saw the birth of political self-fashioning. Like Mucozo, Castiglione's courtier is a public figure, notably above reproach in comportment, speech, and outward appearance—which is, of course, exactly how Garcilaso presents Mucozo to his Spanish readers. But like any good reader of renaissance political discourse, Garcilaso must also have understood that the flip side of Castiglione's courtier was his private will to power—and an attendant mode of artful deception in influencing and manipulating the sovereign to whom he professed to submit: *Il Principe*.[60]

Mucozo's speech thus evokes not the *exemplum* of the noble Indian lord worthy of Christian conversion but, rather, resonating with the wider renaissance "crisis of exemplarity," the far more Machiavellian figure of the state sovereign—in this case, a conquered indigenous sovereign acting on behalf of his state and its rational political interests in an arena of international conflict.[61] Indeed, Mucozo says explicitly that he has acted "in his own interest"—and not out of any recognition of the superiority of Christian ideology but rather in accordance with the law of his people, to which he is obligated. He emphasizes more than once that his actions were undertaken to serve his own advantage rather than Soto's or that of the Spanish, and that he treated Juan Ortiz as he did in order to use him politically as a mediator—"as protector and advocate"—and with the best interests of national security in mind: to prevent harm to his own land. Mucozo goes so far as to repudiate any expression of gratitude from Soto—or even any interpretation of Mucozo's actions as a favor—while simultaneously advising Soto of his required response, which is in effect gratitude: that "Your Lordship, these cavaliers, and the whole Spanish nation . . . would be pleased and show themselves to have received satisfaction." When Mucozo promises to "do similar things from here on in the service of the Spaniards," he is both notably unclear about what acts he means—returning Spanish captives and castaways? sending emissaries on behalf of his people?—and unequivocal about his underlying *raison d'état*: he will base his political actions in the future on the outcomes of his prior acts, "since those he has done ended so well for him." Shuttling between the courtier's posture of humble submission before his superior, *Il Principe*, and the prince's brazen realist political theory, the entire speech is an exercise in rhetorical ambiguity, one that serves ultimately to cast suspicion on the very discourse of Spanish imperial authority in which it appears to participate, and to reiterate the sovereignty of the Floridian Natives whom Mucozo represents.

Against this foil of Mucozo's courtly eloquence and artful, political dissimulation, Juan Ortiz's story is conspicuously muted even as it draws ever closer to the narrative model of his precursor and fellow captive, Cabeza de Vaca. Like the loquacious Cabeza de Vaca, Juan Ortiz, once redeemed, quickly regains his Spanish and warms to the subject of his own suffering: he again "showed the scars on his body, disclosing those that could be seen, and enlarged upon the story of his life that we have given, and again he told of many other tortures he had endured, that caused compassion in his listeners" (41). Yet El Inca makes a point of breaking off the account before the telling can occur—"and we leave him in order to avoid prolixity" (41v)—as if to suggest a certain long-winded vacuity at the heart of the narrative genre upon which Ortiz's story is modeled. Indeed, when Ortiz is summoned before Soto "to inform him of what he knew of that region, and in order that he recount to him particularly that which [he knew] from having been in the power of these two Caciques" (41v), Ortiz's explicit performance of ignorance slyly undermines Cabeza de Vaca's attempt to parlay his cross-cultural knowledge into a new kind of commodity—as he puts it in the *Relación*, an "account of all that [he] was able to observe and learn in [his] nine years" of captivity (25). For Ortiz, Garcilaso tells us, "although he had been so long in that [land,] knew little, or nothing" about it (41v).

Moreover, Ortiz's ignorance of the land parallels his lack of understanding of his cross-cultural experience in a way that again recalls and undermines the narrative of Cabeza de Vaca. Like Cabeza de Vaca, Ortiz approaches the Spaniards only to be misrecognized by them as a non-Spaniard. But in El Inca's version of the redemption moment, this scene illustrates not the captive's ability to assimilate to the indigenous culture (as in Cabeza de Vaca) but the *opposite* of cross-cultural understanding on the captive's part:

> The Indians seeing the Spaniards told Juan Ortiz it would be prudent to secure their persons and lives by taking to the hills until the Christians recognized them as friends: in order that they, taking them as enemies, did not

spear them in the open field. Juan Ortiz refused to take the good counsel of
the Indians, trusting in [the fact that] he was a Spaniard, and that his people
would know him as soon as they saw him as if he came dressed as a Spaniard,
or were in some way differentiated from the Indians so as to be known as a
Spaniard. [But Juan Ortiz] like the others was wearing nothing but some loin
cloths for apparel, and a bow and arrows in his hands, and a feather of about
three feet in height on his head for finery and ornament. (38v)

This elaborate description of Ortiz's appearance—particularly the nearly
comic detail of the ornamental plumage half a fathom in height adorning his
head—casts the retroactive irony of understatement upon Cabeza de Vaca's
account of his encounter with the Spanish, who, "seeing [him] so strangely
dressed and in the company of Indians," predictably fail to identify his nationality. Unlike Cabeza de Vaca's account, however, Garcilaso's narrative
endows the Indians with a specific point of view about the instability of cultural identity and its potential for violence in the moment of first encounter—
and their "good counsel" on this matter turns out to be all too right. Garcilaso
directly attributes the ensuing attack upon the Indians not only to Ortiz's refusal "to heed" the people with whom he has lived for ten years but also to his
utter failure to recognize the reality of his own cross-cultural experience—his
inability, that is, even to entertain the idea that in indigenous dress, weap-
onry, ornamentation, and context, he might *not* appear to the Spaniards to be
"diferenciado de los Indios": differentiated from the Indians.

Lest the point of this failure of vision be missed, Garcilaso stages a comic
but pointed scene in which the Indians rebuke him, "each one [of them] with
much fury, and anger scold[ing] Juan Ortiz for his little warning and great
inexperience" (40). When it turns out that one of the Indians has been lanced
by a Spaniard during the melee, the Indians hold Ortiz personally responsible
and judge him to be deserving of punishment, so much so "that with difficulty they restrained themselves from laying hands on him, and would have
done so had the Spaniards not been present" (40). Constrained by the Spanish
military presence, the Indians fight back with the only weapon they have in
the absence of their author's sword and plume (his coat of arms bore the
motto "*con la espada y con la pluma*"): their spoken words. Of course, when
the Indians "avenge their anger with a thousand affronts," it is Garcilaso's
pen that inscribes these furious words (40). They are words, moreover, that
might as easily and indeed more appropriately have been directed toward that
earlier survivor of Indian captivity, Cabeza de Vaca, after the enslavement of
the Indians who had traveled with and protected him: the Indians call Ortiz
a "stupid, foolish, impertinent [man] . . . [whose] sorrows and all past misfor-
tune had improved him very little, or not at all" (40).

As Garcilaso tells it, in other words, Ortiz's example undermines the whole
point of the captivity narrative as instantiated by Cabeza de Vaca: the captive's

positive transformation in the aftermath of his suffering. Through the words of the Indians, Garcilaso in effect pronounces this suffering not as a cleansing scourge but as divine retribution for something unnamed—afflictions "that had not been given to him in vain," for "he had really deserved much worse" (40). This is a harsh revision of the written self-portrait proffered by Cabeza de Vaca, who after all ends his narrative by casting himself as more Christ-like than *los cristianos.* In Cabeza de Vaca's self-serving narrative, the redeemed captive thus distinguishes himself morally from both the Indians and the Spanish. In Garcilaso's recasting, however, the redeemed captive is, in the words of the Indians, "neither Spaniard nor warrior"—his post-captivity actions reveal neither an added moral value nor a cultural one (40). "In sum," Garcilaso writes, "no Indian came from the hill who did not scold him, and all spoke to him in almost the same words, and he himself declared [these words] to the rest of the Spaniards, to his greater dishonor" (40). With this summation of the episode, Garcilaso turns full circle from Cabeza de Vaca's model of the redeemed captive as the transformed sufferer and perfect instrument of empire: the figure of transparent cross-cultural translation who can speak to, convert, and pacify the Indians. For if Soto seeks precisely this figure in Juan Ortiz—"an interpreter and translator in whom he could trust" (37)—Garcilaso offers up in its stead an imperial scene of translated humiliation, of imperial translation *as* humiliation, in which the only messages the translator can offer to those he is meant to serve are the Indians' words recounting his own cross-cultural failures.[62]

Americas Exceptionalism

Garcilaso's adaptation of the Don Luis story provides a vantage point for understanding much of his larger project in *La Florida*, even as it marks the first significant textual incarnation in the early modern afterlife of the sixteenth-century translator from Ajacán. This afterlife, I believe, offers us a productive frame for thinking about American literary studies more generally, precisely through the Inca's sensibility of unsettlement. What Garcilaso helps us to see, in particular, is the signature accomplishment of Cabeza de Vaca's narrative: its establishment of the ethical superiority of its protagonist through a discourse of primitivism that consolidates the author's own power— a discourse powerfully resisted in El Inca's prehistory of Don Luis. Cabeza de Vaca achieves the ethical foundation for his critique—of sixteenth-century Spanish civilization and its culture of conquest—by virtue of his experience of the primitive realm, from which he emerges, paradoxically, as more modern, more humane, and more true to the new letter of "peaceful" law than his fellow Spaniards. The effects of primitivism, however, require *both* the narrative journey into the indigenous, New World heart of darkness and, crucially, the return that separates Cabeza de Vaca from Lope de Oviedo (and, later, from Garcilaso's Diego de Guzmán). The narrative's doubling of Cabeza de Vaca and Lope de Oviedo requires its subsequent suppression of the trajectory represented by Lope de Oviedo himself, for it is this trajectory—the movement toward indigeneity without return, a movement incarnated and literalized in Don Luis—upon which Cabeza de Vaca's account depends for its narrative authority. Just as the Indians addressed by the *requerimiento* must be embraced as subjects even as they are excluded by their lack of Christianity in order to lend political meaning to conquest and genocide, Lope de Oviedo's trajectory must be enlisted as the narrative's foundational point of exclusion, the untold story against which Cabeza de Vaca's narrative return defines itself: his emergence as a protagonist, as primitivism's modern, ethical hero, borne on the wings of a translated and self-translating authority. But Cabeza de Vaca's apparent acquisition of translational mastery—an achievement of absolute authority across the linguistic divide separating the Spaniards from the Indians—conveniently elides two problems that are also quite often suppressed within transnational American studies: the ambiguous role of the translator and the ever-present possibility of mistranslation.

At the same time, if the *Relación* presented its earliest readers with Cabeza de Vaca's epic emergence by demanding that they simultaneously forget the never completed narrative trajectory embodied by his double and foil, Lope de Oviedo, the now canonical account has induced the same response in the realm of contemporary scholarship—prompting us effectively to repeat the silence mandated by the veterans of the Mexican conquest in the early pages of the text: "We should not even speak of it." To attend to stories that are referenced but never told requires a great deal of speculation, of course, as well as an open-ended process of noticing what these stories are *not* despite the fact that we cannot know what they *are*. The story of Don Luis de Velasco, precisely because it hinges upon the "corrupted" narration of Alonso de Olmos, comes into being—like the untold story of Lope de Oviedo, like the story of Diego de Guzmán and, as we shall see in the next chapter, like the story of a young Spanish "captive" known as Hernando de Escalante Fontaneda—in a context of Spanish-Native, cross-cultural relations that result not in a *mestizo* or *ladino* identity but, rather, working in an inverse direction, in an indigenously acculturated subject of Spanish descent for whom we have no term. Provisionally defining this subject by negation, we must imagine the possibilities of cross-epistemic translation that are simply not available within the vast colonial archive to which we have access—and this despite the potentials of Mignolo's "border thinking," those new modes of knowledge production made possible by modern and colonial expansion and the enforced incorporation of foreign languages and conceptual frameworks within an invaded culture's worldview. As Mignolo observes, these emergent conditions did not produce "border thinking" symmetrically: "Europeans, in general, did not have to incorporate Indigenous languages and frameworks into their own."[63] As one of the many exceptions to Mignolo's generalization, Lope de Oviedo would have embodied a kind of epistemological threat to the colonial regime perhaps even more acute than the indigenous manifestations of border thinking that existed visibly all around the Spaniards in Florida and northern Mexico, and the English in North America—each time, to take a mundane example, that they encountered an Indian (like Samoset or Squanto or, as we will see in the next chapter, like Don Luis in Florida) who already knew their language.

In this sense, Lope de Oviedo's untold story simply could not be articulated outside a new, dual, and improvised way of knowing—a mode of understanding to which Cabeza de Vaca undoubtedly had access, but which he had every reason not to acknowledge or promote in his narrative. To put this another way: By casting Lope de Oviedo's return to Native life as cowardice, Cabeza de Vaca was simultaneously denying any intellectual substance to the decision. To engage with Lope de Oviedo's marginal presence in the *Relación*—as well as the concerted unrealization of his narrative trajectory—is thus to look back through layers of historical suppression in order to imagine, despite all the information we lack about his point of view, the conditions of possibility in which he (along with Alonso de Olmos, Diego de Guzmán, and Fontaneda) thought and acted as he did. To do so is to entertain an expanded, nonprimordial conception of indigeneity—but without the attendant romanticizing that consistently dogs the scholarly stories so often told about both captivity and "playing Indian."[64] That there is no story here to romanticize is perhaps a condition of possibility, rather than an insurmountable obstruction, for future scholarship.

Cabeza de Vaca's story, on the other hand, has yielded much material over the last decades for our collective critical romanticizing within the field of early American studies. But perhaps his self-mythologizing narrative—read alongside the arc of its contemporary critical reception—might also serve as a kind of critical mirror on ourselves, an oblique and transtemporal perspective upon the emergent exceptionalism of transnational American studies, particularly in its incarnation as *Americas* studies. The field registers this reconfigured exceptionalism in a number of ways, though it does so perhaps most clearly in a geographical sense: insisting upon its expanded, border-crossing parameters while placing a critical primacy on the American hemisphere as the origin of the modern world itself—and thus occluding other hemispheres, other continents and histories, to which it is intricately tied.[65] There is also the reflexive exceptionalism of field self-representation, or disciplinary self-description, an idiom that, read alongside the *Relación*, resonates with the celebratory pronouncement of the field's new cross-cultural scholarly credentials—a pronouncement that elides the work of translators while drawing upon it to shore up the ostensible distance from its own former parochialism.

Read in light of the story of Don Luis, the peculiar and informing tension between the narratives of Cabeza de Vaca and Lope de Oviedo adumbrates our field's seemingly intractable relationship to the logic of imperialism. This heady sense of epistemic expansion is not fully separable from imperial desire—an intellectual-political affinity that is symptomatic of the field's headlong slide from the rigors of institutional history into a largely ahistorical anxiety of disciplinary imperialism: the field's near obsession not only with U.S. imperialism, its primary object of study, but also with its own imagined ability somehow to replicate imperialism itself, which it construes as the dreadful potential, lurking behind every corner, of imperial complicity at the scholarly level. At the same time, even as we declaim the ethical and political dimensions of our expanded purview, our oppositional undoing of the national framework, we often ignore the new exclusions produced precisely by our inclusive embrace of the larger hemisphere. As ideological manifestations, these exclusions will remain difficult for any of us within the field to identify without a collective, sustained, and flexible effort to do so—and without the understanding that such "inclusive exclusion," as Devon Carbado has argued in a different context, entails not only exclusion via obfuscation but also exclusion via the uses to which the newly included itself is put.[66]

What purposes do the ever-inclusive parameters of Americas studies serve—what are the uses of its emergent transnational objects of study, imported with ever-growing sophistication and great aesthetic care from abroad? Here again, Cabeza de Vaca's narrative may offer some insight into the latent primitivism within the discipline's transnational structure of feeling: its critical penchant for the "alternative" ways of knowing—the indigeneity, the hybridity, the supposed non-Westernness, the "colonial difference," as Mignolo puts it—of the wider hemisphere.[67] Transnational American studies achieves much of its disciplinary cosmopolitanism—its scholarly modernity, its ethical platform for critique, its mantle of translative mastery—through the very gestures of inclusive exclusion that it also disavows. The solution to this problem (if there is one) is our own return of sorts, *not* to the national paradigm, but across the too-easy critical distance we have assumed between ourselves and the texts by which we have come to define the field. Like Cabeza de Vaca himself, we may end up suppressing the more compelling and revealing stories in favor of those that consolidate our image of ourselves.

Don Luis in La Florida

During the same decade of Don Luis's transatlantic career living among Spaniards in Mexico, Cuba, and Spain, a thirty-year-old Spanish Creole man named Hernando de Escalante Fontaneda was discovered in Florida, where he had been living among the Calusa Indians for seventeen years. The Adelantado Pedro Menéndez de Avilés had just founded St. Augustine and was also in Florida at the time, and he quickly drafted the Creole man into his service as a fully bilingual and bicultural translator. Like Cabeza de Vaca, Juan Ortiz, and Alonso—and like Don Luis—"Fontaneda" faced the unusual circumstance of returning to his birth language after a prolonged absence.[1] Born in Cartagena de Indias, he had been shipwrecked at thirteen years old on the Florida coast during a voyage intended for Spain. By the time he was found by Spaniards in Florida in 1566, he had lived well over half his life among the Calusa. After serving as Menéndez's interpreter in the Floridas for several years, the now middle-aged Creole man went to live in Spain, where he produced a narrative of his experiences in 1575, now known in English as the *Memoir of Hernando de Escalante Fontaneda*.[2]

Written almost a decade after his return to life among the Spaniards, Fontaneda's narrative has long been considered one of the most extensive repositories of information about the Indians of South Florida in the first half of the sixteenth century and, more generally, one of the most valuable firsthand accounts of early American Indian culture from that era.[3] Yet the text has received little sustained attention from literary scholars, in part because the memoir is strikingly impersonal. One would perhaps go too far in saying that the *Memoir* actively refuses to disclose any subjectivity, but it is certainly true that we learn almost nothing about Fontaneda's own experience of his cross-cultural life—or of being "*cautivo*" (captive), as he calls it in the memoir (5:539). To the extent that he does present himself within the account, moreover, Fontaneda self-fashions as an explicitly anti-indigenous ex-captive subject, one who can hardly be advertised as the kind of figure of tolerance or cross-cultural understanding to which captivity survivors such as Cabeza de Vaca and Juan Ortiz have sometimes been likened by literary critics.[4] Unlike Cabeza de Vaca in particular—who advertised himself, as we saw in Chapter 3, as a peaceful and pacifying ex-captive, a knowledgeable cross-cultural colonial ambassador—Fontaneda refers to the Indians as "great traitors" and ultimately advocates, in the starkest of terms, their mass incarceration and enslavement (5:544).

It would be easy enough to understand Fontaneda's motive for advocating violence and slavery simply as a form of revenge upon his former captors. Indeed, in some ways Fontaneda and Don Luis operated along parallel trajectories, each living in captivity across cultures for large portions of his life, each in little contact with his culture of birth, and each ultimately exhibiting or advocating violence toward the culture to which he appeared to have assimilated. But I do not think Fontaneda wanted retribution upon his former captors any more than Don Luis wanted revenge upon the Jesuits—despite Garcilaso's powerful literary construction of his motivation as such. For Don Luis, as I have been arguing throughout this book, was acting against an imminent European settlement in his homeland, not punishing the Jesuits for their treatment of him (despite what some historians have suggested).[5] For reasons that will become clear, I believe that Fontaneda was also engaged in a project of unsettlement, albeit a very different one—and that neither Don Luis nor Fontaneda should be understood within a framework as simple as personal revenge for their experiences of captivity: long and substantial experiences that would certainly have given each of them uniquely complex forms of knowledge and perspectives upon settlement in the Americas.[6] The attribution of revenge suggests a short-sighted and, more important, a *prepolitical* motivation; it is the motive that is all too often and quickly assigned to the ubiquitous figure of the "treacherous native"—or, in Fontaneda's case, the nativized Creole.

Indeed, as I argue in the first section of this chapter, Fontaneda's account embodies a more complex narrative and indeed juridical engagement with Spanish conquest than its violent and explicitly anti-Indian pronouncements seem to suggest. The *Memoir* may in fact be subtly intervening within the legal history of Spanish conquest and settlement by proposing a series of patently illegal actions—a proposal that indirectly but powerfully lays out for sixteenth-century readers (potentially members of the Council of the Indies and Philip the II) a kind of *de jure* case *against* further settlement of Florida, while ingeniously offering a *de facto* set of reasons, again, *not* to settle. To apprehend these counterintuitive aspects of the text, we need to set aside the interpretive framework that assumes the inevitability of an eventual Spanish conquest of Florida in order to examine the potential *effects* of Fontaneda's narrative in its own time, when the future settlement of Florida was anything but guaranteed. For in the discrepancies between the text's articulated values and its silent knowledge of its own potential effects, we may begin to see beyond the anachronistic but deeply structuring assumption of conquest's inevitability. Fontaneda's account offers up both an idiosyncratic critique of Spanish colonial discourse and its attendant laws of settlement *and* a narrative that works doggedly toward the goal of *un*settlement—precisely, that is, toward discouraging future Spanish attempts to colonize Florida. Defining himself incongruously (and thus pointedly) as a *ladino* narrator, Fontaneda performs a kind of generic rupture within the early American writing of settlement—a rupture that can, more generally, help us to theorize the colonial narrative production of both subaltern and ambiguously privileged subjects of conquest.[7]

By the time he wrote his narrative in 1575, Fontaneda would likely have heard and perhaps even read in epistolary form the story of Don Luis's destruction of the Spanish settlement at Ajacán. Just as significant is the near certainty that Don Luis, before he returned to Ajacán in 1570, would have known the story of Fontaneda. In fact, the chances are quite high that Don Luis and Fontaneda met in person given that the former was also in the Floridas in 1566, and was also in the service of Menéndez. Fontaneda joined Menéndez in February of that same year; and Don Luis, by that August, had already been traveling with Menéndez for some time when he was sent off on the first and unsuccessful voyage back to Ajacán.[8] (As we saw in Chapter 2, the expedition was accompanied by military backup and Don Luis claimed not to be able to locate the entrance to the Bahía de Santa María.) In any number of ways, the points of overlap between the trajectories of Fontaneda and Don Luis are unmistakable, beginning with the priest who knew them both: Father Juan Rogel.

Rogel, as we have seen, recorded the first account of what happened in Ajacán, as told by Alonso de Olmos. But long before Don Luis destroyed the Jesuit settlement in Ajacán, Rogel was an idealistic priest stationed in Florida, where he grappled with the problem of interpreters in his dealings with the Calusa, and in particular the indigenous leader known as Carlos. The second section of this chapter turns accordingly to Rogel's writings from that period, which recount his stay first in Havana and then, for several years, at his new post in Florida as a Jesuit missionary to the Calusa Indians. While Rogel's letters from this period coalesce around the problem of unreliable translators and the attendant anxieties of interpretation that emerge, they also shed light on a little-discussed but—in the *longue durée* of early modern Spanish expeditions in Florida—highly influential inter-indigenous circuit of narrative transmission and human migration connecting the Calusa and colonial Cuba. At the same time, Rogel's accounts suggest the pointed interest of the Calusa themselves in shaping the process by which colonial translators were made, which in turn allowed them a startling flexibility in engaging the discourse of Christian evangelism and often refusing it not on cultural or spiritual but epistemological and philosophical grounds. In this way, Rogel's Floridian writings offer a means of revisiting from a new angle the often repudiated but nevertheless enduring representation of orality as conceptual lack. Taken together, these writings reveal the compelling traces of a truly hemispheric indigenous consciousness—a deeply *political* understanding of the threat to indigenous sovereignty throughout the hemisphere that left the Calusa with a growing conceptual map of New World colonialism that shaped their strategy with the encroaching Spaniards and enabled them to unsettle the entire South Floridian coast.

The first two sections of this chapter, then, address Floridian writings from before the Ajacán settlement, setting the regional and geopolitical scene for a work explored in the chapter's final section: *Relación de los trabajos*, a firsthand, early seventeenth-century travel narrative in which Don Luis reappears in Florida alive and well years *after* his destruction of the colony in Ajacán. Written by the Carmelite friar and man of letters, Andrés de San Miguel, about his 1595 shipwreck off the coast of what are now called the Georgia Sea Islands and his subsequent journey across the Floridas, *Relación de los trabajos* presents a baroque chapter in the afterlife of Don Luis, one that sunders the early modern topos of interpretive transparency with a particularly *ladino* form of *desengaño*, or disillusion. Andrés's remarkable text reveals how far and wide the story of Don Luis was traveling in this era, generating a figure for Native dissidence across time and space that embodied a potential for indigenous revolt on a hemispheric scale. In this sense, the most conceptually valuable contribution of the unreliable translator in this chapter is the dogged insistence on historical contingency within the accounts that transmit him: Don Luis was unsettling to these writers' faith in an inevitable teleological triumph of the Christian West in his own time, and is perhaps unsettling to modern scholars' sense of the inevitability of conquest in our own.

"*El más ladino de todos*": The *Memoir of Hernando de Escalante Fontaneda*

In 1566, five months after his infamous massacre of the French and his founding of St. Augustine, Pedro Menéndez de Avilés traveled into South Florida in search of his missing son, Juan Menéndez, who had wrecked at sea near the coastline earlier that year. Pedro Menéndez, as the adelantado and governor of the vast territory of La Florida, had come to the region to establish a stronghold against the French and supervise the construction of a port of safety for Spanish treasure ships, which had become increasingly vulnerable to pirates and tropical storms as they passed the treacherous channel between Florida and the Bahamas, carrying Mexican and Peruvian wealth from the Caribbean to Spain. Menéndez was charged with putting an end to these massive forfeitures of Spanish income, and in the process of doing so he hoped to recover Juan, lost to the same Atlantic treasure circuit. While the adelantado never found his son, he did manage to establish contact with the Calusa Indians and their leader, whom the Spaniards soon came to know as Carlos.[9] As a result of this encounter, Menéndez also made a profoundly unsettling discovery. In South Florida, he learned to his surprise that the Spaniards were not the only post-conquest beneficiaries of indigenous mining throughout the hemisphere from Mexico to Peru. The Calusa, Menéndez learned, had been amassing their own fortune each time a Spanish ship foundered on the shoals near the Florida Keys: Carlos had gold, silver, and—according to some sources—hundreds of Spanish-speaking castaways living as Calusa subjects throughout his Floridian realm.[10]

Viewing the matter as a European and a conquistador, Menéndez understood these hispanophone Atlantic refugees to be Carlos's captives and slaves, and he therefore sought to ransom them—in part for his own use as potential interpreters. According to a letter the adelantado wrote to King Philip in October 1566, Carlos would eventually release to one of Menéndez's representatives a number of these Spanish-speaking subjects, including five Spanish Creole men, five women described as "*mestizas*," and "one black woman."[11] But in a twist that recalls Lope de Oviedo and Alonso de Olmos, again registering the illegibility and unpredictability of cross-cultural identity in the colonial American world, two of these Spanish or Spanish Creole men released to Menéndez "chose not to come and remained" with the Calusa.[12] This failed act of recovery in turn shadows the heroic story that the adelantado tries to tell of those captives whom he does manage to bring back to life among the Spaniards.

Of these, Menéndez particularly praises "two Christians," "whom it appears . . .they have had for [almost] twenty years [and] who, in order to thank me for what I have done for them in bringing them out [showed] a strong desire to help" in the project of colonization and conversion.[13] Not only do these two Spanish Creole "Christians" strongly support Menéndez's agenda, however, but one of them turns out, in a stroke of good luck, to be a person of potential social significance: "One of them [was very good looking,] of noble parents, the son of the late García D'Escalante, a Conquistador of Cartagena, and he is called Hernando D'Escalante."[14] As Menéndez then explains, this captive is a young man of aristocratic birth who began living among the Calusa at "ten years of age"; he was "one of two brothers . . . being sent to Salamanca" from the family residence in Cartagena de Indias "when their ship was lost" at sea: "The people aboard escaped, but over the years the father of this [chief] Carlos had killed 42 of the captives already, among whom was [this captive's] elder brother."[15] From Menéndez's perspective, then, the man we now know as Hernando de Escalante Fontaneda must have seemed an ideal sole survivor for an unproblematic Spanish redemption narrative: aristocratic, handsome, and tragically bereft of an elder brother who was brutally murdered along with the other shipwrecked captives. Fontaneda's multiple allegiances to Spanish culture could not appear more transparent, as did, apparently, his "strong desire" to support Spanish settlement in Florida.

Following Menéndez's lead, contemporary historians consistently describe the event of Fontaneda's return to Spanish life as a rescue or a recovery.[16] As in the case of Alonso or even Cabeza de Vaca, however, we do not know the meaning or the extent of this captive's desire, if any, in the matter of his delivery from the Calusa. We know only that Fontaneda was born on the Caribbean coast of South America, and was shipwrecked on the Florida coast in 1549 during the voyage of a treasure ship intended for Spain, where he was to have received a metropolitan education.[17] Destined for a very different kind of tutelage, Fontaneda was, by his own account, not ten but thirteen at the time of his shipwreck; by the time he was discovered by Spaniards, he was thirty and had thus lived for seventeen years among the Calusa. Not surprisingly, Menéndez was eager to draft into his service this remarkable Spanish Creole man—though oddly, and perhaps tellingly, the adelantado never mentions Fontaneda again after the letter narrating his rescue.

Both the trajectory of Fontaneda's youth and the extraordinary narrative that he produced in 1575 after his return to living among Spaniards articulate a quintessentially Atlantic narrative: a story set in a historical moment of unprecedented and fatal economic expansion that is figured aptly in the wreck of the treasure ship carrying Fontaneda as a boy from South America to Spain. Fontaneda's account is also profoundly shaped by an explicit endorsement of indigenous slavery—by the mid-sixteenth century, an illegal but still continuing practice throughout the Spanish Americas—which has been central to the narrative's continued *mis*reading in scholarship. Indeed, Fontaneda's account anticipates and even invites such misreading, sustaining throughout its narration a stubborn illegibility of Creole identity that lies at the heart of the story's most subversive colonial figure: the unreliable translator.

Addressed to an unnamed "Very Powerful Lord," Fontaneda's account begins by offering a straightforward descriptor of its subject: *Memoria de las cosas y costa y indios de la Florida, que ninguno de cuantos la han costeado, no lo han sabido declarar.* Yet this title also suggests both the ambivalence of its author's unnamed subject position and the text's self-consciousness of its singular place in a world of textual uses and effects. This ambivalent singularity is largely invisible today, however, simply because most contemporary scholarship on Fontaneda follows the lead of the nineteenth-century archivist and translator Buckingham Smith, who gave the title of Fontaneda's text simply as *Memoir of Hernando de Escalante Fontaneda* (1854), altogether eliding the pointed exclusion of its original if awkward Spanish title, which translates into English (roughly) as *Report of the things, the shore, and the Indians of Florida, which none of the many who have coasted there have known how to describe.* "Describe," moreover, may not quite do justice to the term *declarar,* which in this context implies a more official kind of knowledge: to declare, to offer official firsthand testimony, even to make a notarized report, as the term could easily be translated. The final clause at once acknowledges the "many" European explorers who have made contact with Florida while also separating the author from these others, and implying the memoir's narrating subject, unnamed by the title, as the sole source of accurate information when it comes to declaring it. The other accounts of Florida have been inept, Fontaneda suggests, but this one will serve its purpose:

> There is no man who so well knows that region as I, who here write this; for I was a captive among them, from a child of thirteen years until I was thirty years old. I know four languages . . . . There is no river nor bay there that can be hidden from me; and had they treated me as I deserved, the Indians at this day would be the vassals of our powerful king Don Felipe, whom God preserve many years! (5:539–40)

It is easy to see Fontaneda's agenda, writing in Spain, as a self-aggrandizing one. Like Cabeza de Vaca before him, he makes a case here for his own unique forms of knowledge: Not merely bilingual, Fontaneda possesses "four languages," and he claims not only to know the land of Florida but to know it within a hypothetical context of dissimulation, so well that no part of its geography "can be hidden from [him]." Most significantly, he registers Florida's still largely unconquered status in 1575 and implies that he once had the power to subordinate the Floridian Indians, who otherwise "at this day"—had Fontaneda been "treated . . . as [he] deserved"—would be "the vassals of our powerful king Don Felipe." The conditional tense of this assertion is its most salient feature: unlike Cabeza de Vaca's narrative, clearly designed to gain royal approval of a future conquest in Florida, this one contains no promise or plea to return to Florida and put to good use the cross-cultural skills of pacification and dominance that he purports once to have wielded. Fontaneda's interest lies in pronouncing an opportunity now lost—and not to be recovered.

At the same time, Fontaneda's account makes heavy rhetorical use of its own laconic style, repeatedly breaking off to announce what it chooses not to tell. "There is much [information], of all kinds, that I will not tell about," Fontaneda warns the unnamed "Very Powerful Lord" to whom the memoir is addressed, "because I would not finish [the account])" (5:532–33). The narrative repeatedly returns to the matter of the unsaid, highlighting those subjects Fontaneda will not treat, usually by insisting that "if we were to enumerate, we would never be through" (5:535). But when Fontaneda mentions the Floridian Indians living across from the Islands of Bermuda, of whom he insists he has "little memory," he straightforwardly refuses to elaborate: "I do not wish to expand" (5:534). This foregrounding of narrative demurral—the holding of the text's own content at arm's length from the reader, regardless of the purported reason—creates a kind of abortive *occupatio*, the trope of falsely disavowed description. It provides a rhetorical shortcut of sorts, allowing Fontaneda to return quickly and repeatedly to the most significant point in his larger narrative trajectory: the utter lack of treasure to be found in the Floridas. As he puts it succinctly at the outset of his memoir: "These Indians have no gold, less silver, and less clothing; they walk around naked except for only some breechcloths woven of palm" (5:532–33). Because there is no earlier mention of another group of Indians preceding this formulation, his statement appears to offer not a comparative assessment of the Calusas' relative wealth, but rather a rhetorical emphasis on their utter dearth of riches— "no gold" and "less silver"—which then finds an apt cultural analogy in their nakedness.

Yet the ensuing mention of breechcloths would seem to disrupt this analogy, or at least to imply that Fontaneda's claim that there is "no gold" in Florida merely hyperbolizes the insufficiency of the gold that is, in fact, present. Indeed, as the account proceeds, Fontaneda begins to qualify his initial claim more and more anxiously. As he explains, "If [the Spaniards] found some gold, it would have come from far away from these lands" (5:536), for "there are no mines of either silver or gold, and if there are, [the Natives] do not know of them" (5:538). An alternate explanation for gold among the Florida Indians, he finally concedes, is that it came from the Spanish: "they are Indians poor of land, that there are no mines of either gold or silver, and which is to say they are rich entirely from the sea, that many vessels have been lost very loaded with gold and silver" (5:541). To substantiate this claim, Fontaneda cites the loss of riches during his own shipwreck as well as the eyewitness testimony of other castaways, one of whom "saw [the Ais Indians] go and return with great wealth, in bars of silver and gold, and bags of *reales*"—all of which were, he says, taken from a foundered Spanish treasure ship from the very fleet that Menéndez's own son was overseeing (5:541–42).[18] Noting that the loot from this famous lost ship included "articles of jewelry made by the hands of Mexican Indians," Fontaneda establishes pointedly that any treasure of indigenous design to be found among the Floridian Indians is in fact not native to the Floridas at all (5:544). In opposition to all persisting rumors of treasure in Florida, Fontaneda reiterates his position again and again ("they are rich, as I have said, from the sea and not the land," 5:544), finally summarizing with a description of the entire Florida shoreline: "From Tocobaga to Santa Elena [off South Carolina], which comprises a shore of six hundred leagues, there is neither gold nor silver native to the country, but only [riches] as I have said from the sea" (5:544).

The relative correctness of Fontaneda's assessment that neither gold nor silver could be mined in Florida is less meaningful, perhaps, than the fact that his insistence on this matter ran counter to the prevailing beliefs of the day, many of them also founded on the words of those who had been in the country for long periods. The few survivors of the Narváez expedition, for example, had come home with tales of Cíbola and the Seven Cities of Gold, and Cabeza de Vaca's remarks about the mineral wealth of Florida would become what Rolena Adorno calls "an emblem of northern riches during the subsequent two centuries," influencing generations of Spanish and later English explorers in North America.[19] Thus for Fontaneda to insist precisely on the *absence* of gold and silver—and to go out of his way to explain the appearances of gold that prior accounts had claimed—was both unorthodox and perhaps even personally disadvantageous; his pronouncements were not the exciting sort on which one could dine out in the gold-crazed world of sixteenth-century Spain. Why would he insist so doggedly that the rumors of gold and silver were false if he did not hope to *discourage* rather than to promote further European conquest in the Floridas? Why else, if not to further his primary though unspoken aim—unsettlement?

Fontaneda's *stated* position on further colonization of the Floridas was, to be sure, one of violent affirmation. Calling the Indians "*traidores*" (traitors) toward the end of his narrative, he urges the Spaniards to deal with them brutally:

> I hold it certain they will never be peaceful, nor Christians even less . . . . Let the Indians be captured in a good manner, offering them peace; and putting them under the decks, husbands and wives together, and distribute them as vassals among the Islands, and even in Tierra Firma for money, as some old nobles in Spain buy vassals from the king, and this way, there could be artful means of diminishing them. This I say would be a clever thing. (5:544)

The sangfroid of this passage, with its brutal, simplistic logic, is unmistakable. It elicits Stephen Greenblatt's observation that Fontaneda failed to learn "identification with the other" from living most of his life among the Florida Natives, developing instead only "a ruthless will to possess."[20] In Voigt's study of captivity narratives, Fontaneda thus becomes a striking foil to her exemplary figure of the ex-captive as peaceful mediator, notably El Inca Garcilaso de la Vega. In Voigt's comparison of their texts, Garcilaso's *La Florida del Inca* (1605) evinces a nuanced, multivalent discourse that "could not be further" from the cruel proposal of Fontaneda's memoir, the former text thus "reveal[ing] the limitations as well as the violence" of the latter.[21]

But Fontaneda's violent proposal may be a somewhat modest or Swiftean one—however counterintuitive it may seem to imagine this sixteenth-century Creole narrator engaged in such an effort, given the absence of a clear-cut, literary-historical context that might support or explain it. To be sure, Fontanenda's proposal is not, strictly speaking, a satire, for the force of its double meaning is not directed toward the enlightenment of his readers but, rather, as I have been suggesting, toward the influencing and shaping of their future actions. The first element that signals the less than straightforward meaning of the proposal is its odd foregrounding of a long-standing controversy over the incompatibility of vassalage and slavery in the New World context, dating back to Ferdinand and Isabella's 1498 proclamation that Amerindians were vassals of the crown—political citizens of extended Spain—and thus could not be enslaved.[22] In the broader milieu of sixteenth-century Atlantic jurisdictions, Spanish colonizers and Creoles had developed an intricate philosophical and religious discourse allowing them to generate forced indigenous labor through legal loopholes, initially through that gaping chasm known as the *requerimiento*, first drafted in 1513.[23] Read aloud to indigenous Americans, this notorious document demanded— whether or not the addressees understood or were even present—immediate submission to the monarchy, the colonial administration, and the Christian religion. Failure to comply provided the necessary justification for just war and enslavement: "But, if you do not [submit], and maliciously make delay in it, I certify to you that, with the help of God, we shall powerfully enter into your country, and shall make war against you in all ways and manners that we can."[24] The Indians' inevitable misunderstanding of this brutal performative resulted precisely in the convenient loss of their status as "*súbditos y vasallos*" (Spanish subjects and vassals), "*libres y sin servidumbre*" (free without servitude).[25] Failure to comply meant devolving from *vasallos* into *esclavos*, slaves to be sold and disposed of. The document thus laid the legal foundations for continued enslavement of "vassals" despite the inherent incongruity of vassalage and slavery, as pronounced by Ferdinand and Isabella and laid down in Spanish colonial law.

If Fontaneda suggested a potential justification for enslavement of the Indians of Florida by calling them "traitors," his proposal to sell them "as vassals" simultaneously invalidated that very possibility: to call the Indians "vassals" was by definition to invoke the crown's 1498 policy of protection of indigenous inhabitants of the Americas from precisely the fate he was ostensibly advocating. Remarkably, Fontaneda's language partly echoes the wording of the *requerimiento*, which by 1575 had been widely repudiated by critics in both Spain and the Americas as a meaningless ritual premised on the intent to enslave according to the letter (but not the ostensible spirit) of the law. In a telling phrase, Fontaneda advocates the enslavement of "husbands and wives together distributed as vassals among the Islands, and even upon Tierra Firma for money" (5:544), just as the old "requirement" had promised "we shall take you and your wives . . . and shall make slaves of them, and as such shall sell and dispose of them as their Highnesses may command."[26] What Fontaneda suggests as "a clever thing" might easily describe the scandalous subterfuge of the *requerimiento* in its actual practice, which was founded so deeply on the assumption of eventual enslavement of the Indians as the ultimate goal that in some cases the Spaniards put the Indians in shackles *before* even reading them the document.[27] Or, in Fontaneda's bitter formulation: "offer[. . .] them peace; and [then] put . . . them under the decks . . . and distribute them . . . for money" (5:544).

By 1575, when Fontaneda produced his memoir, the transparent use of the *requerimiento* for the purposes of acquiring Indian slaves was widely recognized. In 1526, the *Ordenanzas sobre el buen tratamiento de los indios* had sought to reform the abuses of the *requerimiento* by embracing the concept of a peaceful conquest, and in 1542, the *Nuevas Leyes* made more definitive changes, explicitly outlawing all forms of slavery in law 22. Such reforms catalyzed the development of new, perfectly legal forms of forced indigenous labor, particularly the so-called *repartimiento* system—to which Fontaneda apparently alludes in using the phrase *repartillos,* urging that the Indians be distributed elsewhere in the Americas. This aspect of his proposal further highlights the strange disjuncture between Fontaneda's apparent familiarity with the terms of the New Laws (suggested by his wording) and the patently illegal nature of what he was advocating. For the legal parameters of the *repartimiento* system allowed the forced labor of Indian men (but never women and children), designated by the indigenous leaders themselves, for public works, over temporary periods, and with the payment of wages; the *repartimiento* that Fontaneda suggests thus violates every aspect of the law (as often happened in practice, of course, but *not* for public avowal): the seizure of husbands and wives together—not only without consultation of indigenous leaders but in self-described duplicity; not for public works but for the profit of the captors (*por dineros*); and not over a temporary, defined period of service but as a permanent measure of diminishing the Indian population in Florida.

In 1573, just two years before Fontaneda published his memoir, Menéndez himself had approached Philip II and petitioned for the right to pursue the enslavement of the Floridian Indians "in a war of fire and blood"—a just war, Menéndez was careful to specify, waged in response to those who have "broken the peace many times, slaying many Christians." Such a war would not harm "the friendly Indians," Menéndez promised, but would serve as "a great example . . . so that they may observe and fulfill the amity they establish."[28] King Philip apparently saw through the distinction and not only refused the petition but also brought forward that year the well-known *Ordenanzas de descubrimiento, nueva población y pacificación de las Indias*, which sought more specific protection of the Indians, including the prohibition of Spanish violence and theft perpetrated against indigenous inhabitants of the New World. Even at the level of grammar, the *Ordenanzas* of 1573 sought definitive reform, demanding that the word "conquest" itself be eliminated in favor of the euphemism "pacification."[29]

None of this is to suggest that these changes produced a unified ideological reaction in the colonies. The practices that were outlawed by the various

Ordenanzas and *Nuevas Leyes* persisted unevenly, for varied durations and in different degrees, across the empire and at its edges, and were always shaped by the specific responses of different indigenous polities. And to be sure, the new discourse of pacification was not universally accepted, and particularly not by *conquistadores* and their Creole descendants. But the simple fact of the change itself—in both the laws and the discourse—would have been hard to miss by anyone who had any kind of investment in Spanish-indigenous relations in the Americas, and would have been especially striking to a man who had served as Menéndez's interpreter and at the front line of these relations. After nearly a decade of living (again) among Spaniards and Creoles, Fontaneda could not fail to have noticed that the basic tenets of the changing colonial laws set certain limits on what it was plausible to say in a public, notarized document potentially available to the Spanish crown. Menéndez himself, who went so far as to suggest to the king in 1573 that the Floridas would be better off if its Indians were "dead, or given as slaves," was scrupulous about the *legal* details of his proposals, carefully qualifying that (were his requests granted) enslaved Floridians would serve twelve-year terms and their buyers would be obligated to try to bring them to Christianity.[30] Similarly, even the most celebratory account of conquest, such as Bernal Díaz del Castillo's *Historia verdadera de la conquista de la Nueva España*—which the old foot soldier-turned-encomendero was composing and correcting between 1550 and 1584, during the period when Fontaneda wrote his narrative—was careful to couch all approval of indigenous slavery in the kinds of theological and legal arguments that would distinguish between "vassals" and "slaves," between "peace," "just war," and falsely waged war—explicitly acknowledging that, as in the opening pages of his memoirs, to "make war on the natives and load the vessels with Indians, as slaves . . . was not just . . . it was neither in accordance with the law of God nor of the King, that we should make free men slaves."[31] One has only to consider that this statement came from a writer who sought in large part to *justify* the violent enslavement of Native peoples to see why Fontaneda's proposal cannot be taken at face value. The significance of Fontaneda's proposal, in other words, lies not in its stated aims but in what might reasonably have been predicted to be its likely effect: by proposing in a notarized document a specifically illegal set of actions in a kind of language that was also, by 1575, forbidden under the *Ordenanzas*, Fontaneda seems not to have expected—or, indeed, wanted—to draw supporters to his ostensible cause. What he wanted, I believe, was simply to discredit the Spanish colonial project in La Florida in the eyes of those who might otherwise back it.

Fontaneda's account thus wields to a narrative advantage his ambiguous position as a legal Spanish subject who has nevertheless lived outside Spanish law—and outside European discourse more broadly—for most of his life. That Fontaneda's point of view regarding the Spanish colonial project is, in fact, a covertly critical one is further suggested by his interest in staging within his text scenes of failed translation, which collectively work to expose the Spaniards' disavowal of the violence inherent in the monolingual point of view. At times these scenes are truncated or foreshortened, condensed to the point that they read almost as aphorisms, as when, for example, the Spaniards decide to murder an Abalachi Indian for his failure to provide them with the corn they have requested. "On their way the Spaniards hung the cacique of Abalachi, because he did not want to give them maize for [their] provision on the trip," observes Fontaneda before he recasts the scenario in entirely different terms: "Or because, say the Indians of this town of Abalachi, their *cacique* had around his neck some large pearls and in the middle of these one very large one, that was about as large as an egg of the turtledove, which there are [there], and they nest in some trees at times; and this is what the Indians say" (5:538).

The almost nonsensical shift to the size and nesting location of turtledove eggs highlights the utter disconnect between the Spanish perception of the cacique's refusal to provide maize and the Abalachi Indians' belief that their leader has been killed for his sizable pearls. The narrator alone holds the privileged position of knowing "what the Indians say," and he makes sure that the Spaniards' failure to understand that their own words and actions have not been interpreted as they ostensibly believed and wanted comes across in all its absurdity. At the same time, Fontaneda uses the opportunity of his inside position to expose the Spaniards' monolingualism as a flimsy alibi for their own avaricious interests, which go well beyond the demanded provision of food, straight to the question of indigenous riches—and which the Indians, on the other hand, cannily identify as the deeper motive for the murder.

Yet Fontaneda's authorial voice remains strangely dislocated even in those scenes of the narrative that deliver the most critical insights about the project of settlement. Though the narrative is noticeably reticent about his own experience of captivity, it allows us a glimpse of his persona, all too briefly, when a new castaway washes ashore one day. As Fontaneda recounts it, the Indians "took the Spaniard that reached the shore whom they found starving, and I saw him alive and talked with him. It was a consolation, though a sad one, for those who were lost afterward to find on shore Christian companions who could share their hardships and help them to understand those brutes" (5:541–42). Fontaneda's description of the encounter reiterates a series of familiar colonial tropes of opposition: Indian "brutes" versus "Christian companions"; hardship versus consolation; figurative death (*muerto de hambre*) followed by rebirth (*yo le vi vivo*). Yet the account also manages subtly to redefine the meaning of Indian captivity in this instance: the Natives "took" the Spaniard (*tomar*) after finding or seizing (*coger*) him on the shore, where he was starving or dead of hunger (*muerto de hambre*), and then Fontaneda, to use his curious wording, "saw him alive and talked with him"—almost as if the Indians, while retrieving the young Spaniard's famished body from the shore, had mistaken him for dead. Both the status of the New World castaway and the nature of consent in this context are inherently unstable, as Fontaneda's next descriptor makes explicit: The Spaniard, he remarks, is either "*recién cautivado ó hallado*" (newly captured or found)—perhaps depending on one's point of view (5:542). In this sense, the scene might be said to allegorize the limited perceptions of his *Spanish* readers, along with all those who do not understand, as Fontaneda puts it, "the language of the Indians" (5:542). For what his sixteenth-century readership might perceive as a capture may in fact be a rescue—just as a perceived death (consignment to life among the Calusa) may represent, contrary to conventional uses of the trope, a rebirth.

This scene sets the ideal stage upon which to dramatize the brutal logic of monolingualism in a contact zone, which Fontaneda proceeds to do next in describing the experience of other Spanish captives: "The Indians who took them would order them to dance and sing and [the Spaniards] would not understand it, and as Indians are so warlike, and those of Florida the most so, they thought [the Spaniards] did not want to do it out of rebelliousness; [the Indians] killed them" (5:542). Fontaneda's pronouncement that Indians are "warlike," and those in Florida the most so in the New World, may well have served his more general agenda of discouraging settlement in that part of the Americas. It also highlights his own status as a potential military resource: a seasoned warrior, in effect—and one who, through his familiarity with the bellicose ways of the Indians, knows just what the weaknesses of the Spanish are. In the scene that unfolds, his rare knowledge, enacted through his translations, enables him to interpret, predict, redirect, restrain—and thus subdue—the supposed savagery of the Natives.

At the same time, of course, Fontaneda exposes the linguistically impossible terms of the *requerimiento* as practiced by the Spanish, who routinely (mis)interpreted the Indians' nonperformance of Christianity or Christian rituals as rebelliousness to be punished, at the conquistadors' convenience, with death or violent enslavement. Fontaneda notes twice that the inverse version of this arrangement—where the Indians complain about their captives' failure to dance and sing on command and misapprehend it as "rebelliousness" to be summarily punished by death—is a matter of concern for the cacique (as it supposedly was to a number of Spanish sovereigns): The Indian vassals kill their Spanish prisoners and *then* "said afterwards to their cacique that for their being bellicose and rebellious they had killed [the Spaniards], that they did not want to do what they were commanded: the cacique asking why they killed [the Spaniards], they would answer this which I have said" (5:542).[32] The repetition dramatizes, in satirically abbreviated form, the long history of the Spanish monarchy's moral qualms concerning the harm and enslavement of its transatlantic Indian "vassals," and the colonial administration's response: a defense of their violence via the punitive terms of the *requerimiento*, which of course sidestepped the central matter that the Indians did not speak Spanish.

The nature of his critique becomes even clearer when Fontaneda stages a dialogue about the behavior of some new captives between the cacique and himself, along with "a negro, and two other Spaniards, recent captives" (5:542). Fontaneda's cacique is willfully blind to the possibility of linguistic difference as he inverts the self-serving Indian stereotypes used to shore up Spanish colonial policy: do the Spanish captives disobey, the cacique asks Fontaneda, because they are "bellicose and rebellious," "do not care about death," or love their Christian idols too well and thus will not yield "to a people opposed to their law" (5:542)? All these musings were of course common in Spanish accounts of Indian intractability. Observing finally that the newly arrived Spanish castaways "for their own fault are captives," the cacique directly mirrors the language of the *requerimiento* ("we protest that the deaths and losses which shall accrue from this are *your fault*, and not that of their Highnesses, or ours"), and he repeats the apocryphal, colonial trope of Spanish apotheosis by reminding Fontaneda that these castaways are those "whom we [once] took to be gods descended from the sky" (5:543).[33]

As their conversation continues, Fontaneda creates a fundamental difference between the static perspective of the Spaniards' *requerimiento* and, quite to the contrary, the cacique's willingness to assimilate new information and adapt his policies accordingly. When Fontaneda announces the truth about the captives' lack of comprehension of the Calusa language—"The truth, lord, as I understand it: They are not rebellious, nor do they do it for any evil purpose, but it is because they do not understand"—the cacique is dubious but nevertheless allows an experiment of sorts when Fontaneda requests one: "Speak to [the captives], so that I may see it, I and this your free negro" (5:543). The cacique grants the request and does so laughingly, saying, "'*Se le tega*,' *recién venidos*" ('Se-le-tie-ga,' newcomers) (5:543). The Spaniards, of course, do not understand—and neither do readers of Fontaneda's account: The narrative withholds an immediate translation of *Se-le-tie-ga*, thus keeping Spanish-speaking readers in a state of suspended comprehension, and in effect forcing a kind of self-recognition, an admission of the deadly fallacy that underpinned both the *requerimiento* and the anti-Indian violence it endorsed.

Fontaneda's introduction of the "free negro" into this scene accurately reflects the diversity of hispanophone castaways living among the Calusa, not all of whom, as we have seen, were Creole or Spanish. But this moment in the narrative also further undercuts the colonial racial hierarchy with which contemporaneous Spanish readers would be familiar by positing a "negro" interlocutor at the center of Calusa knowledge production in this scene. Whether the "negro" is designated as "free" because that was his status before or (more likely) after the onset of his life among the Calusa is never specified.[34] Whatever the case, his role in the unveiling of a failed colonial linguistic logic is a striking one. As Fontaneda explains, the "free negro"—also bilingual and also laughing—confirms the result of the experiment, telling the cacique, "Lord, Escalante tells you the truth; that they do not understand it" (5:543). The repeated laughter in the scene signals the inside joke that all participants are, at some level, in on. For the captors, understanding and being understood by the captives is at best a low priority, and at worst an impediment to their own interests. Yet Fontaneda's cacique concludes the discussion with an unmistakably humane pronouncement, insisting upon the presence of translators who are able not only to speak but also to *understand* the captive's language: "They must command them to do nothing," he demands, without a translator "who understands [their] language" (5:543).

Fontaneda may well have a vested interest in representing the indispensability of interpreters, and certainly he uses the scene to promote his own interpretive skills: The cacique singles him out as a sort of spokesperson to explain the supposed disobedience of the Spanish captives because Fontaneda, among the many captives there, is the most gifted translator. But in promoting his own bilingual fluency—"que yo era el más ladino de todos" (that I was the most fluent of all)—Fontaneda offers the most powerful clue to the alternative point of view structuring both this scene and the larger *Memoria* as a whole (5:542). As Adorno has observed in her elaboration of *ladino* as used in the sixteenth- and seventeenth-century New World context, the term (employed as an adjective) referred to indigenous or mestizo speakers of Spanish and signified "linguistic purity"; "proper pronunciation, usage, and cultivated speech in Castilian"; and, by extension, indigenous or mestizo "acculturation to Spanish ways," since "language proficiency, literacy, Christianity, and custom all converged in the concept."[35] But there was also what Adorno calls a "conflictive nature" inherent in the sign *ladino,* which also carried the connotation of "cunning and craftiness" and a suspected "guilt of insubordination after submission."[36] The bilingualism signified by the term *ladino* was in no sense multidirectional: the adjective was *not* applied, in other words, to Spaniards or Creoles with fluency in indigenous languages.

Fontaneda's use of the term *ladino* as a self-descriptor is thus curious, to say the least. Whether he describes his proficiency in the Calusa tongue or in Castilian, the term unsettles his cultural purity, his status as a native speaker of Spanish, whether Spaniard or, in his case, Creole. As a *ladino* Creole, Fontaneda dramatically reverses the point of view implied in the term: the cacique turns to Fontaneda because of his native knowledge of Spanish, which is, rather than the Calusa tongue, figured here as the language of the other. On the other hand, if we assume that Fontaneda means by *ladino* his fluency in the Calusa language, then he necessarily implies his own acculturation to indigenous ways and a definitive separation from his original culture and its worldview. In either case, that is, Fontanedo's *ladino* status skews the simple directionality of the pro-conquest, anti-indigenous perspective that his memoir has been understood to assume. As "el más ladino de

todos" (the most fluent of all), Fontaneda highlights his own singular linguistic and indeed narrative power—a power that is derived, paradoxically,
from both knowing about and *missing* the grand Western education in Spain
that was once intended for his development as a wealthy young Creole heir.
At the moment in which he produced his memoir, that is, Fontaneda was in
a position to understand the workings (and limitations) of Spanish colonial
thought better than the Spaniards themselves, using its terms and premises as
a simultaneous insider and outsider, while telling a powerful story about the
untenable prospect of further colonizing Florida.

Fontaneda's account thus functions as a compelling narrative of unsettlement, articulated from an oblique, *ladino* point of view: from his repeated
insistence that there is no gold or silver to be found in Florida to his long lists
of the names of Spaniards who died or were murdered while attempting to
explore Florida, to his avowal that the renowned "discoverer" of Florida, Juan
Ponce de León, is to be scorned as a *"cosa de risa"* (laughing matter) (5:537), to
his implication that the Spanish have not succeeded and will not succeed in
Florida not only because the Indians are "archers and men of great strength"
but because they have precisely the kind of epistemological advantage that
colonial discourse assumes within itself—the Natives, he says, already "know
the greater part of our tactics" (5:539). *Why* is Fontaneda so intent on discouraging his readers from the land of his adolescence through his middle
age—the land where he was, as he puts it ambiguously, "captured or found"?
No one, of course, can presume to know what this experience actually meant
to him, particularly given how little we know about any other part of his life:
nothing of how he got to Spain, his subsequent life there, or even, before that,
the nature of his career as a translator for Menéndez.

But perhaps we can gain some oblique perspective on Fontaneda from
the anecdote he tells, late in the narrative, of two Calusa caciques in whom
Menéndez had once invested high hopes: Carlos II, the son of Fontaneda's
former master; and Don Pedro, the current ruler of the Calusa at the time
Fontaneda composes his *Memoria* (5:539). "Pedro Menéndez brought [the two
caciques] to Havana in order to regale them," explains Fontaneda, "but they
became worse that way than before the regaling that he offered them" (5:539).
Yet the effects of this cross-cultural experiment might have been "still worse,"
Fontaneda warns darkly, "had they been christened": "but, as I refused it,
they were not baptized; because in their conversation I understood them: that
baptism was not lawful for them, that they were heretics as they have [since
then] rebelled again and worse than before" (5:539).

In this brief story of a thwarted apostasy—an unveiling of abiding heath-
enism before the intended conversion process can be tainted by its subject's
inherent corruption—Carlos II and Don Pedro figure the illegibility of colonial identity within a narrative trajectory that oddly reverses but parallels
Fontaneda's own. Brought in ships from their Florida homeland to a colonial

city, the caciques are, like Fontaneda himself, of elevated rank, and thus handpicked to serve one day as Menéndez's faithful Christian conduits to the Calusa. But Carlos II and Don Pedro eventually dash the hopes of their would-be benefactor: As Fontaneda reminds readers at the opening of the anecdote, Carlos II has, by the time of the memoir's production, been executed for treason by Menéndez; nor is Don Pedro's future more promising, since both Indians eventually rebel again, or return to their old ways, and become "more wicked" after their cross-cultural experience in Cuba. Neither receives the intended baptism, an outcome that, according to Fontaneda, would have left matters "still worse." That Fontaneda has legal consequences in mind is suggested by his pronouncement in the next sentence that baptism would have been "unlawful" or illegitimate—a circumstance in which he himself claims to have played a central, preventative role as the discoverer of their true heretical status (5:539).

But if this account of devolving Indians strengthens the agenda of Fontaneda's *Memoir*, suggesting the poor prospects for settlement in La Florida via the intractability of even its most promising indigenous inhabitants, the anecdote also embeds the major plot points of his own *ladino* narrative as a story in which two young Calusa elites travel by ship to another part of the hemisphere, as once did Fontaneda himself, and are afforded a first-hand comparative view of settlement and unsettlement. Crucially, Carlos and Don Pedro appear actively to *withhold* from the Spanish their perceptions of colonialism in Cuba, for it is only Fontaneda's comprehension of the language they speak between themselves that allows him to discover their secret unlawfulness and prevent the baptism that would make matters more troublesome for colonial officials in Florida. Viewed in light of this withholding from the Spanish of the substance of their conversation (about which Fontaneda too is notably reticent), their attitudes and actions after their trip to Havana might easily be interpreted not as an unthinking rebellion or reversion to their old ways but as a strategic response to what they have learned about the nature of Spanish settlement elsewhere. Further, what they know about conquest *after* the trip to Cuba is, like their behavior as seen by the Spanish, "worse than before": in Cuba they undoubtedly see what Las Casas called the devastation of the Indies at first hand. Whatever Fontaneda's actual interests in telling this anecdote, he was of course the only participant in these events who spoke both Spanish and the Calusa language and went on to record his account. His ambiguous *ladino* narrative is the only story we have today of Carlos and Don Pedro's trip to Cuba, where they would have witnessed the utter decimation of its indigenous inhabitants underway.

In these and other ways, the narrative signs of unsettlement haunt Fontaneda's account from beginning to end. Though we cannot know precisely why, it seems that on some level this Atlantic castaway—and, by his own terminology, former captive—simply did not want to see the indigenous peoples of Florida share the same fate as those in other parts of the Americas. This sentiment is even apparent, and perhaps especially so, when Fontaneda appears to endorse Florida's conquest most enthusiastically. The closing of the *Memoria* exemplifies his extraordinary virtuosity in double-gesturing:

> With this I will end, and say no more, for, if the conquest of that country were aspired to, I would give no more account of it than I have given, although it would be suitable for His Majesty for the security of his armadas that go to Peru and to New Spain and other parts of the Indies, which pass, of necessity, by that shore and the Bahama channel, and many vessels are wrecked, and many people perish; for the Indians oppose them and are great archers: and so, as I say, it is best to make some little fort so they can secure that channel, with some income that can be drawn from Mexico and from Peru, and from the islands of Cuba and from all parts of the Indies, for the relief and maintenance of the soldiers that guard that little port; and this is what would be best, and another thing further is to go in search of pearls, for there is no other wealth in that land; and with this, I conclude and if necessary, I will sign it.—Hernando de Escalante Fontaneda. (5:545–46)

In this final passage, Fontaneda appears explicitly to endorse the conquest of Florida as "best for His Majesty" and suggests building a protective fort on the coast as well as undertaking a search for Floridian pearls.[37] But Fontaneda's other, simultaneous gesture here is to remind readers that the Florida straits are places where many vessels wreck, many persons die, and the Indians are powerful archers and oppose the Spaniards. The fort that protects passing Spanish ships will no doubt be both minimal (a "*fortezuela,*" as Fontaneda calls it in a telling diminutive), under attack and other catastrophes that necessitate the soldiers who man it, and expensive, dependent upon "income" from abroad. Even Fontaneda's pragmatic reminder that income that can be drawn from Mexico, Peru, Cuba, and all parts of the Indies serves more to underscore the tacit point that there are much better bets for getting rich (and staying alive) in the New World. His last-minute, nearly offhand suggestion also "to go in search for pearls" nicely sets up one last reminder, after so many, that there is simply "no other wealth in that land."

Oddly, Fontaneda concludes his text by agreeing, as if the matter were in question, to put his name to the *Memoria*. Perhaps this final sentence indicates the hand of another party in the text's original transcription, a possibility that would not have been unusual in this period, even for a literate Spaniard or Creole—and certainly not for someone who had been educated and reached adulthood in a non-literate society.[38] But whether or not Fontaneda made use of a scribe in producing his account, he registers a surprising degree of ambivalence about entering into the particular narrative contract instantiated with a signature: he will sign the account, he says, "if necessary" (si fuere necesario lo firmo). Buckingham Smith, the nineteenth-century U.S. archivist who made the first and only English translation of this text—which, to repeat the point, scholars still depend upon today for any discussion of Fontaneda— interpreted this final line either incorrectly or so broadly as to be almost un- recognizable. In Smith's version, Fontaneda concludes with a prediction: "and as this account may become important; I sign it."[39] This mistranslation tells us much about a conceptual propensity, particularly strong in the U.S. historical tradition, to read the history of Atlantic conquest and settlement through the proleptic lens of the future, particularly when it concerns the territorial boundaries of what would one day become the United States. But in this case Smith may have been unwittingly correct in suggesting that Fontaneda un- derstood that the account might "become important." In fact, it did—in the crucial sense that it influenced the shift of future Spanish expeditions *away* from La Florida for decades afterward, preventing further conquest in that part of the American hemisphere.[40] In this sense, Fontaneda's narrative of unsettlement proved in its own moment to be extraordinarily successful.

The Hemispheric Consciousness of the Calusa

The year 1566, then, marked a period of strange convergences in the Calusa territory of Florida. Fontaneda re-entered Spanish-speaking society after nearly two decades of life among the Indians and began his work as an inter- preter for Menéndez, who also that year brought Don Luis from New Spain to serve as a translator on the planned expedition to Ajacán. These two transla- tors (one who called himself *ladino*, and the other called *ladino* by those who sought to vilify him) thus coincided in Floridian space a decade before their respective projects of unsettlement—one narrative, the other militant—came to fruition. Father Juan Rogel, the Jesuit priest who would initially record the story of Don Luis as it first came to light, was also on his way to Florida in 1566 to help start a mission to the Indians, a new settlement that would quickly be unsettled.

Rogel's account of this era of unsettlement begins with a long letter written from Havana between November 1566 and January 1567, where he was staying en route to Florida, and it commences on a superlative note, announcing high hopes of a successful conversion project among the Floridian Indians.[41] He has not yet met the Calusa leader Carlos, Fontaneda's former Señor or Lord, but Rogel already pronounces him to be "the greatest of the caciques . . . in all this coast of Florida."[42] The adelantado Menéndez and cacique Carlos are already, Rogel says, "both great friends," the latter having "given his word to the Adelantado that he will become a Christian." Carlos has even sent along to Cuba "one of his sisters . . . whom they say he loves very much and another of his relatives, to whom they say that the kingdom of Carlos has belonged by right."[43] Rogel clearly interprets Carlos's actions—particularly the bequeathal to the Spaniards of his beloved sister—as proof of his intention to convert to Christianity and, more generally, to submit to Spanish authority. What Rogel does not mention (and perhaps does not yet know) is that Carlos's sister—known to the Spanish as Doña Antonia—has come to Cuba specifically as Menéndez's wife. At the time of his union with the middle-aged and (according to Spanish colonial historians, anyway) unattractive Doña Antonia, Menéndez was already married to a Spanish woman of distinguished family, María de Solís; his new marriage was of course considered illegitimate under Spanish law. Yet Menéndez agreed to this legally false union at the insistence of Carlos in order to secure a diplomatic peace with the Calusa—an expedient that was soon afterward a source of embarrassment to early Spanish historians of the conquest.[44] To the contrary of Rogel's interpretation, in other words, Menéndez seems to have submitted to Carlos's authority rather than vice versa. Indeed, in the next sentence of his account, Rogel offers a nearly paradoxical observation that would suggest as much: "There is another good sign that Carlos wants to become a Christian in that he sent to ask for some Spanish people to defend himself from another cacique who makes war on him."[45] On some level, that is, Rogel appears already to apprehend the possibility that Carlos is less interested in becoming a Christian than in manipulating the Spanish to consolidate his own power and to shore up the security of the Calusa within an indigenous arena of international conflict.

Perhaps this is why Rogel decides to wait in Havana for Menéndez's arrival before making the trip to Florida, so that "in his company . . . the word of God and what I should teach them might have more authority among the heathens."[46] If Rogel manifests a bit of guilt about this delay in getting started on his mission in the far less comfortable Floridas, he soon realizes that he can begin his work with the Floridian Indians from right there in Cuba: "[S]ince we have been here, eighteen Indians have come from the provinces of Florida, twelve of them from Carlos, and six from the other cacique, who is called Tequesta, who also is near here. . . ." [47]

Why have eighteen Indians—apparently organized into two groups associated with the respective leaders, Carlos and Tequesta—come to Havana from Cuba? And under what circumstances have they come? Rogel appears to anticipate at least the former question because he notes that "they come here because of the reputation for the good treatment that the Adelantado gives them there, and [the good treatment] here, [from] the people of this town."[48] The colonials in Cuba give the Floridian Indians "trinkets [*regalados*] that they are very pleased with," Rogel observes, and for this reason "they all very willingly wish to become Christians and thus they come every day to the church where I am, so that I may teach the Christian doctrine to them."[49] In Rogel's initial impression, in other words, it is easy to manipulate the Floridian Indians toward becoming Christians, given that they will take leave of homeland and people and travel by sea to Cuba just to receive trinkets and good treatment from the Spaniards in Havana. The passing on of Christian doctrine is also an apparently straightforward process, accomplished, as Rogel explains, "by means of some interpreters that they brought with them, people who know how to speak the Spanish language."[50] These Floridian Indians in Cuba are thus "the first fruits [*primicias*] of the great conversion which is to follow in all of this Florida."[51]

But Rogel's narrative of spiritual harvest soon begins to founder. He remarks that he has become hesitant to baptize anyone who is not about to die (recalling the perhaps feigned illnesses of Don Luis and Aguirre, discussed in Chapter 2) "until I shall be satisfied that they will not return to the vomit of their idolatries"—and until that point when "they know very well everything that the Christian is obliged to know."[52] This will not be accomplished quickly, he observes, "because of their being simple folk [*gente ruda*]" and—despite the presence of interpreters—"of scant understanding."[53] Indeed, as the account progresses, Rogel's trust in his interpreters appears to devolve quite explicitly. "I have taught [the Floridian Indians] the prayers in Castilian, because I do not dare to translate them into their language," he explains. The problem, he notes, is that "I do not put much trust in these who are the tongues or interpreters on account of their knowing little of the Castilian language because of their having been among the Indians since they were children, and on account of their not being very intelligent, for they are a brown-skinned woman and a mulatto."[54]

Thus, the same translators who so conveniently "know how to speak the Spanish language" turn out to know "little of the Castilian language." The problem, moreover, is both cultural and racial: the interpreters have had little exposure to Spanish culture, and they are of African descent (*una morena y un mulato*). If this remark reveals an unsurprising assumption of non-European intellectual inferiority, it also suggests the interesting possibility that the two non-Native but dark-skinned translators who "have been among the Indians since they were children" were raised in part to perform the very interpretive role they are now playing in Havana—and to Rogel's apparent dissatisfaction.

Despite these misgivings, though, Rogel concludes his discussion of his prospects in Florida with an optimistic pronouncement of "Indian reverence for the things of the Christian religion," which he bases upon two anecdotes related by Spanish soldiers who have been in Florida.[55] One is a quite familiar story, an old colonial chestnut about Indian gratitude to the Spaniards for praying to their Christian god and thereby bringing rain in a time of drought and dying crops. The other anecdote, however, curiously revives the problem of the interpreter:

> The other [story] was that a son of a cacique, who was called Guale, swore
> at and beat a young little Spaniard whom the Adelantado had placed there

that he might learn the language. And to cause him greater grief, [the son] said to him that he was going to remove a cross that was placed in a certain area, and he did so and removed it. And the Spaniard said to him that he would beg the cacique of heaven to punish him for it. And it happened that within three days of his having said this to him, that son of the cacique died. . . . On seeing this, his father and his vassals restored the cross to where it was with great veneration and they maintain it with great reverence. And they fear the Spaniards and they do not dare to make them angry.[56]

Like the story of the miraculous deaths of three Ajacán Indians who sought to open a chest in order to desecrate the crucifix within, this one too is transmitted across numerous interlocutors and has clear hallmarks of literary invention, from the trinity of days between the Spanish boy's prayer for retribution and its enactment in the cacique's son's death to the unproblematic restoration of the cross by the father and his vassals. The upshot for Rogel, of course, is the Indians' supposed fear before a vengeful Christian god. Yet perhaps the more salient point, given a larger context that includes the dark-skinned translators in Havana, is that these Floridian Indians had an abiding interest in the process of making translators, and in choosing those whom they trained in their language. That Menéndez had placed the *españolito* among them—so "that he might learn the language" precisely in the service of the adelantado's larger purposes of conquest—may explain the rough treatment he received: the cacique's son apparently preferred that this would-be translator, unlike the dark-skinned interpreters in Havana, should fail in his efforts to become *ladino*. Missing the subtext of his own anecdote, Rogel decides to bypass the problem of his own supposedly unskilled interpreters by learning the Calusa language himself: "I have begun to formulate a vocabulary of the language of Carlos," he announces, and "I am planning to continue it there by means of a Spaniard, who they tell me is there, who knows both languages very well and is a capable man."[57] This *ladino* interpreter remains unnamed, but he is likely none other than Hernando de Escalante Fontaneda.

After his arrival in Florida in March 1567, however, Rogel apparently finds his hopes disappointed; he never mentions this "capable" and promising "Spaniard" again. But in his first missive about his year-long experience in the land of Carlos—a long, corrected letter to Father Jerónimo Ruiz del Portillo, written in April 1568—Rogel does note, with evident distaste, that he has "heard the confessions and [given] communion to all the Christians of [Menéndez's] fort *with the exception of an interpreter who was publically cohabiting with a female infidel*."[58] Such interpreters were far more commonly Native than Spanish, and yet we can infer that this particular offending interpreter is either Spanish or Spanish Creole because Rogel distinguishes him from the female "infidel" with whom he lives openly in an unmarried state.

Whether or not Fontaneda was indeed the transgressing translator living openly with *una infiel*, it is clear that Rogel understands both the indispensability of translation to his colonial conversion project and the unreliability of translation as an instrument of empire. It seems that Rogel's interpreters also understood this, and found in the tension between these two circumstances some of their most successful strategies for countering settlement. Unlike many colonial accounts, Rogel's long missive to Ruiz del Portillo makes constant reference to his use of translators, always noting that his communications with the Calusa have been accomplished "through an interpreter." As he puts it midway through the letter, "I sought always to have an interpreter by my side."[59] Rogel's need for the constant availability of a translator stems in part from his observation that the Calusa will not often accompany him to the cross to receive preaching, or if they do will "not pay attention to what [he says] to them"; his "mode of operation" therefore, is to wait for the Indians to come to him of their own volition and then to dispense "the truths" he wants them to hear by means of the translator already by his side.[60] Rogel is clearly proud of having developed this "method" and sees himself as having manipulated the Indians toward Christianity by receiving them on their terms and then, as he puts it, "luego entrando con la dellos salía con la mía"—'soon entering with theirs I exited with mine': in other words, he shifts the conversation they have initiated toward his own agenda and interests.[61]

But despite the self-described success of Rogel's method, what comes across most clearly in his missive is *not* in fact his own manipulative prowess in controlling the terms of discussion with the Indians but rather their apparent flexibility in challenging the discourse of Christianity on its own terms. When Rogel tries to force the Indians to abandon their own religious objects, their refusal is not only unwavering but philosophically insightful: "I showed them clearly and to their face [*al ojo*] the falsity and deception of their idols," Rogel complains, and "they threw up to me our adoration of the cross."[62] The Indians respond, in other words, by constructing a cross-cultural analogy that points up a central logical flaw in Rogel's position: that Christianity endorses the veneration of its own sacred objects while condemning this practice in non-Christian religions. The primary cultural work of Rogel's interpreters, it seems, is not only to expound Christian doctrine to the Indians but to allow the Indians to engage in substantive theological debate with the Christians. In this particular case, the Native response to Rogel is in effect to deconstruct the binary logic of monotheism—to illustrate if not the relativity of belief systems then their compatibility in distinction from one another, the "sameness" of their differences.

Rogel makes a special effort to evangelize to a cacique known as Felipe, one of the Indians in the group sent to Havana for instruction while the priest was waiting there for Menéndez.[63] But when he tries to convince Felipe of the superiority of Christianity, Felipe appears to lead the priest into a similar logical labyrinth. "I said to him," Rogel reports, "that [God] had told … and revealed … to us" the divine truth of resurrection, whereupon

> [Felipe] asked me how I knew that which God had said to us. I replied to him that we had it written down so, since very many years ago, ever since the time that he spoke it and revealed it. And with this he was brought up short [quedó atajado] and replied that the things that we have in our law have a much greater semblance of truth than did theirs even though they appeared more difficult and obscure. Because we have the things of our law in writing, thus they never change; and as they do not have it so, but only by tradition, by the second or third passing down of it, it becomes entirely changed. And thus it appears that he became more convinced to accept this truth about the immortality of the soul and the resurrection of the dead.[64]

This fascinating passage in Rogel's missive attempts to represent an idea that we have seen repeatedly flouted by Native interlocutors in earlier chapters: the colonial mystification of literacy, the belief that the technology of writing possessed by Europeans proved so dazzling to the indigenous peoples of the Americas to whom it was ostensibly unknown that it left them vulnerable to the invaders' discursive manipulations and, ultimately, to conquest and destruction. Writers across the centuries, from the conquest of Mexico in the early sixteenth century to the age of high structuralism in the twentieth—from Hernán Cortés to Tzvetan Todorov—have represented the absence of literacy as conceptual lack, and its presence as *the* decisive factor in the successful European invasion of the New World. Drawing upon the letters of Cortés and other Spanish colonial sources, Todorov infamously argued that under the new and unpredictable circumstances of the conquest, the oral cultures of New World Natives, specifically indigenous Mexicans—who preserved memory through speech and thus supposedly understood the present through the past of their ancestors—never stood a chance when faced with the flexible and improvisational discursive culture of European literacy.[65]

Rogel too comprehends the technology of writing as a kind of trump card in his encounter with the cacique Don Felipe. In his view, it provides an answer to Felipe's question about how the Spaniards can know what God says to them, though the degree of its power as a response depends upon whether Felipe's question is, in fact, to some extent rhetorical, a question of religious relativism: "how I knew"—better than he or anyone else—"that which God had said to us"? Misapprehending the potential levels on which the question might be answered, Rogel offers up as his answer not just the written word of Christian scripture on the matter of resurrection but the fact of European writing itself—the fact that "we have the things of our law in writing" while "they do not have it so." In Rogel's staging of the scene, orality wilts before literacy: Felipe is "brought up short" and appears to concede the victory, becoming "more convinced to accept the truth about the immortality of the soul."

Yet on one crucial matter, Rogel's account would appear to *contradict* Todorov's central thesis about Native discourse. By Rogel's own description, it is the literate Christian discourse that locates the production and interpretation of meaning in the past, "very many years ago," and that cannot, in effect, shift to accommodate new horizons of knowledge in the present and future; it is "the things of our law" and the larger Christian worldview that "never change." On the other hand, the orality of Native discourse operates far more flexibly, and would appear to adapt to the changing circumstances of its users, for "by the second or third passing down of it, it becomes entirely changed." In Rogel's telling, in other words, Todorov's discursive oppositions and their attendant temporal and cognitive qualities appear to hold stable—but they have switched sides of the encounter between literacy and orality. Even as Rogel strains in the passage to present the triumph of writing, his own account of Felipe's response—"[he] replied that the things that we have in our law have a much greater semblance of truth . . . even though they appeared more difficult and obscure"—sounds far from the clear concession that the priest believes it to be. Of course, the *semblance* of truth depends for significance upon its potential distinction from the truth's *actuality*—and in the possible opposition between the two lies Felipe's lack of concession to those "more difficult and obscure" doctrines upon which Rogel is insisting. It comes as no surprise, therefore, that Rogel concludes this episode by admitting that he is left in "doubt and perplexity" by his encounters, and that, despite the cacique's amiability, "I always saw a great resistance in [Felipe] to believe."[66]

Part of this resistance, as Rogel explains it, comes from the Native discursive feature that Todorov, translating from the Nahuatl concept of *huehuetlatolli*, terms "the speech of the ancients." According to Todorov's well-known line of argument, the Aztec theologians were doomed to be "gradually stifled by the abundant discourse of the Franciscans," and "the greater efficacy of the Christian discourse" more generally, precisely because the essential feature of their Native discourse was recursion to the words of their ancestors.[67] Here again, Rogel's account of his mission among the indigenous Floridians would seem in part to conform to Todorov's observations of indigenous Mexican discourse:

> They go to the burial place to speak with the deceased ones and to ask their advice about the things that they have to do as if they were alive. And I believe that the devil speaks to them there, because from what they say to them there, they learn about many things that happen in other regions or that come to pass later on. They also tell them that they should kill Christians and other evil things.[68]

If the Aztecs relied upon "the speech of the ancients," the Floridians too look toward the past and seek counsel from "the deceased ones" in order to understand the present exigencies of conquest. Just as the Aztecs, according to Todorov, generated meaning in reference to the past to the extent that prophecy and memory became indistinguishable—"prophecy is memory"— the Florida Natives similarly learn from their communion with their ancestors "many things . . . that come to pass later on."[69]

Yet here again, Rogel's account suggests a telling reversal of the hierarchy of discursive sophistication proposed by Todorov. Indeed, the passage clearly registers Rogel's anxiety that the supposedly recursive discourse of the Floridians is a powerful one, in fact laden with valuable information about the present and future: from conversing with the "deceased ones," Rogel attests, the Natives learn not only things "that come to pass" but "many things that happen in other regions" as well—a startling claim that raises as many questions as does the Natives' supposed ability to predict future events. Rogel attributes the informative value and the dangerousness of this Floridian "speech of the ancients" to its possible origin in "the devil"; he believes that it is "the devil [who] speaks to them there" precisely *because* the words of the "deceased ones" signify meaningfully across time and space, yielding accurate information about both the future and circumstances in "other regions"—and, not least, provoking violence against the colonizers. To adapt Todorov's own terms, the "greater efficacy" of the Native discourse would, in less than a decade, successfully overwhelm the Christian one: after all, the Indians would drive the Jesuits out of Florida by 1572—Don Luis's act of unsettlement, indeed, catalyzing the final withdrawal.

To pursue and understand the "greater efficacy" of Native discourse in the instance of South Florida requires no less speculation, of course, than Todorov himself employed—which is why his account of the Mexican conquest remains instructive, despite its problematic, even notorious implications. To read this passage from Rogel's account both through and against Todorov's thesis is to discover the traces of a hemispheric indigenous consciousness, a political understanding of the assault on indigenous sovereignty throughout the hemisphere in the wake of conquest. Whatever else Rogel's description of the recursive speech of the "deceased ones" may tell us about sixteenth-century Native religious ontology, in other words, it *also* suggests that when the Floridian Natives convened at the burial place of their ancestors, they entered into a conversation about the wider hemisphere—exchanging information gleaned from shipwrecked captives or Indians returning from Cuba, for example—that left them with a growing conceptual map of New World colonialism: one that guided their words and actions in dealing with the Spaniards, allowed them to strategize successfully enough to seem even to predict the future, and ultimately mobilized them to overthrow the Spanish settlements along the South Floridian coast.

The existence of such a sixteenth-century hemispheric circuit of indigenous knowledge would help to explain an enduring mystery among historical anthropologists about the complex nature of the Calusa society first recorded by the Spaniards. As William Marquardt explains, "almost all the known people who achieve the measure of complexity [found in Calusa culture] are agriculturalists . . . able to produce and distribute a surplus." Because the Calusa were not agriculturalists, Marquardt observes, scholars have divided roughly into two explanatory camps. One camp understands the Calusa exception as the result of Florida's "bounteous environment," which both allowed for and necessitated complex political organization in order to distribute the foods gathered thereof; the other sees this same complexity, which the Spanish would observe in the mid-sixteenth century, as the result of contact earlier in that century with Europeans and their influential "mercantile/imperial economy."[70]

Coming to this disagreement as a disciplinary outsider, I am no doubt oversimplifying the strengths and importance of each argument in order to register the implications of each. The former depends on the topos of the abundant New World Eden, where the living was easy enough to allow the Floridian Natives to develop a complex political system almost despite themselves. The latter explanation assumes to its detriment that political complexity emanates outward from Europe, moving always in one direction only. Yet Rogel's observations throughout this and his other accounts might easily lead to a different conclusion altogether: that the political complexity of the non-agriculturalist Calusa grew from a multidirectional flow of people, goods, and information between the Indians of South Florida and those of the larger hemisphere, and between the Floridian Natives and those of Cuba, in particular. Certainly, in the post-contact period, numerous Floridian Natives traveled often to Cuba with Spanish ships, as we have already seen in Rogel's account of his arrival in Havana, and there would have had contact not only with sixteenth-century Cuban Natives but with Natives brought from Mexico and elsewhere in the hemisphere to the colonial capital. And though the historian and translator John Hann finds "no clear documentary evidence" of Native trips between Florida and Cuba made independently of the Spanish, we must consider the narrative evidence offered in an account such as Fontaneda's, which explicitly referred to a long tradition of contact between Floridian and Cuban Natives before the arrival of Europeans.[71] Julian Granberry has suggested an even wider range of hemispheric connection in a study that shows the development of the Timucua language of South Florida from an indigenous language originating at the mouth of the Orinoco river in the Vaupés-Caqueta region of present-day Colombia.[72] Given such long-standing circuits of communication and contact among the indigenous peoples of the hemisphere, long preceding but also following the arrival of Europeans, it is perhaps not, after all, surprising that the Indians Rogel observed in Florida were able to predict certain events attending colonial encounter in other parts of the hemisphere. Nor is it surprising that the cacique Carlos would turn out, as Rogel repeatedly complained, to hold a particular hatred for him as a priest, given the clear connections elsewhere in the Americas between Native conversions and successful Spanish colonization.[73] After all, as late as 1698, when some Spanish priests finally made a new effort to establish a mission among the Calusa, and approached the Indians tentatively with some tools brought from abroad, the Calusa refused them—"asking why they had not brought blacks who might dig with the hoes."[74] They knew, in other words, exactly what Cuba looked like in the late sixteenth century, after the decimation of its indigenous inhabitants and the importation of African labor, and they were determined to avoid a similar fate. Perhaps they also knew what happened when Don Luis destroyed the Spanish colony of Ajacán, forestalling European colonization for more than thirty more years: for by 1595, the story of Don Luis had traveled far, and Don Luis himself was said to be living among the Indians of coastal Florida.

Don Luis Resurrected: Andrés de San Miguel and the *Ladino* Baroque

In 1595, two decades after Don Luis's return to Ajacán—after the deaths of the Jesuits, the violent "recovery" of Alonso, and Rogel's subsequent declaration that he had been *engañado* or mistaken in his account of the events—a Spanish ship was carrying South American silver from Mexico and Havana to Spain when it hit a storm and then wrecked off the coast of what are now the Georgia Sea Islands. Those who made it to land feared both starvation and cannibals, but the Indians whom they encountered gave them food and shelter and helped them as they made their way southward. After 111 days, the survivors of the shipwreck eventually reached St. Augustine and from there skirted in a new boat along the coast of Florida and then crossed to Havana. On the last leg of this journey, they met a new group of Indians in southern Florida who spoke about their mysterious leader, a Spanish-speaking cacique. When the cacique came out to meet the Spaniards, he introduced himself to them as Don Luis.

We know about this uncanny claim to a firsthand sighting of Don Luis—which occurred long after Menéndez failed to find and punish him following his destruction of the Jesuit settlement—thanks to one of the survivors of the shipwreck, a Spanish teenager called Andrés de Segura. Andrés returned to Spain after his group made it to Havana, but he returned to Mexico the following year, where he kept a vow he made during his shipwreck travails: to join the Carmelite friars as a lay brother. In Mexico he took the name by which he is now known to seventeenth-century Mexican history: Andrés de San Miguel. Over the next forty years, Andrés became a mathematician, scientist, and hydrographer, helping to design a modern drainage system for lakes in the Valley of Mexico; an architect, designing the Convento de San Ángel in Mexico City among many other Carmelite monasteries; and, most important for this story, an author, writing works on botany and astronomy, among other topics.[75]

Sometime before his death in 1644, most likely during his residency in Mexico City in the 1630s, Andrés also composed an account of his 1595 shipwreck in Florida, which positions itself explicitly as a critique of failed Spanish leadership and colonial greed and cruelty leveled from the point of view of the Church in New Spain.[76] Andrés is thus able to contrast the cruel Spanish treatment of Florida Natives—"poor souls to whom nobody had paid any attention because they had neither gold nor silver"—with the upstanding Spanish Creole project of indigenous conversion, the "lofty goals" of the various sacred orders of the New World.[77] In this sense, Andrés's account participates in the New World baroque, as defined by José Lezama Lima: its critical mode is less counter-reformation than counter-conquest.[78] Baroque too is the text's narrative authority, which derives not only from the discursive power of the "written Church" in a period of weakening Spanish economy and state power but also from Andrés's status as a seventeenth-century man of science who offers detailed, ethnographic descriptions of the indigenous cultures he encounters at first hand as a participant-observer traveling through Florida.[79] This narrative authority operates in a continual, baroque tension with its own dual perspectives: Andrés de Segura's youthful, firsthand point of view and the mature, ostensibly all-knowing vantage afforded Andrés de San Miguel in hindsight. This interplay between past and present, appearance and reality, innocence and knowledge, allows Andrés's text continually to restage the baroque topos of *desengaño*, the disillusion that, as José Antonio Maravall and other theorists of the baroque have argued, allows this post-Renaissance mode so effectively to call into question the absolutist authority of its sixteenth-century discursive antecedents: in this case, the simultaneously economic and religious project of New World imperialism.[80]

Andrés headlined his narrative as a *Relación de los trabajos que la gente de una nao llamada neustra señora de la merced padeció y algunas cosas que en aquella flota sucedieron*—"An Account of the Difficulties that the People of a Ship Called *Our Lady of Mercy* Endured and Some Things that Occurred in that Fleet."[81] The title strangely elides both the narrative's founding event (the wreck of the ship) and its major content (the survivors' travels in Florida), suggesting through its final reference to the fleet that the narrative's primary location is upon the sea rather than on the land—suggesting, that is, that *Our Lady of Mercy* survived with the larger fleet in which it sailed. The ensuing shipwreck comes as something of a surprise, as does the utter absence of the fleet from most of the narrative. Yet the fleet's role is nevertheless a significant one, for it betrays *Our Lady* in its moment of need, five days after the ships have sailed from Havana, when the storm hits. "As we had lost the rudder," Andrés explains, "we began to fire off pieces at once, asking for help":

> But in so great a number of ships . . . going close together, there was not
> one that would help us or ask what our trouble was. And thus, with great
> affliction and tears from some who considered their death certain, we went
> along . . . in pursuit of the other vessels constantly firing pieces, asking for
> help. But all the rest of the vessels, each one followed their own fortunes . .
> . without taking notice of anyone else in such great tribulation . . . And we
> saw that we could not count on human remedies . . . [82]

The straightforwardness of Andrés's plodding title is thus belied not only by
the suspenseful events which follow in the narrative but by the sharp critique
of the Spanish silver fleet embedded within it. In this sense, Andrés shares
Cabeza de Vaca's concern with illustrating the travesty of misused authority; like his famous forebear's account of shipwreck, this one too details the
cowardice of "those who were in command during the time of fair weather"
but who "did not have the courage in order to take charge" during the
tempest—"idle and false men" who plotted to save only themselves "in such
great secrecy that the poor souls who kept themselves busy, working day
and night without stopping . . . to keep the vessel above water, as they never
thought of committing such a betrayal."[83]

But unlike Cabeza de Vaca's account, in which weak authority serves as
a flattering foil for the narrator's own self-described qualities of leadership,
Andrés's *relación* never shores up the fragments of disorder under a figure of
beneficent authority.[84] Instead, his narrative highlights the victims' repetition
of the initial crime perpetrated against them when the remaining men on the
ship, under the direction now of the "good purser," build a new launch and
(Andrés among them) set themselves adrift while some of the sailors are still
on board the sinking ship. While the narrator insists that "it should be understood well that [those left on board] were not among the number whom
God wished to set free from that danger with life," his recollection of one of
those left behind calling "in a high and imploring voice" for the launch to return undercuts his certainty: the earlier "betrayal" of the ship's first leaders is
not so different from what the narrator here attributes to divine providence.[85]
Once on land, the narrative stages another compulsive repetition of the initial act of betrayal, when the "good purser" again leaves behind a group of
unhappy castaways who are begging to be let aboard the survivors' newly
devised sloop. Where Cabeza de Vaca's narrative transcends the calam-
ity of shipwreck and corrupt authority with the authoritative clarity of the
author-protagonist's own virtue, Andrés's account resists any such stability
of meaning, its discrepancies collectively forming an interpretive pattern in
which the narrative first pronounces the meaning of an event that it describes
and then later calls it into question with ensuing details or occurrences.

Often the narrative stages these moments as the visual revelation of a prior
failure of vision: a "phantom" or "dream island" that leaves the storm-tossed

sailors overjoyed and then disappears with the break of day; a terrible hunger
that causes the shipwrecked sailors to "see ourselves more clearly and we did
not know ourselves, after having seen ourselves leave the ship so fat and robust"; a meal of tide-borne rotting scraps that the sailors eat like "little dogs . . .
without taking notice that they were rotten" but afterward "knew very well
[were] some shanks and legs" of their companions.[86] As in Fontaneda's narrative, then, the point of view in Andrés's account is never precisely clear, its dis-
junctive details manifesting a baroque play of perspectives that double back
upon themselves. And if the moment of the shipwreck always marks a kind of
rupture in the epistemological certainty of the narrative that emplots it, then
this text too suggests a broken model—in this case the model of successful
New World translation: an unsettling of renaissance interpretive transparency with a particularly *ladino* form of baroque *desengaño*.[87] This *ladino* baroque, as I am defining it, hinges on the delayed recognition that translation
has failed, that comprehension across language and culture has not, despite
initial impressions, been achieved.

For example, after the purser and the men accompanying him have left
behind the unhappy castaways, the two separated groups experience very different encounters with the Indians of Florida with varied degrees of success
in communicating across languages. The landed group has been left behind
only a few hours when their fortunes take a dramatic turn for the better, as if
their betrayal by the purser and his men were an act of divine intervention:
as Andrés notes elliptically, "it appears that God was waiting for something
else." Their good fortune comes in the form of "a small pirogue . . . in which
there were two young Indian men and an old Indian woman, mother of the
head chief of the kingdom of Asao." A scene of communication between the
Indians and the Spaniards ensues—but, crucially, involves physical gestures
rather than words. After trading with the Indians—exchanging "a rosary and
a little blanket and some other little things" for corn and acorn cakes—the
Spaniards "gave the Indians to understand by signs how [the other group]
had gone with the sloop in search of [a main] river. With that, the Indians
departed leaving [them] consoled with the fire and the other things that they
gave them."[88]

The narrative makes a point of casting this scene of communication as a
seamlessly successful one, though of course the Indians' departure does not
necessarily signify comprehension of what the Spaniards have acted out in
signs. One might conclude, in fact, the opposite—that the Indians left because they did *not* understand the signs but knew, on the other hand, how to
acquire a verbal translation. For on the following day, a group led by the chief
of the village arrives:

> He spoke the Castilian language very well and was a Christian. He pulled
> back at the beginning and refused to come to the shore, fearing lest [they]

might be Englishmen, who were accustomed to mistreat them. But, having been assured that [they] were Spaniards, [the Indians] came ashore. They asked him to carry them [to the village of Christian Indians] and he agreed to this readily.[89]

Here again, the narrative's perspective upon what has been communicated leaves room for doubt: the Spanish-speaking cacique refrains warily from coming to shore until he has learned something about the Spaniards from listening to what they have to say, but what precisely persuades him to come ashore is impossible to know. Yet Andrés's narrative presents this scene of communication as a transparent one: in his view, once the Spaniards have made clear in Castilian that they are not cruel Englishman, they get the help they need from the Indians to arrive safely in the Franciscan mission of San Pedro Mocama. The castaway Spaniards, unhappily left behind by their purser's group (including Andrés), now enjoy the considerable fruits of an ostensibly successful translation: "Our companions were already among Christians," notes Andrés somewhat plaintively, "which is what it seems God intended by means of them."[90]

On the other hand, Andrés's group finds itself within a very different scene of translation. Aboard their sloop that night, they too spot a pirogue approaching:

> . . . the purser told all of us that no one should move or raise his head. And he began to call to them in as many ways as necessity taught him, at times in Mexican of which he knew something, and at times in Spanish, telling them that we were Christians and had been shipwrecked. He repeated the cries to such an extent that they brought the pirogue over to our sloop. There were two Indian men and one Indian woman in it, and they carried a smoldering log. We asked them by sign language to go over to the bank and light a fire. . . . They jumped ashore with ease and lit a fire.[91]

The palpable fear registered in this nighttime scene belongs now to the Spaniards rather than the Indians, and the narrative stages the purser's attempt to negotiate the situation with language as a desperate one. His knowledge of Indian languages, including "Mexican," owes to duress—"necessity [has] taught him"—and proves to be non-functioning. It is not his actual use of language but the repetition of his "cries," in the narrator's view, that draws the Indians toward the sloop; and it is finally "sign language" rather than words that elicits the desired action and the ensuing fire on land.

Yet even the seeming transparency of their ultimate success with sign language only sets the stage for more *desengaño*. When the Spaniards finally make it through the strong current to shore, they find the fire unsatisfactory—the flimsy product of "miserly Indians"—and they set about gathering large pieces of wood with which to stoke it. Finally, they achieve a strong blaze: "and with its light we saw our Indians more clearly and [saw] that they were carrying some things that we recognized as belonging to those who remained on the island."[92] While the reader understands that the companions' belongings have been traded for corn and acorn cakes in the previous scene of the narrative, Andrés and his companions, of course, do not.

This, too, is thus a baroque scene in which the narrative calls into question its own prior account of successful intercultural comprehension. Where the Spaniards had previously had confidence in their own mastery of the situation via sign language, they now see anew by the light of the fire the uncanny evidence of their own vulnerability—the "things" separated from their former owners, indeterminate signs which mutely but powerfully testify to a host of possible realities, past and present: By what (potentially violent) means have these Indians come to possess the belongings of the companions left behind on the island, and what does this scene of delayed recognition now bode for their own future?

By the time the Indians have guided Andrés and his companions to the Guale Indian village of Asao, the narrative's motif of translative *desengaño* has evolved into a founding assumption of linguistic opacity. "They received us" there, Andrés notes, "with happy faces and affable expressions and words that we did not understand just as they did not understand us."[93] Throughout the ensuing scenes set in the Asao village, the narrative acknowledges the limits of its intercultural understanding, even as it draws a number of ethnographic conclusions based on detailed firsthand observation. For example, upon their arrival in the village at dusk the first thing that Andrés and his companions observe is a group of Indian men in "a large and clean plaza," who "receive" the Spaniards and then begin throwing their lances or poles after a stone that is repeatedly thrown across the plaza. The narrator concedes, "I did not understand the game very well"—and then simply describes what he sees next: " it appeared to me that the one who ran the best and arrived first took his pole and the stone and, without hesitating for a moment, threw it back again in the direction from whence it had come. . . . "[94] Yet the seemingly objective narrator has nevertheless already drawn a number of interpretive conclusions about what he has observed through the dusk in this scene: he assumes that the Indian men he sees are "the head chief and his leading men, who were many," and that their actions with the lance are performed for the benefit of the newly arrived Spaniards: "They soon attempted to entertain us with a certain game."[95]

In the memorable scene that follows, however, the narrator observes another indigenous performance, which he again describes in detail, but this time he appears unable to assimilate it to a preconceived frame of reference:

> Once the fiesta had ended, we all entered into the council house together
> and we all sat down, Spaniards, chiefs, and leading men, on a bed made

of tree branches, which was raised more than a yard from the ground. In the council house and close to the door on its right side there was a little idol or human figure, badly carved. For ears it had those of a coyote and for a tail that of the coyote as well. The rest of the body was painted with red ochre. . . . Close to the idol's feet there was a wide-mouthed jar full of a drink that they call cacina and around the jar and the idol were a great number of two-liter pots, also full of cacina. Each Indian took one of these in his hand, and with reverence they went about giving it to those who had played, who were each seated on a bench. Each one took and drank his. As a result of this their bellies became like a drum and as they went on drinking, their bellies kept on growing and swelling. They carried this on calmly for awhile, and we [were] waiting to see how that fiesta would end, when we saw that, on opening their mouths with very great calmness, each one began ejecting by way of [their mouths] a great stream of water as clear as it was when they drank it, and others, on their knees on the ground with their hands, went about spreading the water that they ejected to one side and the other. All those who did this were leading men. That solemn fiesta ended in this fashion.[96]

Though Andrés here again uses the word "fiesta" several times to describe the actions he observes, he no longer understands them as a form of entertainment for the benefit of the Spaniards. Instead, he and his fellow travelers are held in suspension—"waiting to see how that fiesta would end"—as witnesses to a scene they do not understand. As if to contain the incomprehensibility of this episode with a display of ethnographic knowledge, Andrés goes on in the ensuing sentences to detail the size and appearance of the cacina plant and the method of its preparation as a tea. Crucially, however, he draws here on his knowledge of life not in Asao but in colonial St. Augustine, where "Indians and Spaniards drink it in the morning." Cacina is the New World beverage of La Florida, Andrés suggests, a cultural staple of shared indigenous-Creole tradition. As he notes with authority, "This is the common drink of Spaniards and Indians. . . . they say it can prevent the stone. . . . [b]ut it will never serve as a real treat like chocolate." Yet about the vomiting Andrés can only say that he is "not entirely certain": "It may be that the vomiting of it is peculiar to the serious men among them," he speculates, for "later I saw an old Christian chief called don Filipe, because he knew that was the king's name, who was accustomed to throw it up every time he drank it."[97]

Andrés's encounter with an "old Christian chief called don Filipe" raises a number of questions. As noted earlier in this chapter, in 1566 a future cacique who would become known as "don Felipe" (a common name for converts) was among the contingent of Floridian Indians who visited Havana and met with Father Rogel in what he then took be a "good sign" of his potential harvest of Christian souls in Florida. And, as we saw before, this same cacique "don Felipe" promised Menéndez that he would become a Christian but then engaged Rogel in a series of theological debates during the missionary's stay in Florida. Historical chronology precludes Andrés from meeting the same don Felipe whom Rogel knew, however, for by the time of Andrés's Floridian travels in 1595, the earlier cacique Felipe had long since been executed by the Spaniards for the very subversion that Rogel complained of soon after his arrival in Florida.[98] Yet the uncanny similarities of name, Christian conversion, and cacique status collectively suggest that Andrés likely thought he was meeting (or at any rate had in mind) the former Felipe, now two decades older, as an aged cacique. Indeed, Andrés could easily have heard of don Felipe from Rogel himself, who was working in Vera Cruz as a doctor and priest when Andrés arrived in 1595 to stay for nearly a year shortly before his fateful shipwreck and his journey through La Florida.[99] But whether or not Andrés knew of, had in mind, or intended to reference the former cacique Felipe, his passing mention of an "old Christian chief" of the same name summons the specter of indigenous unsettlement associated with the former Felipe, bequeathing a kind of longevity or afterlife to the dissident Calusa leader whom the Spaniards had executed in 1570. In this sense, Andrés's reference to Felipe—"who was accustomed to throw [the cacina tea] up every time he drank it"—casts a somewhat ominous light upon the vomiting ritual he has just described.[100]

And as it turns out later in the narrative, after his arrival in St. Augustine Andrés learns from a soldier there a crucial piece of information that calls into question the meaning of the fiesta he has observed in the Asao village. Though Andrés insists that the kind treatment shown to him and his fellow travelers by the Indians of Asao, along with their apparent willingness to be baptized, must "arise from . . . love of the people and of their faith," he also undercuts this claim profoundly by noting that just prior to his visit there, the Asao Indians had killed a Spaniard: "a soldier [who was] passing through these villages, whom the governor had sent that he might go up to Santa Elena by way of the coastline to look for shipwrecked people on it." When Andrés and his companions arrive, in other words, they do not realize that the Indians of Asao have just done away with their potential means of salvation, the very person who had in effect been sent to rescue them. The game played to "entertain" the arriving Spaniards and the vomiting ceremony that they witness in the council house now appears very different, particularly when Andrés learns that "[t]he image or human figure that was in the council house was the figure of this Spaniard, made to scorn him and placed there [by] the Indians."[101] The Indians of Asao thus perform their vomiting ritual not before "a little idol," as Andrés had previously believed, but before the figure they have quite specifically fashioned to represent the interloping Spaniard they have just killed.

Though this detail is of course highly mediated, coming to Andrés as it does from a Spanish soldier whose own source is never specified, it nevertheless radically shifts the reader's parameters of interpretation in parsing the meaning of the performance—which is perhaps why Andrés withholds it in the narrative until after the scene has occurred. For the sequence of events and the potential function of the ritual must be reconsidered in light of this detail: the Spaniards arrive in Asao and are led into the council house, where their Indian hosts sit beneath the representational figure of a Spaniard they have recently killed and then quite purposefully begin another process of elimination—a bodily purgation in which they eject water from their mouths and then spread it away with their hands, "to one side and the other." While we cannot know the symbolic value of this ejecting process with any certainty, it is worth noting here that historical anthropologists have long documented the widespread use of a purgative "black drink" among southeastern Native groups before, during, and after the colonial period when it was first observed by Europeans. Tea-drinking and vomiting served potential medicinal purposes, ridding the body of contamination, but apparently functioned more often on a spiritual level to empty the drinker of anger and falsehood. More recently, ethnohistorians have linked such self-induced vomiting rituals to what might be called a Native philosophy of anticolonial purgation—a practice originating among the southeastern Indians of North America and then stretching geographically and temporally north of the Ohio Valley and well into the eighteenth century. By the early 1760s, the followers of the Delaware prophet Neolin, one of the greatest of the early Native visionaries to advocate pan-Indian nativism, a pan-Indian project of unsettlement, had adopted and widely propagated the southeastern Native practice of drinking an emetic tea to induce ritual vomiting as a specific means of ridding practitioners from the contamination of "White people's ways and Nature."[102] Viewed in the *longue durée* of the black drink, in other words, Andrés's seeming ethnographic authority on the purgative uses of *cacina* emerges, quite literally, from the shadow of the murdered Spanish effigy hanging in the council house—and, in a broader sense, from the subjugated history of hemispheric indigenous acts of unsettlement dramatized by the scene he narrates.

After the scene in the Asao council house, the narrative brings Andrés to the village of San Pedro, where this time he witnesses what we might call the apparition of an indigenous revolt that will occur in the future. In this strange scene, Andrés and his companions are reunited with the castaway group of Spaniards they had earlier left behind and, despite the tense circumstances of their earlier separation, the latter group greets Andrés's cohort without apparent resentment: "They all received us one by one and embraced us with signs of love and joy. . . ."[103] But if the expected remonstration for the earlier betrayal never occurs, the Spaniards are instead visited by a figure who will, unbeknownst to them, come to stand for a different kind of retribution—the "chief" of San Pedro, who had until then "been absent":

> He and the chieftainness were Christians and spoke the Castilian language very well. He had very good carriage and countenance, of great strength. He was named don Juan and dressed well in the Spanish manner. And when the chieftainness went out she wore a cloak like a Spanish lady. When we learned that they were arriving at the riverbank, we all went to give them a welcome. All those among their vassals who learned of their coming, who were many, flocked to the same reception. On jumping on land, he took the path toward the council house once he had spoken to us and all of us with him. But the Indian men and women [and] the big and little children began as great a wailing in a high voice as if they had dropped dead before their eyes. And they went along following them thus and crying up to the council house, where he sat down on the bench . . . and all the Indians got down on their knees before him continuing their crying, while he listened with great calmness and seriousness until from fatigue he got up and left. And the Indians, on ceasing their crying, got back to their feet and left, drying their tears. Those who were absent because they had not been present at the reception and those from distant villages came later. When there were many assembled, the chief came . . . and the Indians went down on their knees before him and performed their wailing until he rose up and left. Then they returned to their houses. The coming to weep was continued in this manner for many days. They told us that their vassals had to do the same with our chiefs when they returned to their land. Later, while I was in St. Augustine, I went to the river every day to fish, and from there I would hear someone begin to cry in a high voice every afternoon, and that the whole village would soon follow in the same tone. And when I asked the reason, I learned that their chief had died, and that accordingly they had to cry for a whole year. All this people cry in this manner for their chiefs living and dead.[104]

As with the scene in the Asao council house, here too Andrés appears to be at pains to contain that which he does not understand within a frame of ethnographic mastery. Thus the mysterious visits of "don Juan" and the repeated crying of the San Pedro Indians are made legible by the final lines of the passage, in which Andrés learns from an unnamed source—whether Spanish or indigenous he does not specify—that the Indians near St. Augustine are weeping "every afternoon" for a whole year because their chief has died. Neatly wrapping up the mysterious events at San Pedro, Andrés stabilizes the meaning of the weeping in two apparently very different contexts and concludes—as a first-person, participant-observer in St. Augustine, 1595—that "[a]ll this people cry in this manner for their chiefs living and dead."

Yet by the time Andrés composed his account as a lay Carmelite friar in seventeenth-century Mexico, a certain Floridian chief, also called "don Juan," had become infamous in the historical annals of the Spanish in Florida. In 1597, some two years after Andrés's sojourn in Asao and San Pedro, this Guale cacique don Juan led a systematic uprising against the Spanish that became known as Juanillo's Rebellion, and which represented what has been called the "earliest documented anticolonial rebellion in North America."[105] As with the act of unsettlement led by Don Luis, the Guale Indian rebellion particularly distressed the Spanish colonial establishment in Florida and abroad because it was organized and perpetrated by a Hispanized Indian chief, a *ladino* cacique fluent in Castilian and supposedly devoted to the Christian worldview and the colonial project it supported. Moreover, as David Thomas and others have argued, the Juanillo Revolt was not simply an isolated event but the culmination of a series of related uprisings and attacks collectively marking almost thirty years of concerted Native effort to undermine Spanish colonial control—a kind of climax of unsettlement, in other words, and one which almost led King Philip III to terminate all missionary effort in the Floridas.[106]

While scholars today delineate as distinct historical figures the two "don Juans"—the Guale cacique who led Juanillo's revolt and the chief of the San Pedro Timucua Indians—the similarities between the two are compelling: name, *ladino* status, Christianization, and geographical proximity.[107] And it is worth noting, given the latter connection, that the don Juan whom Andrés encountered was not living in San Pedro while Andrés was there, or at any rate had "been absent" before the strange scene of wailing that marked his arrival. Perhaps because of the information that Andrés received in St. Augustine (that the chief there had allegedly died), he retrospectively, in writing his account, casts the San Pedro Indians' wailing also as a kind of mourning without loss: "as if they [don Juan and the chieftainess] had dropped dead before their eyes." But reconsidered in light of the imminent Juanillo Rebellion, and the series of interconnected Guale revolts running from the 1570s through the late 1590s, it is possible that the wailing at San Pedro had another meaning entirely: a meaning, as Andrés believes, directed at don Juan upon his arrival—but perhaps arising from the fact of the Spaniards' presence in the village.

Whatever the wailing signifies, don Juan listens to it "with great calmness and seriousness" and then departs again—though perhaps it is not after all "from fatigue" that he gets up and leaves, but because the wailing has served its purpose. Andrés himself never states explicitly that the Guale uprising is the context through which we must retrospectively filter his narration of this odd scene in San Pedro, but he does cite specifically in this particular section of his account from Fray Juan de Torquemada's monumental history of the indigenous Americas, *Indian Monarchies* (*Los veinte y un libros rituales y monarquia indiana . . .*)—and Torquemada makes clear reference in that text to the Juanillo Rebellion that occurred in 1597.[108] In this sense, then, whether or not the two don Juans described previously were indeed distinct historical figures, the very mention of the San Pedro "don Juan" in Andrés's account necessarily evokes the shadow of the other don Juan, and of the Juanillo Rebellion soon to come after Andrés's departure from Florida. And while Andrés purports to celebrate his sojourn in Asao and San Pedro as the provident hand of God laying the foundations for the Franciscan mission in Florida—and the shipwreck itself as a fortunate fall, as "the beginning and origin of this sacred order"—here too his narrative depends on a different but related repression of chronological history.[109] For as Andrés well knew by the time he wrote *Los trabajos*, the Franciscans first came to Florida not in 1595, as he suggests, but in 1573, and they came precisely because Florida had been abandoned by the Jesuits the year before—when they learned of Don Luis's apostasy and his destruction of Ajacán.

Andrés never directly mentions the flight of the Jesuits from Florida, but the last part of his narrative performs one final, spectacular scene of baroque rupture when it brings its shipwrecked protagonist into contact with a quintessential figure of *desengaño*: an Indian called Don Luis. With this encounter, moreover, comes a swift, uneasy rupture in the narrative authority of the entire account. The scene occurs after Andrés has made his way to St. Augustine and is traveling by a small boat to Havana, "staying along the coast from headland to headland."[110] Along the way, the ship encounters some pre-lapsarian Indians who "neither sow nor gather, nor . . . have any more concern about their food or their clothing than animals . . . and yet do not lack anything, and live to be very old, happy with their lot." But the ship does not meet, Andrés remarks, the Xega Indians, "inhumane, cruel, and enemies of the Spaniards," diametrically opposed to the Edenic figures in the old Columbian binary organizing representations of the indigenous other: "We saw none of these, nor did we go on shore in their land." Instead, in the next sentences of the account, Andrés encounters a figure who disrupts this binary, none other than Don Luis himself:

> . . . and near the land of La Habana, almost straight ahead from the port, there are other Indians, very friendly with the Spanish, whose cacique was then a don luis. The soldiers said of him that he had been in Spain: he spoke the Spanish language as well as if he had been raised in court. I understand that it was he that the inca said killed the fathers of the company, because the name, the language, and the land would make one understand so: this cacique came to meet us in a big canoe made in the Spanish way with 16 rowers, all standing up and he, in the stern, also standing: in arriving at the boat, he came aboard it and was received by all the Spanish as a great friend [which] he was of all of them: his clothing was that of nature which he adorned with a breechcloth. He was different from the rest in the spiritedness and valor of his persona and in the respect that all showed

him, and in the ample beadwork with which he adorned his body, circling
with strings four or six fingers wide his neck, upper arms, wrists, under the
knees, the narrow part of the feet, above the ankles: in this, the king differentiated himself from his underlings: this cacique brought more amber
than all the others in all the coast who met us, and having negotiated and
taken leave, so fluent and friendly [*tan ladino y amigo*], he got in his canoe
and stood himself above the stern [and] began to go toward land, and a
few feet in he was thrown into the sea, and having returned to get into the
canoe he went for one of the rowers, and grabbing hold of his hair threw
him in the sea, and at once he sank to the bottom, and taking his oar the
cacique raised it with both hands above his shoulder, and was waiting like
that for the Indian to bring himself to the surface in order to hit him with
it, and tired of waiting for him and of us seeing him so armed, he let the
oar go and went to his seat, and later the Indian appeared above the water
and got in the canoe, and they went off leaving us amazed that a man could
be so long under the water without drowning himself: with this example,
it won't [be difficult to see] how they leap, go down, and come up on the
whale until they have driven in the stake.[111]

Thus, here, not in Ajacán but near Havana, we find Don Luis, again, as a
chief, his Spanish not only fluent but elevated, as if he had been raised in the
royal court. Lest the coincidence appear too unlikely, Andrés offers his own
summation of the evidence, citing "name," "language," and "land" as proof of
this cacique's identity as the indigenous "traitor apostate" whose story concludes Garcilaso's *La Florida*. Crucially, this passage self-consciously depicts
the figure Don Luis not before but *after* he has already committed the murders of the Jesuits, the "fathers of the company." For in referencing "El Inca,"
who dates the episode (inaccurately, it turns out) as "before [15]68," and in
positioning "don luis" near Havana in the year of his shipwreck, 1595, Andrés
provides a clear chronology: in his telling, Don Luis kills the Jesuits in Ajacán
and then, two decades later, is living near Havana, leading a group of Indians,
who may or may not also be from Ajacán. At the same time, the reference to
Garcilaso introduces a marked tension in the text between two very different
narrative points of view: the late sixteenth-century "we" who encounters
and observes Don Luis without, presumably, having heard of his hand in the
Jesuits' demise, and the "I" telling the story in the seventeenth century, the
older Mexican friar, architect, scientist, and reader of history that Andrés had
become by the time he was composing the account years later.

The tension between these two narrative points of view generates much
of the passage's critical irony. The late-sixteenth-century, first-person plural
narrative renders up Don Luis lavishly, as the primitive exotic visual object of
its own colonial gaze. He enters the narrative line of sight dressed in "*el natural*," naked save the mere adornment of a loincloth, and encircled in strings

of beads erotically figured as "*dedos*" or fingers, which take a tactile and detailed inventory of his body: throat, arms, wrists, knees, feet, and ankles. The scene suggests the promise of abundance (and indeed, Don Luis brings the Spaniards more amber than "all the others in all the coast"); and it casts its central figure in the familiar European terms of royal hierarchy: Don Luis is not only a cacique but a king with vassals. The scene that follows the meeting of Don Luis and the Spaniards on the boat thus plays out a kind of slapstick devoted to the abuses of power: Don Luis seeks an impulsive and arbitrary revenge on one of the rowers, presumably for the injury to his pride, sustained in falling from the canoe. The passage narrates the attempted revenge over a stretched-out syntactical and visually dramatic moment, during which Don Luis waits to assault the rower with his oar, while the rower hides beneath the surface of the water. Yet in the first-person plural narrative perspective, this moment is no more remarkable than Don Luis's circles of beads; strikingly, what leaves this collective narrator amazed and astonished, *espantados*, is the length of time the rower can survive while submerged—and the ethnographic light this sheds on whaling practices.

Andrés thus introduces a narrative blindspot, or a disjunction between the collective, sixteenth-century narrator's interest in this scene as an ethnographic moment and the later, seventeenth-century historian's first-person, singular perspective, one that necessarily knows more than the chronologically prior point of view. Viewed from the later perspective, the scene offers not an ethnographic study but a study in personality in all its instability and ambiguity: a study in the nature of appearances versus reality; in deception (Don Luis abandons his attempted revenge because he does not want the Spanish to see him "*assi armado*"—so armed; poised for assault); and, with the reference to "the fathers of the company," a study in colonial unsettlement. The passage marks the incursion of the later point of view upon the earlier one not only thematically but at the semantic level as well, by means of the "conflictive nature" of the term *ladino*. In signifying both bilingualism and acculturation, on the one hand, but also cunning, deception, and craftiness, on the other, *ladino* provides the semantic hinge in this passage between two conflicting narrative points of view: that which sees Don Luis as "*tan ladino y amigo*," and that which acknowledges *ladino* as a term that marks a separation between the describer and the described (as Adorno points out, it is not a term of self-identification) that inscribes the latter as unknowable and potentially threatening.[112] At the same time, however, for the first-person, singular narrator to reference Garcilaso—and thus to assign both a history and a fleshed-out identity to the cacique encountered in Florida—is also in a sense to resuscitate Don Luis from the death grip of the historical past, to assign him autonomous powers of movement and relocation, from Ajacán to a site near "la Habana," and to give him a powerful written afterlife: engaged in a new strand of history, leading Indians "*muy amigos de espanoles*" in appearance, though perhaps not in reality, Don Luis lives on as an indigenous leader, a cross-cultural negotiator, and an agent of unsettlement—and not only in the comedy of the oarsman, as our plural narrator elaborates it, but, via the singular narrator's citation of El Inca, in the tragedy of La Florida, and what Garcilaso's Don Luis himself called its "desolate" state in the aftermath of conquest.

Andrés's claim to have met Don Luis near Havana in 1595 gives us yet another speculative point on the map of the translator's itinerant career. More significantly, though, it plots a further site on a conceptual map: a tactical map of indigenous consciousness of the hemisphere as a geopolitical entity, encompassing not only metropolitan Spain and the royal seat of imperial power along with Mexico, Peru, Florida, Ajacán, and a place "near Havana," but the accounts of Spanish conquest and indigenous response that traveled across discrete languages, histories, and cultures. The precise parameters of this hemispheric consciousness and the broad, cross-cultural networks of knowledge it might have supported remain difficult to specify. But a speculative history of its elusive but undeniable effects would have to embrace the series of surprise Indian attacks, some occurring within weeks of each other, leveled on Spanish settlements all along the coast of La Florida in the years after Don Luis's unsettlement of Ajacán in 1572, as well as the so-called Guale Uprising of 1597, during which Floridian Natives attacked and burned Spanish missions just after Andrés claims to have sighted Don Luis near Havana.[113]

The story of Don Luis powerfully crystallizes this era of dissident unsettlement by embodying in a single Native subject the hemispheric potential of indigenous revolt in a land where Floridian Indians had been subjected to Spanish slaving missions since even before Ponce de León's "discovery" of the peninsula.[114] When the cacique whom Andrés encounters in Florida calls himself "don luys," the relative truth or falsity, accuracy or inaccuracy, of his declaration is beside the point. The statement functions rather as a performative utterance, one that calls Native sovereignty into being along with the concomitant threat of unsettlement in the face of colonial imposition.[115] To name himself as Don Luis is, irrespective of the cacique's verifiable but unverified identity, to recall a figure who would not die—and to insist upon the unsettling survival of Don Luis and his story beyond the space and time of Ajacán.[116]

PART III

The Translation of Don Luis

FROM THE TREATY OF GUADALUPE HIDALGO TO THE
GOOD NEIGHBOR POLICY

The Politics of Unsettlement
in the Nineteenth Century

In the colonial era, the story of Don Luis was a record of indigenous acts of unsettlement at Ajacán and beyond: the thwarting of a potential Spanish occupation of Don Luis's homeland, and the concomitant forestalling of European colonization there for decades to come. From its first iterations, the story embodied the insurgent possibilities of translation in the colonial context, the inter-indigenous transmission of knowledge from throughout the Americas and across the Atlantic, and the threat of Native revolt against European empire on a hemispheric scale. From the Spanish point of view, it was a story of colonial failure to be kept hidden from competitors during the European struggle for empire, particularly as the metanarrative of Spanish imperial ascendency in the Americas grew increasingly fragile, under continuous assault by the competing narrative complex known popularly as the Black Legend.[1] The English settlers who arrived at Jamestown in 1607 had likely not yet heard the story of Don Luis, but they were steeped in anti-Spanish translations of Las Casas.[2] Busy fashioning themselves in chaste and temperate opposition to the "all-devouringe Spaniard," they sometimes recorded in their writings—but did not seem to wonder about or to investigate—the signs that a Spanish settlement had preceded their own colonial endeavors.[3] Not until the mid-nineteenth century—by which time the notorious account of Pocahontas's self-sacrificing love for an Englishman had become a national U.S. myth, the subject of numerous popular American plays—would the English-speaking world finally learn about Don Luis and his destruction of the Spanish colony at Ajacán.[4]

This chapter elaborates the very different story of unsettlement that was generated by Don Luis's afterlife in the nineteenth-century United States. Emerging from the global race for empire in which Don Luis once traveled, the United States had now entered it; and the story of Ajacán proved powerfully unsettling to the idea of English priority in Virginia, the purported birthplace of a nation now competing to expand its own territorial boundaries. Because the legal basis for such expansion was largely defined by the history of colonial settlement, it is perhaps not surprising that the unsettling (re)discovery of a Spanish colony in Virginia was made by a translator, lawyer, and historian working for the U.S. State Department during the 1840s, Robert Greenhow. As I argue here, Greenhow presents a nineteenth-century U.S. counterpart to the figure of the *traduttore/traditore* examined above in the context of the colonial Americas. But unlike Don Luis—and the many colonial figures of unreliable translation examined in the preceding chapters—Greenhow produced patently false translations for the U.S. government, manipulating long-standing tensions between literature and history to lay the legal groundwork for national expansion into the hemisphere.

I turn first to Greenhow's early politico-scholarly endeavors involving the Oregon dispute with Britain and its relation to one of the most puzzling texts of nineteenth-century U.S. literary history: *The Journal of Julius Rodman* by Edgar Allan Poe—an unfinished novel of Western exploration that is best understood, as the second section suggests, within a frame of narrative unsettlement that has much in common with the strange, impersonal account produced by Fontaneda in the sixteenth century. The third section of the chapter explores what Greenhow did with the story of Don Luis and the sixteenth-century Spanish settlement in Ajacán when he found it in *Ensayo cronológico para la Historia General de la Florida* by the eighteenth-century Spanish historian Andrés González de Barcia. Writing on the eve of the U.S.-Mexican war and concerned with competing land claims, Greenhow willfully erased the Don Luis story as presented by González de Barcia, whose history notes very clearly that the Spanish exploration of the Chesapeake resulted in successful arrival on Virginian soil and clear communication to the Indians, via Don Luis, of their "discovery" of Ajacán. The trajectory of Greenhow's scholarly career introduces the articulated, geopolitical stakes of the story of Don Luis in the mid-nineteenth century, when the early modern doctrine of discovery was dramatically reconfigured with the U.S. Supreme Court case of *Johnson v. M'Intosh* (1823), shaping both international policy and the consolidation of U.S. legal ascendancy over the indigenous lands of North America—which had dramatically increased with the American acquisition of more than half of Mexico occurring at that very moment. Ultimately, these new lands depended for their continued legality—like *Johnson v. M'Intosh*—upon the first discovery of Virginia by the English.

By the end of the century, Don Luis would make his way into a diverse array of texts explored in the subsequent sections of the chapter, from the writings of America's preeminent Catholic historian, John Gilmary Shea, to William Cullen Bryant's *A Popular History of the United States* to Alice Fletcher's *Indian Education and Civilization*, the official congressional report that underwrote the Dawes Act of 1887. While Shea insisted on recovering the story of Don Luis from the annals of Spanish colonial history, arguing in multiple forums that the "first settlement of white men on the soil of Virginia" was not an English one, and that it deserved permanent national prominence, Bryant apprehended a very different theoretical energy within the story, recasting Don Luis's narrative of unsettlement as Anglo-America's primal, counterfactual, nationalist fantasy: the origination of a Spanish-American United States that might have prevailed.[5] Fueled by the symbolic racial logic of the Black Legend, Bryant's counterfactualism presented a rhetorical means of eliding the structure of settler colonialism as practiced by the English and then their American successors—a structure that in effect stages an unending race war over the territory to which it claims legal priority.

The story of Don Luis had to be significantly modified, therefore, for its inclusion in Fletcher's congressional report, which was written in support of the federal allotment plan that mandated the division of tribal territories into private, individual property, and that infamously instantiated the massive loss of Native-held lands that would endure through the Franklin Roosevelt administration. Read in light of its odd revision of the story of Don Luis, however, Fletcher's writing suggests that the taking of this land was not the ill-advised, unfortunate consequence of the Dawes Act but in fact the unspoken point of a legal ritual of claiming territorial possession. The final section of the chapter turns to two contemporaneous Omaha translators who knew and worked with Fletcher. In her political writings from the late nineteenth century, Susette La Flesche Tibbles offered a pointed analysis of the relationship between settler colonialism and the allotment agenda, while her half-brother Francis La Flesche undertook anthropological work that emphasized the epistemological limits of the project of ethnology, and particularly its problematic dependence upon translation. Tracing a history of Western misapprehension of indigenous religious philosophy from the era of colonial missionaries through the emergence of anthropology as a discipline, Francis La Flesche worked to create a scholarly legacy for future indigenous intellectuals by producing anthropology specifically as a means of Native knowledge production.

Robert Greenhow and "Oregon Country"

Throughout the 1840s, the translator Robert Greenhow, a quiet man of letters who loved old books and maps, was suffering periodically from neurasthenia.[6] Nietzsche might have diagnosed him with the disease of antiquarianism, a nervous disorder symptomatic of a scrupulous interest in the past for its own sake without regard for its contemporary use-value—an interest that, as Nietzsche saw it, in turn suppressed the health and instinct of youth and the present.[7] But a closer examination of Greenhow's scholarly work suggests the opposite: it was the contemporary uses to which history could be put that interested him—and the potential impinging of the past upon the present that left him a nervous wreck. Today Greenhow has—like so many translators—been largely forgotten. But during the early nineteenth century he worked under the official title of "Librarian and Translator" at the U.S. Department of State, and was, based upon his translative and scholarly services, among the three most highly-ranked officials in that wing of the government.[8] It was while working for the State Department that Greenhow discovered the story of Don Luis and began to use his status as a translator and historian to lie about the past.

Greenhow undertook this work, in part, by exploiting the historical propensities and prejudices of his own moment. He was writing during the period that preceded the professionalization of American history, as Peter Novick and others have documented it: an era described as "a time when all historians were 'amateurs' of history," "amateur gentleman-scholar[s]" who used their private funds to support their research and writing.[9] Greenhow's situation was by definition distinct, then, from that of the amateur gentlemen; he may have preceded the advent of the "professional historian" in the late nineteenth century, but he was, after all, on the official payroll of the State Department. Moreover, the late-nineteenth-century professionalizers of history would disdain Greenhow's famous peers—notably William Hickling Prescott and George Bancroft—as "literary historians," hopeless romantics who wrote under the spell of Walter Scott's novels, and misconstrued history as art.[10] Though this criticism oversimplifies in its sweeping characterization of early nineteenth-century historical sensibilities, which were—as they are now—varied, marked by the generic tensions between literature and history, and dependent on context, it is not hard to see where this assessment came from.[11] In the early nineteenth century, William Gilmore Simms could declare without qualification that "the chief value of history consists in its proper employment for the purposes of art!" (23). Simms was both a novelist and historian, and in his view the nonliterary historian was weak and ineffectual, a "mere chronologist," for whom "dates and names . . . are every thing" (24), and he accordingly dismissed what he called "that class of modern historians, the professed skeptics," with their "learned ingenuity," "keen and vigilant judgment," "great industry," "vast erudition and sleepless research," and "coldly inquisitive" mode of presentation (23). Not history but art was "the greatest of all historians": "It is the artist only who is the true historian" (25). Edgar Allan Poe, also writing at the Romantic, nineteenth-century crossroads of literature and history, readily agreed. "There is no greater error," he wrote, "than dignifying with the name of History a tissue of dates and details, though the dates be ordinarily correct, and the details indisputably true":

> Not even with the aid of acute comment will such a tissue satisfy our individual notions of History. To the effect let us look—to the impression rather

than the seal. And how very seldom is any definite impression left upon the mind of the historical reader! [Yet] we shall often discover in Fiction the essential spirit and vitality of Historic Truth—while Truth itself, in many a dull and lumbering archive, shall be found guilty of all the inefficiency of Fiction (145).

Nineteenth-century readers "very seldom" encountered histories literary enough to merit the name of History, Poe contended. By contrast, readers were "often" treated to the "Historic Truth" in perusing "Fiction." Poe conceded that "Truth itself" might be found through painstaking historical research, but without proper literary elaboration it would remain useless to its readers.

Yet the "dull and lumbering archive," unrefined by literary appeal, is exactly what Greenhow sought to showcase in the writing that he produced while working for the State Department, beginning with his 1840 "Memoir, Historical and Political, on the Northwest Coast of North America." Against the prevailing nineteenth-century Romantic views of the differences between history and literature, Greenhow's project in this historical work stands out for its relentless accrual of those dry "dates and names" scorned by Simms and Poe—for the sheer weight of accumulated evidence tenaciously resisting the pull of narrative. In fact, his scholarship seems almost to relish its fetishization of the antiquary's "disinterested love" of the "Facts of History" over and above, indeed at the expense of, any literary appeal.[12] And Greenhow appears determined to present himself in this work precisely as the "coldly inquisitive" scholar pursuing facts, uninterested in either the "spirit" or "vitality" of the past. But Greenhow's historical sensibilities did not merely run counter to the prevailing romanticism of his day. As I show here, he was self-consciously exploiting his reader's expectation of that romanticism, and developing in his scholarly work a method of manipulating historical sources to suit specific political interests while appearing to recede into "a tissue of dates and details," abstractly removed from real History's political fray.

As the title's generic designation suggests, the 1840 *Memoir, Historical and Political, on the Northwest Coast of North America* was produced specifically for diplomatic and other official political uses. What it presented was a detailed summary of the existing literatures of European exploration in North America and the competing imperial land claims underpinning the U.S. dispute with Britain over the Pacific Northwest boundary: the so-called Oregon Question. Greenhow submitted the memoir to the U.S. Senate's Select Committee on the Oregon Territory, which in turn entered the document into the *Congressional Record* for the 26th Congress in February 1840; on February 10, the Senate ordered an immediate printing as well as an additional 2,500 copies to be sent to the Senate itself.[13] But the Senate apparently believed it to be advantageous to U.S. interests for this historical work to find a still wider audience, for it would eventually commission and subsidize Greenhow's "revised, corrected, and enlarged" version of the memoir as a book, *The History of Oregon and California and Other Territories of the North-West Coast of North America*, published by Little and Brown in 1845.[14]

Despite the context of its production, Greenhow's history eschews the political role of the scholar in undertaking the work: "The writer has now completed the task assigned to him," he notes modestly on the final page, "by presenting an exposition of the most important circumstances relative to the discovery and occupation of the northwest coasts and territories of North America, by the people of various civilized nations, and of the pretensions advanced by the Governments of those nations in consequence."[15] Indeed, Greenhow appears almost to diminish the lack of power inhering in his own position as translator of the archives of Spanish, Russian, British, French, and U.S. literatures of exploration, a position which he casts in a humble geographic metaphor: "To indicate farther the course which should be pursued on the part of the United States with regard to their claims," he opines, "lies not within [my] province" (200). But if Greenhow disavows any disciplinary land claim on the "province" of U.S. foreign policy, he unequivocally states the upshot of his project within the realm of international relations: that *the titles of the Unites States to the possession of the regions . . . derived from priority of discovery and priority of occupation, are as yet stronger, and more consistent with the principles of national right, than those of any other Power. . . .* " (200; emphasis in original). Precisely when it is most at pains to suggest the neutrality of the scholarly role, in other words, Greenhow's historical work pursues the agenda of legitimating U.S. territorial "possession" through carefully selected and redacted research into the archives of the colonial Americas. It was while constructing this argument for U.S. "titles" to the Northwest Oregon territory, moreover, that Greenhow discovered the story of Don Luis—though, as we shall see, he would not actively suppress the story until later in the decade.

Throughout his writing on the disputed Oregon territory, Greenhow described and sorted the materials at his disposal by continually reconceiving and playing upon the distinction between literature and history that was preoccupying his contemporaries, always taking the side of the latter over the former—the side of the "modern skeptic" over the Romantic. But Greenhow also worked stealthily in the gap between history and literature, manipulating the long-standing battle between them. To do so, he laid out a series of generic specifications that enabled him to distinguish between, on the one hand, "true" accounts, characterized by "authenticity and general correctness," and, on the other, three closely related genres: "false" accounts, which have their "origin, generally, in the knavery and the vanity of their authors"; "reported discover[ies]," in which an author deliberately inscribes a "falsehood or amplification" in reporting another's oral statements or written work, usually to "induce" a patron to sponsor "a voyage which [the writer] then projected"; and, finally, the "pretended discovery," comprised of "mere fictions," which are "invented for the purpose of exercising ingenuity, or of testing the credulity of the public."[16] Greenhow then deftly negotiated these distinctions, highlighting an "exemplary fiction" from the genre of the "pretended voyage," for example, in order to demonstrate the veracity of a different, but equally disputed account (79). This minute detailing of various discovery narratives often disguises, moreover, the extent to which his own argument rests on what we might call the pure force of literary-historical assertion: precisely by writing history as a kind of *literary* history, Greenhow can announce that a particular account will be simply "removed from the class of *fictions*," or firmly settled there, through mere attribution of genre (86). Greenhow thus offers for the reader a purportedly neutral kind of *literary historical* work that he performs in the larger service of *historical* work. The hidden payoff becomes clear only in the larger political context of the history, which is bracketed off until the end of the text: questions of genre allow Greenhow subtly to recast both the strongest forms of evidence supporting the British case and the weakest forms supporting what will ultimately evolve as his larger argument for U.S. dominion in "Oregon Country" as a kind of literary history rendered in the service of historical truth: a literary history that allows History finally to triumph over Fiction, and therefore the United States to triumph over Britain.

For example, in turning to what he calls the "most celebrated fiction of the class" of pretended discoveries—those accounts produced "with the view of obtaining emolument or employment"—Greenhow painstakingly details the example of Lorenzo Ferrer de Maldonado, a Portuguese explorer who claimed in the sixteenth century to have found the fabled Strait of Anian, a northwest passage from the Pacific to the Atlantic (79). Ferrer Maldonado's manuscript account of his alleged discovery was titled *Relación del descubrimiento del Estrecho de Anian en 1588*, and was copied, circulated, and ultimately printed soon after his return to Spain, and sometimes deemed accurate up through the eighteenth century. By the nineteenth century the account no longer held up, but Greenhow's lengthy discussion of "Maldonado," as he calls him, provides a prime opportunity for the nineteenth-century translator to perform a kind of distractive gesture, citing extensive, fantastical passages from the Ferrer Maldonado text as a strong foil against which to present his ensuing case for the veracity of yet another disputed account: "*A Note made by Michael Lok, the elder touching the Strait of Sea commonly called* Fretum Anian, *in the South Sea, through the North-west Passage of Meta Incognita*," published in 1625 in Samuel Purchas's *Pilgrims* (86–87). Greenhow notes that the latter account has been "for a long time, considered as less worthy of credit" than that of Ferrer Maldonado—considered, that is, as another "pretended voyage" from the realm of fiction (86). The State Department historian avers, however, that "more recent examinations from that part of the world"—the Pacific

Northwest—suggest otherwise. He concedes that the account related by Lok "is certainly erroneous as regards the principle circumstance related"—that a "North-west Passage" was discovered (86). But at the end of his discussion of Lok's account and its central figure—a Greek sailor employed by the Spanish, "called, commonly, Juan de Fuca, but named, properly, Apostolos Valerianos"—Greenhow asserts again that "more recent examinations in [the Northwest] quarter have, however, served to establish a strong presumption in favor of its authenticity and general correctness, so far as the supposed narrator could himself have known" (87–88). In other words, Greenhow argues, Juan de Fuca told the truth about finding a strait on the northwest coast of North America; his account may thus be placed in the class of authentic but inadvertently "erroneous" narratives: Fuca, that is, is a "supposed narrator" but he is not an unreliable one, for he "could [not] himself have known" that the strait he found was not a northwest passage connecting the Pacific and Atlantic (88). As before, moreover, Greenhow cites no sources for these "recent examinations" demonstrating Fuca's "authenticity"; his argument rests instead on straightforward assertion: and thus he maintains that Fuca's account "has been removed from the class of *fictions*."[17]

But the seemingly neutral question of genre, as Greenhow presents it, holds a subtext concerning foreign relations that the translator obviously knows but slyly never mentions. To argue for the veracity of Fuca's account, as Greenhow does, is to deny the priority of the English discovery, by the British captain John Mears, in 1788, of the body of water separating Vancouver and Washington and known today as Juan de Fuca's Strait—and "first discovery," as we shall see below, was the fundamental principle that guided nineteenth-century U.S. policy on the acquisition and disposition of disputed territory in supposed accordance with international law. If Fuca's account is "removed from the class of fictions," it turns out, then the right of first discovery goes to Spain (for whom Fuca sailed) rather than England; and Spain had, by the time Greenhow was producing his history in the early 1840s, long ago ceded Florida and any northwestern land claims to the United States under the Treaty of Adams-Onís. The hidden payoff of Greenhow's ostensibly neutral literary historical work, in other words, becomes clear in this context: with Fuca securely designated as the first discoverer of the northwestern strait, England lost one crucial piece of its potential case for claims to the land, thus clearing the way for legitimate U.S. possession of the disputed Northwest Territory.

Edgar Allan Poe and the Unsettling Narrative of *Julius Rodman*

Greenhow's nimble shuttling between literature and history, the fictional and the authentic, would ultimately trip him up, however, when he encountered an authorial persona—a strange, Fontaneda-like writer armed with digressive tactics worthy of El Inca Garcilaso de la Vega—who was determined to unsettle his scholarly agenda to establish U.S. priority in Oregon Country. The precise circumstances of this encounter are unknown, but the evidence of its occurrence can be found in a fascinating implosion in Greenhow's chapter on the earliest overland claims to the Northwest.[18] The U.S. case for priority is not strong at this juncture of Greenhow's argument, and the translator is at pains to contain the threat presented by the 1792 expedition of Alexander Mackenzie, a Scotsman working in the service of the North West Company, who crossed the Rocky Mountains and then reached the Pacific in 1793, thereby potentially establishing first discovery for Great Britain. Greenhow records the information about this expedition succinctly, without dwelling on details that would prolong the discussion, as he often does in cases where he proposes to move a narrative to or from the "class of fictions"—a manipulation that would be highly unfeasible in the case of Mackenzie's much celebrated and publicized journeys. Just after discussing Mackenzie, however, Greenhow draws the reader's attention to a new source, one whose genre he does not specify, describing it only as a "journal . . . recently discovered in Virginia, and now in the course of publication in a periodical magazine at Philadelphia."[19] "It is proper to notice here," Greenhow writes in the *Memoir*, "an account of an expedition across the American continent, made between 1791 and 1794 . . . under the direction of Julius Rodman" (140).

The text to which Greenhow is referring is, of course, Poe's *Journal of Julius Rodman*. This bizarre piece of writing is the only other Poe work besides *The Narrative of Arthur Gordon Pym* that has been considered a novel, though of course genre proves difficult to determine with certainty given that *Rodman* was never completed. Like *Pym*, *Rodman* presents itself to readers as a nonfictional travel narrative: "Being an Account of the First Passage Across the Rocky Mountains of North America ever Achieved By Civilized Man" (44). And like the first chapters of *Pym*, which initially appeared in the 1837 run of *Southern Literary Messenger*, *Rodman* too emerged in serial publication—as Greenhow notes in the careful citation in his *Memoir*: "Burton's Magazine and American Monthly Review, edited by William E. Burton and Edgar A. Poe. Mr. Rodman's journal is commenced in the number for January, 1840, and is continued in those for the next following months" (140). But whereas the first chapters of *Pym* appeared in the *Messenger* under Poe's own name—and only in its final, novel form did the text announce itself as a "pretended fiction," with "the name of Mr. Poe affixed to the articles" "in order that it might certainly be regarded as fiction" (1008)—*Rodman* dispenses with the *mise-en-abîme* of novel-as-nonfiction-disguised-as-fiction and relies instead on the venerable and far simpler literary device of the found manuscript. It appears in *Burton's Magazine* framed by the ostensible voice of its editor, signed only as "G. M." (44). Moreover, while Pym was received in its own time largely as a bad literary hoax—one early reviewer complained of its "impudent attempt at humbugging the public"—*The Journal of Julius Rodman* has maintained a more favorable reputation, if not in aesthetic terms than as a more convincing literary ruse. And the prime evidence supporting this judgment of *Rodman*'s persuasiveness has always been its inclusion in Greenhow's official scholarly report regarding U.S. claims to the Oregon territory.

Greenhow's inclusion of this "recently discovered" manuscript in his *Memoir*—a document that was eventually submitted to the Senate and entered into the Senate record—would constitute the basis for a winking footnote in the annals of Poe reception history. As the eminent Poe scholar David K. Jackson put it in a 1974 note in *Poe Studies*, the strange incident of *Julius Rodman*'s entrance into the Senate record "attests to Poe's contemporary success in imparting verisimilitude to his fictional narrative" (47). "If Poe saw Greenhow's account," Jackson contended hypothetically, "he must have been highly amused" (47). Furthermore, Jackson observed, because Greenhow had earlier contributed articles to the *Southern Literary Messenger* during the period of Poe's editorial work there, he "must have either met or corresponded with Poe" (47). Yet as the title of the note suggests ("A Poe Hoax Comes Before the U.S. Senate"), Jackson believed the "hoax" to be Poe's alone; Greenhow's participation in the hoax was entirely "unintentional," as Jackson saw it. Poe's literary creation of an ingenious "verisimilitude," in Jackson's view, led to "Robert Greenhow's acceptance of 'Julius Rodman' as a factual and not a fictional account of a journey of exploration" (47). Greenhow's own words about the Rodman account support the scholarly persona of painstaking neutrality and careful moderation that the rest of his *Memoir* cultivates. "From what has been published" thus far in *Burton's Magazine*, Greenhow cautioned, "it is impossible to form a definitive opinion as to the degree of credit which is due to the narrative, or as to the value of the statements, if they are true; and all that can be here said in addition is, that nothing as yet appears either in the journal or relating to it, calculated to excite suspicions with regard to its authenticity" (141).

Employing a full arsenal of rhetorical strategies of qualification for this commentary on Rodman's "statements"—"if they are true"—Greenhow offers a series of abnegations couched as affirmative propositions: "It is impossible to form"; "Nothing as yet appears." But his careful empiricist acknowledgement of the limits that facticity places on utterability—or "what can be here said"—hardly constitutes an endless deferral of the "definitive." Rather, Greenhow refuses quite specifically to enter into a particular economy of knowledge—that is, to place a wager on or to invest in either the "degree of credit . . . due" or the gross "value" of Rodman's account. He attempts instead to rig the market from the outside, without risking any of his own scholarly capital, via something like a *rumor* of the text's "authenticity"—a vague assertion that there is nothing "either in the journal or relating to it, calculated to excite suspicions."

But the *Journal of Julius Rodman* was, as every Poe scholar knows, indeed "calculated to excite suspicions"—and not merely in the overblown racialist sensationalism attending its story of "the first white Man that ever crossed the Western Wilderness," or in the parodic extremes to which it brings the ideology of the sublime.[20] It was also "calculated to excite suspicions" through its blatant textual lifting from authentic accounts of expeditions—including that of Alexander Mackenzie—all of which Greenhow himself had read and even cited in his own *Memoir*. In other words, Greenhow *had to have known* that the Rodman account belonged to "the class of fictions," and yet he entered it into his *Memoir* as a text that might well hold up in a test of "its authenticity." And though Greenhow acknowledges that the published part of the account "relates only to the voyage up the Mississippi"—that "no idea is communicated" of the journey beyond this now domestic geography—he also directs readers' attention to the "editor" of the journal and to its official "Introduction": "where it is stated that they traversed the region 'west of the Rocky Mountains, and north of the 60th parallel, which is still marked upon our maps as unexplored, and which, until this day, has been always so considered'" (141). Greenhow in effect constructs a definitive reading of the text, mediated through his own scholarly authority in citing from this authoritative reader—one who ostensibly knows the end of the story and can predict the successful outcome of the exploration "north of the 60th parallel," into virgin land.

The historiographical motive for Greenhow's maneuver seems initially odd given that Poe's obvious fiction actually undermines the case for U.S. priority in exploring the west by insisting almost comically in the "Introduction" that the "credit" for "the *first* passage across the Rocky Mountains . . . should never have been given" to the far more officially national endeavor of Lewis and Clark (47). But the need for Poe's text becomes quite clear by the end of Greenhow's memoir, in his summation of the British case for sovereignty in the Northwest: "the exploration . . . of Lewis and Clark," argue the British, "could not be cited by the United States as strengthening and confirming their claim to that territory, because, '*if not before, at least in the same and subsequent years*, the British Northwest Company had, by means of their agent Mr. Thompson, already established their posts on the head-waters or main branch of the Columbia'" (153). The Lewis and Clark expedition, in other words, was undermined by the British as too belated to count in favor of a U.S. claim on the Northwest; Greenhow thus stood in danger of losing the primary building block of his argument. The fictional Rodman journey, on the other hand, predated not only Lewis and Clark and "Mr. [David] Thompson," the British explorer, but also the even earlier Mackenzie: as Poe's "Introduction" states, "Mackenzie succeeded in [crossing the Rockies] in the year 1793," but "Mr. Rodman was the first who overcame those gigantic barriers; crossing them as he did in 1792" (47). Citing from Poe, in other words, Greenhow inserted crucial evidence of U.S. priority in "Oregon Country" into the official Senate record and, by extension, the larger historical record.

No one knows what Poe intended to do with his unfinished *Journal of Julius Rodman* before he abandoned and stopped acknowledging it. But Greenhow's motivations are, to my mind, transparent: he was testing the historiographical waters to see if Poe's narrative—a narrative he must have known was fabricated and, in places, plagiarized—could survive in U.S. history as fact. It must be emphasized again that Greenhow swam against the romantic current of his moment in doing so: he was most decidedly not arguing, as would many of his peers, for the higher "Historical Truth" made available by literature. Quite the opposite: Greenhow was taking advantage of a long-standing and still enduring disciplinary antagonism between history and literature— and doing so under cover of the specifically Romantic-inflected and derided figure of the "modern skeptic"—to alter the historical record in a profoundly duplicitous way. He was also protecting his reputation as a distinguished scholar by purporting to reserve final judgment on the Poe text's authenticity even as he also encouraged this judgment: indeed, in Greenhow's index, Poe's narrative gets its own, unqualified entry: "Rodman's journey across the continent from the Missouri to the Pacific" (227).

But what was Poe's role in this strange episode? The timing of his publication of the first installment of *Rodman* strongly suggests that Poe—in the midst of financial crisis, on the brink of being fired yet again—made a deal of some kind to write *Rodman* to meet the very demand for which Greenhow used it. It seems more than coincidental that in the very month before Greenhow submitted his memoir before the Senate's Select Committee on the Oregon Territory, Poe happened to publish a pseudo-travel account of a westerly expedition that ostensibly preceded the British Mackenzie expedition, as the overblown subtitle to the *Journal of Julius Rodman* announces: "Being an account of the *First* Passage Across the Rocky Mountains . . ." The fictional "editors" of Rodman's *Journal* are indeed suspiciously to the point, as we have seen, when they insist that the "credit" for "the *first* passage across the Rocky Mountains . . . should never have been given to Lewis and Clark." Poe appears almost to wink at the fact that he is publishing the Rodman *Journal* just in the nick of time to make it into Greenhow's memoir to the U.S. Senate—much in the same manner as our fictional Rodman makes it across the Rockies just in the nick of time to beat the British Mackenzie to it.

It is certainly possible, of course, that Poe was writing his serialized account partly in hopes of winning the Burton's contributor's contest (which as assistant editor he was ineligible to enter under his own name). But he was also likely writing this particular northwestern account on a commission from Greenhow or someone else involved in the territorial Oregon dispute. Otherwise, it becomes hard to explain why, if Greenhow didn't believe that he had a deal of some kind with the author of *Rodman*, he would take a chance on using something that he had to have known was if not falsification then fiction, given that its true author might reveal himself at any time. Believing that the author had a vested economic interest in remaining quiet is the only circumstance, to my mind, that adequately explains Greenhow's decision to try to pass off as factual an account so obviously "calculated to excite suspicions." For in producing a text precisely so calculated, Poe in effect reneged on whatever deal he made: that is, he double-crossed Greenhow and by extension the State Department by producing an account that not only flaunted its own fictionality and lack of authenticity on every page but also satirized the very context of imperial dispute in which it may have been commissioned to intervene.

In other words, like Fontaneda (discussed in Chapter 4), Poe generates within the text of *Rodman* a narrative of unsettlement, a narrative ostensibly supporting but in fact devised to hinder settlement, in this case the U.S. claim to the Northwest. As in Fontaneda's account, the crux of Poe's *Rodman* lies in the discrepancies between the text's articulated values and its silent knowledge of its own potential effects. Indeed, examined in the context of Greenhow's larger body of work, *The Journal of Julius Rodman* reveals an interplay between Rodman's (often plagiarized) voice and the editorial voice that undercuts at every turn the manuscript narrative it purports to present with such gravity and momentousness. Poe's fictional editor continually delights in highlighting the coerciveness of his own particular narrative contract—"We feel sure that all our readers will unite with us," that "our readers will think with us"—while also constantly signposting his own "omissions" and "abridgement" and the "small liberties" that he has taken with the original manuscript. The discovery of the journal similarly calls into doubt the authenticity of the manuscript itself: Rodman supposedly wrote his journal many years after the fact from an outline diary at the request of the scientist Andre Michau, the same French botanist whom Jefferson tried to commission to make a westward exploration. But as the editor notes, the manuscript never reached its intended reader, and while it was "always supposed to have been lost on the road by the young man to whom it was entrusted for delivery," Rodman's journal has not been lost but rather "procured from the messenger [and] concealed," and seemingly by Rodman himself, for it is "discovered years later by his family, after his death, in a secret drawer." So the culpability lies not with the messenger but with the author, who has purloined his own missive: as so often with Poe, an allegory of writing, of textual indeterminacy, frames Rodman's journal from the beginning.

More broadly, then, the editorial voice framing Rodman's account reads like a personal taunting of Greenhow at every turn, undercutting the authenticity and therefore the potential usefulness of Rodman's alleged claim to have crossed the Rockies before any "civilized man." The editorial narrator also advertises the "romantic fervor" of Rodman's account, which he opposes to the "lukewarm and statistical air which pervades most records of the kind"—an unflattering description that perfectly encapsulates not only his own scholarly voice but Greenhow's. The editor goes out of his way to expose the disingenuousness of the objective neutrality that such tepid, numerically laden prose is meant to convey. The editor claims, for example, that the chief attribute of the journal is its romantic virtue: Rodman's "burning love of Nature, the rapture at his heart" as he "stalked through that immense and often terrible wilderness." But these romantic platitudes are revealed as a transparent pretext in the next lines: in an abrupt shift, the editor demands— suddenly all business—that the reader "will turn to a map of North America . . . to follow us in our observations." What follows is a fastidiously dry listing of latitudes, longitudes, parallels, meridians, dates, and explorer names as the editor plods doggedly through the competitive history of European and Anglo-American expeditions in the Northwest—a historical survey tinged with a faint ridiculousness by the editor's new phrasing for his category: the "earliest travels of any extent made in North America by white people." The shift from the subtitular phrase "civilized man" to "white people" is a subtle one, marking a sort of logical stutter along the trajectory from early modern conquest to nineteenth-century U.S. expansionism, and shadowing the whole editorial frame with the oxymoron of imperial "discovery," with the obvious but occluded priority of Native peoples.

More important, however, Poe's fictionalized editor goes out of his way to put holes in the case for U.S. over European priority in the Northwest by undermining the other American contenders for that title as well as the writings that documented their efforts: Thomas Jefferson is described as "erroneous" in calling John Ledyard the first to attempt northwestern exploration, while Washington Irving "appears to be mistaken" in naming Jonathan Carver's trip as the first overland attempt. Both are supplanted in the editor's account by non-American figures, particularly those British figures who prove pesky stumbling blocks in Greenhow's legal argument for U.S. priority. And Greenhow must have been furious to discover Poe's hilarious description of Rodman's explorer party, which we only see when the editor finally gets around to presenting the Rodman account itself. For while Greenhow's memoir to the Senate committee promises an account about "an expedition . . . by a party of citizens of the United States, under the direction of Julius Rodman" (140), Poe's Rodman turns out to be an Englishman by birth, and his motley group includes fourteen explorers, six of whom the account defines as "Canadians," five as hailing from the "State" of Kentucky, two as "Virginians," and one as "a negro belonging to" one of the Canadians (80–81). Greenhow is thus left in the precarious and indeed foolish position of having to rewrite the group under the patently false sign of U.S. nationalism.

Poe never admitted in print to authoring Rodman, except circuitously so in one famous letter that he wrote to Burton, the main editor of *Burton's*

Gentleman's Magazine, after Burton had written to Poe apparently complaining that Poe owed him $100 and had also been sending out a prospectus for a new, competitor Philadelphia journal. But Burton also apparently accuses Poe in the letter of something that Poe alludes to but doesn't name specifically. "You do me gross injustice," Poe tells Burton: "you have wrought yourself into a passion with me on account of some imaginary wrong . . . As I live, I am utterly unable to say . . . what true grounds of complaint you have against me . . . I cannot permit myself to suppose that you would say to me in cool blood what you said in your letter of yesterday." At the end of the letter, though, Poe refers, as so often, to his financial crisis and adds, "I can give you no definitive answer (respecting the continuation [of] Rodman's Journal) until I hear from you again. The charge of $100 I shall not admit for an instant. If you persist in it our intercourse is at an end, and I shall refer you to an attorney. But I cannot bring myself to believe that you will. We can each adopt our own measures. . . ."[21]

Whatever accusation Burton had leveled at Poe in his letter, Poe's warning here rings distinctly of blackmail, suggesting that the disclosure of wrongdoing would be detrimental to Burton's interests as well—and perhaps to the reputation of Burton's journal, which had published *Julius Rodman*. The following year finds Poe working for new editors and writing frantic letters to the Washington writer and government bureaucrat Frederick William Thomas, asking him to entreat various congressmen for a job. Desperate to find a way to insinuate himself into a political appointment, Poe writes, "I mention in particular the Secretary of War, because I have been to W. Point, and this may stand me in some stead. I would be glad to get almost any appointment . . . so that I have *something* independent of letters for a subsistence."[22] Perhaps what we see in *Rodman*, then, is Poe's attempt at a different kind of government assignment, not from the Secretary of War but from the third highest-ranking employee of the State Department, Robert Greenhow. Poe was fast approaching what Gerald Kennedy has called the "American turn" in his fictions when he wrote *Rodman*.[23] Perhaps in this early failed attempt to use letters precisely to "have *something* independent of letters," that inestimable combination of literariness and rage that characterizes so much of his work took him over—and with such force that he double-crossed the State Department and, like Rodman, effectively purloined his own promised account from its intended receiver.

Don Luis and the Doctrine of Discovery

In the spring of 1848, eight years after Poe's *Rodman* slyly unsettled the territorial agenda of Greenhow's *Memoir*—and after the "Oregon Question" had finally been settled in a compromise with Britain—the State Department translator was finishing up another scholarly project, seemingly unrelated to the urgent political matters of the day. In the intervening years another territorial dispute—this time involving Texas and the Southwest—had exploded into a U.S. war with Mexico. Once again, Greenhow's expertise as a translator played a shadowy, little-documented role in the international crisis. In 1837, Greenhow had traveled to Mexico at the behest of President Van Buren on a secret intelligence-gathering mission, during which he met with the Mexican president and foreign minister and outlined the U.S. position regarding the newly independent Texas as well as a number of claims by American citizens against the Mexican government.[24] When tensions escalated over U.S. interest in acquiring Texas as well as New Mexico and California, Greenhow was at the center of the diplomatic effort to resolve the impending crisis until 1846, when he was accused by Secretary of State James Buchanan of mistranslating correspondence from the foreign minister of Mexico. Greenhow blamed the translational errors on his colleague Nicholas Trist, the chief clerk at the State Department, whom he accused of trying to sabotage him by altering the original translation. Whether the mistranslation was Greenhow's or Trist's, and whether intentional or careless, is unclear. But there was bad blood and clear rivalry between these two employees of the State Department who spoke and read Spanish—and it was Trist who was famously chosen for the secret diplomatic mission to Mexico that resulted in the Treaty of Guadalupe Hidalgo. Greenhow apparently sank, once again, into a nervous depression during this period—which is why historians have assumed that his turn to antiquarianism in the spring of 1848 was to escape the stresses of contemporary politics during the Mexican War.[25]

A superficial glance at his 1848 scholarly endeavor would seem to confirm this notion. If Greenhow had written his 1840 memoir specifically for the U.S. Senate and the 26th *Congressional Record*, he produced this later piece of work for a very different venue: the Virginia Historical and Philosophical Society, an antiquarian organization founded in 1831.[26] Modeled on the New York Historical Society and the American Antiquarian Society of Massachusetts, the Virginia Historical and Philosophical Society drew on private funds to carry out its designated mission to preserve books, manuscripts, historic documents, and natural history specimens relating to the state and its history. The antiquarian mission of this society was, as Jonathan P. Cushing put it in his 1833 address (citing the society's constitution), "to procure and preserve whatever relates to the natural, civil, and literary history of this state" (13). Its stated goal of filling the "library [with] all the rare and valuable materials, for a full and correct exposition of the physical resources, and the intellectual power and moral worth of the sons of Virginia" and the "cabinet and museum [with] all those specimens in geology, mineralogy, zoology, and botany, which are necessary to illustrate our natural history," and "to brighten the glory of the commonwealth," seems at first far removed from the legalistic world of international affairs overseen by the U.S. Department of State where Greenhow was still employed, and for which he had produced his work on "Oregon Country."[27]

Curiously, however, Greenhow's generic designation for the piece he submitted to the society was the same: he titled it *Memoir on the First Discovery of the Chesapeake Bay* and sent it off that May to Richmond.[28] The information outlined in the memoir had been, he said, "obtained in the course of researches among the Old Spanish Chroniclers of the New World"—"works [that] have been most lamentably neglected by our historians; few of whom have, indeed, possessed a knowledge of the language in which they are written, sufficient for such investigations."[29] To Greenhow, this was no mere matter of asserting his historiographical and linguistic prowess, however: the Spanish chronicles contain "innumerable . . . facts," "unnoticed, though recorded in full in those venerable volumes"—facts "relating to the countries now included, as well as to those about to be included, within the limits of our republic" (481). Clearly referring in the latter clause to the imminent U.S. territories ceded by Mexico in the Treaty of Guadalupe Hidalgo, signed three months earlier and then ratified by the U.S. Senate in March, Greenhow evokes the larger political context for the strange disclosures presented in his accompanying memoir on the Spanish "discovery" of the Chesapeake Bay.

Greenhow avowedly undertook the memoir "with the hope that the Society may succeed . . . in rescuing from destruction the historical monuments and records of our Ancient Dominion, and in bringing to light those which lie in obscurity" (482). Presenting himself as a scrupulous modern historian, sifting through the "dull and lumbering archive" and determined to excavate lost records of the Virginian past, Greenhow begins with a dramatic flourish by dismantling a foundational received truth of Old Dominion history: "The Bay of Chesapeake is usually supposed to have been first seen, and entered by the English . . . who founded the earliest European settlement on its waters in 1607 . . . Accordingly in all our histories, the discovery of the Chesapeake is attributed to the English" (483–84). But "there is evidence . . . apparently incontrovertible," Greenhow admonishes, "that the Chesapeake was known to the Spaniards, and that an expedition had been made by them for the occupation of its coasts, at least twenty years before any attempt of the English to establish themselves in any part of the American continent" (485).

Greenhow dutifully cites his source for this evidence, but only by its Spanish title—*Ensayo cronológico para la historia general de la Florida* or "Chronological Essay on the General History of Florida"—which he does not translate for the benefit of monolingual readers. Nor does he provide any context for this massive, early eighteenth-century history of the North American continent, known as La Florida among sixteenth- and seventeenth-century

Spaniards ever since its discovery by Juan Ponce de León. Yet the conceptual framework within which the *Ensayo cronológico* was produced in 1723 was pointedly relevant to Greenhow's political moment, and would have been immediately recognizable to the U.S. translator, for its Spanish author, Andrés González de Barcia Carballido y Zúñiga, was explicit about his purposes in the introduction: to "restore . . . to the Spanish what is justly theirs, giving clear and distinct notice of the peoples, capes, rivers, ports, and bays that encircle their continent" of La Florida.[30] Like Greenhow, in other words, Barcia self-consciously merged scholarly interests with those of the state; he was an influential man of the court, a member of the Royal Council and magistrate of the Council of Castile and the Council of War as well as a landmark figure in early Enlightenment Spanish historiography.[31] As a founding member of the Spanish Academy, Barcia set out to create what Jonathan Carlyon has called "the first comprehensive Spanish American colonial library" by collecting, editing, annotating, and synthesizing a compilation of critical editions of early modern works relating to the Spanish Americas.[32] The project represented a massive exercise in relegitimating Spanish historiography, one that would restore the intellectual authority of Spanish letters in the wake of the Black Legend's denial of modernity to the Spanish-speaking world and its assault on hispanophone accounts of the Americas. For this historiographical assault was inextricably tied, as Barcia made clear, to the shifting of imperial power from Spain to England—and in Greenhow's moment, of course, to the United States.

Thus, in the particular case of the *Ensayo cronológico,* Barcia and the authenticating editors of his text presented the 1723 history of Florida as a response to the specific problem of "*Autores Estrangeros*" ('foreign authors'), who were, they charged, "envious of the glories of Spain" and "ambitious for the grandeur and honor" of Spanish New World discovery. These authors, they claimed, wanted "to have the glory of others who were the first Conquistadors"—and therefore sought "to obscure": they "introduced into the historical record . . . many confusions," relating to "the demarcations of Florida," and the "proper names" of places. Barcia's history, therefore, would *textually* return to its rightful owners, via meticulous historicization, what had been robbed by foreign authors who "seek only to steal, along with the land, the fame of those whom they should venerate." Moreover, Barcia sought to expose historiographical mendacity in its particular relation to unlawful occupation in the realm of international law: "the main guile of this foreign avarice, this tyrannical greed," he maintained, "consists of [foreign authors'] improbable usurpations, detailing false proofs that they represent as just conquests." History not only supported but in some cases achieved conquest, Barcia explained, by "mak[ing] the settlements of the Spaniards appear as the habitations of foreigners"—easily establishing "with the pen what so many others have failed to do with the sword." But if conquest could be accomplished by discursive means when military ones failed, it was foreign cartography in particular that posed the worst threat:

> Until now, geographical maps held value by juridical law, but already . . . these maps are worth nothing, except to know the outline of the Indies. Nor is it only Florida that is confused, or obfuscated, by different names, so that the map is not proof of ownership. This is the capital deception for unjustly establishing ownership and legal appurtenance: to change the names of oceans, rivers, bays, capes, ports, provinces, in order to inhabit empty roads and populate wilderness.

The prefatory material to the *Ensayo cronológico* thus justifies the writing and publication of Barcia's history by describing Spain's falling fortunes in the New World as a kind of disciplinary crisis, one in which discursive productions of geography and cartography have lost their legal standing and thus most of their value. This clears a new functional space, however, for Barcia the historian, who will undermine the fraudulent record created by "foreign authors" through a kind of self-consciously interdisciplinary intervention: transforming Spanish cartography into an overarching, chronological historical narrative that authenticates itself with its own set of proofs and corroboration in the form of citations from other accounts. Ultimately, then, Barcia's work is a concerted effort, in the face of what he calls "published lies," to stabilize original Spanish land claims via the symbolic possession of geographical naming in a time of shifting imperial boundaries—a moment very like Greenhow's own at the end of the U.S.-Mexican War.

When Greenhow came across Barcia's text—whether he found it himself or whether it was brought to his attention by another interested party—he was thus facing a profoundly authoritative scholar who had created an oppositional discourse of Spanish historical and territorial priority in the New World that registered doubly: in its original, early eighteenth-century moment when Spain's American fortunes, which had fallen into decline, were increasingly threatened by English and other European powers; and in Greenhow's mid-nineteenth-century moment, barely two decades after Spain's loss of colonial Mexico had paved the way for a U.S. invasion, when the question of rightful territorial possession was very much in dispute.[33] One might even say that Barcia's account of the Spanish "discovery of the Chesapeake" and the story of Ajacán could not have emerged in the U.S. context at a more inopportune time. Greenhow would surely have known this, raising the question of why he would publish his 1848 *Memoir*, derived from Barcia's text, in the first place. But Greenhow also certainly knew that in an era of resurgent interest in Spanish accounts of the New World—the era of Irving, Prescott, and Simms, to name a few of the literary figures then delving in the archives—the contents of Barcia's *Ensayo cronológico* would eventually make their way into the Anglophone public sphere—unless, that is, Greenhow somehow discouraged a reading of the text and contained its unsettling import. His first step was to transform Barcia's oppositional historicism into mere antiquarianism—a maneuver which was itself, of course, an act of historiographical warfare.[34]

Greenhow introduces Barcia by noting that the "name . . . given on the title page of the work," "Gabriel de Cardenas Z. Cano," "is fictitious, being an anagram of that of its real author, Andrés González de Barcia" (486). As if word games in Spanish were not intimidating enough to brush off future Anglophone readers, Greenhow goes out of his way to discourage future research into Barcia's history given its "extreme minuteness on all points, with little regard to their importance" which "render [. . .] the book intolerable to the general reader" as a work of frustratingly antiquary limitations (486). Accordingly, Greenhow offers his own translative services for nineteenth-century U.S. historians in order to narrate the sixteenth-century story of the Spanish in the Chesapeake Bay. As Greenhow tells it, the story begins in good Black Legend style with "the ruthless Adelantado of Florida, Pedro Menendez" [sic], who—competing with England—"ordered surveys to be made of the countries farther north" because he "foresaw the absolute necessity of extending the dominion of Spain" (486–87). Citing here from Barcia, Greenhow presents the project of settling the future Virginia:

> . . . in the summer of 1566, '[Menendez] dispatched . . . a captain with thirty soldiers and two monks . . . to the Bay of Santa Maria . . . to settle in that region, and to convert its inhabitants to Christianity. [But] the captain . . . was overcome by his crew . . . So they sailed . . . for Seville, abusing the King and the Adelantado for attempting to settle in that country, of which they spread the worst accounts, though none of them had seen it.' Thus it appears that the Chesapeake . . . was so well known to the Spaniards in 1566, that an expedition was made for . . . taking possession of the surrounding country. We do not learn that the attempt was repeated. (487–88)

For Greenhow, of course, the crucial issue in citing from Barcia is settlement: Menéndez's dispatch of the monks and soldiers "to settle in that region" and their subsequent "abusing [of] the King and the Adelantado for attempting to settle in that country." Not only do the soldiers' negative accounts of the country constitute legal falsehoods, according to Barcia's account, but the very assertion of their fraudulence, based on the premise that "none of them had seen it," undermined any territorial rights potentially deriving from the doctrine of first discovery. As Greenhow explains, in a curious phrasing that evokes his hyper-qualified commentary on the Rodman account: "We do not learn that the attempt was repeated."

Greenhow concludes his memoir on an oddly deflating note: "To the utilitarian the question will appear of no importance," he concedes, "nor can any direct advantage be derived from speculations as to the change which might have been made . . . had the Spanish expedition . . . proved successful"

(490–91). Yet in the next sentence, Greenhow employs this very hypothetical to telegraph a dramatic counterfactual history in which the English would not have settled in Virginia because "James the Second of England, would not have readily granted a commission to his subjects to encroach upon territories held" by the Spanish (491). These are the contingencies of history, Greenhow seems to suggest; in fact, it is precisely the different possible outcome of this colonial moment that underscores the meaning of Greenhow's Anglo-Saxonist present. The "importance" of Greenhow's memoir, then, lies not, contrary to its title, in its establishment of the "First Discovery of the Chesapeake Bay [by the Spanish]"—but in its fully documented, official scholarly pronouncement of a lack of Spanish settlement on the Chesapeake in 1566, or at any subsequent date. As Greenhow puts it, "This is all that Barcia says of the bay of Santa Maria; and nothing has been found with regard to it elsewhere . . . No allusion to such a bay is made in any account of any voyage . . . by any other Spanish historian except Barcia" (489–90). In this sense, in his studies of Spanish colonial history, Barcia has offered what Greenhow terms a "good service in the cause of American history" (486).

But if any nineteenth-century readers had actually opened the eighteenth-century Spanish source that Greenhow warned was not just hard-going but "intolerable," they would have seen immediately that Greenhow's own translative contribution to "the cause of American history" hinged on a blatant suppression. For Barcia noted very clearly there that the 1566 Spanish attempt to settle in the future Virginia was of course "repeated," specifically in the year 1570—well before the ill-fated Roanoke voyages, and decades before Jamestown—and this time it resulted in successful arrival and settlement on New World soil. In the "Year 1570," Barcia wrote, a group of Spanish Jesuits, under the direction of "Father Vice Provincial Juan Baptista de Segura . . . tried a method of entering in the Province of Ajacán. . . . They walked together until they entered the Province of Ajacán, bearing the hardships of the journey, and the hunger. . . . in the hope of converting many people to the office of the Church" (Año M.D. LXX). Barcia's history records not only the arduous journey by land, moreover, but the later interactions with the indigenous, the high hopes of the missionaries, their faith in their Native translator, and ultimately, their demise at the behest of Don Luis. That there *was* a settlement made by the Spanish in 1570 is never in question. Thus, when Greenhow insisted in his memoir that the failed 1566 voyage to Virginia is "all that Barcia says of the bay of Santa Maria; and nothing has been found with regard to it elsewhere," he was committing a blatant act of scholarly suppression, one entered into the official U.S. historical record over a century after the publication of Barcia's history.

Here again Barcia's volume speaks presciently to the mid-nineteenth century in which Greenhow was machinating: "Already foreigners are frequenting our Indies," complains Barcia's second prefatory statement, "and

they treat the Spanish as Indians" ('*y tratan a los españoles como a indios*').
Thus, a legal category of eighteenth-century Spanish colonial discourse fore-
tells a racial categorization of nineteenth-century U.S. Anglo-Saxonism: as
Greenhow's close family friend, John C. Calhoun famously put it: "Are we
to associate with ourselves as equals, companions, and fellow citizens the
Indians and mixed races of Mexico? I would consider such associations as
degrading to ourselves and fatal to our institutions."[35] Unlike Calhoun,
Greenhow appears to have supported annexation and the all-Mexico movement, which begrudged Trist for securing only *part* of Mexico's territory for
U.S. acquisition. (He also supported the annexation of Cuba, to the point of
seeking out advice for Narciso López, who met with Greenhow's wife before
undertaking the first of his three filibustering expeditions.) Soon after the
war, President Taylor appointed Greenhow as a special agent in Mexico and
then in California to put his scholarly and linguistic skills toward researching
the flood of competing land claims made in the recently acquired territories.[36]

In writing about the so-called "First Discovery" of the Chesapeake, then,
Greenhow was indeed contributing his "services to the cause of American
History." On the one hand, he produced an account of Spanish failure that
would bolster a predictably triumphant version of Anglo-American historical success. But even as he outlined the sensational hypothetical possibility
of a Spanish Virginia, Greenhow was in a sense also closing up legal loopholes—willfully erasing the historical evidence of a Spanish settlement, however temporary, that preceded the English in Virginia. The Spanish may have
had "First Discovery" of the Chesapeake, but Greenhow's memoir was determined to show that Spain could not ever claim "First Discovery" of Virginia
itself. Greenhow knew the importance of discovery well, of course, from his
firsthand experience in supporting the U.S. case during the dispute with
Great Britain over "Oregon Country"; like the text of *Julius Rodman*, every
facet of his case for U.S. rights to the Pacific Northwest was based in some
way on this early modern premise, which had governed the imperial contest
of European powers in the New World. In this sense, it was perhaps inevitable
that Greenhow would understand a Spanish discovery of Virginia as a veritable threat to national security: a catastrophic shard of the colonial past that
had to be smoothed into neutrality, an explosive historical narrative that had
to be hastily revised.

As Greenhow knew very well, the principle of first discovery had been
written into federal law by the 1823 Supreme Court case *Johnson v. M'Intosh*.
The question introduced to the court in that landmark case concerned the
rights of individuals to buy land from Indian tribes, and in finding that only
the U.S. government could ultimately make such purchases, Chief Justice
John Marshall famously laid the groundwork for the ensuing legal conquest of Indian lands across the rest of the nineteenth century, creating what
amounted to "a new judicial philosophy of indigenous subordination."[37] In

doing so, Marshall turned to the original Virginia letters patent issued by King James I in 1609 and resuscitated the concept of discovery, inventing what Robert J. Miller calls "the primary legal precedent that still controls native affairs and rights" in the United States today.[38] In its Anglo-American form, discovery had waned even during the colonial period when Protestant theorists of international law sought to discredit Spanish claims on the New World by casting Spanish discovery as mere symbolic possession, associated with Catholic popery and the papal donation, and by creating their own ostensibly more substantial justification of New World possession based in the agricultural renovation of the wilderness. Though still hewing to the agricultural principal in part of his argument, Marshall nevertheless restored the *primacy* of discovery by defining it doctrinally as the "original fundamental principle" governing land rights in the United States and in the territories it hoped to acquire: "that discovery gave title to the government by whose subjects, or by whose authority, it was made, against all other European governments, which title might be consummated by possession"—"that discovery gave exclusive title to those who made it."[39]

The doctrine of discovery was thus a principle of international law that had governed European powers during the colonial period but that, as the Marshall court laid it out, extended naturally to the new nation:

> The United States, then, have unequivocally acceded to that great and broad rule [of discovery] by which its civilized inhabitants now hold this country. They hold, and assert in themselves, the title by which it was acquired. They maintain, as all others have maintained, that discovery gave an exclusive right to extinguish the Indian title of occupancy, either by purchase or by conquest.... (587)

As these last two infamous clauses indicate, the doctrine that allowed the nineteenth-century United States to compete with European powers over disputed territories such as "Oregon Country" also became the foundational logic of federal Indian policy denying Native sovereignty over tribal lands. But if the doctrine of discovery was crucial to national expansion on every front, its logic was also particularly fragile during this period. Even those who invoked it to create national policy understood how much it depended on the misrecognition of monarchical rights that had been ostensibly terminated after the American Revolution. As the Marshall Court conceded a decade later in *Worcester v. Georgia* (1832), the early modern doctrine appeared, from a nineteenth-century vantage point, "extravagant and absurd" (544): it was "difficult to comprehend" how "feeble settlements made on the sea coast ... acquired legitimate power by [England] to govern people, or occupy lands from sea to sea"—how discovery "gave the discoverer rights ... which annulled the pre-existing rights of the ancient possessors" (543–44). The Marshall Court wanted it both ways, in other words: wanted to distance the United States from the "extravagant" doctrine of an early modern, imperial Europe that was now a competitor for land, and yet also to claim via that same doctrine an aggressive legal foundation for national U.S. expansion that was specifically based in English rights of "First Discovery" that were inherited by, or defaulted to, the people of the former British colonies.

Under the Marshall ruling, what the United States could do with these former English rights was virtually limitless because possession was ambiguously defined and could be argued in multiple, self-contradictory ways as long as it always rested upon first discovery, or "admitting the prior title of any Christian people who may have made a previous discoverie." Title could be claimed, in other words, not merely in the case of continued occupation or improvement of the arable land but even when "not in actual possession of a foot of the land"—a large loophole that left room for the seizing of Indian lands that could not be claimed by a preponderance of U.S. citizens already settled upon it. The doctrine of discovery was thus indispensable to almost every aspect of the U.S. national appropriation of Native-owned lands throughout the rest of the nineteenth century; as Lindsay G. Robertson puts it, the Marshall Court's decision "gave rise to a massive displacement of persons and the creation of an entire legal regime" when "the American political descendants of the discovering sovereigns overnight became owners of lands that had previously belonged to Native Americans."[40]

But subordinating possession to discovery had other potential effects as well. If the United States had inherited England's rights of first discovery after the American Revolution, then so too had Mexico inherited the rights of Spain in 1821 after its own wars of independence from the former imperial power. Taken to its logical extreme, then, *Johnson v. M'Intosh* could perhaps even be recruited to argue, alongside the evidence of a Spanish colony in Ajacán, that Mexico had—and perhaps still has—a viable claim of first discovery on Virginia. And a Spanish discovery of Virginia so soon after the U.S.-Mexican war might have proven to be, at the very least, a national embarrassment, a public relations disaster.

No one was in a better position than Greenhow to understand that the spring of 1848, when the discourse of Manifest Destiny rose to a peak following the Mexican War and the incorporation of former Mexican lands into the United States was not an ideal time to go muddying the ideological and jurisdictional waters of "First Discovery" by announcing the historical irony of Spanish priority in the future state of Virginia, Mother of Presidents, the very birthplace of the nation. This is not necessarily to suggest that Greenhow understood the story of the Spanish settlement as a source of imminent military danger, threatening a potential nineteenth-century Spanish or Mexican *reconquista* of U.S. land. But the story of Don Luis that Greenhow discovered in Barcia *did* endanger U.S. interests in a powerful, symbolic way at a particular historical moment in the mid-nineteenth century—when arguments

about the divergent historical development of the hemisphere were emerging in full force as a narrative about an antidemocratic, racially amalgam-
ated, and economically deteriorating Spanish America practically begging
for U.S. intervention.[41] And in an important sense, Greenhow's suppression
of the story of Don Luis was critically deployed precisely to ensure the *future*
of uneven development in the hemisphere: to consolidate U.S. legal ascendancy over the indigenous lands of North America, which had dramatically
increased with the U.S. acquisition of more than half of Mexico occurring
at that very moment, and which depended for their continued legality—like
Johnson v. M'Intosh—upon the first discovery of Virginia by the English.

John Gilmary Shea and the "Log Chapel on the Rappahannock"

Greenhow's suppression of the story of the Spanish colony at Ajacán—a settlement that in effect superseded the priority of the English at Roanoke or
Jamestown—might have lasted indefinitely had it not been for the work of the
nineteenth-century scholar John Gilmary Shea, now known as the "preeminent Catholic American historian" of his day.[42] An extraordinary multilingual scholar who not only studied and synthesized a broad range of Spanish
colonial documents relating to the New World but also amassed an exceptional collection of American Indian grammars and vocabularies including
a number of original documents written in Native languages, Shea in fact
encountered Don Luis even before Greenhow did, and transmitted his story
from Spanish to English, from González de Barcia's *Ensayo cronológico* to the
United States Catholic Magazine, in 1846. It is possible that Greenhow—whose
wife was a Catholic, and whose marriage took place in a Catholic church—
saw this contribution to the magazine, in an issue circulated some two years
before he published his own historical piece erasing the presence of a Spanish
settlement in Virginia.[43]

Founded in 1842 and running monthly issues over the next seven years,
the *United States Catholic Magazine* was published during a decade of intense
anti-Catholic resentment and rioting, particularly in Philadelphia and New
York. Its mission was not only to decry such violence but also in large part to
insist upon and carefully record the history of Catholic contributions to the
formation and development of U.S. nationhood—particularly the Church's
historiographic contributions. Addressing the charge of Catholic supersti-
tion and benighted ahistoricism, the journal reminded readers to the contrary that Catholic writings on the New World were far more relevant to
scholarship than Protestant ones: "The zeal of Spanish Catholics in registering useful facts and events, and thus promoting the interests of literature,
presents a remarkable contrast with the barrenness of English Protestant
documents in reference to the history of early times."[44] To see the scholarly

results of this contrast, the magazine argued, one need only compare Prescott and Bancroft; the former had relied upon 8,000 pages of manuscript provided by the Catholic church for his history of the conquest of Mexico, while the latter had faced utter scarcity of materials in writing about early America and resorted to empty pontification to make up for a lack of facts. Spanish-American historiography superseded its U.S. counterpart, in other words, because of the firsthand accounts of Catholics. Moreover, the United States owed what little knowledge of its past it did have not to Protestant but to Catholic historicism: "had not the Jesuit missionaries recorded the result of their observations, we should possess but very few documents concerning the early history of our country." Shea thus closely anticipates the observation made by Jorge Cañizares-Esguerra that "[c]ompared to the vast amounts of scholarship put forth by Spanish American Creoles, British colonial historiography appears negligible and derivative"—an empirical fact that belies the long-held tendency in much U.S. scholarship to view Latin American and Spanish productions of knowledge as implicitly "derivative and second-rate intellectual pursuits."[45]

Shea's piece in *United States Catholic Magazine* is part of a larger series called "Our Martyrs," in which he pays tribute to Catholic missionaries in the North American colonies.[46] As its title suggests, Shea's narrative series casts the deaths of Catholic priests throughout the colonies as a nationalist prolepsis—an account of "our" U.S. Catholic martyrs, or those who "laid down . . . life for the faith in the territories of the United States." Just as the ambiguous syntax of this clause elides the Catholic religion with devotion to the American state and its boundaries ("faith in the territories of the United States"), the articles in the series similarly record Jesuit colonial history as a story of the U.S. past, a story in which the major action is important only insofar as its characters "entered the territory now embraced by the United States" and, preferably, died within it. Don Luis thus appears in Shea's 1846 entry on "John Baptist Segura, and his companions": the story of the deaths of the Jesuits at Ajacán.

Drawing on Barcia's *Ensayo cronológico* and Garcilaso's *La Florida*, Shea begins his account in Havana, where Father Rogel and Brother Villareal have been stationed and have "applied themselves to the study of the languages spoken by the natives" of Florida. Shea's description of Rogel's first encounters in Cuba with the Floridian Indians and their languages presents a fascinating contrast with Rogel's own descriptions of that period in his letters (as discussed in the last chapter). Reading backward from the outcome of the missionary efforts in Florida and Ajacán, the nineteenth-century historian assumes none of the translational transparency that shapes the sixteenth-century version of the story. The first missionaries in Florida fail, Shea notes, because "as they were compelled to employ an interpreter, they preached without much fruit." Nor is the "academy or college for Indian youth" opened by Rogel in Havana more successful; here, the priests fail in their own concerted "efforts to learn the language" of the Floridian Natives because "the Indians continually gave them wrong names for things when asked." Rogel may have opened an Indian school in Havana, in other words, but his Native students are controlling the access to bilingualism supposedly made available to its Spanish instructors.

Into this complex Cuban scene of instruction comes "Don Luis de Velasco, Lord of Vasallos," brought by Menéndez to accompany the new mission to Ajacán. Shea's description of Don Luis follows the basic outline presented by the earliest Jesuit writers—"a native of Florida and brother of the cacique of Ajacán," "educated [in Spain and Mexico] and instructed in the Christian religion," "he was, at his own request, baptized, receiving in baptism the name of the viceroy." But Shea also speculates upon the central problem of Don Luis's apostasy from Christianity in an unprecedented way. Pointing out that Don Luis accompanied the Dominicans on an attempted voyage to Ajacán in 1566, "voluntarily," Shea concludes that the translator truly hoped to convert his people to Christianity at that time: "Of his sincerity no doubts were entertained." To understand what happened to change Don Luis from sincere convert and helpmate in the project of Indian conversion, Shea turns, remarkably, to the prehistory in Spain provided by Garcilaso (discussed in Chapter 3). Noting that Don Luis traveled in Spain with five indigenous companions, as described by Garcilaso, Shea speculates that these Native transatlantic sojourners were "not, like Don Luis, voluntary companions of Melendez [*sic*], and that, from representations of theirs, [Don Luis] conceived that hate which, carefully dissembled, was to bring death to those who confided in his honor." If the distinction between "voluntary companions" and involuntary or enslaved ones proves murky and unreliable in this colonial context, the suggestion that Don Luis underwent a significant experience in Spain is nevertheless a compelling one. For what Shea ultimately indicates here is that Don Luis's worldview, unsurprisingly defined by the nineteenth-century historian as "hate," was powerfully shaped by the "representations" of the Natives from elsewhere in the Americas who are also in Spain. Parsing the early modern texts from his nineteenth-century vantage point, Shea points to the inter-indigenous transmission of information that lies at the heart of the story of Don Luis—a figure who was, in Shea's estimation, not only "possessed [of] a good head," but indeed "an apt scholar."

But Shea's 1846 account of Don Luis and the failed settlement of Ajacán does not present the one element of the story that would have been most unsettling to his nineteenth-century U.S. readers, and certainly to Greenhow: its specific location within the "territory now embraced by the United States" in the nation's putative birthplace of Virginia. As do earlier hispanophone writers, Shea refers to Don Luis's homeland as Ajacán, and following Garcilaso's lead in *La Florida del Inca*, he places Ajacán in La Florida. Though the state known by the mid-nineteenth century as Florida had very different boundaries than did the undemarcated expanse of land called La Florida during the sixteenth century, Shea nevertheless makes the translation from Spanish to English as if the geography were identical. He does, however, register some discomfort with the process, conceding in a footnote that he has "not . . . been able to locate to his own satisfaction the names of provinces, towns, etc. in Florida by means of the old maps to which he has had access." Shea has found in his archive of Spanish materials the story of Don Luis as first told by the Jesuits—but he has apparently not apprehended what was by the mid-nineteenth century the central irony of its primary setting in the future Virginia.

This irony, as we have seen, was not lost on Greenhow, who in 1848 entered the geographical location of Ajacán into the historical record and seized upon the counterfactual historical fantasy of a Spanish North America while also suppressing the story of actual settlement—and unsettlement—that unfolded in its (future) Virginia setting. By 1855, however, Shea would publish a new account of the events at Ajacán in a book-length study, *History of the Catholic Missions in the United States*, which retrieved the suppressed settlement from the Spanish archive, and re-transmitted it into English—this time correctly joining the story to its proper setting: as Shea put it in this version, "Ajacán, in St. Mary's Bay, which lying 37 North must be Chesapeake Bay . . . in Virginia." This version of the story deviates little from Shea's earlier account, but the fact of Spanish settlement in "Virginia"—rather than, as Greenhow told it, a mere, un-landed discovery of its Chesapeake Bay—is unmistakable, down to the detail of the "rustic altar [that] witnessed daily the holy sacrifice."

Shea does not mention Greenhow or his scholarly suppression in his 1855 version of the story of Don Luis; his interests seem to lie, as before, primarily in honoring the missionary work of Catholics and Catholic historians in the early American colonies. But soon thereafter Shea began to follow emerging historical work on Ajacán, and to become more aware of its potential symbolic import in a country now deeply divided by sectional conflict. When he learned that the *Southern Literary Messenger* contributor and Virginia historian Charles Campbell was working on a book-length study of "Old Dominion" history, Shea sent him his own findings on the Spanish settlement in Virginia.[47] And what Campbell did with Shea's information resembles Greenhow's slippery performance in his submission to the Virginia Historical Society during the previous decade. In *History of the Colony and Ancient Dominion of Virginia* (1860), Campbell pointedly removed the location of Ajacán from Virginia to North Carolina, and he hedged his bets further by redefining the status of the colony as a matter of mere visitation: the "Jesuit missionaries, accompanied by Don Luis, *visited* Ajacán, but were treacherously cut off by him" (my emphasis). Campbell cites both Greenhow and Shea in his book, but he clearly privileges the former over the latter, for he suppresses the information sent to him by Shea about the Spanish settlement in Virginia in at least two significant ways. This suppression suggests the extent to which the writing of colonial history was bound up in sectional conflict during that decade. To present a Spanish colonization of Virginia would have potentially undermined a significant component of Southern nationalist mythology—of chivalrous John Smith and royal Pocahontas as the forebears of the "Mother of States"—and thereby ceded a certain degree of historical prestige to the North, with its Pilgrims and Puritans, and with its cadre of historians eager to debunk the story of Smith's rescue.[48] If Jamestown were not the first European settlement in Virginia, then—in the zero-sum game of settlement priority practiced in the decade before the Civil War (and arguably now)—the significance of Cavalier history necessarily lost ground to the histories of Plymouth and Massachusetts Bay.

But Shea was not willing to let the historical record stand uncorrected. The eruption and ultimate outcome of the Civil War did not, apparently, distract him permanently from Ajacán, though he did turn his attention away from colonial history after Lincoln's death in order to produce *The Lincoln Memorial* (1865), a biography of the late president and a collection of firsthand accounts of and responses to the assassination.[49] By 1872, however, Shea was back on the Ajacán case, making an address on the subject of the Spanish settlement to the New York Historical Society.[50] In 1875, he developed the talk into a new essay for *Catholic World* in which he told the story of Don Luis, making sure this time to rebuke Campbell, though without naming him specifically: "Though his attention was called to it, the latest historian of Virginia, misled by a somewhat careless guide, robs his State of the glory which we claim for her." Greenhow was of course the "guide" upon whom Campbell relied in suppressing the settlement at Ajacán, though as we have seen he was anything but "careless." What for Shea was "rob[bing]" Virginia of the "glory" of a sixteenth-century Catholic settlement, followed by a martyrdom, was for Greenhow and Campbell a means of securing the story of English priority in the Old Dominion against the encroaching possibility of being undermined by a Spanish predecessor.

Shea clearly understood this discrepancy on some level, for he made certain that both the location and the status of Ajacán as a colony were impossible for readers to miss if they glanced at the title: "The Log Chapel on the Rappahannock." The geography of Ajacán was certain "beyond all peradventure," Shea asserted, as was the matter of its settlement, with what turned out to be its now explicitly racial mid-nineteenth-century valence. Shea narrated the episode at Ajacán as—over and above discovery or, in Campbell's hedging parlance, mere visitation—"the first white habitation in that part of America," where "the first white occupants" of the "Old Dominion" created a religious settlement: "by actual possession, by erecting a chapel, by instituting a regular community life, by instructing, baptizing, and hallowing the land by the Holy Sacrifice of the Mass." Even after narrating the *un*settlement of Ajacán, Shea notes that it was not an English standard that was hoisted during Menéndez's punitive expedition to the Bahía de Santa María, where "the Spanish flag floated for the last time over the land of Ajacán" (856).

Within two years of this publication of the *Catholic World* piece, moreover, Shea had taken his argument about the Ajacán settlement to a historical venue of more general interest, *The Indian Miscellany*. Published in 1877 as a popular volume exploring the history of "a race whose annals must erelong constitute their only monument," the book included mainstream pieces by Ephraim George Squier and William Cullen Bryant as well as Shea's contribution.[51] Shea's title now focused not on the Jesuit "chapel" but on the structural quality of intended permanence it once signified: "The Spanish Mission Colony on the Rappahannock: the First European Settlement in Virginia." Lest readers miss the significance announced in the title, the piece goes on to proclaim that this Spanish colony potentially implicates even the most hallowed figures of Virginia history, noting the likelihood that "Don Luis de Velasco honorably received at Mexico and Madrid, was a kinsman of Pocahontas treated as a princess in England." The "history of the first settlement of white men on the soil of Virginia" is *not*, Shea discloses repeatedly, an Anglo-American history—and, as he argues, this fact deserves permanent national prominence:

> The walls of the Capitol at Washington, might well be adorned with a painting of a scene that occurred almost in sight of its dome—the founder of Saint Augustine, the butcher of Ribault, the chosen commander of the Invincible Armada, as he stood surrounded by his grim warriors, placing the standard of Spain in the banks of the Potomac. (343)

The idea proposed here by Shea registers several levels of irony. There were (and are today) eight historical paintings placed in the Washington Capitol by 1855, four of which represent scenes from the American Revolution, and four of which depict scenes of exploration and colonization in the New World. Of the latter four, two paintings offer episodes of Spanish exploration—the "Landing of Columbus" and the "Discovery of the Mississippi"—which nineteenth-century U.S. historiography differently, but with equal success, appropriated into a nationalist teleology: Columbus had been cast as a proto-American since the early nineteenth century, and De Soto's expedition into the Southwest was, by the 1850s, widely understood as a symbolic auguring of the U.S. annexation of Mexican territory after the war of 1846–48.[52] But a Spanish settlement in the so-called Old Dominion was quite another matter, as Shea surely understood, for it displaced and rendered belated the English colonial history of Virginia that was already represented in the Capitol by the "Baptism of Pocahontas" painting, which had been placed in 1840. Finally, the visual subject matter proposed by Shea—Menéndez hoisting the Spanish flag during the punitive mission to Ajacán—presents a scene neither of discovery nor colonization but of unsettlement, for it occurs *after* Don Luis's destruction of the Spanish colony. Whatever Shea ultimately meant in making this dramatic proposal, it was compelling and startling enough that, as we shall see in the next chapter, James Branch Cabell would include it as an epigraph in *First Gentleman of America*, his novel about Don Luis.

William Cullen Bryant and the Popular Don Luis

But Shea's determination to foreground the Spanish colony in Virginia—which Greenhow's (and, to a lesser extent, Campbell's) efforts had suppressed—paid off decades before Cabell's novel appeared in 1942. Remarkably, thanks to Shea, the story of Don Luis would make its way back from the oblivion to which Greenhow had consigned it and appear in what was advertised as the first popular history of the United States, published in 1876 to celebrate the centennial anniversary of the American Revolution. Commissioned by Scribner's and edited by the preeminent American man of letters, William Cullen Bryant, *A popular history of the United States: from the first discovery of the Western Hemisphere by the Northmen, to the end of the Civil War, preceded by a sketch of the pre-historic period and the age of the mound builders* was designed as a four-volume history spanning the nation's pre-European-contact past all the way through the Civil War, which had ended a decade earlier.[53] Though Bryant was advertised as the main author (the unofficial title "Bryant's Popular History of the United States" appeared in the front matter, along with his picture), he died just after the publication of volume 1, an unfortunate event for the publishers, who were then forced to admit that the bulk of the writing was always in fact meant to have been handled by the writer advertised on the title pages as Bryant's co-author, Sydney Howard Gay.[54] But if Gay wrote the bulk of the subsequent history, Bryant was nevertheless central to the production of the first volume in conceiving the structure the project would take, writing its long preface, and closely editing each portion of the manuscript. Bryant had by this late point in his career developed a complex poetics of the national past that would shape the emergent genre of popular history, a genre intended to reach, in the poet's words, "that large class who have not leisure for reading those narratives which aim at setting forth, with the greatest breadth and variety of circumstance, the annals of our nation's life." Modeled on the recent and highly successful production of popular history in Britain, the Bryant volume was both market-driven and didactic, meant to condense and distill history in order to shape its readers into ideal national subjects: by "prompt[ing] the good citizen," as he explained in the Preface, "to cherish . . . confidence in regard to the destiny reserved for our beloved country."[55] As we shall see, it was a vision of national history into which the story of Don Luis could not easily assimilate.

What Bryant sought to make legible for mainstream readers was the ineluctable emergence out of seemingly unlikely circumstances and events of what was, by the centennial of the American Revolution, a nation "so great and powerful" that it *required* a new history, one that would embrace the Civil War as a necessary stage of national development. Arbitrating between the merely providential view that all was foreordained and the quasi-scientific observation of causes and effects, Bryant developed an explanatory model provided by literature to engross his readers in what he called "a mighty drama . . . put upon the stage of our continent, which, after a series of fierce contentions and subtle intrigues, closed in a bloody catastrophe with a result favorable to liberty and human rights and to the fair fame of the Republic." The outcome of the Civil War, the preservation of the Union, was to be understood as an effect of colonial history: that "out of this fortuitous planting of our continent in scattered and independent settlements, has arisen the strongest form of government, so far as respects cohesion and self-maintenance, the world has seen." It was precisely the history of settlement, then—laid out in "records . . . preserved as those of no other nation have been," and therefore free from the "shadows of tradition" that obscure historical truth—that ensured the foregone conclusion of the Civil War: that "the entire people of the North rose as one man to breast and beat back this bold attack upon a system of polity which every man of them was moved to defend," leaving its Southern enemy "ravaged and desolate," while preserving the future of the nation.

Of course, colonial history is not always easily funneled into a single outcome within a national storyline. Bryant's narrative of the Civil War has an explicit national moral—that "the existence of slavery in our Republic was at utter variance with the free institutions which we made our boast"—that is nevertheless undermined by the residual effects of antebellum internationalism. More noteworthy in Bryant's Preface than the quick mention of slavery's contradiction of the national principle of liberty is the potential threat posed by the Civil War to the Monroe Doctrine: "When the slave states first revolted . . . the people of the Old World, even those who wished well to the Northern states, adopted the conclusion, that the Union could endure no longer"—a belief which quickly "reliev[ed] the European powers from the danger of aggression in this quarter." While Britain "instantly declar[ed] the slave States a belligerent power—a virtual acknowledgement of their independence," France went even further, "posting a dependent Prince in Mexico with the view of intervening in that quarter." Bryant's reference here is to the so-called Maximilian Affair, which led to the short-lived Second Mexican Empire (1864–67), a monarchical regime supported by Napoleon III that installed a Habsburg archduke as the emperor of Mexico. Though the *Imperio Mexicano* was regarded as illegitimate by the U.S. administration and formally protested by the Lincoln administration (then hamstrung by the Civil War), it was taken seriously enough that President Johnson would dispatch upward of 50,000 troops to the southern border to protect against incursions.[56] "Till the close of our civil war," Bryant warns, the nation faced the threat of foreign invasion from Mexico: "the armed cohorts of France hung like a thunder-cloud over our southwestern border," a "grim mass [poised] to move northward."

Bryant thus situates the history of the Civil War within a transatlantic and hemispheric contest—a nullified Monroe Doctrine, the long arm of European imperialism, a looming Franco-Mexican invasion—that yields up what he defines unabashedly as "the only great nation on the globe." The power of this exceptional state is of course centered in the North, which had at once brought to submission the U.S. South, and the "brutal instincts" of that "region which had been the seat of the war," and secured its dominant status over the greater, hemispheric South surging against its southwestern border. This newly consolidated imperial nation had honed its military skills in Indian dispossession on the staging ground of the Civil War, during which U.S. combatant violence on the frontier, contrary to popular historical belief, increased rather than declined, while federal troops mobilized against the South often engaged in combat with Native populations during the effort to suppress the Confederacy.[57] Once again, the writing of history tacitly justifies Bryant's present, imperial moment, during which, following the conclusion of the Civil War, the United States was entering the ferocious final decades of the Indian Wars.

And it is just here that the *Popular History* articulates its most revealing vision regarding the history of American unsettlement. After a lengthy and tedious disquisition on national debt, depreciated currency, and states' rights, Bryant announces, in an abrupt non sequitur, that he must now speak to the plan of the larger history, for he has "yet something to add" regarding "the works of the Mound Builders which lie scattered by thousands over our territory, from the Gulf of Mexico to Oregon." The Mound Builders were important enough to his conception of the "Popular History of the United States" that they would receive not only their own chapter in Volume 1 but a separate mention in the title itself. Bryant's better-known expression of his interest in the ancient indigenous cultures (dubbed "Mound Builders" by nineteenth-century archaeologists), appears in his 1832 poem, "The Prairies." Here, Bryant's speaker notoriously contemplates the "mighty mounds/That overlook the rivers, or that rise/In the dim forest," and then elaborates the prevailing pseudo-scientific theory of the day about these ancient inhabitants:

> A race, that long has passed away,
> Built them;—a disciplined and populous race
> Heaped, with long toil, the earth, while yet the Greek
> Was hewing the Pentelicus to forms
> Of symmetry, and rearing on its rock
> The glittering Parthenon. These ample fields
> Nourished their harvests, here their herds were fed,

When haply by their stalls the bison lowed,
And bowed his maned shoulder to the yoke.
All day this desert murmured with their toils,
Till twilight blushed, and lovers walked, and wooed
In a forgotten language, and old tunes,
From instruments of unremembered form,
Gave the soft winds a voice. The red man came—
The roaming hunter tribes, warlike and fierce,
And the mound-builders vanished from the earth.
The solitude of centuries untold
Has settled where they dwelt.[58]

In Bryant's dark pastoral vision, the "red man," a people of "rude conquerors," thus cruelly destroyed the Mound Builders, including "wi[ves]" and "sweet little ones" who were "Butchered amid their shrieks with all [the] race." As many critics have noted, Bryant's poetic lament for the Mound Builders proffered a thinly-veiled apology for Indian removal by disavowing the American Indians' original inhabitance of the continent, casting them not as the dispossessed but as the savage dispossessors of a prior and superior civilization, the Mound Builders, thus naturalizing the genocidal expansion being undertaken by the United States: "Thus change the forms of being. Thus arise/ Races of living things, glorious in strength,/And perish."[59] Just as the Mound Builders have vanished, "The red man, too,/Has left the blooming wilds he ranged so long," making way for Anglo-American possession of the West, the "Advancing multitude/Which soon shall fill these deserts."

The concept of a prior inhabitance, unjustly and violently usurped by foes of settlement—by the agents of unsettlement—had been a key topos of Spanish colonial disavowal as well. Cortés proclaimed, for example, that Moctezuma and the Aztecs had stolen the Mexica throne from its original owners, and were thus willing to see it "restored" to the Spanish conqueror, whom they took to be the returning and rightful king.[60] But like nineteenth-century Anglo-American culture more broadly, Bryant had a strong investment in *not* seeing the parallelism, the twinned forms of denial of indigenous possession of the land that linked his North American "prairie" to Mexico and the southern part of the hemisphere: "ye have played/ Among the palms of Mexico and vines/Of Texas, and have crisped the limpid brooks/That from the fountains of Sonora glide/ Into the calm Pacific," he apostrophizes to the "Southern winds," but then asks rhetorically, "have ye fanned/A nobler or a lovelier scene than this?" The sublime landscape of the U.S. prairie diminishes its Spanish-American counterparts—Mexico; Texas; and Sonora, California: "'southern' locales" that, as Jennifer Greeson observes, will "be touched by U.S. might during the subsequent fifteen years." Ultimately, Bryant insists, there is "a fresher wind" than the one hailing from the hemispheric south.[61]

There is something chilling about the shift, across more than forty years, from Bryant's poetic meditation on the Mound Builders to his quasi-scientific historical production on the same subject in the *Popular History*. Touting new archaeological evidence, Bryant now contends that advances in science "prove clearly, what was previously doubted by many, the existence of a semi-civilized race, dwelling within our borders, who preceded the savage tribes found here by the discoverers from the Old World, and who disappeared at some unknown era, leaving behind them no tradition, nor any record save these remarkable monuments." As his defensive tone suggests, the theory of gene-alogical separation between the Mound builders and the American Indians had by this point in the nineteenth century become quite controversial.[62] The subsequent chapter on the Mound Builders—which Bryant may not have written himself but certainly edited carefully and approved—nevertheless goes out of its way to convince readers that any such skepticism should now quail and retreat before the obvious truth: "It is to set aside all the facts of his-tory, as well as all rational conjecture, to suppose that a race now apparently so hopelessly incapable of improvement had . . . fallen from the condition of a partially cultivated people . . . to that of savage hunters in a country which had become a wilderness through their own voluntary degradation." The legal context of land possession still lies at the heart of this strained discourse on the Mound Builders: again and again the writer aims, in his curious phrasing, to go "behind the Indians"—those "who were in possession of the country when it was discovered by Europeans"—to apprehend "the shadowy form of another people," and thereby to prove prior "occupation of this land" that nullified any Native right to it.

Indeed, the Mound Builders are nothing less than an ancient auguring of the America to come: a "singular civilization" of "a vigorous and original growth," "a civilization developed by themselves," with "an industrious and agricultural people" of "active and intelligent labor." The incipient greatness of this civilization of farmers and workers rivaled "the whole of Europe," which "was still in the darkness of primeval barbarism" while it flourished. And despite its practical focus on labor and industry, the civilization of the Mound Builders was fully capable of creating great art; its works could stand "as distinctly original and independent of any foreign influence"—just as nineteenth-century Americans insisted their art could stand in the face of European charges of imitative aesthetics.

By far the most striking aspect of the Mound Builders here is the avow-edly hemispheric geography within which the *Popular History* locates them. Where "The Prairies" demotes the Spanish-American locales wafting on the "Southern winds," Bryant and Gay's *Popular History* eagerly associates its an-cient, proto-American civilization with the southern Americas. The chapter first lays out tantalizing correspondences: while arguing that the Mound Builder artifacts "far exceed anything of which the existing Indian tribes are known to have been capable," the writer notes that they do, however, "come fully up to the best Peruvian specimens, to which they bear in many respects a close resemblance." Though the chapter does not suggest why this might be so—or why, for that matter, the Mound Builders had material "they could only have got from Mexico"—the implication becomes clear once the argument more directly broaches the question of their disappearance. Like "The Prairies," the account speculates that these proto-Americans were "driven away by a savage foe against whose furious onslaughts they could contend no longer"—an obvious justification for demolishing that same brutal Native enemy in his nineteenth-century moment. Yet perhaps, the chapter suggests, they were "driven from the country to seek new homes south and west of the Gulf of Mexico"—indeed, the whole mystery of their disappearance "ceases if we look for the farther development of their civilization in Mexico and Central America" (31–32). The proposition neatly explains what has already been established in the chapter as the similarity of Mound Builder art and the ancient indigenous art found elsewhere in the Americas—proving the "apparent growth" of the now disappeared "northern race" into the "higher civilization of that of the south."

If the chapter betrays a degree of ambivalence about the proposition that the proto-Americans became the ancient Mexicans, Central Americans, and Peruvians once they were chased away by the savage American Indians, it concludes with an odd statement of emphasis: "It certainly is not a violent supposition." Ultimately, though, the logic of Bryant and Gay's own sedimented analogy suggests that such a supposition is violent indeed. Just as the priority of the proto-American Mound Builders justifies westward expansion across the continent, the alleged dispersal of those prehistoric people throughout the Americas bequeaths priority once again to the United States, justifying a *southward* expansion. If the true and rightful and proto-American possessors of North America fled southward and created an even "higher civilization" which was then subjected to Spanish atrocities—as, indeed, much of the *Popular History* will suggest in typical Black-Legend style—then the "only great nation on the globe" has a mandate to destroy not only the "savage foe" of Native America but the rapine spoilers of the southern hemisphere as well. The spurious archaeological vision of the Mound Builders, then, is also a theoretical justification of Anglo-American settler colonialism—a justification that capaciously bridges the Americas only to redivide them along lines convenient to U.S. imperial interests: the American Indians are sharply separated from the indigenous peoples to the south, just as the violence of Spanish-American conquest throws into relief the ostensible temperance of English and Anglo-American settlement.[63]

The story of Don Luis, however, disrupts the historical telos instantiated by the Mound Builder theory in several ways. Transmitted by Shea and incorporated into Bryant's *Popular History*, the Ajacán narrative problematizes the neat North-South divide upon which the national U.S. plotline depends: Don Luis is both a North American Indian (a kinsman of Powhatan, Shea surmises) and a Spanish-American Indian (baptized in Mexico and fluent in Spanish). Moreover, the Spanish settlement in Ajacán undermines the narrative of Anglo-American priority that the Mound Builder thesis upholds by disavowal. Both of these factors suggest that it was likely Gay the scholarly empiricist rather than Bryant the myth-maker who made the decision to include the Don Luis story. This seems especially plausible given that the two editors would disagree notably over Gay's skeptical treatment, later in the volume, of the story of John Smith's rescue by Pocahontas. Bryant went so far as to rebuke Gay for being "a terrible image-breaker" responsible for destroying "that beautiful image of Pocahontas interposing to save Captain Smith from the numerous savages."[64]

In this sense, the story of Don Luis exists in a compellingly iconoclastic relation to the Pocahontas myth, corroding the "beautiful image" that Bryant so admired in the Jamestown story. On the one hand, the *Popular History* introduces him as "an Indian convert" and, like Pocahontas, as a quasi-royal subject, "a brother of the cacique of the Axacan or Iacan country, as a portion of Virginia was called, whence he had been taken some years before to Mexico, and christened by the name of the viceroy, Don Luis de Velasco." Yet as a Virginian-Mexican, he embodies a very different model of cross-cultural indigeneity for a primal colonial scene—a hispanophone Native who sides ultimately with the "numerous savages" who would attack John Smith rather than with the European colonizer, and whose many contradictions call into question the virtues of conversion and assimilation his English counterpart is meant to symbolize. As the *Popular History* tells the story, Don Luis is at first gentlemanly and genial when the reader finds him in Spain, where he "gladly avail[s] himself of such an opportunity to return to his own country, promising to use his influence with his brother and his people on behalf of the missionaries" (220). But no sooner has he arrived on Virginian soil than he suddenly exemplifies not merely "treachery and hypocrisy," qualities to which the sixteenth-century Spanish accounts often referred, but also the nineteenth-century racial maxim that blood will tell. It is "the instinct of Indian blood"—"stronger than the rite of baptism"—that causes him to "forg[e]t that he was a Christian" along with all the "pious promises of the neophyte" (221).

It is unclear in this version of the story whether Don Luis is acting as a cornered isolate who destroys the Spanish colony because he must, to save face, "prove [himself] to those whom he had once abandoned for civilized life and the religion of the white man"; or whether he is in fact acting out of a coherent point of view based upon the effects of colonialism in Mexico, the land of his baptism, and the wider Americas; and is thus engaged in a military struggle against Spanish settlement—albeit one that is drawn here from an Anglo frontier scene: "the war whoop rung through the woods; a band of painted savages surrounded the chapel, Don Luis at their head dressed in the cassock of [a] murdered priest." None of this reconciles with the *Popular History*'s casting of Don Luis's act of unsettlement in the familiar American literary terms of boyish pastoral retreat, when he "resume[s] the companionship of his youth and the free and savage life of the woods." Perhaps most unsettling in its implications, this version of the story of the colony at Ajacán unmistakably echoes another familiar American scene as well in depicting a "devout and courageous" band of settlers "landed on the banks of the Potomac." The writer of this section of the *Popular History*—almost certainly Gay—details these Catholic pilgrims' inland journey to the Rappahannock and the construction and naming of their chapel: "'*La Madre de Dios de Iacan*'—'the chapel of the mother of God at Iacan,' or Axacan." In this telling, the Ajacán colony undermines the priority not only of Jamestown but of Plymouth as well.

Perhaps this is why, at the opening of the next chapter of the *Popular History*, the distinctive voice of Bryant suddenly returns, as if Gay the "terrible image-breaker" has made a mess of things with Don Luis, and his senior editor—once known as the "father of American literature"—has had to step in to do some damage control. Like Greenhow, Bryant begins the chapter by deploying the counterfactual mode, but where the State Department translator sensationalized the Spanish "discovery" of the Chesapeake, the poet-historian appears studiedly casual. "It is not always unprofitable, and it is often interesting, to reflect what might have been the course of human events," he remarks, "but for the intervention of some slight action, seeming at the moment to be of trifling importance." The "slight action" to which Bryant turns next is telling; he invokes nothing less than the foundational "discovery" of America: "Had Columbus, for example, refused to deviate on his first voyage from that directly westward course which he had laid down as the only true one, his first landfall would probably have been the coast of Florida" (224). Had Columbus deviated, in other words, he would have discovered not a Caribbean island but the territory of the future United States. This counterfactual premise has a global scope, as he sees it: the whole "history of the world would have flowed in another direction," swerving from modernity, causing "the progress of the human race [to be] arrested for centuries." With the fate of the Ajacán colony clearly in mind, he ponders the possibilities suggested by a kind of counterfactual map: "We may venture upon almost any latitude of conjecture as to what might have been, had the Spanish march of conquest and possession been directed to the territory now occupied by the United States rather than to that of the rich and semi-civilized peoples of Mexico and Peru" (224).

Such counterfactual speculation leaves Bryant uneasy; the account shifts here back to a traditional historical narrative about the ostensibly real-world past and begins busily reconstituting the hemispheric North-South divide that shapes his preferred theory of the Mound Builders, and which the figure of Don Luis has in effect just disrupted. To do so, he quickly enumerates the central theses of the Black Legend: that there was in North America "none of that dazzling acquisition of wealth that came from the spoiling of the semi-civilized nations of the South"; that "the North American Indians, unlike the natives of softer climates whom the Spanish subdued so easily, would fight to the death with the fierceness of wild beasts rather than quietly submit to the white men, or if reduced to slavery would die in obstinate despair"; that "there were no slaves and no gold in this inhospitable region"; and that "people and country were proved to be alike valueless, in the estimate of the Spanish conquerors, the one feeble colony at St. Augustine alone being an exception [which] owed its origin to a cruel fanaticism and was held together by the spirit of religious propagandism" (225).

The narrative is all too familiar, yet Bryant's small stutters in rehearsing it are revealing, particularly his acknowledgement that the enslavement of Natives was practiced in the North American colonies alongside his assertion that "there were no slaves." Implying by contrast the widespread enslavement of indigenous populations in Spanish America, Bryant trips over his own opposition—for of course there were indeed slaves in colonial North America, albeit imported from outside the "inhospitable region" and then systematically reproduced under the regime of biopower exercised within it. But it is the uneasy slide from mineral wealth to territory—from "no gold" to a "country" deemed "valueless"—that drives the symbolic oppositions of Black Legend discourse and the central problem it conceals: the problem of land. Throughout the century over which Bryant presided as preeminent man of letters, this land—the "territory now occupied by the United States"—of course needed to be cleared precisely of those prior inhabitants whom the Spaniards had putatively rejected as unfit for slavery, worthless as "wild beasts." *This* was the central ideological contribution of the Black Legend as deployed by Bryant and other U.S. writers during the nineteenth century—and as it continues to shape our thinking now, however forcefully we reject its tenets: its spectacular concealment of the enduring structure of settler colonialism as practiced by the English and then their American successors.[65]

Bryant's exercise in counterfactual history, then, is ultimately necessitated far more by the Spanish colony in Virginia, the Mother of the States, than by the ostensibly outlying "exception" of the "feeble" St. Augustine. The real point of the exercise lies in maintaining rather than shifting the ontological status quo: it is the appearance of imagining alternate historical outcomes while in effect denying their possibility and insisting upon the desirability and inevitability of the present.[66] Bryant speculates upon a Spanish North America only to maintain with religious finality that "[i]n the providence of God it was not to be," and "[i]t was happy for the world that it was so" (225).

To put this another way: the story of Don Luis had an outcome that apparently took Menéndez and the Jesuits by surprise. The retelling of the story in a prominent venue like the *Popular History* thus necessarily invited a certain degree of counterfactual, historical speculation: what if Don Luis had acted otherwise, and had served as the ideal colonial interpreter that he was expected to become? This alternate outcome was unsettling enough to Bryant to evoke what I would characterize as a conditional *un*discovery of America, subject to his own nightmarish version of the hypothesis: "If the history of South America had been repeated in the north it would have been better that the Atlantic had still been held to be a sea of darkness into which no ship manned by mortals could penetrate and live" (225). It is a dramatic, nearly histrionic hypothetical—and the story of Don Luis, as understood in the nineteenth century, offered the clearest and most spectacular specter of its potential realization. Bryant's final commentary on the matter accordingly reinscribes both a providential vision of history and a statement of territorialization: "At length it was plain that not the Spanish but a people of another blood, another faith, and another destiny were to possess the land" (225). The symbolic logic undergirding the oppositions of the Black Legend is thus ineluctably racial, and it works here in the service of settler colonialism's unending race war over the territory upon which it claims legal and other kinds of priority.

Don Luis and the Dawes Act: Alice Fletcher's
Indian Education and Civilization

The story of Don Luis, then, marked the centennial celebration of the American Revolution with its appearance in Bryant's *Popular History*; the tale was, by 1876, a familiar one in the nineteenth-century writing of the colonial past. But the uses of that history were also swiftly changing during the century's last decades, and when the story of Don Luis reappeared in 1888, it had undergone some slight but telling modifications. It had also returned to its early nineteenth-century home in an official government document—this time "A Report Prepared in Answer to Senate Resolution of February 23, 1885": *Indian Education and Civilization*.[67] In its generic shift from a popular history to institutional report, designed for congressional persuasion and legitimation, the story of Don Luis, in this late nineteenth-century version, opens a window onto the vexed and interdependent relation between historical narrative and national Indian policy.

Indian Education and Civilization was originally conceived as a United States Centennial project of the government's Office of Education in 1876, and as such was taken up by General John Eaton, then serving as the U.S. Commissioner of Education within the Department of the Interior.[68] The complex bureaucratic origin of the report itself tells an important story about the flexible structure of settler colonialism. The U.S. government had created the Department of the Interior immediately after the U.S.-Mexican War, transferring the Office of Indian Affairs (OIA) from the Department of War into the newly-opened bureaucratic wing at the same time. This organizational shift recognized an obvious, seemingly straightforward increase in the OIA's purview: the end of the war and the acquisition of more than one-half of former Mexican territory (counting Texas) had meant the incorporation of many new Indian tribes and languages into the territorial United States, easily doubling its Native population. But the shift from "war" to "interior" instantiated an ideological transition as well: war is predicated upon the recognition of separate nations even when it disputes their sovereignty; the interiorization of Indian peoples, on the other hand, structurally elides the concept of Native nationhood, even when nominally recognizing it, by bureaucratically disavowing it through the category of natural resources.[69] To put this another way, the 1849 placement of the OIA within the Department of the Interior marked not simply a shift toward new federal policies of "civilization" and assimilation, but a next step in what Patrick Wolfe calls the "logic of elimination" underwriting the U.S. settler state.[70]

Understood within this context, *Indian Education and Civilization* reveals much about the intersecting contributions of literary, historical, and anthropological writing to the political work of late nineteenth-century colonial invasion. In 1885, Eaton passed on the project of writing and preparing the Interior Department report to a Special Agent of Indian Affairs and self-described ethnologist, Alice Fletcher, who had lived among and studied the Sioux Indians earlier during that decade before being hired by the OIA to mandate and enact a federal allotment law among the Omaha Indians in Nebraska.[71] Fletcher's sojourn among the Indians, during which she wrote letters describing what it was like to camp under an open sky during winter and to survive a life-threatening illness far from eastern civilization, marked her as an extraordinary woman in the eyes of her peers. She had lectured widely on topics ranging from the Mound Builders—they were both the ancestors of the country's Indians, she concluded, *and* possibly also pre-Adamites, and thus a separate species from Euro-Americans—to Indian songs and ceremonies.[72] She had attended east-coast Indian reformer events and had worked closely with Frederic Putnam, the first director of Harvard's Peabody Museum, collecting Native specimens for his collections and taking composite photographs of "full-blooded" Indians using techniques that were modeled on those of the British eugenicist Francis Galton.[73]

Perhaps most important from Eaton's point of view, Fletcher had presented a much acclaimed exhibit titled "Indian Civilization" at the 1885 New Orleans Exposition, for which she used before-and-after photographs to show the putatively positive effects of individual land ownership among the Omaha

Indians. Her mission was not only to showcase the advantages of land allotment but to undo the serious damage suffered by the government's reputation after the 1881 publication of *A Century of Dishonor*, Helen Hunt Jackson's
widely read outcry against the centennial of U.S. mistreatment of Native peoples. Fletcher had been tapped for the project, in other words, to present a different face of the U.S. government vis-à-vis the American Indians: ostensibly
benevolent, distinctly female, even quasi-maternal. All these qualifications
made her Eaton's—and by extension the Department of Interior's—choice to
author what became an important congressional report, a veritable handbook
on the forging of new Indian policy.[74]

Those who would shape policy need history to serve at their convenience, of
course, which is why *Indian Education and Civilization* includes what Fletcher
calls an "outline sketch" of the colonial past—or, as the Commissioner of
Education puts it in the report's prefatory material, "a historical résumé of the
relations between the Indians and the American colonists prior to the War
of the Revolution, and of the origin and progress of the Indian policy of the
Government from that date to the present time, with statements respecting
the agencies, reservations, lands, legal status, population, trade, and education
of these wards of the nation" (9–10). As this description suggests, Fletcher's
report constructs a straightforwardly teleological narrative of the past, one in
which colonial history gives way ineluctably to the "War of the Revolution"
and the subsequent national "Government," with its coherent "Indian policy"
advancing forward into the present in fully documented segments of time.
The defining, originary matter of the "lands" gets sandwiched neatly between two subsequent inventions of settler colonialism—"reservations" and
"legal status"—while the initially neutral structure of "relations between the
Indians and the American colonists" seamlessly gives way to the benevolent
government paternalism which the larger report is designed precisely to authorize: "agencies" caring for "wards of the nation."

Don Luis appears in the first chapter of this "résumé"—"The Sixteenth
Century"—which covers in fewer than ten pages everything from the "origin
of the American Indians" through the failed efforts of Spaniards in North
America to evoke from the indigenous people any "real progress toward civilization." This failure is in fact Fletcher's central point, drawn straight from
the Black Legend: that under the cruel policies of the Spaniards, Indian "contact with the white race was attended by wars, slavery, and other evils connected with the presence of soldiers" (22). Though Fletcher will in subsequent
chapters have criticisms of English policy as well, the trajectory that she seeks
to outline is a progressive one: from sixteenth-century Spanish brutality to
a benevolent, Anglo-American future in the late nineteenth century. (Along
the way, she will also discuss Virginia and the southern colonies, which she
appears to view as part of an extended South America, where treatment of
the Indians contrasted sharply with the humane policies developing in the

North. Like Bryant's, in other words, her version of the Black Legend includes the U.S. South.)[75]

The history of the Ajacán settlement, however, disrupts the trajectory of Fletcher's report in several important ways. First, it complicates the story perpetuated by the Black Legend by presenting the compelling exception of a soldierless mission, a Jesuit "peaceful conquest" organized around the very premise that Fletcher embraces: that the "conversion of these Indians" depended upon their separation from the "vices and immoralities" of the military. Fletcher's cited source for the Ajacán section of her report is Shea's *History of the Catholic Missions*, which makes clear that the colony was specifically planned around the perceived "necessity of removing the missions from the vicinity of the Spanish [military] posts." Fletcher sidesteps this obvious contradiction by simply not mentioning it in her brief and perfunctory segment on the failed mission, one of several that she must document on her way to a bright Anglo-American future of bringing civilization to the Indians.

But the shadowy figure of the Ajacán mission's translator and guide—"an Indian chief belonging to one of the Virginia tribes," who "was baptized by the name Don Luis Velasco"—presents Fletcher with a more troubling contradiction. Her entire report is devoted to the promotion of Native assimilation as the ideal national policy for addressing the "Indian Problem"—and the story of Don Luis is at root a story of assimilative failure if not also of assimilation's flawed assumptions. Indeed, the story of an educated, Christianized Indian who experienced a decade of Western civilization before choosing unequivocally against it does not square easily with a report promoting federal policies based upon its own titular values of "Indian Education and Civilization." This surely explains why, despite the brevity of her account, Fletcher contributes to the tale an entirely new detail, one that is never mentioned in Shea's account or prior histories, and which is thus almost certainly her own invention. Don Luis, she contends, had a personal motive for his destruction of the Ajacán settlement after "regain[ing] his people": he "had been separated [from them] against his will by Spanish marauders" (21). Unlike other historians' speculations about why Don Luis acted as he did, Fletcher's assertion here has the distinction of not only ignoring prior historical understanding but actually inverting it: Shea clearly stipulates (whether accurately or not) that Don Luis was a "voluntary companion" of the Spaniards. Invoking his victimization by villainous Spanish slavers despite a notable absence of such an episode in prior accounts, Fletcher's version of the story posits an individual passion versus a collective rationale behind Don Luis's unsettlement of the colony—and thus neatly contains the story's most subversive possibilities in this context: the obvious doubts that it might register about the central tenets of *Indian Education and Civilization*.

As in the case of Greenhow, moreover, the problem of territorial possession tacitly underwrites the story of Don Luis as well as the larger report.

Indeed, the report itself might more accurately have been titled according to a straightforward statement that Fletcher made in an 1886 article while she was working on the government text: "The Indian question in its civil aspect is two-fold," she wrote, "education and land." Civilization, then, is a proxy term for territory—and in fact Fletcher made it her mission while writing *Indian Education and Civilization* to deploy the full weight of American Indian history as laid down in its pages to dramatically change federal policy regarding the future of indigenous land. In 1885 she approached Massachusetts senator Henry Dawes to discuss his impending legislation regarding Indian land allotment, which had recently passed the Senate, impressing him enough to gain herself an appointment to the influential lobbying committee that would ultimately push this controversial law through the House, becoming federal law as the General Allotment Act in February 1887.[76] Of course, historians now recognize that this infamous law—which claimed to safeguard Indian land by allotting legal property rights and deeds of title to individuals—was wholly disastrous for Native Americans, depriving them of two-thirds of all remaining landholdings over the next half century, and indeed decimating their human population, which reached its lowest numbers on record during that period.[77]

But the so-called Dawes Act came into existence as it did because of Fletcher's powerful historical intervention. When she went to see Dawes, she had been combing the archives of colonial settlement and had at her fingertips the details of every prior Indian treaty made across the centuries along with its outcome. And while Dawes had envisioned a law protecting Indian landholdings through the preservation of a "tribal patent" or deed of collective ownership, Fletcher wanted to see the Indian liberated from "the tyranny of the tribe as to his property."[78] Persuaded by her historical authority, Dawes changed the text of the act to mandate land allotments to *individual* Indians rather than tribal collectives, to make allotment compulsory rather than conditional upon the voting consent of tribal members, and to enact allotment immediately by breaking treaty law rather than waiting to renegotiate it. Fletcher's specific, reformist reasons for enacting each of these changes in the Dawes law are perhaps less important than her stated belief that "the lands held by many of the Indian tribes are too vast ever to be fully utilized by them," and indeed that the "extent of [Indian] territory retards the advancement of the Indian," "leav[ing] him without ambition or any stimulus to action," "the victim of conceit and pauperism."[79] It is no coincidence that the grammatical emphasis of Fletcher's prose here is upon the land rather than the Indians who are designated for "education and civilization": "vast tracts lie like a dead weight on the white community," "unused acres may not be touched by civilizing work," "waste land irritates the settlers." Historians have long noted that the defining *effect* of the Dawes Act was its creation of a land surplus that could be sold off to these "irritate[d]" settlers once the allotments were made—and its designation, of course, of individual property that could be sold far more easily than could collectively held lands.[80] What Fletcher's writing suggests, perhaps predictably, is that taking the land was the tacit *point* and not the ill-advised, unfortunate consequence of the Dawes Act. It was a legal ritual of claiming territorial possession as much as was the unfurling of the Spanish royal standard on the isle of Guanahani in 1492. As Dawes himself would later put it, describing his own role as distinguished from Fletcher's in the conceptual development of the General Allotment Act, "I stand in reference to that [legislation] very much as Americus Vespuscious stands to Columbus."[81]

The Translators of Nineteenth-Century Indian Reform: Colonial Settlement and the Native Critique of Anthropology

But if Fletcher and Dawes remained unaware of the ideological engine driving their rhetoric, the contemporaneous Omaha translator Susette La Flesche—who knew Alice Fletcher well—offered an unflinching assessment of the relationship between settler colonialism and the land which underlay the allotment agenda. "If it were not for the lands which the Indian holds, he would have been a citizen long before the negro," she contended in 1881—a point that anticipates Wolfe's observation that "Indians and Black people in the U.S. have been racialized in opposing ways that reflect their antithetical roles in the development of U.S. [settler colonialism]": an obstruction to territorial acquisition, on the one hand, and a source of enslaved labor, on the other.[82] The competing rhetorics of Indian civilization and savagery masked this fundamental problem driving American settlement, La Flesche suggested: "the clever operators of the Indian Ring," she wrote, "not caring what [the Indian] is, but looking on him for what he has, and the opportunities he affords . . . pounce on him and use him as a means."[83]

Born on an Omaha reservation, educated at a mission school, and a multilingual speaker of the Omaha-Ponca language as well as French and English, La Flesche grew up to become a translator in both the specific and general senses of the term: as an interpreter for non-English-language Indian testimony and as a lecturer, writer, and activist addressing the non-Indian world about indigenous rights.[84] La Flesche was serving as a translator for the Ponca leader Standing Bear and touring the United States to protest the forced removal of the Ponca Indians when she first met Alice Fletcher. She closely observed the reformer's attitude toward the Omaha people whom she studied and proposed to help, and soon came to mistrust her. It was not lost on La Flesche that Fletcher opposed granting immediate citizenship to the Indian peoples whom she termed "wards of the nation" as a part of the allotment plan. La Flesche had initially supported the allotment plan but only as a part of bringing the full legal rights of U.S. nationals to all Native peoples; "Allow an Indian to suggest," she wrote, "that the solution of the vexed 'Indian Question' is *Citizenship*."[85] As the quotation marks suggest, La Flesche had a certain ironic distance upon the language of Indian reform, and she cannily read the term "ward" in particular as key to the logic of elimination: "As a 'ward,' or extraordinary being, if [an Indian] is accused of committing a crime, this serves as a pretext of war for his extermination." Nor was La Flesche naïve about the productive uses to which the "Indian Question" could be put to sustain the livelihoods of those who sought to answer it: "The Indian . . . affords employment to about ten thousand employees in the Indian Bureau, with all the salaries attached, as well as innumerable contractors, freighters, and land speculators." Fletcher was one of those employees, of course; and as La Flesche indicates here, it was not merely ideological on her part, but in her own economic interests, to promulgate the concept of Indian wardship.

As it turned out, Fletcher would end up formally adopting La Flesche's half-brother, Francis La Flesche—who not only played the role of Fletcher's adoptive son and thus literal "ward" but also served as her translator throughout her career as an anthropologist.[86] This relationship in turn put distance—publicly if not privately—between the La Flesche brother and sister, especially after Susette La Flesche married the Indian reformer Thomas Henry Tibbles, for whom she too worked as a translator. Like La Flesche, Tibbles opposed some aspects of Fletcher's allotment agenda, particularly its lack of a provision for immediate citizenship, and he jockeyed to offset her power and influence among the Omaha Indians. The close personal relationships of these two Omaha translators with those for whom they acted as interpreters thus paralleled each other while putting the La Flesche siblings, at least outwardly, on opposing sides of a power struggle within the Indian reform movement. Moreover, both relationships eventually disclosed signs of a similar strain, a tension that ultimately suggests a long-standing ambivalence on the part of each translator.[87]

Susette La Flesche publicly supported her husband's work in her lectures and editorials, but her own writing sometimes seemed to undercut the self-aggrandizing puffery of Tibbles's account of his own role as a reformer. In *The Ponca Chiefs*, for example, a work ostensibly addressing the mistreatment of the Ponca people and the trial of Standing Bear, Tibbles included an entire chapter on a character based upon himself as a heroic Western frontiersman who "did not pretend to be civilized," "carried perhaps the marks of more gunshot and other wounds than any other one man in a thousand miles of him," and who—when learning of the mistreatment of the Poncas—"brought his fist down on the table and said, 'Those Indians shall not be taken back to die in the Indian Territory.'"[88] Susette La Flesche was enlisted to provide for this work of protest—and authorial self-promotion—"an Introduction, written by an Indian Girl," and she was accordingly identified on the cover page not as

"Susette La Flesche," which she had been called for most of her life, but under her indigenous name from a private childhood ceremony: "Inshta Theamba (Bright Eyes)." Whatever La Flesche thought of the role she was asked to play in constructing this textual apparatus, she wrote an introduction that offset the bloated self-congratulations offered in Tibbles's text by cutting straight to the true importance of the work. "This little book is only a simple narration of facts concerning some of my people," she began. La Flesche's introduction, moreover, did not include heroic characterizations of individual white reformers but emphasized instead a collective national readership that was guilty of "indifference" before the "evil shown forth" in the government's treatment of Indians. Against Tibbles's grandiloquent prose, La Flesche counterpoised the "little thing, a simple thing, which my people ask of a nation whose watchword is liberty": "They ask for their liberty and law is liberty." La Flesche's hope for the book, she indicates, is that it finds a readership within "every home in the land," for she envisions not a lone frontiersman saving victimized Indians but instead the collective might of a public sphere: "The people are the power which move the magistrates who administer the laws."

Susette La Flesche's introduction thus translated Tibbles's bombastic and self-satisfied tirade into a "simple narration of facts" focused on democratic possibility rather than a single gun-slinging reformer. Meanwhile, her brother Francis La Flesche was also playing a compelling translative role in Fletcher's simultaneous quest to "put the public and the press more fully in possession of the facts of Indian life"—a quest that was, as this acquisitive language suggests, simultaneously ethnological and political.[89] All outward appearances suggest that Francis La Flesche dutifully aided Fletcher as a translator and research assistant throughout her career as an ethnologist and a Special Agent at the Bureau of Indian Affairs; in later years, after his adoption, he shared a house with her and cared for her until her death. But as with his sister's writings, Francis La Flesche's scholarly work tells a more complex story. While translating indigenous tongues into English for Fletcher, La Flesche was also acquiring another language for himself: that of the emergent discipline of anthropology.[90] As time went on, La Flesche subtly distanced himself from Fletcher's work, undertaking a study of law and embracing a new role as a writer of fiction, in such a way that his adoptive mother's progress as both an ethnologist and Special Agent was often thwarted by her inability to acquire or fully understand the information she wanted.[91] Moreover, the anthropological work that La Flesche produced after this scholarly separation from Fletcher began to emphasize the epistemological limits of ethnology itself, and particularly its problematic dependence upon (mis)translation.

In 1903, for example, La Flesche was asked to respond to the unveiling of Cyrus E. Dallin's statue "The Medicine Man" by delivering an address to the Fairmont Park Art Association of Philadelphia. Soon afterward printed in the *Journal of American Folklore*, the address—"Who was the medicine man?"—cannily avoided saying much about the sculpture itself until the last two paragraphs, where La Flesche briefly congratulated Dallin for having "risen above the distorting influence of the prejudice one race is apt to feel toward another" in creating his work. But La Flesche simultaneously established his own distance from the representation by referring to Dallin as "your artist" and "your sculptor" while also marking the limits of his willingness to engage with the work: "I cannot discuss, from the standpoint of an artist," he demurred, "the Medicine Man as he is here portrayed."[92] Instead, La Flesche took the opportunity to trace a history of Western misapprehension of indigenous religious philosophy and knowledge production from the era of colonial missionaries through the emergence of anthropology. Missionaries were "well meaning and zealous men" who nevertheless "did not stop to inquire if the people had any idea of a Power that made and controlled all things"; in first overlooking the presence of Native thought, even as they claimed expertise in Native culture, they laid the foundations for the continued misrecognition of Native knowledge production across the centuries: "It was not possible therefore for the white people to gain, through the medium of these teachers, any definite knowledge of the real thoughts of the Indian concerning the Supreme Being" (4). Missionaries find direct descendants, moreover, in "those who have undertaken to study [the Indian] as an object of ethnological interest"—anthropologists who have recorded Native cultural productions without an attention to Native frameworks of knowledge, and "in such manner as to obscure their true meaning and to make them appear as childish or foolish" (5).

La Flesche locates the source of this problem in mistranslation: the "linguistic difficulties" faced by ethnologists who fail to acknowledge that "Indian tongues differ widely from the English language, not only in the construction of sentences but in general literary form." Failures of translation in turn yield the misrecognition of alternative knowledge frameworks: the "different lessons" drawn from "a different standpoint." The point here is not merely that Indian "mental capacity" is misjudged, for the Western anthropologist's production of knowledge is also distorted: "So when scholars give a literary translation of an Indian story, both its spirit and its form are lost to the English reader." The anthropologist's drive to acquire information is catastrophically—and, he implies, permanently—thwarted: "The true religious ideas of the Indians will never be fully comprehended" (12).

Despite this cautionary note, however, La Flesche persisted in his anthropological work. By the time he wrote *The Osage Tribe: Rite of the Chiefs; Sayings of the Ancient Men*, published in 1921 just a few years before Fletcher's death, he had found what might be called a solution to the problems of translation outlined in his earlier address on the Medicine Man: a three-part representation of Osage religious rituals that included first, a "free English translation of the intoned or recited parts of the rituals"; second, a transcription of the rituals in the Osage language as recorded on "dictaphone records made by *Wa-tse'-moⁿ-iⁿ* and other members of the tribe versed in tribal rites"; and third, a word-for-word English translation "as literal given as it could be made under certain difficulties" (54–55). Neither of the forms of translation offered in this tripartite scheme was without problems. La Flesche warned that the free translation had been wrenched from its performative context and altered "for convenience in reading, and to avoid the monotony of constant repetition," while the metaphrase or literal translation was replete with the "tropes, figures of speech, and metaphorical expressions [that] were freely used by the *Noⁿ'-hoⁿ-zhiⁿ-ga* to convey their ideas, thus making it difficult for the uninitiated to fully understand the ritualistic language" (55). It was perhaps the second mode of representation—the transcription—upon which La Flesche was pinning his hopes for posterity: as he explained it briefly in the introduction, "The original form is included in this volume in order that the educated Osage may read the rituals of his ancestors in his own language unconfused by the English translations" (55). La Flesche was, in other words, simply bracketing the confusions of translation, the distortions of Western ethnology, by producing within his scholarly work a legacy for Native readers—by producing anthropology specifically as a means of Native knowledge production, and for future Native uses.

As Native interpreters and intellectuals working for nineteenth-century Indian reform, Susette La Flesche Tibbles and Francis La Flesche thus provide a compelling gloss on the story of Don Luis as recorded in Alice Fletcher's report for the U.S. Senate, reminding us of the alternative histories that reside in the often unexamined relations between translators and those whom they ostensibly serve. As we have seen, Don Luis would reappear with odd regularity in a range of disparate documents and contexts throughout the nineteenth century, from the writings of John Gilmary Shea to Fletcher's *Indian Education and Civilization*—and despite the willed attempt by Robert Greenhow to suppress both the historical evidence of the colony of Ajacán and the unsettlement of America that Don Luis's story embodied. But even his appearance in the first popular history of the United States, by William Cullen Bryant, could not save Don Luis from the fate assigned to him by the novelist explored in the next chapter of this book: as James Branch Cabell would argue about the story of Don Luis in 1947, "oblivion is its right doom."[93]

The Good Neighborly Don Luis

ROANOKE, AJACÁN, AND THE HEMISPHERIC SOUTH

By the late 1840s, as we saw in Chapter 5, Robert Greenhow of the U.S. State Department could be credited with several impressive scholarly and political achievements. He had willfully falsified colonial history to present-day ends: first by bolstering the U.S. case for Oregon territory by entering a fictional manuscript from early Virginia into the Congressional Record as historical fact; and second by consolidating the historical borders of the United States just after the Mexican War by suppressing the story of Don Luis and the "First Discovery" of Virginia in an official report to the Virginia Historical Society. One year after the conclusion of the war, Greenhow was turning his attention to Cuba, and to what his wife—in a secret missive to Senator John C. Calhoun—called "the incorporation of that ocean gem, in our Sisterhood of States." As proslavery Southerners, the Greenhows viewed the potential annexation of slaveholding Cuba as a key defense against "agitation in regard to the abolition of Slavery in the District of Columbia" and against the "encroachments of the North upon Southern rights." It is hard to know how Greenhow might have brought colonial history to bear on what Rose Greenhow called "the progress of the Cuba affair," but the general pattern of his career suggests that he would have found a way to do so, had the project of acquiring Cuba ever gotten fully off the ground. Instead, the Greenhows went to Mexico City where, as we have seen, he worked to settle the land claims of U.S. citizens in the aftermath of the war and Mexico's loss of nearly half its national territory.[1]

In 1916, another scholarly Virginia historian, Woodrow Wilson, was elected to his second term as president. Wilson had campaigned on the famous anti-intervention slogan "He kept us out of war," and he had publically repudiated the hemispheric expansionism of the previous century, drafting a Pan-American treaty endorsing the unity of all the Americas and pledging to keep the United States from acquiring more territory by conquest.[2]

Wilson cited his regional origin as the source of his hemispheric foreign policy: "I came from the South and I know what war is, for I have seen its wreckage and terrible ruin."[3] If, by his own account, the Civil War gave shape to Wilson the "Peace Without Victory" neutralist, it is also fair to say that the historical echoes of the U.S.-Mexican War formed the Wilson who would shortly lead the United States into armed conflict on a global scale. Popular culture continues to enjoin readers of American history to "Remember the Lusitania"—the British ship sunk by German submarines in 1915—but it was the so-called Zimmermann telegram from two years later that finally catalyzed the U.S. entrance into World War I: the intercepted German communiqué to Mexican officials asking for a military alliance in exchange for "an understanding on our part that Mexico is to reconquer the lost territory in Texas, New Mexico, and Arizona."[4]

The force of the Zimmermann telegram derived not only from the specter of invasion it raised but from its offer of a *reconquista*, an implied invitation to return to a prior historical scene in hopes of forcing an alternative outcome. The telegram proposed not just an act of war, that is, but an act of unsettlement: an unsettling of contemporary international boundaries based on the logic of defunct historical borders from the previous century, and also, of course, the concordant literal unsettlement of the dominant culture this act would have demanded. Its importation of the geopolitical past into the wartime present—its use of the language of *reconquista*—served to register the constructedness, instability, and malleability of national borders. Yet the Zimmermann telegram also showcased the dependence of all geopolitical borders on historical precedents, subject to varying degrees of ideological fragility and of varying temporal removes from the present.

As Wilson's antiwar pronouncement of his Southern origin suggests, the status of the U.S. South was closely intertwined with the contradictory hemispheric politics of this early twentieth-century moment. The relation of the U.S. South to the hemispheric South was an old and vexed one even in Greenhow's time—and, as Jennifer Greeson has shown, the writing of colonial history had long provided a means of establishing symbolic distinctions between the two Souths, two regions that shared an uncomfortably obvious number of common features within a larger world system.[5] To write, as Greenhow did in Black Legend style, of Spain's "ruthless" conquistadors and "wretched colonies," was to insist—even as he looked to Cuba for U.S. annexation—on the fundamental unrelatedness of his own South to the Latin American fate that Virginia had nearly missed. After the Civil War, however, the geopolitical proximity of the hemispheric South to the U.S. South yielded an even more ambivalent and charged set of symbolic terms, given the "wreckage and ruin" experienced by the former slaveholding states, the increase of intermittent U.S. military interventions throughout the hemisphere beginning in

1865, and widespread national U.S. discussion of "using our great resources in guiding the reconstruction of the world."[6]

This hemispheric moment is helpfully delineated by what Arthur P. Whitaker long ago called the "Western Hemisphere idea," which informed twentieth-century U.S. culture and international politics from the Pan-American Movement in the last decades of the nineteenth century to the articulation of the "Bolton thesis" in 1932 to the Good Neighbor Policy instantiated by Franklin Delano Roosevelt in 1933.[7] Advancing the notion of a common pan-American bond that set the disparate peoples of the American hemisphere apart from Europe and the larger world, Western Hemisphere discourse envisioned a triumphal United States leading the wider Americas to a glorious future of economic modernization—when, as Secretary of State James G. Blaine put it during the 1889 Pan-American Conference in Washington, D.C.—"the personal and commercial relations of the American states, north and south, shall be so developed and so regulated that each shall acquire the highest possible advantage from the enlightened and enlarged intercourse of all."[8] Yet as the ambiguous reference to "American states, north and south" suggests, the United States' own South was positioned as both the national agent and the regional object of this project of development, regulation, and enlightenment.

Of all southerly "American states," Virginia—precisely because of the venerable colonial history that Greenhow had sought to defend from Spanish incursion—held a special place in the national conversation about the problems and possibilities of enlightening the South, whether national or hemispheric. Virginia was simultaneously abject and superior: abject as a part of the U.S. South—"the Nation's Problem," as Roosevelt would put it in the summer of 1938—but also superior to the rest of the U.S. South, by popular national fiat as well as its own self-description.[9] In his infamous essay on Southern cultural poverty—"The Sahara of the Bozart," first published in 1917 (a few months after Wilson received the intercepted Zimmermann telegram)—H. L. Mencken lambasted the whole region of the U.S. South as a "gargantuan paradise of the fourth-rate": "there is not a single picture gallery worth going into, or a single orchestra capable of playing the nine symphonies of Beethoven, or a single opera-house, or a single theater devoted to decent plays, or a single public monument that is worth looking at. . . . [not] a single Southern prose writer who can actually write."[10] Virginia did not escape condemnation ("Virginia has no art, no literature, no philosophy, no mind or aspiration of her own"), but Mencken singled out the state on the basis of both its former and present status within the region: "in the great days indubitably the premier American state, the mother of Presidents and statesmen, the home of the first American university worthy of the name, the arbiter elegantarum of the Western World"; "by long odds, the most civilized of the Southern states, now as always. . . . the best of the South today" (139–42).

Even the "worst" of Virginians, Mencken avowed, "show the effects of a great tradition": "They hold themselves above other Southerners, and with sound pretension" (141).

Mencken does not mention Jamestown among the Old Dominion's qualifications as the "premier American state," but he might as well have (139). With its chivalric legend of Captain John Smith and Pocahontas as well as its storied class of minor nobility, Jamestown played an important symbolic role in establishing Virginia's mystique—its reputation for having what Mencken unapologetically described as "men of delicate fancy, urbane instinct and aristocratic manner—in brief, superior men—in brief, gentry" (137). Mencken did not invent the myth of Virginia gentility, of course, but his particular use of Virginia exceptionalism within his larger excoriation of U.S. Southern cultural sterility (Southern letters especially) became an ideological cornerstone for the group of Southern writers who published their Agrarian manifesto, *I'll Take My Stand*, in 1930.[11] The Agrarians resurrected the century-old "cavalier myth" of the U.S. South: the legend that the South's ostensible difference from a Northern culture of middle-class shopkeepers and religious fundamentalists was attributable to its original settlement by noblemen and squires, aristocratic Royalists fleeing to a New World haven for the so-called distressed cavaliers.[12] By the early twentieth century, few could hold onto this mythology in "its overt form," as the journalist and historian W. J. Cash would put it; yet the Agrarians nevertheless transmuted Mencken's Virginia exceptionalism—based solely on what Cash spurned as a "narrow world" of Virginia planter society—into a theory of Southern difference that gave the cavalier thesis the new authority of sociological analysis.[13] Virginia's plantation elite had migrated throughout the greater South, went the theory, allowing their aristocratic traditions both to spread and to shape the sensibility of the entire region, endowing it with a culture of small farmer-philosophers and gentlemen extending far beyond the Old Dominion and yet indelibly stamped with Virginian superiority. The national context that produced heightened Southern literary alienation was thus both intertwined and in contradiction with a regional context of disputed Southern meaning. Was Virginia the exception or the exception that became the rule? Was Mencken right, or were the Agrarians?

In the hemispheric idiom of the early twentieth century, both of these contexts, national and regional, figured within a larger global milieu shaped by the vexed and mutually defining relation of the U.S. South and the hemispheric South. Mencken captures this global context offhandedly throughout "The Sahara of the Bozart" by characterizing the South during Reconstruction as the victim of a kind of uneven global development. "It is as if the Civil War stamped out every last bearer of the torch, and left only a mob of peasants on the field," Mencken argues: "One thinks of Asia Minor, resigned to Armenians, Greeks and wild swine, of Poland abandoned to the Poles. . . . the South is an awe-inspiring blank—a brother to Portugal, Serbia and Albania. . . . an intellectual Gobi or Lapland" (138–40). "If the whole of the late Confederacy were to be engulfed by a tidal wave tomorrow," he proposes, "the effect upon the civilized minority of men in the world would be but little greater than that of a flood on the Yang-tse-kiang" (136–37): But given the South's status as a "late empire"—one of dazzling imperial potential as the center of a slave-holding dominion stretching down the southern hemisphere—the most acute irony is, finally, its comparability to Latin America (138). "The south produces nothing and reads nothing," Mencken scoffed; "it is culturally about as dead as Yucatan."[14] "One could no more imagine a Lee or a Washington in the Virginia of today than one could imagine a Huxley in Nicaragua" (140).

The parallel impossibility (as Mencken would have it) of a great military leader in Virginia and a great scientist in Nicaragua—Thomas Huxley had defended Darwin's theory of evolution in England, and Mencken famously saw anti-evolutionism as a symbol of provincial ignorance—evokes the un-spoken connection in this derogation of the U.S. South: Nicaragua had been occupied by U.S. military forces for five years when Mencken penned his arti-cle in 1917.[15] Mencken's analogy thus subtly exploits a shared imperial relation. Like Nicaragua, the "late empire" of the U.S. South was now itself the prod-uct of a recent imperial occupation, an enabling yet crippling contradiction for the literary culture of the modern United States.[16] Thus on the one hand, the Agrarian poet Allen Tate could laud Jefferson Davis in his biography of the Confederate statesman as "the best Secretary of War the United States ever had," his "greatest aim . . . Southern expansion into Mexico or Cuba or Central America," while on the other hand, William Faulkner's Jason Compson roiled over "them up there in Washington spending fifty thousand dollars a day keeping an army in *Nicaragua* or some place."[17] As Jason well understood, the U.S. military occupation of Nicaragua, an agriculturally rich producer of cotton, correlated on a number of levels to the economic and social conditions of the post-Civil War U.S. South—which is why some elite Southern families, as Mencken notes offhandedly, "went to South America."

With this set of regional, national, and global contradictions in mind, the remainder of this chapter turns to two literary works that emerged during the last years of the Western Hemisphere era: Paul Green's symphonic drama, *The Lost Colony*, first staged in 1937; and a 1942 novel that I suggest responded sharply to Green's play, James Branch Cabell's *The First Gentleman of America*—a virtually unstudied novel that features Don Luis de Velasco as its protagonist. Both works take up the colonial history venerated by Greenhow, and both tell stories of unsettlement. Both emerge from a historical tradition in crisis, marked by the logical impasse of conflicting state, regional, and na-tional self-representations, when the meaning of the U.S. South was defined not only by its long-standing relation to the larger American nation and an emergent U.S. empire but by its new, uncanny twin: the hemispheric South to which it had once looked longingly as a source of extended power, but with which it was now inextricably intertwined by the Great Depression, the Good Neighbor Policy, a history of military occupation, and the very idea of the Western Hemisphere. As we shall see, Green's *The Lost Colony* articulates colonial Roanoke as the origin of the U.S. nation, the antithesis of Virginia, and a tragic instance of Spanish atrocity that sharply differentiates the histories of the English and Spanish Americas. As a pointed response to Green's play, Cabell's *The First Gentleman of America* enacts a broad investigation of the Western Hemisphere idea itself through a generic conquest of irony even while celebrating an inevitably dominant Anglo-American version of history. Its strategies of containment, both historical and generic, shed light on why the story of Don Luis mattered in the first half of the twentieth century—and on why, as Cabell himself would suggest, it continues to be forgotten.

"The First Colony": Roanoke vs. Virginia

On August 18, 1937, Franklin and Eleanor Roosevelt traveled south to the Waterside Theater just outside Manteo, North Carolina, to attend a production of Paul Green's outdoor play *The Lost Colony: A Symphonic Drama of American History*. The Roosevelts had not graced the Waterside Theater on the opening night of Green's play—July 4 of that same summer—but their attendance this particular night nevertheless marked another symbolic date for a production of *The Lost Colony*: the birthday of Virginia Dare, the so-called first English child born in the New World. Roosevelt's official remarks following the play made parallel references to the originary significance of the settlement and the child for the U.S. national narrative: "We do not know the fate of Virginia Dare or the First Colony," Franklin observed. "We do know, however, that the story of America is largely a record of that spirit of adventure."[18] The President's remarks might have been scripted by the playwright himself, so closely did they adhere to the counterintuitive message of the drama: that England's short-lived, ill-fated attempt to colonize Roanoke Island would come to define the U.S. nation in the twentieth century, in the year of the settlement's 350th anniversary. As Green later told the story of the play's genesis, a North Carolina newspaper editor had predicted the opportunity for "nationwide, even worldwide publicity" for the state if it could find a way to showcase such a colonial-era anniversary as their neighbor to the north had done with great success thirty years earlier: "You see," the editor said to Green, "1937 will be here soon. . . . We ought to have a great exposition—something like the Jamestown Exposition of 1907."[19]

From the beginning, then, Green understood *The Lost Colony* in relation to Jamestown and especially the vast, commercial context of its commemoration during the 1907 World's Fair Exposition—which had, despite broad financial failure, garnered two presidential visits and eventually resulted in the founding of the Norfolk U.S. Naval Base.[20] But the commemoration of Jamestown had found its cultural logic in Virginia's originary status as the site of the first *permanent* English colony in North America. Roanoke, North Carolina, by contrast, offered only the site where the English had first *attempted* colonization in the late sixteenth century—where the English had tried and failed to begin a New World colony, and where they had given up the whole colonial project until the first decade of the next century. The primary contribution of Green's play was thus to convert a spectacular colonial failure into a correspondingly spectacular protonational success—nothing less, in the subtitle's phrase, than a "symphonic drama of American history." *The Lost Colony* was North Carolina's answer to Virginia, its bid—lacking the distinction of historical success—for the distinction of historical priority in the larger national narrative.

Green's play positioned itself advantageously in its address to a larger moment of overlapping state, regional and hemispheric contexts, arguing for Roanoke's primacy within a national tradition even as it also repudiates and distances itself from the history of the Spanish in America. As a symphonic drama, *The Lost Colony* in effect challenged Mencken's complaint that the U.S. South boasted no music or plays, despite the "little theater movement" that had swept the rest of the country ("Everywhere else the wave rolls high—but along the line of the Potomac it breaks upon a rock-bound shore"): "There are no committees down there cadging subscriptions for orchestras; if a string quartet is ever heard there, the news of it has never come out; an opera troupe, when it roves the land, is a nine days' wonder [and] there is no little theater beyond. . . ." At the same time, Green's play disputed the priority of Virginia within the U.S. South, taking on both the cavalier thesis of the Agrarians and Jamestown's status as the so-called cradle of America.[21] Green arguably succeeded on all these fronts with his play: *The Lost Colony* has run continuously nearly every summer since 1937.[22]

In recounting the history of the Roanoke settlement and advancing an argument about its role in defining U.S. tradition, *The Lost Colony* also elaborates a particular historical sensibility: progressive, based in the common people, yet driven by the individual dreams of great men, and—above all—insistently earnest. Only the softest, most superficial of ironies are permitted in the script: Queen Elizabeth's jocular asides about her promiscuity or about a man's lack of tact as a suitor, for example. On the matter of History per se, the drama's guiding sensibility emerges clearly in the original 1937 stage directions for the characters of the Chorus and the Historian, who occupy "a sort of niche or alcove built into the bank at the immediate left front of the proscenium":

> Here as if seen through a transparent gauze is a group of fifteen or twenty men and women who constitute the commenting and interpretive chorus

throughout the play. They are dressed in gray smock-like vestments. Down in the middle forefront of them and seated at a little table with a light and a great open book is the elderly historian and chorus leader who is also dressed like the chorus. He begins reading aloud. . . .

The play's relation to the colonial past is a collective or communitarian one—its history will be articulated by a Greek Chorus, made up of representatives of the general Elizabethan population depicted in the play—that nevertheless rests on the disciplinary authority of one man, set apart from the others not only as the chorus leader but as the "elderly historian." He may be dressed like the others, but the Historian is the only character with access to the official text of the past, the "great open book" of History before him. Later editions of the play make the distinction even more explicit, describing this character as "a kindly, elderly man, dressed in a scholar's dark robe" rather than the "smock-like vestments" of the general chorus. But the scholarly and the ecclesiastical are essentially flip sides of the same vocational coin when it comes to the play's Historian, who offers a fundamentally benevolent view of history as a progressive unfolding of preordained events: as the central protagonist John Borden puts it in the final scene, "Somehow a destiny, a purpose moving deeper than we know" (125)—and going forward, always, without any acknowledgement of contradiction, without any ironic perception of history as a form of knowledge.

Indeed, to the extent that *The Lost Colony* registers an awareness of the connection between its own historical moment of first production and the historical moment that is its subject, it does so with the fundamental earnestness at the heart of all prolepsis in the philosophy of history. "Friends, we are gathered here this evening to honor the spiritual birthplace of our nation and to memorialize those brave men and women who made it so," intones the Historian: "And in the symbol of their endurance and their sacrifice, let us renew our courage and our hope. For as we keep faith with them so we shall keep faith with ourselves." In attending to the "pioneers" of Roanoke and how they "lived, struggled, and suffered," viewers will thus see the reflected but wholly un-ironic meaning of their own "endurance and . . . sacrifice" during the decade of the Great Depression. The Roanoke colonists may be destined to "walk [the] way of death," as the chorus announces, but their eventual disappearance from the historical record nevertheless marks what Governor John White, at the beginning of Act II, somewhat eerily terms "the permanent beginning of English colonization in the new world" (100)—as if he already knows that the colony itself, on the other hand, will not be permanent. The play has begun, in other words, to hedge its definitional bets in emplotting Roanoke within a national narrative.

This emplotment depends in large part upon a distinction that the play tacitly invokes between Roanoke and the future Virginia, most prominently through its characterization of Roanoke's colonial sponsor, Sir Walter Raleigh, as well as the four historical colonists who are its main players: Ananias Dare and his fiancée and then wife Eleanor White Dare; John Borden; and Old Tom, a "masterless man" who could be any one of the twelve historical Thomases who voyaged to Roanoke. The name "Virginia" is of course prominent throughout the play, both because Virginia was the general English name for the whole North American expanse stretching up to Maine, including Bermuda (but excluding Spanish Florida) and because of Virginia Dare, named for the land in which she was born. But Green's play privileges not just the historical specificity of the island-setting of Roanoke but the name "Roanoke" itself, when it takes up the subject of future national meaning. The name "Virginia," on the other hand, is often associated with those values the play subtly defines itself against. Old Tom, for example, is the play's preeminent spokesman for the national future and the American ideals supposedly incipient in the settlement, and he never once speaks the name Virginia. Instead, the inebriated reveries of this English vagrant, both Shakespearean fool and proto-American visionary, advertise the ostensibly anti-aristocratic spirit of the colony as distinct from that of the future Virginia—the Virginia, that is to say, mythologized by Mencken and the Agrarians. "[A]s the world knows, the queen's power depends on the common people, and the people are all poor," Tom pronounces in the first act: "And Sir Walter too. Never will he make a colony on Roanoke except through us. It is now the time of the demos. . . ." (41). But this clever beggar-cum-political savant is not a static figure; Old Tom will transform as a colonist and come to celebrate the supposedly classless ideal embodied by Roanoke: "[H]ere where there is no remembrance I who was lately nothing am become somebody. . . . Roanoke, thou hast made a man of me!" (128).

It is hard not to read this paean to the self-made man through the lens of the play's historical amnesia, as there is also, apparently, "no remembrance" when it comes to Sir Walter Raleigh, who has been dramatically refigured to serve the anti-genteel sensibility of the script. Raleigh plays a prominent role in the first half of *The Lost Colony*, set in England, where he is cast not as a soldier aristocrat who had participated in the brutal quelling of Irish rebellions, but rather as a "poor boy from Devon" who has never forgotten his humble roots.[23] "'Tis well known the great Sir Walter hath a soft heart for such [vagrants as Old Tom]," notes a passing soldier in England (41), while Raleigh himself purports to take a democratic view of his own political popularity, for which, as he tells his patron Queen Elizabeth, he "owe[s] the people many thanks" (51). No longer a courtier par excellence, symbol of chivalric nobility and royal patronage at its most exhilarating and dangerous, this Raleigh is instead the play's proto-American, but distinctly non-Virginian, New World dreamer. Moreover, the play centers its second half around the character of colonist John Borden, who stands in as Raleigh's spiritual heir (the historical Raleigh never having set foot on Roanoke) and the true romantic match for the already be-trothed Eleanor. As Borden reminds her in the first act, Eleanor is marrying Ananias Dare at her father's behest, "for pride and place and family name," though Borden, a mere "tenant on her father's farm," offers "the toil of a man's true hands that would work for you" (57–58). Dare may be right for Eleanor in England, where manual labor "counts for naught," but the play makes clear that he is not right for Eleanor in Roanoke, where his obsequious regard for royalty cannot replace the value of hard labor, for which Borden stands: as the latter puts it tersely, describing his relation to Eleanor, "I plough [her father's] land." Like Raleigh, Borden is also a "poor boy from Devon" and a would-be populist in a world organized around the privileges of rank. When asked if he will be "obedient to orders" in Roanoke, he answers affirmatively but with a glaringly proto-American qualification: "as independent men should be—no more" (57).

The conclusion of the play will bring John Borden and the eventually wid-owed Eleanor Dare into their destined union as the true spiritual inheritors of America. The drama organizes this America quite specifically around Roanoke rather than, indeed in opposition to, the Virginia territory within which it lies—and in fact the particular vision of Southern history against which *The Lost Colony* tacitly defines itself: the South that is merely England elsewhere, made by Virginia cavaliers into an anciently descended culture of southern squires and latter-day chivalry. The play makes this antagonism particularly clear during the scene in which the new English territory first receives its name. At Raleigh's suggestion, Elizabeth has just taken a puff from an Indian pipe brought back from the newly discovered land—a farcical moment that is clearly comical rather than reverential; as the stage directions would have it, the queen "falls to coughing and sputtering," her ladies and courtiers "surround[ing] her solicitously." The humor lies both in the public moment of royal gracelessness and in her furious reaction: she "throws the pipe back at Wanchese," the Indian from whom she had taken it, and then "looks angrily at Raleigh" before "quickly recovering her dignity." When she rises, the "people fall to their knees" and "Virginia" enters history as an after-thought, a recuperative gesture, a royal saving of face:

> Conscious of the great worth of our loyal servant, Sir Walter Raleigh, and of all those brave and daring subjects who crossed the unknown sea to spread the name and conquest of England further, I accept this day the tokens of their loyalty and service. And I do designate and order that from this time forth the new and western empire shall be named—(*she pauses for effect while everyone listens in suspense.*)—"Virginia" in honor of myself, England's virgin queen. . . .
>
> VOICES. Long live the Queen! Long live the Queen! Long live the Queen!
>
> —(*RALEIGH STANDS WITH BOWED HEAD LOOKING AT THE GROUND. . . .*) (55)

The scene thus suggests on a number of levels that the history associated with the name "Virginia" derives implicitly from monarchical self-congratulation, false self-mythologizing (a prior dialogue has already established her lack of virginity), and an imperial ambition—for "conquest," for a "new and western empire"—that the play will disavow in the name of an alternative U.S. historical trajectory embodied in Roanoke. "Virginia" emerges here as a continuation and an endorsement of monarchical rule and its chivalric code of value, as the people's shouts make clear, while Raleigh's response suggests a demurral—both from Elizabeth's designation and, more broadly, from the Agrarian tradition of Southern history that derives precisely from such a conception of Virginia. The scene is one of the few in the play to register any form of historical irony—but only in relation to Virginia. Crucially, Raleigh himself stands apart and does not participate in the actions or the language that produce this ironic history of Virginia; his dream of Roanoke consistently returns the play's historical mode to the reverential and the proleptic.

Rejecting the Virginia cavalier myth promulgated by the Agrarians, *The Lost Colony* instead advances an argument closely resembling the "frontier thesis" of Southern history, which would be most famously articulated more than a decade later in *The Mind of the South* (1941) by Green's fellow Carolinian man of letters, W. J. Cash. Cash's landmark study memorably privileged the yeoman farmers of the Carolina piedmont region and rough frontiersmen to the west over the so-called Virginia gentry as "the best people that the South has ever produced in any numbers."[24] This quasi-populist romanticism might be taken straight from the pages of *The Lost Colony* and its dramatization of Roanoke rather than Jamestown as the true spiritual origin of America. As its central representative, John Borden embodies what Cash would describe as "those qualities of physical energy and dogged application which, in the absence of degeneracy, are preeminently the heritage of the laborer." The leveling qualities of the frontier ensure that John and Eleanor come together at last in Roanoke, effectively defining its history by what Cash elaborated as a "characteristic of the frontier tradition everywhere": "that it places no such value of wealth and rank as they command in an old and stable society"; and that it believes that the personal qualities that make great men are "at least as important as possessions, and infinitely more important than heraldic crests." Indeed, Borden no sooner arrives in Roanoke than he finds himself promoted to captain and joint governor of the colony—exemplifying Cash's theory of the frontier's "predestined inheritance," a natural aristocracy comprised of men of "great personal courage," "substance and respect," who "possessed precisely the qualities necessary to the taming of the land." As Borden puts it none too subtly in the face of Roanoke's near demise, "I swear we will fight on and on here until this wilderness is won" (125). Cash termed this "the process of [the] rise to power" on the frontier, and in his view it was, as for Borden in Green's play, "simplicity itself."

It goes almost without saying that the frontier populism of Cash's thesis, and of its dramatic forerunner in *The Lost Colony*, is just as invested in naturalizing social hierarchy as the so-called cavalier thesis. Indeed, the "simplicity" of its vision depends upon a subtle relationship between race and region that informs the play from beginning to end. The drama calibrates the American-ness of its Roanoke protagonists—their simultaneous non-English-ness *and* non-Virginian-ness—by their refusal to engage in the discourse of noble Indian savagery and its rhetorical sympathy for Native priority. Part of what distinguishes the courtly Dare from the self-made Borden is his embrace of precisely this discourse, which is literary-historically aligned not with Roanoke but with Virginia and Pocahontas—the "King's dearest daughter," as John Smith called her—in its comparative feudalism and valorization of Indian nobility. In the first scene of Act II, set in Roanoke itself, Dare reprimands Borden—"in a prim schoolmasterish manner" that has no place in this frontier setting—for attempting to stop their fleeing Native interpreter, Wanchese: "Soldier John Borden, once more I command you to your place—in the ranks. If the noble Indian has traffic with his people in the forest, we have no right to stop him" (81). The play's populism and proto-Americanism are thus defined in part by the text's disdain for any concept of Native rights, ridiculed here through the figure of the noble savage.

Of course, Wanchese—like the historical translator and Native guide upon whom he is based—will betray the English not long after this scene, which occurs just after his return to Roanoke from London. In this sense, he is Don Luis's Anglophone cousin and, as we saw in Chapter 1, another in a long line of unremembered Native translators who drew upon their transatlantic and cross-cultural experiences to unsettle the project of European colonization.[25] While *The Lost Colony* does not concern itself with Wanchese's motives for doing so, it does stage a failure of translation in this scene by having Wanchese and the medicine man character, Uppowoc, exchange words in a shared language that is never interpreted for the audience: "Mish-wi aga, Wingina?" asks Wanchese, to which Uppowoc replies, "Ne bah na-tee-o, Wingina" (81). The opacity of their exchange signals the end of Wanchese's role as a colonial figuration of successful, transparent translation (as Manteo will remain); in the next lines he will not only defy Dare but will exit the play's view altogether until he puts his new position into English later in the scene: "You white people must go. You must leave our land now" (85).

As a whole, the scene establishes that Dare would be far more suited to life within a Virginia cavalier legend than he is to frontier leadership: his subsequent refusal to allow the colonists to encroach on Wanchese's tribal fishing grounds—"There's to be no bloodshed. The governor's orders" (93)—nearly costs the colony its already foreshortened life, and is thus an unforgiveable decision, in the play's view. He and the men who follow him are "all cowards," as one character puts it, while strapping John Borden, who would have detained Wanchese originally, is the "only man among them" (93). Old Tom might be added to the list, however; true to his proto-American characterization, he longs to shoot "Old Beelzebub Wanchese" himself when he pronounces the frontiersman's position vis-à-vis Native priority in all its simplicity: "This is our country now, and we be ready to defend it. . . . what a mighty destruction of lives I could manage with this weapon of terror! I am good for a whole army of Indians" (88). Other characters, such as Eleanor's father, John White, put the matter in legal terms that obfuscate Tom's statement of bald violence: "Come now, come," says White to Wanchese, "This is our land. Captains Philip Amadas and Arthur Barlowe made treaty for it" (85). There was no such treaty historically, of course—at least not one that the Indians were part of; Elizabeth simply issued Raleigh a patent defined by the doctrine of discovery.[26] But the earnest pronouncement bespeaks the implied historical argument that defines the play's entire vision of Roanoke—rather than Jamestown—as the true origin of America.

"Africay," Croatans, and the Spanish Fate of Paul Green's *The Lost Colony*

In advancing this argument, *The Lost Colony* was also attempting to recast the prevailing story of colonial beginnings in the U.S. South, positing Roanoke's Indian frontier in the stead of the slaveholding plantation long associated with Virginia. That Virginia was the original fount of U.S. slavery—via the "20 and odd negroes" who arrived in Jamestown in 1619—is an old truism, but it is one that bears closer scrutiny in light of Green's play. Early writers as disparate as William Wells Brown and Nathaniel Hawthorne perpetuated the myth of Jamestown, Virginia as the site of the first importation of African slaves in what would become the United States: in *Clotel* (1853), Brown memorably described "the slave-ship in James River" that carried "the first cargo of slaves on their way to Jamestown, Virginia" as "a parent," "the mother of slavery, idleness, lynch-law, ignorance, unpaid labour, poverty, and duelling, despotism, the ceaseless swing of the whip, and the peculiar institutions of the South"; in "Chiefly About War Matters" (1862), Hawthorne notoriously figures Virginia as the originary site of slavery's birth, and the ship that brought the first African slaves as a "fated womb" that "spawned slaves upon the Southern soil" in "a monstrous birth" that would forever disfigure the purity of the nation's genealogy.[27] The short-lived settlement of Roanoke would seem to escape such historical notoriety altogether—and yet the shadow of African slavery falls across Green's Roanoke, and simultaneously evokes the very hemispheric South from which the play's ending seeks aggressively to distance itself.

When Old Tom first enters the stage, rambling about Raleigh and Roanoke, he refers to Manteo and Wanchese, the two Natives accompanying the English explorers to London, as "two Indian kings like the twin sons of Noah . . . come back to rule the earth." The allusion to a multiple birth, resulting here in "twin sons," oddly recalls the "fated womb" of the slave ship in Brown and Hawthorne, but it is the reference to Noah and his progeny that raises the specter of blackness, the supposed curse of Noah's son Ham. That Noah's sons are twinned in Tom's formulation suggests a tangled genealogy that the original biblical gloss was intended to avoid, ascribing the geography of racial difference through Noah's *three* sons, who were believed to have conveniently populated different continents, with Shem in Asia, Japheth in Europe, and Ham, of course, in Africa.[28] Yet Tom's "twin sons of Noah" hail, confusingly, from the New World, which is perhaps why he sees them as "nothing but poor bedlam men—like myself, mayhap . . ." Nevertheless, Tom is as clear about their racial blackness as Wanchese is in declaring that the "white people must go" from America: these Indians come, Tom says, "out of the darkness of Africay" (39).

Tom's elliptical remark takes on added resonance once the Historian re-enters the play to describe the 1585 voyage to Roanoke under Ralph Lane, which preceded the "lost colony," the more famous settlement of 1587. The historical Lane and his colonists aborted their attempt to settle on Roanoke after they had given up hope of receiving much-needed supplies from England and then saw the chance to go back across the Atlantic with Sir Francis Drake, who had arrived on the island en route from a privateering expedition in the Caribbean. The supply ship they had been waiting for, captained by Sir Richard Grenville, arrived soon afterward—"but too late," as the Historian puts it: so Grenville "left fifteen brave men to hold the fort in the queen's name and sailed for England to report to Raleigh." What the Historian does not mention in describing how the "Citie of Raleigh was left deserted"—when "all hands embarked for England" with Drake—is that the notorious privateer also left behind another group on Roanoke, one far larger than Grenville's fifteen Englishmen. Struggling to make space on his ships for the many Roanoke colonists, Drake put ashore an estimated 300 to 500 African and Indian slaves captured from the Spanish during his Caribbean adventure and intended as the colony's new labor force. Some of these hundreds of former slaves (and perhaps some of Grenville's "fifteen brave men") presumably survived—likely, as in most such cases, by intermixing with the Native population.[29] If *The Lost Colony* makes no mention of this non-English population left ashore on the historical Roanoke, their unspoken presence seems to shape Tom's reference to "the darkness of Africay" he perceives in its Indians.

Perhaps this explains the odd song Tom sings when he is romantically pursued by a Native woman on the island—described by the stage directions as "a middle-aged pudgy Indian squaw" (80): "O once I was courted by a lady of color. . . ." Though the phrase "Indian squaw" is clear enough in its crude racial designation, the construction "lady of color" proves more ambiguous;

the phrasing had been associated for at least the last century with African rather than Native descent. Tom's announcement that he has "christened her Agona—which is to say in the Indian tongue—'Agony'"—suggests the pervasive anxiety underlying the superficial comedy of their slapstick romance (106). The play's staging of their union—Tom and his Agony—functions as a kind of alibi: a middle-aged, non-reproductive decoy from the inevitable history of racial mixture that must attend any story about Roanoke. The romance of Tom and Agona, then, allegorizes the interracial history that the play does not engage—a history that Green himself would in fact invoke explicitly in describing the genesis of the play. As a college student, Green explains in the introduction to the 1954 edition, he wrote a one-act play in his drama class for production in the outdoor Forest Theater at the University of North Carolina at Chapel Hill: "It told an imaginary story of Virginia Dare and how she grew up and lived in the wilderness among the Indians, falling in love with Chief Manteo's son and marrying him—a forest idyll." But neither his class nor the professor found much to admire in the play, and Green himself soon agreed that "it was pretty rotten": "So I threw the play away, and turned back to writing furiously about the poor whites and negroes of my native county in Eastern North Carolina."[30] The story Green tells here is both true and, I would argue, more complicated than he lets on. He is indeed known today (if at all) as a sympathetic white playwright and poet in the early twentieth-century tradition of American writing about race. But his turn away from the colonial history of Indians and Europeans in sixteenth-century Roanoke toward the dualistic history of black-white relations in the U.S. South explains much about both the regional Carolina context in which Green wrote and the "darkness of Africay" that shadows *The Lost Colony* from beginning to end. For the local history of late nineteenth- and early twentieth-century North Carolina was shaped in part by a parallel attempt on the part of the state and federal governments to render the complexity of colonial history and its modern inheritances into a more manageable, black-and-white racial ideology.

Indeed, the Carolina region where Green was born and educated had been marked indelibly not only by the Civil War, but by the so-called Lowry War with which it overlapped. The Lowry band of anti-Confederate rebels took its name from Henry Berry Lowry, the mixed-race leader described by one nineteenth-century observer as evincing in his appearance "a far remote generation of mulatto, and the Indian still apparent."[31] Though the band identified themselves as "Indians," that is, Lowry represented both African and Native descent, as did the multiracial members of his outlaw group. Together they terrorized first Confederate forces and then Reconstruction's white authorities, assassinating the local head of the Ku Klux Klan in 1870. In 1885, a conservative (white) Democratic state legislator, Hamilton McMillan, saw an opportunity to divide the Republican-leaning black and Native vote in that region of North Carolina by proposing federal recognition to the unnamed, racially-mixed Afro-Native people of the area, thereby juridically separating them from black voters who were not of Native descent or did not identify as Indian.[32] McMillan, a former news writer who fancied himself something of a historian, conducted oral interviews with Indian elders in Robeson County (original home of Lowry and his band), who explained that their ancestors were from the east, in Hatteras and Roanoke, and that many of them had been English. McMillan received similar stories from local white residents, who averred that the Robeson County Indians' farming habits were characteristically English, and thus further evidence of their descent from early Englishmen on the east coast of North Carolina. With these interviews in hand, McMillan developed his so-called Croatan thesis—that the North Carolina Indians were descendants of the English colonists of Roanoke and the Indians of Croatan, the famous site to which the English colonists were said to have fled after abandoning the original Roanoke fort.[33] Soon thereafter McMillan gained state recognition for this group as the Croatan Indian tribe, a designation that garnered more Democratic votes and temporarily brought certain privileges to the "Croatans" that were not accorded to black citizens.[34]

By the early twentieth century, however, local and state politicians realized they had little to gain from offering civil privileges to the group now known as Croatans, and found it far more serviceable to revert to black-white racial dualism than to countenance the complex colonial history that lay behind this particularly litigious group of multiracial Indians of partial but visible African descent. The term "Croatan" came to represent a kind of slur; especially when shortened to "Cro"—as in Jim Crow—the name that had once evoked Roanoke's lost colonists and their probable intermixing with Croatan Indians now stood for the racial blackness from which this group of Indians had been distancing itself since at least the nineteenth century. The ensuing years saw the Croatans attempt with varying degrees of legal success to change their Africanized name; they now call themselves the Lumbee Indians but have yet to receive the federal recognition they have pursued since the nineteenth century.[35]

The interracial fate of the lost colonists was thus a vexed issue in the years preceding *The Lost Colony*, particularly so in Green's home state, but at the national level as well. An entry on "Croatan Indians," contributed by anthropologist James Mooney to the 1907 edition of *Handbook of American Indians North of Mexico*, offers an apt illustration of the intricate colonial genealogies that a black-white racial imaginary would so conveniently sidestep:

> The legal designation in North Carolina for a people evidently of mixed Indian and white blood, found in various E. sections of the state, and numbering approximately 5,000. For many years they were classed with the free negroes, but steadily refused to accept such classification . . . claiming to be the descendants of the early native tribes and of white settlers who had

intermarried with them. About 20 years ago their claim was officially recognized and they were given a separate legal existence under the title of "Croatan Indians" on the theory of descent from Raleigh's lost colony. . . . Under this name they now have separate school provision and are permitted to some of the privileges not accorded to the negroes. The theory of descent from the lost colony may be regarded as baseless, but the name itself serves as a convenient label for a people who combine in themselves the blood of the wasted native tribes, the early colonists or forest rovers, the runaway slaves or other negroes, and probably also of stray seamen of the Latin races from coasting vessels in the West Indian or Brazilian trade.[36]

Beneath its neutral rhetoric, the entry tells in condensed version the long story of U.S. racial binarism. "Croatan Indian" is simply a legal category for people "evidently of mixed Indian and white blood"—a proposition undermined in the next sentence: "Croatan Indians" are also "free negroes," according to a long-standing classification which they in turn reject. By the next sentence, the simple "Indian and white" dualism has degenerated into a mere claim, one that was "officially recognized" on the basis of a particular "theory" but which, as we soon learn, "may be regarded as baseless." From this false theory, it is suggested, has flowed a series of privileges that are "not accorded to negroes." According to this logic, the Croatan Indians are thus not really Indians at all, because they embody Native extinction rather than descent—"the blood of the wasted native tribes"—combined with the blood of "the runaway slaves or other negroes"; and with the perhaps not truly "white blood" of the early colonists so much as the unknowable inheritance of "forest rovers." The Croatans are, in short, the impossible receptacles of multiple bloods, which exceed the guarded boundaries of the United States and its rigid racial binarisms: they descend as well from "stray seamen of the Latin races," from "the West Indian or Brazilian trade."

In many ways, then, the story of a union between Virginia Dare and Chief Manteo's son—which Green would write and then quickly reject as "pretty rotten"—represents a far more complex colonial inheritance than the early English and Indian interracialism of, for example, the much vaunted marriage of Pocahontas to John Rolfe in Jamestown. In his introduction to the 1946 edition of *The Lost Colony*, Green mused on the producers' original plan for the character of Virginia Dare, leading up to the 1937 anniversary of Roanoke, "to hold a nationwide beauty contest to select the girl" to play her part:

At that time they didn't know, nor did I, that when the play came to be written she would be a baby and remain so. In all our minds was the legend that she grew up to be a beautiful maiden, fell in love with the Indian chief Manteo's son, married him, and became the mother of a brave race that somehow evaporated into thin air. (142)

The comment illuminates the pervasiveness of the Virginia Dare legend of interracial genealogy—present "in all [their] minds"—and its national import in the minds of the producers, who would have selected her representational figure from a nationwide contest. But Green's memory also suggests, once again, an unwillingness to imagine that genealogy as alive and ongoing—a particularly acute refusal given the alternate (and quite publicly registered) history embodied in Croatan oral tradition. There is no acknowledgment of the ongoing litigation attached to that colonial history in Green's musing—which is instead contained in the very same instant that it is articulated; it has, to use his phrase, "somehow evaporated into thin air." "I would forget baby Virginia Dare except as one of the items in the whole dramatic symphony," Green recalls. More important, in his view, were "the people": "For these were the folk of England, the folk of our race. . . ." (150–51). And indeed, the Virginia Dare who appears briefly in *The Lost Colony* is in fact nothing more than "a little bundle of white": a racial symbol that must be, in Reverend Martin's words, "marked and set down in history for all time to come . . . the first English child to be born in the new world!" (99).

The arrival upon Roanoke of this little bundle of English whiteness sheds further light upon the dialectic of race and region structuring the play as a whole. For the racial anxiety subtending Green's refusal to write Virginia Dare into adulthood is not finally what Leslie Fiedler famously called the American "nightmare of miscegenation"; it is instead the U.S. South's disavowal of its own *mestizaje*—a disavowal of the "Latin races" and "the West Indian or Brazilian trade" in which they circulated—and a renunciation of the encroaching hemispheric south of which it had always been part and parcel, from the colonial period on.[37] Indeed, during the Great Depression of the 1930s—when Roosevelt could simultaneously pronounce the U.S. South as "the Nation's Problem" even as he applied his "Solid South" political strategy to build a hemispheric foreign policy—Green's play had a particular stake in distancing the colonial history of Roanoke from the sweeping historical vision of a hemispheric "Greater America" that was then being popularized.[38]

Accordingly, Green defines the Roanoke colony in opposition to what it casts as a looming threat of *latinidad*, a threat that both frames the colonists' fatal destiny and evokes the story of Don Luis and the prior Spanish colony. An early scene in England introduces the play's most explicit antagonist (along with Wanchese) in the historical figure of Simon Fernandes, the pilot of the Roanoke voyages, originally a navigator from the Portuguese Azores. Little is known historically about Fernandes, a privateer who had worked with the English, including Raleigh, for more than a decade by the time of the Roanoke voyage.[39] Yet in Green's play, Fernandes's villainy is immediately apparent when he emerges onstage as "a swarthy middle-aged sea pilot, with a short mean-looking sword hanging from his belt" and begins "haranguing" the prospective colonists. Emphasizing his foreign Catholic identity, he crosses himself repeatedly while urging his audience to turn away from their commitment to sail to Roanoke. He knows already what has happened to the fifteen Englishmen left behind to guard the fort—"They are dead. The wilderness has swallowed them up as it will swallow you"—and he knows how "the tale [will be] ended" for these future Roanoke colonists as well. The play grants Fernandes a surprising amount of predictive power, including his uncanny claim—given the early twentieth-century history of U.S. intervention in the Americas—that the Roanoke colony marks the beginning not of a "new empire" to be celebrated but of "an empire where King Death sits on the throne." That Fernandes wants to see the colony fail is clear to the audience but not to the other characters—save Eleanor and John, whose suspicions ("Simon Fernandes is no friend of this colony," as John says flatly) solidify them as the play's true bearers of a future (Anglo-)America.

The play works assiduously, in other words, to define the history of Roanoke in opposition to the history of the wider hemisphere, uncoupling Sir Francis Drake and his West Indian slaves from the "Spanish pirates" whom the English colonists fear—and from the general hemispheric "Robberee" in which Spanish *and* English "conquistadors" were, as Jorge Cañizares-Esguerra has argued, *both* actively participating.[40] Dramatically revising the character of Raleigh, the play elides the adventurer's hemispheric longings, his obsessive attraction to Spanish wealth derived from the wider Americas, and his cavalier attitude toward the waiting colonists once Roanoke proved to offer little gold or silver.[41] In fact, the historical Raleigh focused his energy southward, on Guiana, once Roanoke appeared to offer less than instantaneous profit. His account of his endeavors in South America, *The Discoverie of the Large, Rich, and Bewtiful Empyre of Guiana* (1596), makes only a passing reference to Roanoke, when he describes wining and dining some Spaniards "by means whereof I learned of one and another as much of the estate of Guiana as I could. . . ." Raleigh's strategy with these hemispheric travelers apparently involved both hospitality and clever deception, as he boasts in his account: "a fewe draughts [of wine] made them merry, in which mood they vaunted of Guiana and of the riches thereof . . . [while] my selfe seeming to purpose nothing . . . but bred in them an opinion that I was bounde onely for the reliefe of those English, which I had planted in Virginia." Only as an afterthought, in a subordinate clause likely intended to prevent the appearance of callousness, does Raleigh add that the supposed trip to check on the Roanoke colonists was not entirely a ruse, but one "which I had performed in my return if extremity of weather had not forst me from the said coast."[42] The Raleigh of *The Lost Colony*, however, would never betray his English colony for such a patently hispanicized fantasy of South America. The play presents him instead as a veritable martyr to the cause of Roanoke: as Queen Elizabeth describes him, "Night and day he pursues me, sends messages to my door, haunts me in my dreams with 'Roanoke, Roanoke! My people are perishing in yonder world!' "

But in dramatizing its proleptic history of Roanoke as the birthplace of the nation, the play cannot finally elude the shaping force of hemispheric *mestizaje* upon its insistently Anglo-yeoman U.S. South. In the chilling final scene of the second act, Eleanor acknowledges this force while discussing the fate of the colony with her rightful beloved, John. Trying to cheer her spirits, he addresses her "jocularly": "And now let me ask you—could you love an Indian king?" Her physical response alone, as dictated by the stage direction, speaks volumes: "Half-rising from her seat in alarm," Eleanor cries out, "No, no, not you, John—don't talk so." John takes her exclamation—"not you"—as a reference to the plague that has recently befallen so many of the colonists, and he assures her of his continuing health: "Oh, it's not the fever got me. Cross my heart, Manteo's tribe wants me as chief in his place." John's announcement— with its ludicrous fantasy of white superiority—bears no relation to historical events, but it serves here to undo, if only partially, the deeper meaning of the joking question he has just asked Eleanor about her willingness to "love an Indian king." Moreover, her alarm was never about the plague, as she makes clear in her next lines: "And now it comes at you—this thing we have to fear far worse than death. Bit by bit, little by little this wilderness, this everlasting darkness of the forest creeps in upon us. The end is savagery."

What Eleanor fears in John's self-description as a future Indian king, in other words, is the transformative racial and cultural mixing of colonists and Indians: an outcome, in her view, of wilderness, darkness, and savagery. And it was, more significantly, the precise historical destiny that the nineteenth- and early twentieth-century United States consistently ascribed to Latin America: the Roanoke fate "far worse than death" would bespeak the dissolution of that perceived line of racial purity that ostensibly separated the proto-United States from the wider hemisphere.[43]

As if conjured from some collective historical unconscious, a representative of this hemispheric fate arrives suddenly on the island as soon as Eleanor and John give themselves over to sleep: a Spanish ship, en route between Spain and Spanish America, materializes before the colonists, "anchored in the inlet," unmistakable "by the shape of her—[by] their flags and colors." But the dream work performed by this ship is once again the work of disavowal. Its arrival allows the colonists both a new historical justification for their decision to go to Croatan in order to avoid Spanish enemies who will "slaughter [them] in cold blood" *and* an implied alibi for the ostensibly Latin American fate that Eleanor fears. As John Borden puts it unequivocally, "But remember we leave the fort only to return again. We do not give up this settlement." The colonists are going to Croatan, but they will not stay—will not, that is, succumb to the history of *mestizaje* that defines their enemies and the greater, hemispheric South that looms before them. In its own historiographical refusal to "give up this settlement," then, Green's play effectively recasts the failure of the Roanoke colony as a triumph of the frontier spirit that would supposedly come to define the future U.S. nation. But Green's virtuosic rehistoricizing could not fully disentangle itself from Roanoke's repudiations: from Drake's West Indies, Raleigh's Guiana, Croatan's "Latin races"—nor, finally, from the originary history of a Spanish "Virginia" that Roanoke's historical unsettlement merely repeated.

"Mr. Cabell Goes South": Don Luis as the "First Gentleman of America"

The gauntlet of historical priority thrown down by Green's play did not go ignored. In 1942, five years after the initial staging of *The Lost Colony*, a Virginia writer responded with a historical novel that upstaged the symphonic drama with its own attempt to parlay a sixteenth-century failure to colonize into a proto-national success. *The First Gentleman of America: A Comedy of Conquest*, replete with extended dialogues and monologues, and even stage directions, flaunted its own potential for dramatic adaptation. Its author was the single writer Mencken had excepted by name from his excoriation of Southern literary barbarism: James Branch Cabell—"a lingering survivor of the *ancien regime*," in Mencken's description, "a scarlet dragon-fly imbedded in opaque amber."

In the February 16, 1942, issue of *TIME* magazine—alongside updates for the new magazine section that had begun appearing less than two months earlier, "The U.S. at War"—appeared a blandly positive review of Cabell's novel. The review gave the title of the book as *The First Gentleman of America*, a stately but ambiguous advertisement of an unnamed but originary national figure. But the reviewer left out the book's unsettling subtitle—*A Comedy of Conquest*—with its odd generic designation for an imperial effect: not an epic, a tragedy, or a historical romance but a *comedy* of conquest. Eliding the title's implausible coupling of genre and subject, the *TIME* review—oddly called "Mr. Cabell Goes South"—described the book as "an urbane and bloody tale," a novelistic "compact of history, folklore and imagination."

The novel's peculiarity required some explanatory background, offered somewhat haltingly in the opening line of the review: "Author (James) Branch Cabell of Virginia spent several pleasant winters in St. Augustine, Fla., where he got interested in the character of Pedro Menendez de Aviles [*sic*], who founded the town (oldest continuous white settlement in the U.S.) in 1565." Region provides the review's crucial framework: the book is by an author "of Virginia" who has himself gone "South" to Florida. This southward travel is genteelly seasonal, and the book's southerly subject less than urgent—a matter of leisurely curiosity, the passing fancy of a wintering tourist. Pedro Menéndez de Avilés becomes a mere "character" rather than a historical Spanish explorer and governor. And in founding St. Augustine, Menéndez did not inaugurate the oldest continuous *European* or *Spanish* settlement north of Mexico but rather laid a racial foundation of whiteness "in the U.S."—as if the nation itself had always already existed.

But if Florida boasts the nation's "oldest continuous white settlement," it cannot claim the nation's "first gentleman," at least in this novel's argument. As the *TIME* review observes, the "first gentleman" of Cabell's novel is not the Spanish Menéndez but rather, like Cabell himself, a Virginian. Not, however, John Smith, George Wingfield, or John Rolfe, not Washington, Jefferson, Madison, or Monroe: Cabell's "first gentleman of America" is instead "Nemattanon," a "Virginia Indian chief" who, in the reviewer's words, "learned the ways of the Spanish hidalgos, but returned to Virginia to protect his tribe from plundering, torture and slavery." The "first gentleman of America" is none other than Don Luis.

Cabell's strange and today little-read historical novel posits yet another afterlife for the treasonous translator of Ajacán. And like El Inca's *La Florida*, Cabell's *First Gentleman of America* provides Don Luis with an imagined history preceding not only his betrayal of the Jesuits but even the arrival of the Spaniards who first meet him in Ajacán and bring him to Spain. At the same time, Cabell's retelling brings together Spanish colonial history with the Anglophone annals of Jamestown to present Don Luis under a new historical guise: as Nemattanew, a warrior of the Powhatan confederacy whose antagonism against the Jamestown settlers and prowess in battle made him legendary among the English.[44] The novel thus extends Don Luis's historical agency beyond even the late sixteenth-century Florida travels of Andrés de San Miguel and well into seventeenth-century Virginia. As Cabell explains in the concluding Editorial Note in his novel, Don Luis first appeared before the English settlers in Jamestown as "Nemattanon"—or "Nemattanow," in John Smith's account—"near fifty years after the events" at Ajacán when "a very old man came out of the west, into the early established Colony of Virginia, saying all his people were dead" (283). In this incarnation, the translator is again "a chiefe Captain"—writes Cabell, quoting Smith—and is again believed by the local natives to possess special powers, to be "immortall from any hurt could be done him."[45] In Cabell's novelistic hypothesis, this Anglophone embodiment of Don Luis leads the famously catastrophic assault upon the English settlement that almost led to its fatal demise: he is "the main cause of the Great Massacre of 1622, in which, but through mischance, not quite all the English were killed" (284). In other words, while Cabell's Don Luis lives on to mastermind another scene of unsettlement, it is only dumb luck—only arbitrary chance—that the English colony in Virginia turns out to have a better fate than its Spanish predecessor.

The novel's opening epigraph signals precisely the instability and haphazardness of Virginia's ostensibly English origins, proffering a well-known description of the primacy of Virginia in the history of the "discovered" world:

> It is a country that may have the prerogative over the most pleasant places knowne; heaven and earth never agreed better to frame a place for man's habitation.…Here are mountaines, hils, plaines, valleys, rivers, and brookes, all running most pleasantly into a faire Baye, compassed, but for the mouth, with fruitfull and delightsome land. (2)

The passage is taken from John Smith's 1624 *Generall Historie*, in which it occurs just after Smith has navigated the reader through the mysterious geography of this New World—"There is but one entrance by Sea into this Country"—and casually dropped his own name into this third-person account of the English settlers' first arrival in Virginia: after locating Cape Henry, "in honour of our most noble Prince"; and Cape Charles, "in honour of the worthy Duke of Yorke," Smith points us to "The Isles before it, Smith's Isles," which are honored "by the name of the discoverer." Cabell's citation of Smith registers multiple ironies, then, for his novel will indeed explore "the fruitfull and delightsome land" described by Smith—though this land will be known as Ajacán rather than Virginia. The book will indeed feature a "discoverer," but he will not be Smith, whose priority as discoverer the novel repudiates on every front. The first European to sail into the "faire Baye," set foot upon its shores, and converse with its Native inhabitants, in Cabell's telling, is Pedro Menéndez de Avilés. Just as significantly, Cabell's historical protagonist, Don Luis, also lays a major claim upon discovery in this novel, as the first "American" (or "the first gentleman of America") to explore Spain and its New World conquest in Mexico and Cuba.

The First Gentleman of America traces the itinerant career of Don Luis beginning with his youth in Ajacán, where a Spanish ship led by Menéndez sails into the Chesapeake Bay and leaves soon thereafter with the young "Virginian" Indian who will, as the novel stages his story, radically alter the entire historical trajectory of the Atlantic world. Tracking the young man's religious training and christening in Mexico City as Don Luis, the novel explores his further education at the royal court in Spain and his increasing knowledge of its New World institutions, including the offices of the Inquisition and the encomienda system, before his eventual return, via Florida, to Ajacán. Here Don Luis plans and enacts what he himself understands as a momentous turning point in the history of the "two Americas" (70). Cabell casts Don Luis's destruction of the Jesuit settlement as a proleptic subversion of the Spanish colonial project in the future Virginia—an act of deeply considered "patriotism" well-deserving of the originary national status advertised in the novel's subtitle (247). Cabell's novelized retelling of what most historians have treated as a relatively obscure and minor historical incident thus offers a rich opportunity for thinking about how and why a narrative marginal to Spanish colonial history becomes, in Cabell's text, a U.S. national narrative and a decidedly Virginian one: a narrative celebrating Don Luis as "the first patriot in our history," and establishing "the decisive part which [he] played . . . in the history of the yet unborn United States."[46]

The First Gentleman of America was Cabell's first novel to address the subject of his own country—which was precisely why, as he suggested in a letter to his publisher in 1941, he chose the title that he did: it "would show that at long last my theme is American."[47] This statement was true only in the strictest of senses, however. Cabell's earliest works had been novels of manners, often set in what appeared to be Richmond—though Cabell was quick to point out that he had never actually specified a Virginian setting. Most readers assumed this setting, however, for obvious biographical reasons. Born in 1879, Cabell was descended from an old and prominent Virginian family dating back to an ancestor who emigrated from England in the early 1700s and established himself in Henrico Country, which was then the westernmost boundary of the English settlement begun at Jamestown. The Cabell family had been closely involved in Jefferson's earliest planning for the University of Virginia, and it boasted numerous members connected to that institution, including James Lawrence Cabell, a well-known nineteenth-century medical professor and early proponent of racial science and eugenics.[48]

As a novelist seeking public attention, James Branch Cabell had learned to trade on the family's notable ancestry, and though he claimed not to have read, for example, a contemporary genealogical study of Cabell history, *The Cabells and Their Kin*, he cultivated the persona of a genteel Virginian of the old school—Cabell "of Virginia," as *TIME* identified him—in his self-presentation to the world. When Mencken singled him out as a bright light of urbanity and sophistication in the otherwise bleak landscape of Southern letters, other writers and critics quickly followed suit. But even in his early novels of Virginian manners, Cabell's brand of romanticism established him as a national writer as much as a regional one, veering extra-regionally toward the medieval and the metaphysical. By the time he wrote *Jurgen*, the 1919 novel for which he is now best known, Cabell was fully immersed in the fantastical. *Jurgen*'s seduction plots, profanely set in heaven and hell among other unearthly sites, led to a notorious obscenity trial that further solidified his fame.[49] The eminent critic Carl Van Doren could proclaim in a 1925 monograph devoted solely to Cabell and his work that the author was "already a classic if any American novelist of this century is." The earlier Cabell works had been masterfully written but "minor," as Van Doren saw it; "Cabell Major," on the other hand, wrote works that did not inhabit "any tangible province" but instead explored the invented medieval realm of Poictesme, "one of the most exquisite worlds in fiction."[50]

Cabell's 1942 novel on Don Luis and the events in sixteenth-century Ajacán, then, did indeed mark a shift in his work—a turn from the fantastical toward carefully researched history. The novel insists almost flamboyantly on its own scrupulous historicism, anchoring Don Luis's story to precise geographic locations and events as recorded in the official scholarly accounts of numerous historians, from sixteenth-, seventeenth-, and eighteenth-century Spanish accounts of Pedro Menéndez's career to nineteenth- and early-twentieth-century U.S. accounts of early Florida exploration and Mexican cultural history—all of which Cabell listed in the extensive bibliography at the end of the novel. All of the novel's major and minor figures come directly from these sources, as does the precise wording in certain of its key descriptions and dialogues. As Cabell put it on his opening page, in a riff on the standard disclaimer for novels, "the characters and happenings of this book are all pilfered from fact [and] any incidental resemblance to fictitious events or to imaginary persons is unintentional."

But in taking up what he called an "American" theme, Cabell was also in some sense returning to the Virginia setting of his earlier fictional work—a specific regional setting that the novel holds in tension with a temporal setting that predates the advent of "Virginia" itself. Perhaps in doing so, he hoped to recover some of the critical admiration that marked his early career; by 1942, the dominant literary sensibility had shifted dramatically with the Depression and the concomitant turn to realism and protest writing. Cabell did not fare well in this new climate, and by the time the iconoclastic study *On Native Grounds* came out, in the same year as *First Gentleman of America*, Alfred Kazin could declare that Cabell's irreverence and sophisticated cynicism offered little sustenance to the current generation of readers—and that the past one, in judging him superior to William Dean Howells, had been utterly wrong.[51]

By the time Cabell was composing *The First Gentleman of America*, he had come to resent the changing fortune of his literary reception as well as the political climate of New Deal progressivism that lay behind it. Like Poe—another Virginian and Richmond native who could not always control his ironic fury at the absurd pieties of the larger culture—Cabell sought commercial success while holding in contempt the popular, national readership that was necessary to deliver it. He sulked to publishers when they abandoned him, while to his literary friends he despaired of ever again receiving public acclaim—particularly the prestigious kind associated with literary prizes.[52] In turning from fantastical medievalism to the historical terrain of the new novel, Cabell was taking up subject matter that brought him closer to the possibility of garnering such an award. Yet, like Poe, Cabell could not bring himself to adopt the requisite tone of sincerity, as he points out midway through *First Gentleman*:

> Here is rich epic matter. It is matter such as might well justify the high and unhumorous manner of most epics, even at the risk of a dullness which is

admired only by the awarders of Pulitzer Prizes. Do you tell, O Muse,—
one is tempted to hortate,—do you tell of the low-lying, green-and-gray
city which, a great long while before the intrepid colonists of Jamestown
had begun their heroic hopeless struggle against mosquitoes and malaria,
and when the inhuman virtues of our Pilgrim Fathers remained a myth
as yet uninvented, Pedro Menéndez brought into being. Of that city's very
many glories, do you speak, O bright-haired, honey-tongued Calliope, with
a lively eloquence. (183–84)

The "low-lying, green-and-gray city" is, of course, St. Augustine. In its
tongue-in-cheek rewriting of the opening lines of Virgil's *Aeneid*, the passage
gestures toward the wider implications of the Jamestown/Ajacán relation for
the confluence of English and Spanish imperialisms in the New World. Just as
Virgil in recounting the end of Troy and the beginning of Rome had praised
Aeneas's achievement in the face of adversity—"a man much buffeted on land
and on the deep by violence from above, to sate the unforgetting wrath of Juno
the cruel—much scourged too in war, as he struggled to build him a city"—
Cabell pronounces Menéndez's heroism in having "brought into being" St.
Augustine: as he dubs it, the "main glory, in our Western Hemisphere, of
the tourist trade."[53] But in this mock-epic, complete with the invocation of a
muse, the real object of Cabell's satire is not the ostensibly undistinguished St.
Augustine but the ubiquitous chant of historical priority and proto-national
originary status that it stands for here: before mosquito-ridden Jamestown,
before the "inhuman . . . Pilgrim Fathers" at Plymouth.

From Epic to Ironic National History

And, though it goes unsaid, before *Roanoke*: the obvious source of the "rich
epic matter" that Paul Green—Cabell's fellow Southerner and man of letters—had taken up in *The Lost Colony* in 1937. Green had made his own dramatic case for Roanoke as epic—and as the "birthplace of our nation"—both
to great national acclaim and with enduring success in bringing tourists,
including a U.S. president, to North Carolina. The overt politics of Green's
literary initiative were also perfectly suited to the resources and interests
of the New Deal federal government in that decade. Thus Manteo, North
Carolina became one of the countless small U.S. towns that could, as Cabell
put it laconically in *First Gentleman of America*, "thrive trimly by virtue of
many WPA projects" (214). It was not lost on Cabell that the WPA (Works
Project Administration) had funded Green's production, financing both its
large-scale set and the salaries of its original Broadway actors.[54]

That the novel's satiric object is, on some level, Green's symphonic drama
and its epic proportionality registers clearly when Cabell drops the reference

to Pulitzer Prizes, reminding us that the Pulitzer Prize–winning Green approached his own historical material with precisely the sort of "high and unhumorous" "dullness"—embodied, indeed almost personified, in the character of the elderly Historian, "dressed in a scholar's dark robe"—that draws Cabell's scorn. *The First Gentleman of America* undercuts the earnest historical tone set by *The Lost Colony* at every turn, but it also works aggressively, and in a different critical mode, to rejigger the politics of priority, thereby returning to Virginia the originary national status that Green had tried to claim for Roanoke. Don Luis embodied a trump card of sorts, a "first gentleman" who returned proto-national priority to Virginia, by way of St. Augustine, while bypassing North Carolina altogether. As Cabell suggested in a later essay on Virginia history, "Myths of the Old Dominion," North Carolina had nothing to claim with the "little bundle of white" that was born and baptized in Roanoke and represented in Green's play. On the one hand, "White children were as much a matter of course as scrub palmettos in and about Florida when North Carolina produced Virginia Dare"; and, on the other, "That [Dare's] people could not have been North Carolinians is proved, in passing, by the fact that nobody ever heard of any divine favor shown toward North Carolinians. . . . We know only that through her sacrifice, the epic of *Virginia* has been begun in a correct manner such as satisfied the requirements of art."[55]

It went without saying that Green's epic of North Carolina did *not*, in Cabell's view, satisfy such aesthetic requirements. The novel's opening pages take every opportunity to satirize the simultaneously folksy and high-toned prolepsis of American nationalism that characterizes *The Lost Colony*. Cabell's narrator introduces the book's historical narrative with apparent solemnity as "a tale told in the Northern Neck of Virginia," passed down generationally as the oral inheritance of colonial forebears: "the teller of it says it is the same story he got from his grandfather, who got it from his own grandfather, and so on back to that instant when English ears first heard this same story. . . ." (3). The mood of homespun ancestral piety dissolves even before the end of the novel's first sentence when the expected heroism of English national origins fails to emerge: "forthright Anglo-Saxons came into this part of Virginia to bring with them double-dealing and firearms and alcohol and yet other amenities which aid the civilized in dealing with the owners of a backward country such as one might plunder with profit" (3). If narrative irony is central to Cabell's "comedy of conquest," so too is the retroactive perspective of national history—which the narrator, in a send-up of Green's dramatic commemoration of Roanoke as a hallowed site of American origin, raises to the level of absurdity. "Ajacán," the narrator explains, "extended from about the present station of Stratford Hall along the south bank of the Potomac . . . even unto Reedville and Whitestone, where nowadays these thriving centres of the fertilizer industry affront Chesapeake Bay with stenches of rotting fish" (4). Where Green lyrically consecrates the North Carolinian soil from which sprang forth an American spirit, Cabell finds the cynical stink of a self-serving national history.

It is worth pausing here to note that Cabell was well aware of Robert Greenhow's "Memoir on the First Discovery of the Chesapeake Bay" (1848), discussed in Chapter 4; the book in which the essay was collected by the Virginia Historical Society—Conway Robinson's *An Account of Discoveries in the West Until 1519* (1848)—appears in the bibliography at the end of the novel. So too does González de Barcia's *Ensayo cronológico*—Greenhow's primary source—which means, in turn, that Cabell would have understood in quite specific terms the sweeping act of historical erasure that Greenhow committed in his memoir. Where Greenhow had insisted that no Spanish explorers of the Chesapeake Bay ever set foot on land, Cabell explicitly frames his novel with the discourse of first discovery. When the Spaniards sailed into Chesapeake Bay and from there into the Potomac River, Cabell's narrator explains early on, they understood where they were and "landed forthwith"— "a fact which no few historians have overlooked: but the Spaniards (not being extremely learned persons with a theory to establish) did not overlook it" (20, 19). With this passing nod at the limited historical purview afforded by scholarly agendas, the narrator proceeds to enumerate the rituals of possession undertaken by the Spaniards: "rais[ing] up the banner of the two castles and the two lions, to show that all these West Indies belonged to King Philip"; "sound[ing] trumpets in the King's honor"; erecting a cross; and "offer[ing] praise and the correct prayers to heaven" (20). Likewise, when the narrator details the arrival of the Jesuit mission in 1570, he describes the extent of the settlement with an ironic edge that only sharpens the argument for Spanish priority: "One end of [their] mission house was devoted to the priests' living quarters; the other end was fitted up as a chapel. Here the good Fathers performed, every day, the offices of the Church of Rome" (231).

The final section of the novel, "The Werrowance of Ajacán," produces an extended rebuttal of Greenhow's scholarly mendacity by drawing almost verbatim from the Jesuit accounts—and its gloss of these accounts is strikingly attuned to the unwritten record of narrative agency exercised by Don Luis. Thus, when the narrator explains how the Jesuit mission in Ajacán first came to pass, he introduces the persuasive force of Don Luis's narration even as he assigns credit for the idea of the mission to Father Juan Baptista Segura:

> The tale declares that Segura had felt an unparalleled field for his Order to lie open in the earthly paradise which was Ajacán—in the huge, golden and bejeweled cities of Ajacán, and in the unimaginably opulent and fertile provinces of Ajacán—after the good prelate had heard, upon some thirty occasions, about the marvels of Ajacán as these phenomena gleamed through the not utterly opaque veiling of American reticence whensoever Don Luis de Velasco became descriptive as to his native land. (213)

Anyone familiar with Greenhow and González de Barcia will appreciate the
subtle irony of Don Luis's gold-laden narrative of Ajacán and its success in
bringing Segura, and by extension future Jesuit accounts, to believe that the
Ajacán settlement was the priest's own inspired brainchild. As the account
unfolds, Cabell's ironic narrator continues to suggest Don Luis's long-term
role in shaping the outcome of historical events, often by glossing exact lines
from the Quirós and Segura letter of 1570. Where the Jesuits "find the land of
Don Luis to be very different than we thought," Cabell's narrator sardonically
notes that "the surprise of everybody was considerable to find . . . in place
of the genial and all-golden province of fairy land for which the Spaniards
were questing, what seemed to them, in dismayed silence, . . . an exceedingly
uncultured forest." Where Quirós and Segura conclude that their translator
was "not . . . at fault in giving his account of [Ajacán]," Cabell's Don Luis
hams it up to effect a similar conclusion, uttering "never so many shocked
protestations" about the state of his homeland. Where the Jesuits attribute
the discrepancy between Don Luis's account of Ajacán and its actual state
to God's disfavor—"because our Lord has chastised it with six years of barrenness and death which has caused it to be left very depopulated"—Cabell's
narrator hints broadly at Don Luis's misleading agenda as a translator: "You
had best go [from Ajacán]," he urges the Jesuits, "Disastrous magics have been
sent abroad by the deplorable God of this country, and under them the land
has changed." The worsened climate, the missing gold, and the lost cities, Don
Luis explains, are but a "ruthless and insidious attempt by [the Ajacán god] to
belittle [his own] veracity."[56]

At the same time, the final section of the novel plays out Cabell's most
incisive response to *The Lost Colony*. In a series of heady monologues that
recall Green's dramatic, high-toned staging of Roanoke's fate, the narrative
establishes Don Luis's rationale for his choice to destroy the Spanish settlement—a protonational patriotism that earns him (and not John Borden) the
status of "first American." Cabell's Don Luis acknowledges at this point that
his sojourn among the Spaniards has all along been strategic; he has played
"their lackey" for his own reasons (227). Moreover, he has chosen the path of
unsettlement in Ajacán as a matter of higher principle: though it necessarily
means murdering the Jesuits and thus "indulging in crime and unreason," it
is nevertheless the only choice that allows him to remain "magnanimous . . .
heroic and . . . virtuous" (224). To act against the Spaniards, he avows, is to
"obey in short every call of my own conscience, of my own patriotism, of
my own piety, and of all other human high endowments" (224). In the end,
Don Luis explains to Menéndez, he destroys the Spanish settlement in accordance with his deepest values—"loyalty," the "honorable avoidance of discomfort," and "the freedom of [his] own thinking"—which together amount
to patriotism: "as an American," he declares, echoing the Historian in *The
Lost Colony*, "I ought to keep faith with America above all, and among the

ruins of all minor loyalties" (263). In the end, then, Cabell's ironic Don Luis is every bit as proleptic a figure as Green's John Borden. In thwarting the possibility of Spanish settlement in Ajacán, he heroically allows America to remain America—or, rather, to become Anglo-America.

From the Western Hemisphere Idea to Anglo-Atlantis

In an important sense, then, Cabell's novelistic response to Green's symphonic drama was also an extended meditation on the Western Hemisphere idea from which *The Lost Colony* had actively distanced itself. With its expansive multilingual bibliography and its complex synthesis of primary and secondary sources on colonial Florida, Mexico, and Virginia, *The First Gentleman of America* is itself a tour de force of borderlands history, a novelistic homage to Herbert Eugene Bolton's 1932 call for "a broader treatment of American history, to supplement the purely nationalistic presentation to which we are accustomed."[57] In excavating one strand of "Chesapeake" history, Cabell's novel bears out Bolton's maxim "that each local story will have clearer meaning when studied in the light of the others"; in tracing Don Luis's itinerant career in the Americas, the novel sidesteps the "provincialism" that Bolton saw in "Saxon America," where "the story of the 'struggle for the continent' has usually been told as though it all happened north of the Gulf of Mexico" (449, 453). Cabell's Don Luis witnesses what Bolton called "the larger historical unities and interrelations of the Americas," and the work as a whole shores up the essential Bolton premise that "the Americas have developed side by side" (472–73). The novel's primary scene of urbanity occurs in New Spain, reminding readers that—as Bolton put it—"Till near the end of the eighteenth century not Boston, not New York, not Charleston, not Quebec, but Mexico City was the metropolis of the entire Western Hemisphere" (452).

But if Cabell offers a kind of novelized "epic of Greater America" in *First Gentleman*, he also works consistently to undermine the Western Hemisphere idea and its attendant historical and political discourses. For even as the novel traces out the interrelations among the multiple Americas à la Bolton, it does so precisely in order to give parodic voice to the very U.S.-centric historiographical isolationism that Bolton hoped to remediate. Bolton cautioned that early twentieth-century U.S. historians had obscured much in undertaking "the study of thirteen English colonies and the United States in isolation"— and had, furthermore, "helped to raise up a nation of chauvinists" (448). Such historians, he explained, were "prone to write of the broad phases of American history as though they were applicable to one country alone" (449). Cabell's narrator, on the other hand, offers a comparative, hemispheric historical account to the opposite ends: in the explicit service of American and Virginian exceptionalism. Thus, Cabell's Don Luis articulates his opposition to European settlement from a hemispheric point of view—"I had seen the fate of a conquered people in Mexico; in Florida I had seen the fate of a conquered people"; "at no cost will I consent to see [the people of Ajacán] enslaved and robbed and tortured, like the people of Mexico and Florida, and of every other part of the west" (259, 237)—but he always recasts this comparative understanding as a proleptic form of U.S. patriotism. Moreover, in describing the indigenous inhabitants led by Don Luis to kill the Spaniards in Ajacán, Cabell's novel refers to them as "first families of Virginia" (286)—or FFV, the notoriously exclusive and self-serious Virginian hereditary society devoted to adjudicating, verifying, and documenting any claim of descent from the leading colonial families of Virginia history (of which Cabell's own family, FFV par excellence, was a prominent one).[58] Cabell's staging of the Western Hemisphere idea broadens the geographic lens of history only to ratchet up both nationalism and provincialism to absurd extremes.

The inconsistencies and disjunctures in Cabell's Western Hemisphere rhetoric are clearly deliberate, and they appear to be aimed squarely at the prevailing—and equally inconsistent and disjointed—internationalist idiom of the 1930s. Perhaps this explains why Cabell chose to write about Don Luis when he did. By his own account, he first learned the story of Ajacán in 1912, during the decade when he published *Jurgen* to much notoriety. But he didn't start researching and composing his novel during this high-production decade; instead, he waited to resurrect Don Luis until relatively late in his own career, more than twenty-five years later, during a very different hemispheric historical moment. The intervening years marked the end of the era of heightened U.S. intervention in the Americas that had followed 1898 and the beginning, in 1933, of the very different period of U.S.-Latin American relations introduced by Roosevelt's Good Neighbor Policy.[59] This dramatic shift in foreign relations also marked a discursive turn from explicit paternalism to detachment: a famously ironic mode that characterized the next decades' Good Neighbor Policy and its subtler forms of coercion.

Favoring economic rather than military intervention—executive levies and presidential commissions rather than "big stick diplomacy"—the Good Neighbor Policy depended on implied rather than explicit forms of engagement. Its rhetorical sensibility is best represented, in this sense, not by Franklin's inaugural address on respecting the rights of sovereign neighbor states but by his apocryphal observation about the U.S.-backed dictator of Nicaragua who was then busy massacring his opposition: "Somoza may be a son of a bitch," Franklin allegedly said, "but he's our son of a bitch." That Franklin never actually said this, but that he was reported to have done so by *TIME* magazine and later CBS, only suggests the statement's ironic force—and the wide range of its applicability; for in the latter report, Roosevelt is credited with making this sardonic observation not about Somoza, but about Rafael Trujillo, the dictator of the Dominican Republic.[60]

In some sense, the *TIME* review of *First Gentleman* may have missed the point in remarking that the novel's eponymous subject evoked not Menéndez but Don Luis. Rather, Cabell's Don Luis—as the "First Gentleman of America"—summons his twentieth-century counterpart in the years of the novel's writing and emergence: Roosevelt himself. Famous for his rhetorical prowess, especially his brilliant deployment of circumlocution and casuistic stretching in promoting the Good Neighbor Policy, Roosevelt spoke winningly of the "spiritual unity of the Americas" while effecting mystification through pure force of assertion, and demanding adherence to a series of abstract principles in quick succession, as in the 1933 address where he famously enjoined the Governing Board of the Pan-American Union—an organization spearheaded by the United States in 1889 and ostensibly devoted to the unity of the Americas, but in reality deployed as a facilitator of U.S. interests in inter-American trade—that "Your Americanism and mine must be a structure built of confidence cemented by a sympathy which recognizes only equality and fraternity."[61] Americanism, confidence, sympathy, equality, and fraternity: the procession of values obfuscates both the essential bifurcation of Americanism into the United States and the rest of the hemisphere and the threatening imperative of similitude between "your" version and "mine." Moreover, Americanism will quickly stretch away from the principles (of "confidence" through "fraternity") that apparently define it here, reaching toward their intended economic application: "It is of vital importance to every Nation of this Continent that the American Governments, individually, take, without further delay, such action as may be possible to abolish all unnecessary and artificial barriers and restrictions which now hamper the healthy flow of trade between the peoples of the American Republics." The abstraction of "spiritual unity" thus turns out to contain a loophole for nationalist expedience: "We all of us have peculiar problems, and, to speak frankly, the interest of our own citizens must, in each instance, come first."

As did Roosevelt, Cabell's Don Luis meditates loftily throughout the novel on the relationship between what he calls "our two Americas" (300). But where Roosevelt's rhetorical casuistry allowed him to dart around nimbly in the gap between abstraction and application, Cabell's Don Luis addresses the discrepancy full on, holding it up to the light for all to see: the Spaniards have "a glad high sense of duty" and "motives . . . no doubt excellent," he observes, but "once they obey the ideals of patriotism, their actions become pernicious" (218, 240). "In theory, one may admire [European] virtues," he explains sardonically toward the end of the novel, "yet they work out hatefully in practice, when you let any such noble notion get control of a crowd of human beings" (223). Even his own Rooseveltian circumlocution must be disclosed, as when he distinguishes between "my most handsomely chosen words and the amount of truth which, if but now and then, may happen to vitiate them" (222). But when Don Luis recasts a notorious casuist maxim about the potential virtues of case-specific mendacity—"within judicious limits, truth-telling may be a virtue" (222)—it becomes clear that the object of this comic critique is itself the rhetoric of casuistry: the hallmark of Roosevelt's diplomatic discourse.[62] Don Luis, in other words, measures the distance between patriotism's abstract meaning and its "pernicious" application in order to modify the principle; he argues that the Spaniards "compel [him] also, in brief, to become a patriot" (240). He will enact this transformation through a project of unsettlement: by thwarting conquest, "by ridding [his] own dear land" of Europeans, by becoming "an American who preferred the requirements of his native land to the needs of foreign empire builders" (240, 283).

Such a recasting of patriotism might easily have come from Roosevelt, who consistently voiced abhorrence for European colonialism, the purported enemy of a Western hemisphere devoted to good neighborly non-interference.[63] As perhaps the quintessential novel of the Good Neighbor Policy, *The First Gentleman of America* presents a story about the two Americas in which the eponymous protagonist ventriloquizes Roosevelt even as he spoofs the pan-American sensibility upon which he traded rhetorically. Roosevelt waxed lyrical about the family of Greater America: the sister states bound inextricably together by a shared New World past and common ideals in the present. But the familial metaphors shading his public discourse only went so far, for Franklin privately understood Latin America to be fundamentally different from and inferior to its U.S. counterpart on specifically racial grounds: the other America had developed as it had because it was a hybrid race "part cavalier, part Indian, and later on in part negro."[64] Cabell's novel, on the other hand, takes to a parodic extreme this history of hemispheric consanguinity by tracking the inter-American family that Don Luis sires over the course of his travels outside Ajacán. In Spain, Don Luis produces a number of "natural" children who disrupt the *pureza de sangre* of the most hallowed colonial Latin American familial genealogies. Evoking the canonical literary libertine known to the Anglophone tradition simply as "Don Juan," he impregnates, for example, Doña Catalina de Tapia, the wife and niece, respectively, of two so-called first conquerors on Hernán Cortés's expedition, and the matriarch of a venerable colonial line of *encomenderos* in New Spain.[65] The prominent Creole Mexican family he sires is thus both secretly indigenous and anachronistically "Virginian."

But the English history of Virginia is no more stable: in Florida, Don Luis encounters a French Huguenot blonde called Margot, attached to the ill-fated Jean Ribault settlement, and they are rumored, as the narrator explains, to have conceived a child before she escapes the Menéndez massacre of 1565 and makes her way eventually to England.[66] There she marries one George Smith—himself a New World castaway, left behind by John Hawkins on one of his slaving missions—in order to bequeath her son a legal name. Her son, of course, is John Smith—an English-speaking *mestizo* (borne of a French woman and a Spanish-speaking Chesapeake Indian), the half-French, half-indigenous, "Virginian" discoverer of Virginia. In Cabell's writing of a common history of the hemisphere, the ostensibly Anglo-American, racially pure United States and its "hybrid" neighbors to the South are genealogically intertwined to a nearly indistinguishable degree—not only good neighbors but related neighbors: an extended interracial family of Greater America.

That Cabell is not endorsing this common history is clear throughout the novel; he consistently reduces the Western Hemisphere idea to an absurdity of implausible coincidences, mockingly adopting the rhetoric of the Good Neighbor Policy and its pan-American familial tropes. Cabell's Don Luis proves to be a "first gentleman" of both Americas: the forgotten progenitor who stands for the indeterminacy and fundamental impurity of all origins. "[U]nlike other people, he ha[s] no mother"—a "fact" to which he early on has "grown accustomed" (27). His father, moreover, calls himself Quetzal and, as his name suggests, hails from New Spain rather than Ajacán.[67] As Quetzal explains, "I was a god in Mexico a long while before Cortés came into Tenochtitlan . . ." (41). Despite his status as an "American" and a "Virginian" from Ajacán, then, Don Luis understands himself to be descended from an indigenous Mexican divinity, a being of "not inconsiderable" powers in "the two Americas" (83)—another linking figure in the complex interracial gene-alogy of the Western hemisphere.

Here again, however, and in yet another reversal, *First Gentleman* under-mines the common history it almost tauntingly elaborates. Quetzal, it turns out, knows a suspicious amount about Europe, Christianity, and Spanish cul-ture for an indigenous Mexican god. By the end of the novel, he confirms that he is in fact not divine at all—nor Mexican, nor indigenous—but in-stead a renegade Spaniard. Indeed, Quetzal is rumored to be—though he never confirms this—the historical Vasco de Lerma, a Spanish foot soldier in the conquest of Mexico who incurred Cortés's displeasure and ran away to the Indians never to be heard from again.[68] When Don Luis berates him near the novel's conclusion for "pass[ing] himself off as a god," Lerma coun-ters by arguing that his theological deceptions have benefited the indigenous people of Ajacán (269). He has provided "a leaderless barbarian people living in savage discomfort" with "a leader," "a fair portion of bodily comfort," "the refining and sedative influence of law," "the inspiring influence of religion," and—through a long period of Good Neighborly non-interventionist peace—"strength and contentment" (270).

By the end of the novel, the "first gentleman" of America has learned two salient and related truths. The first is that "all his people [are] doomed" to ex-tinction by the eventual advent of European colonization (271). All he can do for them—in the name of his father, Quetzal, and "the protecting of the nation [he] made"—is to "protect [their] people for yet a while longer" by destroying the Spanish settlement in Ajacán and forestalling but never truly preventing the inevitable (274). Quetzal's simultaneous revelation is that, unlike "his people" in Ajacán, his own ancestry is European, though the novel never discloses explicitly "whether or not this Quetzal had once been called Vasco de Lerma" (275). The point instead is that Don Luis comes to know a more essential truth about the nondivinity of the "most impudent, swindling impostor" who is "his begetter": that he is "an old, feeble, and very brave bit of mortal wreckage" who relieved indigenous Ajacán of its "barbarism" for as long as he humanly could (275). To put the matter somewhat differently, the point is that Quetzal is *white*— and thus so is his son, the motherless Don Luis who succeeds him and who, in thwarting Spanish colonization, saves Ajacán from a Latin American fate.

Ultimately, then, Cabell's novel consolidates the very racial boundaries between "the two Americas" that it appears, however fleetingly, to elide. What initially promises to be Don Luis's indigenous Mexican inheritance from his father Quetzal is in fact the inheritance of an ideological whiteness—a racial formation suggested by the sleight-of-hand historical coincidence provided by the Vasco de Lerma rumor and then consolidated by what turns out to be the novel's persistent recourse to the discourse of Atlantism and its promotion of Aryan supremacy. When the novel first introduces the story of Quetzal's alleged divinity, it paraphrases directly from the most popular Atlantist treatise from Cabell's day, Alexander Braghine's *The Shadow of Atlantis*, which came out in 1940 riding a wave of interest in the legendary lost civilization that had been gathering force since the 1882 publication of Ignatius L. Donnelly's *Atlantis: The Antediluvian World*.[69] Braghine applied early twentieth-century race theory from physical anthropology to write an Atlantist history of civilizations in which "Aryan peoples" from the lost island of Atlantis migrated throughout the world and brought with them their superior culture, their riches, and their ability to build pyramids and ancient wonders. These Atlantean Aryans inaugurated the world's great ancient civilizations, Braghine argued, indelibly marking their written and oral legends, until intermixture with inferior races destroyed the Atlanteans in Africa and the Americas, producing the backward degeneration of the nonwhite world.

But the "shadow of Atlantis" could still be discerned by careful readers of history. "In all the Central and South American legends," Braghine writes, "are hidden, it seems, the same facts: from time to time, Atlantean missionaries appeared in America and their activity was clothed later on by poetry and religion" (32). "[A]ll were white-skinned," and all came as "great reformers, leaders, and missionaries . . . among the natives," carrying out "the cultural mission of the Atlanteans in the prehistoric world" of Peru, Columbia, Yucatán, Guatemala, Brazil, Paraguay—and, most significantly for Cabell, Mexico (32). According to Braghine,

> . . . the legends of the Mayas relate that Quetzal-Coatl came . . . from a certain land 'Tlapallan' . . . The Aztec myth relates that . . . he returned

to Tlapallan. Other myths affirm that [he] burnt himself on a funeral
pyre, but that his heart ascended to heaven and was transformed into the
Morning Star. [He] wore a long white cloth and had a beard. His images
often present a pilgrim with a pastoral staff. . . . Immediately after his arrival, Quetzal-Coatl started to preach a new religion and new morals. He
was infinitely kind-hearted, abhorred every violence, and stopped his ears
with cotton when the conversation touched on war . . . He introduced into
Mexico a better social order. . . . (32–33).

The Quetzal of Cabell's novel—who reforms Ajacán by teaching peace and
developing a new religion—appears to be lifted directly from Braghine's
byzantine gloss of meso-American iconography. Cabell presents his own
Atlantean Aryan in a typically laconic way, noting that he is "a visible god,
shaped like a pale-colored human being," and that he instantiates "the immediate improvement of local affairs" (6) Like Quetzal-Coatl, Cabell's Quetzal
has "come out of the heaven which is called Tapallan" (6). When he introduces himself to Menéndez, Quetzal closely echoes Branghine's wording as
well: "Quite properly attested accounts declare that I cast myself upon a funeral pyre, which consumed all of me except my heart. After that, my heart
ascended into the sky, and my heart became the evening star" (41). Quetzal's
Atlantean Aryanism is further reinforced when Don Luis visits the Calusa
Indians of Florida and encounters there a shaman called Hirrigua, a "small,
gray wisp of a man" who, like Quetzal, is rumored to be non-indigenous—"a
foreigner, saved out of a shipwreck by the great-great-grand-uncle Carlos,"
the cacique (106). As with Quetzal, the narrative possibility of historical coincidence—perhaps Hirrigua is Lope de Oviedo or some other survivor of
the Narváez expedition—is superseded here by the trappings of Atlantism.[70]
Hirrigua places a shield on the ground, draws around it the green circle of
the Egyptian God Osiris, which is itself the Atlantean symbol for the universe, and begins to inscribe figures in "Utic," all of which are "dated from
a late period of the Second, or Tiger, Dynasty"—and which Don Luis recognizes as such (106). When Hirrigua speaks, it is in "words which had not
any meaning" to the Calusa Indians—and yet "it is said, with I do not know
how much truth," the narrator hedges, "that Don Luis de Velasco understood
parts of this invocation" (106).

The clear implication here is that Don Luis recognizes Hirrigua's unfamiliar writing and speech—from Utica or Phoenicia, the second dynasty
in the great Atlantean dispersal—because they are both secretly descended
from the ancient Aryan race destined to subdue barbarism and rule the
world. Indeed, Hirrigua, like Quetzal, possesses the supreme Atlantean
gifts of prophecy and divination; he knows Don Luis's birth name without
being told, and he predicts (and history bears out) that Don Luis's current
lover, the Calusa beauty known as Antonia, will one day marry Menéndez

de Avilés, the man who "will bid time quicken. . . and will establish the beginnings of a new order and of new peoples" in Florida.[71] But Hirrigua used his
ancient Atlantean second sight most significantly to offer a very different
prophecy about Don Luis: "It is laid upon you to bid time stand still. . . You
will raise up your war-cry against gods; and your war-cry will prevail against
both Sinai and Bethlehem until, at long last, death leaves you silent" (110). In
other words, unlike Menéndez, who founds St. Augustine in Florida, Don
Luis will stave off Christian settlement and its Old and New Testament gods
(of Sinai and of Bethlehem). In doing so, this Aryan protagonist will indeed
stop time, halting the seemingly inevitable course of history unfolding in his
sixteenth-century moment: that historical trajectory leading ineluctably to a
Spanish (and then Latin American) "Virginia."

The Conquest of Irony

In Cabell's *The First Gentleman of Virginia*, the Good Neighbor Era version
of the story of Don Luis requires the full force of Atlantean Aryanism to
blunt the unsettling implications of a Spanish colony preceding the English
in Virginia. Five years after the novel's publication, Cabell was still contending with these implications, returning to the story in a collection of essays
about Virginia, *Let Me Lie: Being in the Main an Ethnological Account of the
Remarkable Commonwealth of Virginia and the Making of its History* (1947). The
volume takes its main title from a nineteenth-century song about Virginia
that also serves as the book's epigraph: "Just take me back and let me lie/ . . .
Down in Virginia." The original song is earnest in tone, offering its senti-
mental paean through a speaker, possibly a Confederate soldier, who is con-
templating his mortality somewhere outside his home state. In the spirit of its
epigraph, Cabell's collection takes up what the Prologue defines as "the task
which is laid upon every native Virginian author . . . to put together a book of
homage to the remarkable Commonwealth" (21). It does so, however, with a
winking acknowledgement of its own participation in a collective project of
historical falsehood: "[I]n Virginia . . . we shape our history with discretion,"
adopting a "Virginian method of reforming charitably the past for its own
good" (78, 114). As the volume's subtitle suggests, moreover, this charitable
reforming of Virginia history may be understood in "ethnological" terms—
which is perhaps why Don Luis de Velasco provides the subject matter for the
book's first essay, "The First Virginian," as well as a touchstone throughout
the volume.

Unlike the novel's "First Gentleman of America," Cabell's 1947 Don Luis
is decidedly not a crypto-Aryan of Atlantean descent. There are no hints of
Atlantis in *Let Me Lie*, and Cabell refers to Don Luis throughout as an "Indian
Prince" and as "Indian-born" (26, 34). At the same time, Cabell's 1947 Don Luis

is more centrally tied to a future state identity than his forebear: he is "the earliest known Virginian," "her first famous son," "the first of all Virginians who entered history" (25, 32). This Don Luis has entered history self-consciously—and not at the behest of a white father, as in *First Gentleman*—choosing on his own "to become the first patriot in our history" (35). It goes almost without saying that this characterization ran counter to conventional definitions of U.S. patriotism in 1947 just after World War II.[72] More significantly, though, this characterization upended the understanding of Don Luis that Cabell would have taken from the book that provided, by his own account, his first encounter with the history of the Spanish in Virginia: the *Indian Miscellany*, compiled by the notable Catholic historian John Gilmary Shea.

As shown in the last chapter, Shea's essay in that volume, "The Spanish Mission Colony of the Rappahannock," treated the history of Ajacán as an exemplary tale of Jesuit martyrdom that would establish the brave contributions of Catholics in the early history of the future United States. As such, Shea's primary focus was on the arrival of Catholic colonists, rather than on the act of unsettlement in which Don Luis engaged—a mere symptom, as Shea saw it, of a typical tendency among American Indians toward degeneration: "For a time Don Luis remained with [the Jesuits], but as so generally happens in all attempts to elevate the redmen, old habits returned, [and] he became Indian with the Indians rather than Spanish with the Spaniards" (341). Cabell responds sharply to this premise in "The First Virginian": "Inasmuch as the first historians to write about Don Luis de Velasco were sound Catholics, they explained the killing of the defenseless Jesuits upon the sonorous if indefinite ground that, after his return into [Ajacán], Don Luis 'reverted to savagery.' And that explanation, I protest, is plain balderdash" (35).

Glossing Shea's point of view, Cabell proceeds to mount a case for seeing in Don Luis the considered action of a knowing historical agent who has achieved a specific geopolitical understanding of the hemisphere. Ten years of European experience "does not vanish overnight," he observes (35). Moreover, it was the Jesuits who were "provincial and simple-hearted"—and not their translator:

> He had lived in Mexico, he had lived in Cuba, he had lived in Florida; and he unavoidably had observed, in all these colonies, what happened to the native Indians when once the white man had got a foothold among them. It followed that after patiently awaiting . . . for the most advantageous moment, he destroyed the white men who had invaded his country, and he withdrew his people beyond the reach of white men. (35–36)

For Cabell, Don Luis's actions in Ajacán bespoke a higher principle than mere self-preservation. Don Luis had held a royal allowance and had "prospered as a well-to-do nobleman, in and about the most splendid court in Europe" (29); to retain the advantages he had already secured, he "had merely to do nothing" but allow the fate of Spanish colonization to take its course (35). Instead, Cabell concludes, Don Luis "preserved his people from being despoiled and decimated and enslaved; and in order to secure this end, he sacrificed himself"—knowingly giving up the material privileges he had garnered as a an elite colonial subject (36).

In both his novel and his later writings, then, Cabell always kept one ironic eye on the story of Don Luis as told—and, in many cases, not told—by professional historians. In *First Gentleman*, for example, Cabell cited from Shea's "Spanish Mission Colony" in the epigraph to his Editorial Note at the conclusion of the novel. "So ends the history of the first settlement of white men on the soil of Virginia," wrote Shea: "The walls of the Capitol at Washington might well be adorned with a painting of a scene that occurred almost in sight of its dome—[Menéndez]. . . . planting the standard of Spain on the banks of the Potomac." Cabell apparently enjoyed the idea of a national fresco devoted to the story of the Spanish settlement in Virginia enough to highlight it in his novel. By the time he wrote "The First Virginian," however, he had followed Shea's logic to its natural conclusion—but in order to argue for the proto-national and even world significance of Don Luis's project of unsettlement. Don Luis qualifies as the "first Virginian" precisely because he "changed completely the history of the present United States of America":

> But for Don Luis de Velasco, the Spanish reinforcements would have landed unopposed in the spring of 1571, and yet further military forces and more settlers would have followed them during the summer, as was foreplanned. In a situation so far more favorable for a colony than was any other part of the present Virginia, there seems no apparent reason why a Spanish settlement should not have thrived and extended, under the continued favor of Don Luis de Velasco. The present-day Commonwealth of Virginia, and in due course the entire Atlantic seaboard between the Potomac and Florida, would have become a Spanish province; nor would Jamestown ever have been heard of. . . . The Carolinas and Georgia could not conceivably have been occupied by the English when once Spanish military posts had been established to the north and the south of this area . . . . It follows, I submit, that the Indian-born Don Luis changed, and in changing he predetermined, the fate of a continent. He left it free to become English; and but for his intervention no one of the South Atlantic states would, or indeed could, have been settled by British pioneers . . . (33–34)

Cabell's counterfactual line of argument echoes Greenhow, the nineteenth-century Virginian historian who consigned to oblivion the Spanish colony in Ajacán, writing it neatly out of the historical record, while allowing the understated possibility that England "would not have readily granted a commission to . . . encroach upon territories held" by Spain. Cabell, on the other hand, gives his counterfactual history a much wider berth, almost perverse in the immensity of its implications for the future nation. For in destroying the Spanish colony, Don Luis thus saved Virginia and indeed "the entire Atlantic seaboard" from a Latin American fate; and he preserved the Commonwealth, the Carolinas, Georgia—all the South Atlantic states—for the future U.S. nation. Cabell thus assigns a singular causality to the divergent history of the hemisphere from the sixteenth century through the mid-twentieth, neatly overwriting the complex economic and political trajectories of uneven development with a narrative centered on a single literary-historical character: the "Indian-born" man who "predetermined the fate of a continent."

And yet, Cabell laments, "you will not find a full account, or it may be even a mention of Don Luis de Velasco in any orthodox history of Virginia" (37). For Cabell, the absence has everything to do with the ethnic parameters of such official histories: no other state but Virginia, he asserted, could "have ignored resolutely" the story of Don Luis "because it did not involve persons of Teutonic ancestry": "We prefer to begin our history in 1607, with . . . Captain John Smith, who if perhaps an almost appreciably less talented liar than Don Luis, was at any rate Anglo-Saxon" (34, 37). Cabell thus presents his own novelizing of this historical figure as a kind of historiographical gaffe: "Tactlessly, I once compiled an account of the life and exploits of Don Luis de Velasco" (39). But despite what he describes as his "duly impressive-looking, rather closely printed bibliography, five pages long," he notes mischievously that his "staid tome" and "scholastic parergon" was received by the public as a "not unsatisfying romance" rather than a carefully researched historical novel, the fruit of his "patient and pedestrian labors" as a "plodding historian" (40). Because not one of his "on the whole kindly critics" understood that the novel's protagonist was in fact an historical figure, Cabell observes, they reviewed it as "fantasy" or "ironic romance," a tale of the "legendary adventures of a prince of a mythic country"—though with a bibliography exhibiting his "ingenuity in inventing historians."[73]

The ensuing essays in *Let Me Lie* return repeatedly to Don Luis, as if to re-establish both the factual basis of his character and the significance of his place in history. Cabell includes Don Luis in a list of his "great neighbors" in Virginia, "such as George Washington and James Monroe and James Madison and Robert Edward Lee" (118). Writing a sardonic fan letter to Lee, Cabell offers up an extended comparison between the Confederate general and the "first known of all Virginians": "Like him, you hard-headedly preferred to sacrifice, to your own ideas about honor, your private welfare" (176). Don Luis also ranks with "Virginians" as diverse as John Smith, Edgar Allan Poe, and Ellen Glasgow as an author or artistic liar—willing to "set forth the history of Virginia 'in the more freely interpretive form of fiction'"; "our Virginian version of the history of Virginia" is in fact "begun by Don Luis de Velasco" (262, 267). In satirizing what he sees as a post-World War II national amnesia

vis-à-vis the virtues of the Monroe Doctrine, Cabell nods to the Spanish settlement in Virginia to demonstrate a larger historical sensibility—which is, he
says, "very much the same bland fashion in which we have agreed to dismiss
an ill-advised and regrettably premature white settlement . . . which was not
Anglo-Saxon" (137). For all these reasons, Cabell continuously claims disappointment in the reception of *The First Gentleman* as a fiction, averring that
he "would have preferred . . . to convince my fellow Virginians that in the history of our nation's making, the first chapter was contributed by a Virginian
whom they have snubbed and forgotten" (42).

But this dissatisfaction sounds an oddly false note when Cabell reflects
on how his "conscience" "did . . . trouble [him]" over the misunderstanding
of his novel and of Don Luis as fiction—but troubled him only "ever so civ-
illy and with a refraining from violence such as bespoke its long years of
well-bred coercion" (40). Indeed, that Cabell both exposes and makes use
of the forms and functions of "well-bred coercion," and their relation to the
historiographical process, is clear in both his novel and his essay collection.
The First Gentleman of America opens with a mock-heroic dedicatory poem
addressed to a scholar who assisted Cabell in his research for the novel, the
Spanish borderlands historian A. J. Hanna; the verse announces the novel's
titular character as "Nemattanon" (the indigenous name that Cabell posits
for Don Luis before his renaming by the Spanish) and presents the novel's
subject:

> As, but for you, this book had not been done
> Justly, I need (at outset) to proclaim
> How opulent has been your aid.
>
>   —Whereon
> (As, but for you, this book had not been done)
> Nature demands, all-justly, that your name
> Now head this Story of Nemattanon
> and of His Flight into Oblivion.

The latter phrase appropriates the title of one of Hanna's own histories,
also a work of historical recovery as much as interpretation, about the escape of Confederate officers facing treason charges after the Civil War—
their flight from Cabell's hometown of Richmond to Mexico, Florida, and
Cuba, after which they were consigned to oblivion by a U.S. historical narrative invested in a seamless emplotment of the Civil War's end and the onset
of Reconstruction.[74] Like Hanna's hemispheric history, Cabell's novel also
embraces the Greater South circuit connecting Virginia, Mexico, Florida, and
Cuba; and like Hanna's historical figures, his Don Luis, too, was effaced from
the historical record. But the rhymed couplet framing Cabell's citation evokes
a less straightforward "flight into oblivion" for his historical protagonist—an

historical oblivion, in Cabell's case, that is in a way both predicted and ensured by the ironic register of the couplet, and of the novel more generally. In his "First Virginian" essay, after ironically describing "the somewhat rigorously exclusive history of Virginia," Cabell pronounces Don Luis's oblivion even more forcefully, intoning, almost hypnotically, "we omit, and we shall continue to omit, forever, the first Virginian" (37).

Such gestures serve to contain Cabell's interventions into the amnesiac history of Virginia and the larger nation, trumping his ironic register with the more elevated rhetorical modes of romance and epic when the necessity arises. When Don Luis returns to Ajacán accompanied by Cabell's invocations of the Muses, the nod to epic history may be made with tongue in cheek, but there is little irony in Don Luis's concluding pronouncement that he will, in the end, "keep faith with America above all," or in his flat acceptance of the ostensibly inevitable vanishing of Native peoples: ". . . the god I serve, and the country I serve, are both doomed to perish before long" (263). Cabell's "Comedy of Conquest," then, enacts a generic conquest of irony at the moment of unsettlement—in other words, at the precise moment of its greatest potential for undoing the grand narrative of future nationhood. The ending of the novel works powerfully against satire's political possibilities through epic, through romance, and, perhaps most crucially, through comedy's neat closure: as *Let Me Lie* makes clear, the happy ending of an "Anglo-Saxon" America to come.

Cabell reflects upon this generic conquest of irony most directly in the essay "Myths of the Old Dominion," which follows "First Virginian" in *Let Me Lie*. This essay argues for the aesthetic superiority, and thus the national significance, of "the official history of Virginia" precisely because it embraces falsehood for the sake of art (63). Itself a generic mixture, the essay takes the form of a theatrical scene set in the drawing room of Cabell's Northumberland home, Poynton Lodge, where Cabell and one "Dr. Alonzo Juan Hernández," a "noted authority upon Floridian history," engage in an argument over the priority of Spanish versus English settlement and the status of Floridian versus Virginian history (45). The essay allows Hernández to make a number of hilarious points about the self-delusion of Virginia's historical accounts, including its claim of Jamestown as "the first permanent English settlement" and the site where "our nation began" (46). Terming it "transient Jamestown," Hernández observes that there is actually no current settlement whatsoever at Jamestown Island, uninhabited for years "except by mosquitoes and a caretaker" (46–47). Had Don Luis "not destroyed the beginning Spanish colony upon the banks of the Rappahannock," Hernández points out, Jamestown would not be "burdened with a collection of serio-comic sculpture" (51). And even if we discount the priority of the Spanish in Virginia, he argues, Virginia's beloved Pocahontas was borne of the Spanish rather than English historical record: a mere copy, a pale translation of the indigenous Floridian princess

Ulaleh, who rescued Juan Ortiz from the wrath of chief Ucita. Jamestown's John Smith would have come by the story of Ortiz in Hakluyt's English translation of the Portuguese Gentleman of Elvas (as we saw in Chapter 1)—and in which, Hernández says, Smith likely "observed with what ease the fine episode of the rescue by an Indian princess could have been adjusted to some one or other of the many daughters of Powhatan" (53). But Hernández's case for the belatedness of the English in Virginia (and for the concordant plagiarism and untruth of Virginia historiography) short-circuits by the end of the essay, when Cabell's persona intervenes to argue that "art has its own rules," including those of genre, and that the "spirited romance of the founding of Virginia" surpasses in aesthetic terms the "depressing results" of "all the formal histories" of colonial Spanish Florida, which feature "a horde of but half-seen and featureless ghosts who stray confusedly, through a twilight of syntax about an endless flatness of diction" (67, 72–73). In other words, Cabell argues, Florida history remains obscure as a result of its aesthetic inferiority, while Virginia history—given the "poetic abandon which graces all our accounts"—is familiar not only to Virginians, or even Americans, but to "every literate English-speaking person" (72–73). Cabell's essay as a whole, then, elaborates a series of Virginian historical ironies through the voice of the hispanophone Hernández, only to contain them by celebrating the generic virtues of the epic—"stirring," "great," "noble"—and by judging that any revisionist history that would correct Virginia's official narrative would fall prey to "the same pedantic frivolity which would declare the *Odyssey* or the *Aeneid* to be implausible" (74). Virginia history, Cabell affirms, serves both the larger nation and "the higher needs of our patriotism" (74). To put it another way, Cabell's conquest of irony becomes nothing less than a patriotic duty—or as Don Luis puts it, in one of the novel's early and most ironic scenes, "No true-born American has ever ventured to distinguish between the ironist and the idiot" (69).

Epilogue

The First Gentleman of America, then, plays out an ideological comedy in its conquest of irony, its resurrection and projection of its protagonist into a national afterlife as the Good Neighborly Don Luis, a consummate ironist—capable of a Rooseveltian rhetorical prowess—who draws admiration from his Spanish interlocutors even as he works to render the future United States "free to become English."[1] The ultimate irony of Cabell's peculiar novel is precisely this nationalist triumph over irony itself: the reinvention of Don Luis as the U.S.-American patriot who "prevents despair's entrance into the sturdy Anglo-Saxon bosom of any true Virginian" even as he himself is resolutely ignored and forgotten.[2] The "flight into oblivion" that Cabell predicted for Don Luis has been largely realized outside the realm of specialists—and was indeed oddly borne out again in 2003 with the reissue of *First Gentleman* by a marginal fantasy-science fiction press. In this iteration, Don Luis remains consigned to the realm of the supernatural, the fantastic, the impossible, while Cabell's strategies of containment in writing the colonial past return in a melancholy guise, this time to preside over the waning of the so-called American Century. The story of Don Luis de Velasco, like all stories, is thus shaped in each new version by its current teller, from the founding accounts that Paquiquineo gave to Spanish interlocutors to prevent the settlement of his homeland to the Jesuit letters and relations that recorded the unsettlement of Ajacán as a religious martyrdom to the 1942 novel that inscribed Don Luis as the national "First Gentleman."

My own project in this book also constitutes a telling of the story, and like every other iteration it too, of course, has been shaped by my particular motivations as a writer, and it too embeds a dense weave of circumstances—personal, scholarly, historical, political—only some of which are consciously available to me at the moment of this writing. I first learned the story of Don Luis while researching a book I thought I might write about early American literature, Jamestown, and the zero-sum game of U.S. settlement history as celebrated in national rituals of memorialization. As I watched the unfolding of the Jamestown Quadricentennial over the year 2007, I was initially struck by the Pilgrim anxiety shadowing the celebrations, and the repeated claims of the promotional literature to be "correct[ing] history by reminding Americans that the first permanent English settlement was at Jamestown—thirteen years before colonists arrived at Plymouth, Massachusetts."[3] But the story of Don Luis, as it stretched from the sixteenth century across the *longue durée* of settler colonialism to our own moment, pushed me to see how his single feat of unsettlement ineluctably connects the early modern Native hemisphere to our own vexed transnational one. For as Cabell laconically reminds us, only by virtue of its Englishness can Jamestown claim its originary status in U.S. settlement history. Even during the colonial moment, the name of the new "Virginia" territory announced itself, in accordance with Queen Elizabeth's sixteenth-century patents and international law, as untouched by any prior European settlement. Jamestown is the "nation's birthplace"—as House Document No. 13 in the 2009 archives of the General Assembly of Virginia would have it—simply and only because the settlement was *not* Spanish (52).

And yet, in a profound sense, both symbolic and legal, it was. Robert Greenhow understood this, as we saw in Chapter 5, and worked to suppress the evidence of the Spanish colony at Ajacán, closing up the potential legal loopholes created by nineteenth-century Indian law and its subordination of actual possession to the doctrine of discovery. As Greenhow well knew, the colonial logic of discovery defining the landmark Supreme Court case *Johnson v. M'Intosh* might easily have been recruited to argue that Mexico, as the legal inheritor of Spanish colonial rights, had a viable claim on the first discovery of Virginia. The immediate historical context of Greenhow's scholarly dissembling, in the spring of 1848, was a potentially explosive one, for Mexico was in the process of ceding almost half of its sovereign territory to the United States. In the long view, Greenhow's suppression of the story of Don Luis and what it implied about Spanish priority in Virginia, "the cradle of America," helped ensure the future of U.S. dominance in the hemisphere—a future shaped dramatically by U.S. legal ascendancy over the indigenous lands of North America, including those newly acquired from the Mexican government. All of these U.S. land rights depended for their continued legality upon the first English discovery of Virginia—as did, therefore, the very future of uneven development in the hemisphere.

The story of Don Luis thus opens up new and unexpected sight lines on literary and cultural history in the longest and broadest of views, showing how the genealogy of a single early American story—lived, narrated, retold and retranslated, expanded, revised, suppressed, and contained across centuries, continents, and several seas—relates seemingly discrete geographies and histories whose connections remain otherwise invisible to us. We might consider in this regard the name that Don Luis apparently gave for the region where his people lived. Ajacán is an indigenous term, though we do not know whether the written form in which it survives records an indigenous name, a Spanish misunderstanding of an indigenous name, or perhaps a Spanish transliteration of another word, not necessarily a proper name at all—as in Garcilaso's story of the origin of the name "Perú."[4] But when considered across time—in both its sixteenth-century context and, simultaneously, in the very different historical moment of Greenhow's suppression of the story—this lost Native regional formation for what is now eastern Virginia resonates uncannily with its more familiar counterpart in the U.S. southwestern region emerging from the events of 1848. Ajacán, that is to say, might even be understood as the Atlantic world's indigenous iteration of Aztlán.

As the name of the ancestral homeland of the Nahua-speaking people of central Mexico, the Mexica or "Aztecs" whom Cortés encountered and fought in 1519, Aztlán has generated a long and complex genealogy intertwining history and myth. The name first appears in written form in colonial-era Nahuatl codices, which tell different stories about the departure of ancestors from an abundant northern region, feeding Spanish interest in venturing higher into North America in their conquests. Based upon this projected geography, Chicano activism and scholarship in the twentieth century appropriated the term Aztlán to designate the territories of northern Mexico ceded to the United States in 1848, a lost homeland with both spiritual and historico-legal dimensions.[5] Wherever its original geographic site, the name and the concept of "Aztlán" traveled far, between the southwest of what is today the United States and the current Mexican states of Guanajuato, Jalisco, and Michoacán, its coordinates ever hazy and obscure. ("The Mexicans lived in Aztlán, a country situated to the north of California," as one Massachusetts historian put it in 1805.)[6]

Perhaps the name also traveled between Mexico and Don Luis's homeland. In this speculative genealogy of Aztlán, the word and its attendant concept would have circulated via the close relationship (discussed in Chapter 2) between the "First Gentleman of America" and the Mexican Indian known as Alonso de Aguirre, passing across at least two discrete indigenous languages, until it was written down by Spaniards who spoke to the Native translator Don Luis: thus, the indigenous Nahua name "Aztlán" echoes across a Spanish translation as the ostensibly Algonquian word "Ajacán"—or, as it was also often written, in a minor orthographic change that evokes its possible Nahuatl influence, "Axacán."[7] But what did the name signify? It is not difficult to imagine Aguirre, after learning to communicate with Don Luis in Algonquian and traveling with him to Spain and Mexico City, speaking of the Mexica ancestral homeland. Whether he was himself Mexica or not, Aguirre would likely have known many stories of Aztlán, for these were the very years when the Nahua legend took on increasing symbolic significance in the wake of the Spanish conquest. Perhaps Aguirre used the word when Don Luis was in Mexico City witnessing the effects of Spanish conquest and colonization at first hand; maybe he evoked it when Don Luis described his own home-land. For Aztlán, as recorded in the codices, was often cast as a paradise of sorts, unmarked by disease and death, located spatially "somewhere in the far north," and temporally before the arrival of the conquistadors.[8] When Don Luis first spoke the word that the Spanish recorded variously as "Ajacán" or "Axacán," perhaps he was using not the Algonquian proper name for his own homeland but instead a Nahua toponym learned from his Mexican compan-ion—a formulation for his country charged more by history than by mysti-cism, a beloved place "far north," an indigenous "Eden" that Europeans had yet to destroy: Aztlán.[9] For Aztlán, as both a name and a concept, has al-ways signified what we might call a geography of unsettlement, a time and a place that either has not been subject to—or that might one day be recovered from—the devastation of conquest and colonialism.

The point in speculating on a strategic and historical affinity between these two formations is not to create a definitive origins narrative for Ajacán by means of Aztlán but rather to suggest a particular way of comprehend-ing the spatiotemporal coordinates of Don Luis's fugitive American narra-tive, a story whose protagonist-translator was literally never found after he fled, and whose meaning is inevitably elusive, though it has nevertheless signified powerfully in different historical times and places throughout the hemisphere. Regardless of its linguistic origin, then, Ajacán remains inevi-tably tied to Aztlán precisely because, in Greenhow's imperial cartography, this sixteenth-century Native formation stood in symbolically for compet-ing U.S.-Mexican claims on land and history. Just as Greenhow suppressed Ajacán and the Treaty of Guadalupe Hidalgo was signed into international law, the southwestern Aztlán was, in an ideological sense, reborn in Mexico's loss of its territory, though it wouldn't be conceptually formulated and named as such until the 1960s Chicano movement. This rebirth might be contained and disabled as mere historical irony, or recuperated (and romanticized?) as the haunting of a past that will not be laid to rest. Perhaps moving dialecti-cally between these two positions—History and the Gothic, we might label them—we can find another vantage point, a critical mode that would allow us to *use* the story of Ajacán, to apply its disruptive narrative force and its figures of narrative unreliability and mistranslation to a range of the contemporary conceptual inheritances of settler colonialism that currently shape public discourse about U.S. territorial sovereignty, from the formulaic and thus all too consumable "Aztlán plot" described in the anti-immigration polemics of Pat Buchanan and others to the very nature of the U.S.-Mexico border it-self.[10] Indeed, what if we conceived of Virginia as an unrecognized territory of Mexico, according to the rights of first discovery inherited from Spain? Such a speculative geography does more than challenge what is still an anglocentric (and implicitly, to use Reginald Horsman's term, Anglo-Saxonist) narrative of national U.S. beginnings; it unsettles the foundations of U.S. territoriality according to the very logic of settler colonialism that continues to define it in both legal and ideological terms.[11]

One of my hopes for *The Unsettlement of America* is that the broad, transhistorical story of Don Luis will contribute to those counterfactual and reparative practices of reading that resist predetermination by the framework of U.S. settlement. At the heart of the particular American past postulated here is the story of Don Luis's destruction of the sixteenth-century Ajacán colony—a rejection of colonial settlement based not upon a "natural" resistance to new, unknown, and potentially violent invaders but instead upon a deep, prior knowledge of Western imperial history throughout the Americas. Yet if the trajectory of Don Luis's life embeds an account of indigenous knowledge production embracing the hemisphere and the Atlantic world, it remains a narrative that *we* will never fully know, and thus demands a certain level of interpretive humility. In part because of its wide geographic and temporal range, the extraordinary afterlife of Don Luis requires a kind of itinerant critical work attentive to both the commonalities and antagonisms among the many disciplinary formations relevant to its recovery: American literature and translation studies; microhistory and global history; Atlantic history and Indian history; Southern Studies and Western Hemisphere studies; Greater Mexico studies and Native studies. Accordingly, we as critics must remain alive to the potential of translation and *mis*translation between these disparate fields, as well as across the many times and places in which the unsettlement of America has been narrated. We might take some inspiration here from El Inca Garcilaso de la Vega, one of the earliest retellers of the story of Don Luis as part of a broader history of unsettlement linking his childhood in Cusco, Peru to the court of Madrid in Spain—far indeed from the "Log Chapel on the Rappahanock" envisioned by Father Shea in the *Catholic World* in 1875. For El Inca, one of the temptations of historical *translatio* is the invitation "to deceive with fictions and falsehoods" those readers who come to a story seeking confirmation of cherished convictions and beliefs. The story of Don Luis de Velasco works powerfully against such certitudes, confronting centuries of readers with its myriad mistranslations and multiple (re)beginnings—those unsettling fragments of oblivion that, in El Inca's words, "contribute much to the value of our history."[12]

{ NOTES }

Chapter 1

1. "Columbus's Letter" 118, ed. and trans. Cohen; *Diario* (75), ed. Dunn and Kelley. The standard edition is Columbus, *Textos y documentos completos*, ed. Varela (see pp. 222–23).

2. Greenblatt 1990, 24; Cheyfitz 1997, 104. Cheyfitz's concept of the "fiction of translation" has nevertheless been of great importance to my own thinking. That Columbus understood translation to be central to his project is not the point with which I take issue in this project; even before his kidnapping of the Taíno Indians, Columbus had brought along on the transatlantic voyage his own multilingual interpreter, Luis de Torres, who spoke Hebrew, Chaldee, and Arabic. Yet the language-as-imperial-tool model, inherited from Columbus, has also led to the oversimplification and misunderstanding of "the polemical and theoretical positions expressed in the Spanish 'language of empire'" itself, as Rolena Adorno has recently shown (20). Moreover, as ethnohistorians and literary critics alike have suggested, the interpretive sway of the "linguistic colonialism" model can obscure as much about its Native objects as it reveals about the purported discursive complexity of its European subjects. In the ethnohistory field, James Axtell, for example, notes that Columbus's attempt at seizing linguistic power in fact indicates no "cause for smugness in the language department" (23); see his detailed essay on the varieties of interpreters and interpretive contexts in Eastern North America (15–60). At the same time, a long tradition of historical studies has focused on Native translators as cultural brokers rather than (or, in some cases, in addition to being) victims of imperial translation, presenting disparate models of translation in the process. For an excellent overview of this work, see Hinderaker (2004, 357–75) as well as the interdisciplinary collection edited by Gray and Fiering, which emphasizes the concept of the "language encounter"—"a more balanced historical meeting" than the concept of conquest—in which "both Indians and Europeans negotiated difficult and unfamiliar cultural practices" (1–2). See especially Isaías Lerner's essay in this volume, which emphasizes not only the unique linguistic density of Amerindian languages confronting Europeans, but their role in transforming the Spanish language (281–92). In literary studies, Joshua Bellin, Lisa Brooks, Kristina Bross, Matt Cohen (see especially his commentary on Greenblatt [9–10]), Laura Donaldson, Michael Householder, Laura Mielke, Phillip Round, and Hilary Wyss, among others, have shown that technologies of literacy and print were not simply the overpowering imperial weapons once theorized by Tzvetan Todorov; they were elements of both "colonial Native subject formation" and the "syncretic literary practices" formed "within the Native spaces of communicative performance" (Round 2010, 11). Brooks, for example, elaborates a "spatialized writing tradition" in northeast North America that incorporated and altered European literacy upon its arrival, rather than succumbing to it (11), while as Sabine MacCormack observes, at the other end of the hemisphere, indigenous

"networks of communication . . . reached as far as the Inka frontiers and the Amazon valley" (1996, 106).

3. Antonio de Nebrija, ed. Ignacio González-Llubera (3). Cited in Foster and Altamiranda, vol. 1 (1997), 328.

4. Todorov 1996, 123. On Todorov's continuing influence even upon scholars who reject his premise, see Soler 2010 and Camilla Townsend's Commentary on this piece in the same issue. Even when inflected positively, the assumption that empire depends upon language pervades contemporary scholarship; for example, Gray and Fiering note that "the Curse of the Tower of Babel caused enormous suffering" during the "European conquest of the Americas" and wonder how "different it might have been if, as Columbus had hoped, the Native Americans had only one language rather than hundreds and hundreds, and it was a language intelligible to Europeans" (2001, ix). See also Adorno's commentary on how this assumption has constrained scholarship (2011, 20).

5. In developing this reading I rely here in particular on the multilayered concept of sovereignty elaborated in Native studies. The debates on sovereignty in its legal, political, and literary dimensions are wide ranging and complex. The work I cite below has been especially influential for the way it contests the implied opposition of Western knowledge and Native culture—a dichotomy that inevitably casts the history of invasion as a story of European intellectual development versus indigenous cultural resistance. Jace Weaver's essay on the "Red Atlantic" has been indispensable as a model for balancing the conceptual frame of Native political sovereignty with the inter-indigenous transmission of ideas and knowledge in the colonial era (and before), as has Robert Warrior's concept of "intellectual trade routes" (2005, 181–87). I have also drawn upon the different frame provided by José David Saldívar's recent work on subaltern modernities, which importantly builds upon the groundbreaking essay by Aníbal Quijano and Immanuel Wallerstein, "Americanity as a Concept; or the Americas in the Modern World-System," to argue for the divergent and uneven modernities constituted by the ongoing problem of "coloniality." Regarding the geopolitics of Latin American indigenous knowledge production and oral literacies, Mignolo's work has deeply informed my thinking here, especially his attention to "the double process of translation in which Western . . . epistemology is appropriated by indigenous . . . epistemology, transformed, and returned" (1995, 224–25). In a different but related vein, Adorno's field-defining work on the *Nueva corónica y buen gobierno* of the Peruvian Quechua author Felipe Guaman Poma de Ayala (1986) has continuing importance for anyone studying the discursive interventions posed by Native writing, both with and without letters, in the early modern Americas.

6. Though using here and throughout the very general, shorthand phrase "the colonial American context," I am in fact referring to the multiple and heterogeneous contexts of European colonialism in the Americas, which unfolded very differently within and across disparate British-, French-, Portuguese-, and Spanish-American milieus, and differently at different times. The term "colonial" as applied to the Americas has itself been called into question by some scholars, as Ralph Bauer and José Antonio Mazzotti note; see their useful overview of the history of this debate in the introduction to *Creole Subjects*, as well as Michael Warner's "What's Colonial About Colonial America?" I certainly agree that it is problematic to equate colonialism in the context of eighteenth-century British India with colonialism in the "early modern" Americas—or, in a related manner, to import

postcolonial theory uncritically from the latter to the former contexts—and I hope it will be obvious to all readers that I am not interested in using the rubric of colonialism to explore the emergence of "American" or "Latin American" identity. My use of the phrase "colonial American" is instead based upon two bodies of scholarship. I follow Patrick Wolfe among others in assuming a fundamental difference between "settler colonialism" as widely (and continuously) practiced in the Americas, for example—where colonists arrive, stay, found sovereign political orders, and operate under a "logic of elimination," promoting the disappearance of indigenous peoples in the name of establishing their own locality—and other forms of colonialism, such as franchise colonialism in British India, where the extraction of economic surplus by means of Native labor is the primary project, rather than the acquisition of new territory. The broad framework of settler colonialism, however, does not obviate an awareness of distinctions among the English, Spanish, and Portuguese contexts—nor between the U.S. and Latin American contexts—given that the logic of elimination functions quite differently in the latter, where colonization itself has not in some cases even occurred, as scholars such as Jorge Klor de Alva have rightly argued (1995); see especially the essays collected in Moraña, Dussel, and Jáuregui (2008). As Wolfe himself notes, moreover, multiple forms of colonialism can exist in the same time and place (1999, 102–32).

In addition to the scholarship on settler colonialism, I also follow the lead of Quijano and Wallerstein, Mignolo, and Saldívar in assuming that the operations of colonialism in the early modern Americas constituted a dramatic historical shift, influencing without necessarily replicating all future forms of European (and U.S.) colonialism, while also producing a larger and varied coloniality of power that shaped and continues to shape modernity itself and the modern/colonial world in which we now live (inevitably making terms such as "modern" and "early modern" themselves problematic). To take this view may risk a certain form of "Americas exceptionalism" (as I discuss in Chapter 3), but I believe the conceptual payoff—the self-reflexive focus on the limits of knowledge production in a modern/colonial world continuously if variably defined by the historical operations of early modern colonialism—makes the risk worth taking.

7. Lyons 2000, 462.

8. See also Gentzler, citing Else Ribeiro Pires Vieira, on the "fictional turn" in translation studies, which emphasizes the productive potential of fiction in theorizing translation (2007, 108–09). See, e.g., Taíno and Cuban scholar José Barreiro's 1993 novel *The Indian Chronicles*, which postulates a suppressed translation of the diary of Diego Colón, one of Columbus's Native translators.

9. Gruesz 2004, 85–87.

10. Cortés, *Cartas de Relación* 1993, II. Malintzin, known popularly as Doña Marina or la Malinche, was a Nahua captive given to Hernán Cortés upon his arrival in Tabasco during the Conquest of Mexico in 1519. Affirming and embracing the corporeal dimensions of language need not exclude hermeneutic agency, of course. See Gruesz's reading of Gloria Anzaldúa's extended play on *lengua* in the "How to Tame a Wild Tongue" section of *Borderlands/La Frontera*. ("Alien Speech, Incorporated"). On the legacy of La Malinche more generally, see Cypess.

11. Krupat 1996, 32. The first formulation is loosely associated with Latin American colonial history, perhaps because of its most famous translator, Malintzin.

12. Gentzler 2007, 12–13.

13. Even when scholars acknowledge the mutual lack of comprehension between Europeans and Natives, they largely assume that transparent communication is a shared goal: that both groups sought to "remedy the seeming failures of utterance as a communications medium"; see, e.g., Gray and Fiering 2001, 3. Yet this goal is not by any means universal, as Gray and Fiering themselves suggest later in their introduction when they note that "at least some Indian communities used language as a barrier to protect local knowledge . . . it would appear that among American Indians there has long been a sense that language and politics are intertwined" (9).

14. Zamora 1993, 11.

15. Las Casas also drew upon Columbus for other writings, especially his *Historia de las Indias,* using the *Diario,* his own paraphrase of the logbook, as his primary source. In Zamora's argument, Las Casas's paraphrase of the logbook should be understood as a kind of compendium of citations to be used in support of the friar's other writings; we should not assume that it was "a complete or even a representative version" of the logbook. Hernando Colón is often referred to as Fernando Colón or (in English) Ferdinand Columbus.

16. As Zamora notes, Hernando Colón was involved in lawsuits at the time he was writing and had reasons to use the *Diario* to support a particular version of his father (*Reading Columbus* 40).

17. *Diario* 77. Communicating by signs and linguistic translation are not interchangeable practices, of course, and there is a vast and complex literature on the disparate Native sign languages of the Americas (see, e.g., Davis 2010). Here, however, I will read communication by signs as a part of the broad process of translation—and motivated mistranslation—of ideas and information.

18. Womack 2008, 358.

19. Colón, *Historia del almirante,* ed. Arranz Márquez (1988, 134); see also the earlier English translation, *Life of the Admiral,* ed. Keen (1992, 85). Both Arranz Márquez and Keen are working from the Italian edition (the supposed Spanish original is now lost), *Historie della vita,* ed. Rinaldo Caddeo. On the biography's (questionable) authorship, see Rumeu de Armas, *Hernando Colón.*

20. Colón 1988, 136.

21. Ed. Varela, 224. The February 15 letter, published in Cohen, ed., *Four Voyages* as the "Letter of Columbus to Various Persons," was one of four versions announcing the news of the first voyage; this version survives in copies addressed to Luis de Santángel and Rafael Sánchez, and is thus also called the Santángel-Sánchez letter to distinguish it from the March 4 "Letter to the Sovereigns," a copy of which was discovered and published in 1989 by Rumeu de Armas, and later translated into English by Zamora, who also analyzes the discrepancies between the two versions and the history of their dissemination (Greenblatt 1993, 1–11).

22. Columbus, "Letter," 120.

23. Colón 1988, 135.

24. Chanca 1990, 109–37; see also Cohen's translation (129–57). As Wey Gómez argues, Columbus in fact understood his project as a discovery of the tropical South.

25. Chanca 1990, 125.

26. Ibid., 126.

27. Ibid., 127; Columbus, "Letter," 120.

28. Chanca, 1990, 127.

29. *Unsettlement* as elaborated in this book resonates with but also departs from several other more commonly used terms. Unsettlement shares with a term such as *anti-colonial* a sense of the always unfinished and ongoing nature of its work, though the latter usually registers later, nationally-based historical contexts of decolonization. At the same time, *unsettlement*—both because it precedes the era of the modern nation state and because it by definition opposes the settler foundations of nationhood in the Americas—thus also differs from *counterconquest* or *contraconquista* which, as conceived by José Lezama Lima, articulates a break from the former colonizers via a modern declaration of cultural autonomy and a concomitant celebration of *mestizaje*. Neither is *unsettlement* to be confused with the term *anti-conquest*, as developed by Mary Louise Pratt to describe the discursive strategies by which the eighteenth-century European subject secures a sense of innocence vis-à-vis a prior imperial rhetoric of conquest while asserting European hegemony over the colonized or the potentially colonizable. There is still more at stake, however, in making a case for unsettlement by distinguishing among these terms, which are drawn from the disparate but overlapping contexts of British and Spanish American colonialism across many periods. Ultimately, to elaborate a history of unsettlement is to move beyond critique toward reparative possibilities for the future. See, in particular, Coronado's *A World Not to Come*, which powerfully affirms the possibility of "witness[ing] alternative, if at times unfulfilled, paths to our modernity" (8). The gerund form *unsettling* has somewhat different connotations. In Wendell Berry's classic work of environmental criticism, *The Unsettling of America* (1977), "unsettling" refers to modern agricultural reforms, while Richard King (2013) employs the phrase "unsettling America" to evoke Native resistance to stereotype in the twenty-first century.

30. Gillman 2008, 204–05; Castronovo and Gillman 2009, 4; Castronovo 2007, 176; Levine 2008, 11–12.

31. Apter 2005, 6.

32. See Bauer 2003; Hill 2000, 2006; and Voigt 2008.

33. Calloway 2011, 200.

34. Weaver 2011, 422; Warrior 2005, 181; Teuton 2013, 33–53.

35. See in particular Stavans on the fate of American translators (2001, 187–203).

36. Frances Kartunnen's study of translators, *Between Worlds*, provides an excellent example, embracing the premise of "successful" translation openly in the introduction: "Incompetent and wholly unwilling interpreters didn't last long. Given the least opportunity, they fled for their lives, or lost them in violent encounters when negotiations failed. The famous ones are the individuals who had some aptitude for living in two worlds . . ." (1994, xi–xii); see also Kartunnen's more recent essay, which briefly mentions "don Luis" as a kidnapped interpreter, although without noting that he ultimately broke from those he ostensibly served as a translator (2001, 217). As Yanna Yannakakis notes in her excellent study of Native mediaries in colonial Oaxaca, Native interpreters in the colonial Latin American context—to some degree unlike their ostensibly "successful" counterparts in the Anglo-American context—have long been treated with some degree of scholarly hostility, for they "betray our expectation": "At best, scholars have perceived them as enigmatic, but more often they have portrayed them as social climbers, tragic figures, power seekers, and lesser partners in the colonial enterprise" (2008, 5). On Malintzin's role in the Conquest of Mexico, see Yannakakis (5–7) as well as Townsend's

study *Malintzin's Choices* (2006) and Kartunnen (1994, 1–22). Bernal Díaz del Castillo (2005) offers the most detailed contemporary account of Malintzin, or Doña Marina as he called her, in his *Historia verdadera de la conquista de la Nueva España*; see his discussion of Melchorejo and Julianillo as well.

37. See Tilton on Pocahontas's role in sectionalist propaganda (1994, 145–75); likewise, Scheckel observes that the Pocahontas story achieved the status of foundational national myth through a series of popular stage performances during the first half of the nineteenth century (1998, 41–69).

38. On the Allyón settlement and Francisco de Chicora's role in its demise, see Weber (2009, 31–32) and, on the vast and long-standing implications of the legend that Francisco de Chicora created with his tales of a "new Andalucia" overflowing with gold, silver, and Edenic abundance, Hoffman (2004, 3–104).

39. Vaughn's *Transatlantic Encounters* explores the disparate reactions of Wanchese and Manteo (2008, 21–41) along with the experiences of numerous other Native travelers to England between 1500 and the American Revolution. In Vaughn's reading, Manteo provides a suggestive model for most Indians who were brought to England and returned to the New World during these centuries; they became "faithful" interpreters and guides for the English. Wanchese, whom this study casts as possibly "resent[ful]" of Manteo's higher status, and as "blam[ing] the English for an unpleasant disruption in his life," presents a salient counterexample to this model (24). On the Roanoke settlement more generally, see studies by Kupperman (1984), Quinn (1985), and Richter (2011, 102–7).

40. The phrase appears in Gorges' *Briefe Narration*, in Baxter, ed., *Sir Fernando Gorges* vol. 2, 21. On Shakespeare's use of Epenow, see Vaughn (2000) as well as Takaki (1992), who speculates that Epenow was a source for Caliban.

41. Epenow used his linguistic skills after his escape as well, as Gorges notes (1990, vol. II). When Captain Thomas Dermer arrived in Martha's Vineyard in 1619, Epenow, "speaking some English, laughed at his owne escape" when he told the story (29). Epenow's narrative performance apparently had an underlying strategy, for he used the opportunity provided by his rapt audience to effect an attack on Dermer, during which Squanto was "taken" (or perhaps freed) from the English. On Epenow's role in the history of New England exploration and settlement, see Salisbury (1984, 95–96); Silverman (2007, 1–15); and Van Zandt (2008, 54–57).

42. For an excellent overview of the myth of Smith's rescue, see Townsend (2005, 51–56). Scholars who entertain the possibility that Smith was involved in an intercultural adoption or subordination ceremony of some kind include Gleach (2000, 120), Kupperman (2000, 114), and Richter (2003, 71). Other compelling accounts of Smith's captivity and its aftermath include James Horn (2006, ch. 3) and, from a more discursive perspective, Hulme (1992, ch. 4).

43. Percy 1922, 267, 280. On the phenomenon of English runaways to the Indians, see Gleach (2000, 131, 193–94), Edmund S. Morgan (2003, 74), and Woolley (2008, 259).

44. John Demos explores this alternate plotline in his classic study *The Unredeemed Captive*. See also the section on Cabeza de Vaca in Chapter Four of this book.

45. Indeed, in *True Relation*, Smith alludes ambiguously to the possibility of his own journey toward indigeneity, without return, when he says Powhatan "desired me to forsake Paspagegh (Jamestown), and to lie with him upon his river. . . . He promised to give me corn, venison, or what I wanted to feed. . . ." (57). As Smith continues, the account shifts

to the plural first person, as if indicating that Powhatan's "desire" is for all the Jamestown settlers to relocate, to which Smith appears to agree. See Horn's account of this moment (2006, 67–69). Nevertheless, when Powhatan sends Smith "home," and Smith, after much narrative meandering, arrives back in Jamestown, he is greeted as if his actions have been suspicious: "great blame and imputation was laid upon me by them, for the loss of our two men which the Indians slew" (61).

46. As Smith notes somewhat nervously in *The Generall Historie*, "Some propheticall spirit calculated hee had the Salvages in such subjection, hee would have made himself a king, by marrying Pocahontas, Powhatan's daughter." Smith hastens to deny this—"But her marriage could no way haue entitled him by any right to the kingdome, nor was it ever suspected hee had ever such a thought"—contradicting his initial comment about "some propheticall spirit." Then he undermines this claim that he never "had such a thought" about remaining with Powhatan's people by asserting, "If he would, he might haue married her, or haue done what him listed" (274). Thanks to James Horn for pointing me back to this passage.

47. Cheyfitz notes that the "repressed problem of translation" is central to Smith's narrative of his captivity and subsequent events, observing a range of self-contradictory details including Smith's concession of his "want of [Algonquian] language," on the one hand, and his "fantasy of absolute control," linguistic and otherwise, on the other (1997, 79–80). On Smith's Algonquian glossary, see Knapp (1991, 209–10) and Axtell (2001, 38).

48. See especially the first chapter of Bauer's *Cultural Geography* on the "unprecedented inflation in the value of empirical forms of knowledge" during the period of European encounter with the New World (2003, 3).

49. For an excellent example recent scholarship that asks us to reevaluate the nature of English-Spanish imperial rivalry during the early modern period, see Boruchoff on the editorial practices of Richard Hakluyt (2009).

50. In his 1630 *True Travels*, Smith in effect retold this rescue story again, applying it this time to an earlier episode from his life, when he was captured by Ottoman Turks in Hungary and supposedly saved by a noble Turkish princess; see Townsend (2005, 52–53) A number of writers, including James Branch Cabell (discussed in Chapter 6), have speculated that the story of Juan Ortiz was a source for Smith's own account of his rescue by Pocahontas. See especially Lisa Voigt for an excellent analysis of the Juan Ortiz episode in a number of accounts, which she compares to the more detailed and nuanced version found in El Inca Garcilaso's *La Florida del Inca* (2008, 99–153). Voigt also notes that Garcilaso's version of the Juan Ortiz captivity may have been circulating in London during the years when Smith published *Generall Historie* and discusses his "inspiration in Iberian sources" more generally (306–13). For a comparison of Smith and El Inca Garcilaso de le Vega as authors, see Bauer (2003, 115–17).

51. A number of sources mention Juan Ortiz briefly, but the two that recount his story in greatest detail are the account of the Fidalgo de Elvas, written in Portuguese and published in Évora in 1557 under the title *Relaçam verdadeira dos trabalhos q̃ ho gouernador dõ Fernãdo de Souto e certos fidlagos portugueses passarom no descobrimẽto da prouincia da Frolida* [sic]; and El Inca Garcilaso's *La Florida del Inca*, from 1605, both discussed later.

52. Hakluyt's version, which was the first translation into English, was published in London, in 1609, under the title *Virginia Richly Valued, by the Description of the Maine Land of Florida Her Next Neighbor.* The identity of the "gentleman" who anonymously

authored the original text remains unknown, but he was apparently a Portuguese officer during the Soto expedition. For an overview of theories about the authorship and the publication history of the *Relaçam verdadeira,* see Martin Malcolm Elbl and Ivana Elbl (1997). As Elbl and Elbl note, there has been relatively little sustained scholarly attention the Fidalgo of Elvas's account, though it has long been a source of ethnographic material. For a recent exception, see Rabasa on the "strikingly candid" depiction of Spanish atrocities in the Fidalgo de Elvas's account, which (he argues) did not conform to the more commonly "moralizing" Spanish accounts (1994, 161).

53. Cronin 2002, 55.

54. There are relatively few extended discussions, other than Voigt's, of the Juan Ortiz episode in Garcilaso. On the episode's literary qualities, and especially its kinship with the developing genre of the novella, see Dowling, "*La Florida del Inca*: Garcilaso's Literary Sources" (1997, 98–154).

55. *La Florida* Book II, part I (37v).

56. Ibid.

57. See Voigt's illuminating discussion of the episode (2008, 116).

58. In fact, Garcilaso appears almost dismissive of Ortiz's death, burying the news of his demise in a list of other victims, and stressing his other skills over his linguistic ones (533).

59. Zamora 2005, 67.

60. Garcilaso, *Comentarios reales*, ed. Miró Quesada, vol. 1, 15.

61. Zamora 2005, 63.

62. Sommer 1999, 16.

63. Some historians recount this story straightforwardly (see, e.g., Hine and Faragher 2000, 41). Since at least the eighteenth century, however, many historians have been skeptical. The author "M. M.," for example, writing in 1863 for the Canadian periodical *British American Magazine*, notes that the story is "liable to several strong objections," beginning with the improbability that "the learned men who accompanied the French expedition under Jacques Cartier were all so entirely ignorant of the language of the Spaniards, their neighbors, as not to be able to recognize these two very common words" (491). It is worth noting as well that the German naturalist and historian Johann Reinhold Forster included a version of the story in his 1786 *History of the Voyages and Discoveries Made in the North* (trans. from German), in which a "Spaniard" known simply as "Velasco" travels up an arm of the St. Lawrence River and, "finding no metals of any kind, he cried out, *Aca nada*, HERE IS NOTHING; from which expression was formed Canada." Forster, too, is skeptical: "I cannot help stating some objections. . . . The Spanish word for *here* is not *aca* but *aqui* [*sic*]" (438).

64. The phrase comes from Fabian's *Time and the Other* (2000, see esp. 22–36). Walter Mignolo has elaborated on the idea, calling for "the denial of the denial of coevalness" as a "first step toward intellectual decolonization" in the writing of modernity (2011, ix, see also 249–58).

65. Clifford 1997, 18.

66. On public elementary school curricula and the ideological uses of the Thanksgiving "morality play," see Villaverde and Kincheloe (1998, 149–66).

67. Bradford 1981, 99. On Squanto's life and the multiple possibilities for interpreting his actions, see Salisbury, (1982 and 1984, ch. 4); Axtell (*The European and the Indian* 134–35, 252); Kupperman (2000, esp. 116–20); and Vaughn (2008, 70–74).

68. Vaughn suggests that Squanto may have already been to England once even before he was kidnapped by Hunt (70). This is based on Gorges's contention that Squanto was brought to England in 1605 by Captain Weymouth, long before he was kidnapped by Hunt in 1614. John Smith seems to support this suggestion when he mentions leaving an Indian named "Tantum" in Cape Cod the same year (see Peyer 2008, 24). Yet as many scholars have noted, the name Tisquantum was almost certainly not Squanto's birth name but a more general designation linking him to a particular Manitou, which might account for multiple individuals bearing similar-sounding names. See, e.g., Bragdon 1999, 202.

69. On the Black Legend see Maltby (1971) and, more recently, DeGuzmán (2005) and Greer, Mignolo, and Quilligan (1988). The Black Legend is discussed in more depth in Chapter 5.

70. Vaughn 2008, 14, 20. On North American Natives in early modern England more generally, see Vaughn's larger study.

71. Vaughn 2008, 75.

72. Doherty and Doherty 2005, 14; Waldman, 105. The English rescuer narrative is repeated in *The Invented Indian* with the assertion that it is supported by "somewhat better documentation" than other ideas about Squanto's life, but the footnote sends the reader to *Mourt's Relation* which says nothing about such an English rescuer from Spain.

73. Smith 1986, 219.

74. On Spain's colonial laws and the recourse to the "just war" justification for indigenous slavery, see Elliott (2007, 97–101). On the little-studied history of indigenous slavery in North America, see Gallay (2010) and Salisbury, who notes that by 1610 English hunting for slaves along the Atlantic coast was "routine" (1981, 233).

75. On the stunning variety and extent of indigenous uses of European languages, see especially Axtell (2001).

76. On the "polyglot maritime world," see Fuller (2008, 170–71).

77. As Adorno points out, however, the positions of both Sepúlveda and Las Casas have been oversimplified and mischaracterized by contemporary scholarship: Sepúlveda was not arguing against the humanity of Amerindians (though Las Casas, in a powerful rhetorical move of enduring effects, indeed accused him of this) but rather for their necessary entrance into "a relationship of hierarchy" that justified Spanish conquests and the taking of slaves (2011, 28). On Sepúlveda, Las Casas, and the Valladolid debate, see Anthony Pagden (1987, 109–45) as well as Ángel Losada (1979).

78. Indigenous slavery began in Spain with Columbus; see Hugh Thomas (1999, 89–90). Though the Crown denied Columbus's proposal to begin massive importation of Amerindian slaves and in 1511 issued a proclamation that no slaves could be brought from the Americas, many Amerindians continued to be sold into Spain. See Jack D. Forbes (1993, 39–47).

79. Said's classic definition, from *The World, the Text, and the Critic* (1983) has since been modified by numerous readers, including Bruce Robbins (2004).

80. Las Casas, *Brevísima relación de la destrución de las Indias* (A Short Account of the Destruction of the Indies), 1552.

81. This is the theory in Salisbury (1981, 244). For a similar reading in the specific context of shamanism, see Frank Shuffleton, who argues that Squanto's knowledge of the English gave him "an imaginative lever against his tribe's power structure," which he needed as "a man who had lost his power base" (1976, 114–15).

82. Among the historians who have written on Indian diplomacy, see White's classic *The Middle Ground* (2010); Richter (2003); Shannon (2008). In considering the potential transatlantic and hemispheric dimensions of Squanto's perspective, I am guided by the principle of "controlled speculation," whereby details are drawn from one historical context in order to fill in the gaps and silences of another; see Frederick Gleach (2000, 13).

83. Bradford, 99. See Cristobal Silva's fascinating reading of Squanto (Tisquantum) "test[ing] the boundaries of the epidemiological genre" (*Miraculous Plagues*, 54–61).

84. Stephen Greenblatt famously discusses this phrase from Harriot in his 1988 essay of the same name (*Shakespearean Negotiations* 36). See Harriot (1972, 29).

Chapter 2

1. On the limits of the multicultural perspective, see Bauer 2010; Brooks 2008, 234–37.

2. See Mignolo 1995, 224–25; Mignolo and Schiwy 2003.

3. Many of the primary sources connected to the Spanish Jesuit settlement for which Don Luis was employed to serve as an interpreter—particularly the manuscripts of the letters and *relaciones* written by Jesuits and various colonial officials between 1570 and 1622—are collected in Zubillaga (F.S.J.), *Monumenta Historica*. They have also been transcribed and translated into English, and then collected in a dual Spanish-English edition by two U.S. Jesuit fathers, Clifford M. Lewis and Albert J. Loomie in *The Spanish Jesuit Mission in Virginia, 1570–1572*. Throughout this chapter, I cite where relevant from Lewis and Loomie's English translations (abbreviated hereafter as LL)—though I have changed much of their wording in consultation with the original Spanish. More recently, Camilla Townsend has translated and published the significant letter of Father Pedro de Feria to His Majesty (February 13, 1563, "Fray Pedro de Feria a Su Majestad," discovered by Paul E. Hoffman in the Archivo General de Indios, Record Group México, vol. 280), from which I will also cite; see Townsend (2009, 31–33). Historical writing on Don Luis and the Spanish colony dates back to El Inca Garcilaso's *La Florida del Inca* from 1609, the subject of Chapter 3. Twentieth-century and contemporary scholarship relies on the Lewis and Loomie archive (as does this book), but it has also, until relatively recently, relied too heavily on the conclusions that the two fathers drew from their research. Indeed, the Lewis and Loomie volume is a fascinating primary source in its own right. The two fathers write explicitly from the perspective of "the Christian historian," their work following "the dictum of St. Paul," they avow, in forming its argument through "all that rings true, all that commands reverence, and all that makes for right . . . wherever virtue and merit are found." They present the 1570 Spanish Jesuit settlement accordingly as "one of the noblest events in all of early American history," and this premise in some cases profoundly shapes what they highlight and what they subordinate in the history they assemble, including an important gloss on the story of the captive Alonso de Olmos, which I discuss in the final section of the chapter. At the same time, Lewis and Loomie proceed from the assumption that Don Luis's actions—destroying the settlement and either killing or causing the deaths of the Spanish colonists—were iniquitous and illegal: "When a crime has been committed," they note, "it is logical to look for motives." The rationale they provide offers what they call "an interesting study in [abnormal] psychology," laying out as possible motives Don Luis's desire for the "precious vessels" of the Jesuits, which would lead to "greater power and possession of more women"; an "historic Indian

psychology" which "manifest[s] extreme sensitivity to overtones of anger or public criticism . . . heightened by a disturbed conscience"; and the custom of polygamy ("marital
aberrations [are] the cause of Don Luis's downfall"), 44–47. However dated the language
in which they are cast, Lewis and Loomie's assumptions were reiterated (and continue to
be propounded) by historians, from Carl Bridenbaugh, who states that a "lusty" Don Luis
indulging in "old ways" (1981, 13) incurred Jesuit reprimands, which in turn transformed
him from a "proud young man" into a "humiliated native American," so that "hatred"
replaced "submission and respect" (1980, 16–17); to Helen Rountree, who repeats both the
polygamy and the humiliation explanations, noting that Don Luis "succumbed to the
temptation to live well in the Indian fashion" (1996, 16–17); to Alfred A. Cave, who fuses
the two explanations, opining that because multiple wives were expected of indigenous
leaders, the Jesuit "demand was not only insulting . . . but also degrading" (2013, 33–34). It
is worth noting that the earliest Jesuit account of the mission does not mention polygamy;
only later do the Jesuits begin surmising that Don Luis acted out of a desire for what Juan
de la Carrera called "marrying many women in a pagan way" (LL 134). A 2011 study, *The
Ethnic Dimension in American History*, proposes that a "sadly deluded" Don Luis "hacked
the Jesuits to death" because he was "sick of white people"—"a determined people, courageous enough to face an unknown wilderness, restless enough to leave the ties of home,
and confident enough to believe they could succeed in such a daring enterprise" (Olson
and Beal 2010, 30).

A number of recent studies, however, provide fascinating comparative contexts for
understanding the story of Don Luis. Especially helpful for my own purposes have been
Charlotte Gradie, who offers an excellent analysis of Spanish imperial and religious tensions and the kinds of observations that Don Luis would likely have made upon his arrival in Mexico (1993, esp. 166–68); Hoffman (2004), who brings together a number of
documents, not included in Lewis and Loomie, from the Archivo General de Indias, to
offer background on Don Luis's travels in Spain and Mexico; and Townsend (2011, 57–90),
who draws upon the Feria document and, more generally, approaches the story of Don
Luis from a macrohistory perspective informed by Jared Diamond's work to argue that
the settlement of Virginia by the English was virtually inevitable (there are "no important lessons about contingency" to be drawn from his tale, 83). Though I am taking a very
different perspective in this chapter, I am greatly indebted to her astute readings of the record. See also Axtell 1995, 4–5; Elliot 2007; Gleach 1997, 90–97; Horn 2006, 2007; Richter
2007, 2011, 123–24.

4. On the history of this voyage, Don Luis in Spain and Mexico, and the larger context
of Spanish interest in the "American southeast," or the northeastern part of La Florida,
see especially Hoffman 2004, esp. 182–89.

5. See Milanich 2006, 47. By the middle decades of the sixteenth century, "La Florida"
had narrowed to designate the land stretching from the Bahía de Santa María to northern Mexico and what is today "the greater southeastern US" (including eastern Texas,
Arkansas, and Missouri). In other words, the *Santa Catalina* was in 1561 at the outer
northern limit of La Florida. See also Townsend who notes that the exploration was carrying supplies to the attempted settlement of Santa Elena, located in what is today Parris
Island, South Carolina (2011, 58).

6. San Miguel de Gualdape was the first European settlement in what is now the
United States, located in what is now South Carolina, founded in 1526; see the discussion

of the translator Chicora in Chapter 1. San María de Filipino was founded by Tristán de Luna y Arellano in 1559; David Weber calls it "a classic Spanish city, the first in North America" (2009, 68).

7. On the "Chicora legend," see Hoffman 2004 and Weber 2009, 36–40. A classic example of the promotional literature of colonization is the *Relación* of Álvar Nuñez Cabeza de Vaca, a survivor of the catastrophic Narváez expedition in La Florida, who returned to Spain telling tales of gold and silver (along with human treasure, easily "pacified" Indians): northern riches to rival the fortunes already made in the West Indies, Mexico, and Peru. Cabeza de Vaca's 1542 (and now canonical, Norton-anthologized) account established La Florida's colonial promise for generations to come, and is discussed in the next chapter.

8. Townsend suggests that Paquiquineo and his companion were likely Chiskiak Indians, or possibly Paspagegh or Kecoughtan (2011, 59). Charlotte Gradie and others believe they were Powhatan (proper, not confederacy). As Daniel Richter notes, however, we cannot be sure even that Paquiquineo was originally from the Chesapeake (2013, 19). I have referred to Paquiquineo and his companion throughout simply as Algonquian-speaking. The spelling of Don Luis's homeland varies in the earliest documents that record his story. The 1570 letter of Quirós and Segura (discussed below), for example, refers to "Axacam" (LL 87), while the 1572 letter of Juan Rogel refers to "Ajacán" (LL 98) and the 1600 Relación de Juan de la Carrera refers to "Jacán" (LL 125). I have followed Lewis and Loomie in using Ajacán throughout, but I will be considering the homophonic similarities between the version of the name that is spelled "Axacán" and the far better-known name "Aztlán" in the epilogue of this book.

9. See, e.g., the letter of Quirós and Segura (LL 85).

10. As she notes, a Spaniard later "gave the game away" by admitting that the two men had worried about their families, who would not know what had become of them (2011, 59).

11. See Hoffman 2004, 184. Though his indigenous name is recorded as Paquiquineo, I have chosen to refer to him throughout this book as "Don Luis de Velasco" and "Don Luis," the names under which his own narratives of his homeland and his potential work as a translator and guide were circulated—and the names by which the subsequent writers discussed in this book all knew him.

12. The ship stopped first in Portugal; see Hoffman 2004, 184.

13. Hoffman 2002, 184.

14. LL 123, 115. Paquiquineo was not, however, baptized over the course of those five months at court—possibly because his religious education was deemed incomplete. The question of baptism becomes important later on, as I discuss below. The account's mention of Don Luis taking communion may thus be a reference to a later period when he was in Spain rather than during the five months after his first arrival there.

15. LL 115, 125. The term *ladino* is discussed at length in Chapter 4. Lewis and Loomie's translation of the latter phrase is "a clever talker" (133).

16. Cited in Hoffman 2004, 180.

17. For unstated reasons, King Philip was not entirely confident in the testimony of the Spanish officials aboard the *Santa Catalina*; see Hoffman 2004, 185.

18. See Hoffman (2004, 185–86) and Townsend, who notes that Alonso de Aguirre was working as a bearer in the port at the time he made the petition, and that he claimed to

have learned the language of Ajacán from Paquiquineo's unnamed companion, though it was Paquiquineo from whom he did not wish to be parted (2011, 84–85).

19. The Feria letter is in Townsend (2009, 31–33); hereafter cited internally. On the conversions of Paquiquineo and his companion, see both Hoffman (2004, 186) and Townsend (2011, 60).

20. On the "higher status of the baptized" and the differing views of various religious orders about the appropriate time to baptize, see Cline 2000, 82.

21. Townsend offers a different interpretation: that Paquiquineo hoped to accompany Menéndez to Ajacán, but that his "strategy . . . proved disastrous" when Feria interceded to prevent his return (2011, 61).

22. Feria 33. On the political significance of the locus amoenus, see Beverly 2008, ch. 5.

23. For an excellent account of what Don Luis might have observed in Mexico, see Gradie 1993. On the status of forced labor versus formal slavery in mid-sixteenth-century Mexico, and on the litigious context in which Mexican Indians were intervening, see Owensby 2008, 130–66.

24. Menéndez de Avilés, "Habana 25 diciembre de 1565," 175–85; see also the translation by Quinn, "Pedro Menéndez de Avilés to Philip II," December 5, 1565, in Quinn 1979, II:416, 412.

25. Ibid., 177; trans. Quinn, 415.

26. Ibid., 177–78; trans. Quinn, 415–16. As Hoffman notes, this idea of a passage to the Orient originates with Francisco de Chicora, leading to the Vásquez de Allyón expedition (236). Don Luis has clearly apprehended the significance of this concept to the discourse of colonization and has used it accordingly in his discussion with Menéndez.

27. Ibid., 179; trans. Quinn 417. The adelantado would apparently prefer not to have to rely solely upon the lone testimony of Don Luis. In a January 30 letter to Philip, Menéndez informs the king that he hopes to send a Spanish captain "with the Indian of the Bay of Santa María, in order that with his own eyes he may see this arm of the sea." By offering this confirmation of Don Luis's information "so that Your Majesty may make such provisions in relation thereto, as shall be expedient to Your Majesty's service," Menendez hopes to secure what he needs to colonize Ajacán ("Pedro Menéndez de Avilés to Philip II," January 30, 1566, in Quinn 422).

28. On the little-studied history of French attempts to colonize in sixteenth-century Florida, see McGrath 2000. The history of the Spanish in early Florida and particularly Menéndez's role in the region has been well documented; see especially Lyon 1999.

29. "Instructions from Pedro Menéndez de Avilés for the expedition under Pedro Coronas to the Bahía de Santa María," August 1, 1566, in Quinn 551.

30. Diego de Camargo, "August 14, 1566. *La Trinidad* makes a landfall at 37 30′ N," in Quinn 552.

31. Diego de Camargo, "August 24, 1566. Driven from the entry to Chesapeake Bay, they enter a river at 36 N.," in Quinn 552–53.

32. Diego de Camargo, "August 25, 1566. Possession is taken of the land and of the Río de San Bartolomé for the crown of Spain," in Quinn 553.

33. "October 23, 1566. Antonio de Abalia informs the Council of the Indies of the return of *La Trinidad* to Spain," in Quinn 553.

34. Solís de Merás, in Ruidíaz y Caravia, *La Florida*, 258. The *Memorial*'s likely date of composition is 1567; it was first published in 1893 in Eugenio Ruidíaz y Caravia's *La*

Florida; su conquista y colonización por Pedro Menéndez de Avilés. All citations hereafter will be internal. I have also consulted the English-language edition, *Pedro Menéndez de Avilés . . . Memorial*, ed. and trans. Connor.

35. See LL 18. As they note, it is unclear when or how Don Luis got back to Havana.

36. On the discourse of pacification generally, see Bushnell 2006, 66–67; and Bauer 2003, 42–48.

37. On the new imperial policy of peaceful conquest, see especially "Cabeza de Vaca's empire of peace" in Bauer 2003, 30–76.

38. Cited in Weber 2009, 111; and Kenny 1934, 231.

39. Kupperman 2009, 104. It should be noted that this last detail, about Don Luis's demurral of political for spiritual authority, comes from Francisco Sacchini's history *Borgia, the Third Part of the History of the Society of Jesus*, written in Latin and not composed until 1622, some fifty years after the events in question. I place less faith in his account than do Lewis and Loomie, though they make the intriguing observation that he may have interviewed Juan Rogel and others involved in the events (226).

40. The letter I will be quoting is "To Peter Faber" I, 236–38, Letter 58, published in *Letters of St. Ignatius of Loyola* (1959, 62–64). It was originally written in Spanish and, Loyola suggests internally, copied and sent to members of the order. I have also consulted a slightly different translation by Joseph N. Tylenda; hereafter cited internally.

41. Merrim 1995, 61.

42. On the locus desertus, see Glick 1979, 56. I would like to thank my former student Karliana Sakas for pointing me toward these rhetorical terms.

43. See Kelton 2007, 47–100. Kelton discusses the relevant passage in the Quirós and Segura letter, taking Don Luis at his word and hypothesizing that Ajacán may have experienced an outbreak of typhus—but he maintains nevertheless that "massive depopulation did not occur" as a result (75–76).

44. "Juan Rogel to Francis Borgia," August 28, 1572 (LL 106–7). Carrera also recalls seeing a large Ajacán population in his account (LL 125).

45. The figure of the divine European dazzling a bewildered indigenous audience was canonical in accounts of the conquest by the 1550s (in other words, a decade before Don Luis began his sojourn among the Spanish), and it was clearly inflected by the Christian narrative of apotheosis. On the prevalence of this conflation in English colonial writings, see Hamlin 1996, 405–28. Such imagined apotheoses began with Columbus, who believed the Natives were asking the Spaniards "if we had come from the heavens [*cielo*]" (*Diario* 74–5)—and have continued to this day. The idea that the Aztecs perceived Cortés as a God, for example, has persisted in the popular imagination as well as in academic scholarship, despite many studies showing otherwise. See Townsend 2003, 659–87.

46. The child, who disappears from future Jesuit accounts of the mission, either recovers and survives or was never ill to begin with, if we choose to believe those historians who postulate that Don Luis was the future Opechancanaugh (see Bridenbaugh 1980, 10–33, and 1981, 5–49; and Weber 2009, 72): for the "boy of three years" would thus prove to be Opechancanaugh's much younger brother and grow up to become the leader of the Powhatan Indians, known to the English as "Powhatan" and as Pocahontas's father. But this interpretation, however compelling, depends upon what is likely Lewis and Loomie's mistranslation of the original Spanish, which suggests that the three-year-old child, rather than his father, the cacique, is Don Luis's brother. In any case, it is still plausible

that the child—as son of the cacique—grew up to be Powhatan. Through this record of Don Luis's first act of mediation, then, the major Native interlocutor for the English in Jamestown nearly forty years later may have entered the written record in the Spanish Jesuit documents of a pre-English Virginian past.

47. LL 90. Lewis and Loomie note that the reference to great snows in the Quirós letter is mysterious (36). But the reference is only confusing if we assume that Don Luis's primary purpose in speaking and translating is to convey accurate information to the Jesuits, rather than to influence what they believe and, most important, how they present the possibility of future colonization in Ajacán in their letter back to Havana.

48. Lewis and Loomie note that the system of communicating by signal fires is an Algonquian practice (43).

49. This plan to keep the information in the letters secret from the Ajacán Natives may have been a useless one, as Luis Gerónimo de Oré's relación suggests that Don Luis was not only bilingual but literate in Spanish (LL 180); in other words, he could have read the letters.

50. LL 117. The priest is Juan Rogel, discussed later. What he describes is clearly a performance; his description is meant to convey the Indians' deception, a ruse to lure in the unsuspecting Spaniards; the entire scene suggests a sort of proleptic horror, for the Indians are wearing the robes of the priests whom the writer, but not the Spaniards observing the scene, knows to be dead. It should be noted, however, that this account is from Rogel's official *relación*, written long after the events in question, and not from the letter that he wrote immediately from the Bahía de Santa María, far closer in time to the events, which does not mention such a scene. Moreover, Carrera's account suggests that the ship does not land simply because the pilot and sailors do not see the Jesuits anywhere.

51. It is unclear when the captive conveyed this—or how, given his presumed lack of Spanish. Rogel and Carrera both observe that the two captured Indians gave no useful information for quite a while, and the captive who did not escape by jumping overboard did not disclose anything in Havana. But by the time he is brought back to Ajacán, serving as a translator in chains, he has apparently conveyed the news that Alonso is alive.

52. LL 107. See Richter's fascinating account of the use of these objects in Algonquian trade networks (2007, 119–22).

53. See note 3.

54. LL 116. See, e.g., Carrera's account in which the Indians' "responses [to Father Quirós's question and prayer] was a volley of arrows," and Don Luis "replied with the axe he was carrying" to Father Segura's greeting (127). See the discussion of Don Luis's purported silence and his status as a political figure in the next chapter.

55. LL 117. In Carrera's account, in fact, Don Luis registers his purported remorse by calling the fathers "mártires" (LL 128); the narrative purpose here seems clear enough: to put into the mouth of the perpetrator himself the definitional justification for the fathers' canonization. On the politics of canonization during this period, see Po-chia Hsia 2005, 127–43.

56. See, e.g., the 1600 relation of Juan de la Carrera (LL 125) and the 1610 relation of Bartolomé Martínez (LL 152).

57. See Carrera (LL 127).

58. See the relation of Luis Gerónimo de Oré, composed between 1617 and 1620 (LL 172). Our Lady of Candelaria is a Black Madonna and the patron saint of the Canary

Islands; her feast is celebrated on February 2, which is why Lewis and Loomie choose to translate the name as Candlemas.

59. Tanner retold the story of Don Luis by drawing upon Sacchini's Latin account of the Jesuits, written in Rome.

60. Tanner 1675, 450: ". . . in Florida pro Chfristi fide trucidate . . ."

61. Ibid., 448: ". . . pro Christi fide barbare enecti . . ."

62. González Echevarría 1998, 57. His larger argument about the relevance of the *relación* and other genres of the colonial archive to the emergence of the modern novel suggests an intriguing possibility for recovering the indigenous authorial roots of modern literatures of the Americas.

63. Martínez, "The Martyrdom of the Fathers and Brothers of the Company of Jesus whom the Indians of Ajacán, in the Land of Florida, Martyred" (October 24, 1610) (LL 153).

64. LL 148–55.

65. See LL, 114 n. 17.

66. Mignolo 1991, 34; 2000, xxvi.

Chapter 3

1. On Ribadeneyra's biography, see Bilinkoff 1999, especially on his background as a *converso*; and Maryks 2009, 42–45.

2. A modern edition of *Vida del Padre Francisco de Borja* can be found in Ribadeneyra, *Historias de la Contrareforma*. Lewis and Loomie's edition, from which I will cite, includes the relevant section on Don Luis and the Jesuit colony, taken from a manuscript copied by Las Casas, *Obras Escogidas*, and appended to his *Relación* (see n. 1, LL 146), discussed in the previous chapter.

3. On Ribadeneyra as the inaugurator of "modern hagiography," see Bilinkoff 1999, 182.

4. It is noteworthy that Lewis and Loomie, despite praising Ribadeneyra's "facile, clear, and graceful prose" (146), leave out significant portions of his text in their translation, omitting the description of Don Luis "having been taught in the ways of our sanctified religion, received with the greatest shows of joy the water of the sanctified baptism" (LL 143)—perhaps to dial down the dramatic irony of an (implied) false conversion.

5. The Valladolid debate is discussed briefly in Chapter 1 and later.

6. Ribadeneyra 1868. On Ribadeneyra's anti-Machiavellianism, see Skinner 1978, 2:171–72; and Fernández-Santamaría 2005, 30–46; on his political philosophy, see Höpfl 2008, 104–16.

7. Ribadeneyra 1868, 456.

8. Sommer, 1999, 61. There are a number of useful biographies of Garcilaso in both English and Spanish. See especially Varner 2012; Sosa 1994; and Castanien 1969. On Garcilaso and problems of colonial interpretation, see especially Voigt 2008, 41–98; and, on El Inca's understanding of history itself as a "vast enterprise of translation," Zamora 2005, 62–84. See also the discussion of Garcilaso and failed translation in Chapter 1.

9. There were numerous printed versions of this episode of Atahualpa's confrontation with Pizarro; Gonzalo Lamana traces the changing meanings of the scene across multiple texts and points of view, including the English-language texts that deployed it in the service of the Black Legend; see Lamana 1988.

10. See Castanien, 1969, 23–26; González Echevarría, 1998, 74–76.

11. See Varner and Varner, *The Florida of the Inca*, 1981, xxvii; Chang-Rodríguez 2006, 37.

12. Garcilaso's name changes—his adoption of both his father's name and the moniker "el Inca"—have been the subject of much speculation. See Sommer's analysis of the oxymoronic status of the two names in conjunction in her chapter "Mosiac and Mestizo" (1999, 61–91). Jonathan Steigman notes that some scholars believe Garcilaso changed his name to avoid being confused with the son of a prominent family in Spain (2005, 17). Castanien proposes that El Inca was pressured to change his name by members of his own extended family, who were ashamed of his indigenous heritage and illegitimacy (1969, 35).

13. Or perhaps he changed his mind; see Castanien 1969, 34.

14. José Rabasa argues that the repeating phrase "*porque soy indio*" ('because I am an Indian') "constitutes a motif in the work of Garcilaso, plac[ing] him outside European discourse" (2000, 199).

15. Rabasa 1994, 199. There is a long-standing tradition in scholarly studies of Garcilaso of understanding his authorial interests as primarily identified with Spanish and Creole *encomendero* culture—best contrasted with those of a more "authentically" indigenous figure such as the Quechua chronicler Guaman Poma. As Antonio Mazzotti notes, however, the "old dichotomy of the Hispanicized Garcilaso versus the indigenous chronicler Guaman Poma" is not particularly useful for parsing the actual complexities of Garcilaso's texts (2008, 23). At the same time, it would certainly oversimplify to cast Garcilaso as a straightforward advocate for subordinated Andeans: clearly, he sometimes uses the *Comentarios* to position elite Inca interests against those of other indigenous Peruvian groups, as numerous scholars have pointed out (see, e.g., Seed, *American Pentimento* 246). In this chapter, I follow Rabasa and others who see El Inca as more significantly—if ambiguously—committed to the kinds if insights that are afforded to him by virtue of his self-designated status as indigenous ("*soy indio*").

16. See, e.g., Smith 2009, 359; Luebering 2010, 180; Baym 2002.

17. Though Durand produced a landmark collection of his Garcilaso essays, *El Inca Garcilaso, clásico de América*, along with numerous other influential articles, José Antonio Mazzotti notes that Durand has been "systematically ignored" by subsequent scholars (2008, 28). See Mazzotti's important discussion of Durand's argument about the composition of different parts of the *Comentarios* at different times, and his decision to add chapters on the Incan wars, resulting in a mixture of styles and rhythms in the final text (1976, 28–29); this relates to the argument I will be making about Garcilaso's addition of the Don Luis material to *La Florida del Inca*. Major studies on the *Comentarios* include those by Zamora 2005; González Echevarría 1998; Mazzotti 2008; and MacCormack 1993, ch. 8, among others.

18. Chang-Rodríguez 2006, 134. Her ground-breaking collection, *Beyond Books and Borders*, includes important articles on *La Florida* by a range of illustrious critics. Other significant scholarship on *La Florida* includes Voigt 2008, "Captivity, Exile, and Interpretation in El Inca Garcilaso's La Florida del Inca"; and Adorno 2008.

19. Throughout I have cited from the original Pedro Crasbeek edition of *La Florida del Inca* (Lisbon, 1605), available in a facsimile. I have used my own translations, in consultation with the translated edition by Varner and Varner, *The Inca's Florida*. All page numbers refer to the 1605 edition unless I am specifically discussing translation issues in Varner and Varner.

20. Libro VI, Cap. XXII, 347v.

21. *La Florida del Inca*, Libro VI, 830 [291]. This page number appears on the opening page of Book 6 but is an error; the next page is 292. Throughout I will note pagination anomalies as they occur. Garcilaso repeats the statement that the book contains twenty-one chapters in the book's *Tabla*.

22. Varner and Varner 1981, 637. Compare to the introduction to "Libro sesto"—Book 6—of the *Tabla*. Varner and Varner have imported this description to the beginning of Book 6 in the book proper.

23. Libro VI, Cap. XXII 347v.

24. "Proemio al letor," no page number.

25. Libro VI, Cap. XXII 348.

26. Indeed, El Inca's strange and violent version of the story of Don Luis seems tacked on to the history and hardly provides a harmonious conclusion to its late-Golden Age text. Struggling to resolve these contradictions, scholars have arrived at a number of useful conclusions. Voigt, for example, reads the episode as emblematic of El Inca's own psychology, "the conflictive nature of his sympathies and identifications, as the son of an Inca noblewoman and a Spanish conquistador" (2008, 102). Chang-Rodríguez suggests that Garcilaso adds the martyrdoms at the end of *La Florida* because it circles back to his opening caution against French colonization and his primary motivation in writing the entire book: "the fear of losing La Florida for Spain and the Catholic faith" (2006, 28). José Rabasa argues that the episode demonstrates Garcilaso's interest in a "discourse of tolerance rather than a diatribe on Amerindian savagery" (1994, 231). I take a different approach in this chapter to the strange appearance of Don Luis in *La Florida*, drawing in part on Roland Greene's interpretation of narrative *huacas* in the *Comentarios* as "episodes or set pieces that inflect and undermine commonplace notions and draw on humanist antecedents for their power to startle" (220).

27. Garcilaso 350–51. Lewis and Loomie first noted that *La Florida del Inca* contains a reference to the story of the Jesuit martyrdoms in Ajacán (147).

28. On Gonzalo Silvestre as Garcilaso's principal source and the identity behind the construction of "mi autor," see, e.g., Chang-Rodríguez 2006, 15, 26; Voigt 2008, 100; Galloway 1997, 37. It is important to note that the figure of the anonymous (fictional) informant was conventional in historical writing. As Rabasa notes, moreover, El Inca "subvert[ed] the hierarchy with an Indian who wrote history and an hildalgo who provided an oral account" (1994, 216).

29. See Chapter 2.

30. Rabasa 1994, 280; Voigt 2008, 102.

31. Roa-de-la-Carrera 2005, 109–10; Davis 1988, 171.

32. Genesis 4:15.

33. Las Casas 1965, 2:441. On the significance of Montesinos's sermon, see Parratt 2004, 19–20; and Castro 2007, 56–59.

34. See, e.g., Steigman 2005, 13; Varner and Varner 1981, xxvii; and the long analysis of Garcilaso and "mestizo" as a political category in Burns 1988.

35. Galloway 1997, 28. For a description of Garcilaso's encounter with Las Casas, see Adorno 2008, 94.

36. On Garcilaso and the "rhetoric of particularism," see Sommer 1999, 61–91.

37. Garcilaso himself echoes Corinthians on the importance of *testigo de vista*: "in the mouths of two or three witnesses shall every word be verified"; cited in Rabasa, quoting Henige 1994, 224. See also Zamora 2005, 41.

38. See Rowe 1976, 27–32; Galindo 2010, ch. 1. See also Stavig 1999, 237; Stavig and Schmidt 2008, 147.

39. See Mazzotti's groundbreaking *Incan Insights/Coros mestizos* on the presence of Andean oral traditions and symbolism in the *Comentarios*.

40. Chang-Rodríguez 2006, 139, 27.

41. Las Casas 2006, 12.

42. Las Casas 1995, 13:23–48.

43. On the myth of Las Casas's responsibility for instantiating African slavery in the Americas, see Adorno 2008, 64. It is possible that Garcilaso also echoes the Fidalgo d'Elvas in this passage, who commented anecdotally on Indian suicides by hanging in Cuba, probably also with Las Casas in mind: "There is much gold in this land, but few slaves to get it out, for many hanged themselves because of the harsh treatment received in the mines from the Christians. An overseer of Vasco Porcallo, a resident of that island, having learned that his Indians were about to hang themselves, with a rope in his hands, went to await them in the place where they were to meet and told them that they could do nothing nor think of anything which he did not know beforehand; that he was going to hang himself with them, for if he had given them a hard life in this world, he would give them a worse in the other. This caused them to change their minds and return to do what he ordered them"; in "Account by a Gentleman from Elvas," pp. 53–54. See also the translation by Smith, "The True Relation given by a Fidalgo of Elvas," in Clayton, *The De Soto Chronicles*, 1:53–54. As Galloway notes, Garcilaso likely knew the Elvas account (*Hernando de Soto Expedition*, 36).

44. In the *Comentarios*, Garcilaso notes that he encountered Las Casas at the royal court, but the "Defender of the Indians" snubbed him once he realized that El Inca was from Peru rather than Mexico (Livermore 1989, 959). But Garcilaso had other reasons to dislike Las Casas as well; see, e.g., Adorno 2008, 94.

45. Adorno and Pautz have documented Garcilaso's use of the 1555 edition of Cabeza de Vaca's *Relación*, which he drew upon and embellished for his own account of the Soto expedition in La Florida (where it converged with incidents from the Narváez expedition); 2:122–27; 3:129–44; 150–54. Adorno has also written extensively on Garcilaso's engagement with Cabeza de Vaca in his writing, and has quite rightly pointed out that Garcilaso in fact "not only privileges Cabeza de Vaca's testimony regarding the Spanish interactions with the Amerindians of La Florida, but also models key episodes of his own narration . . . on Cabeza de Vaca's work"—in her view, to "affirm the importance of the narrative tradition" in which they both participate (2008, 281–82). I will argue later, however, that Garcilaso's engagement with Cabeza de Vaca is far from positive or identificatory.

46. On the figure of the captive in the colonial Americas, see the excellent studies by Voigt and Operé.

47. All quotations from the text of Cabeza de Vaca's 1542 *Relación* come from the authoritative modern edition by Adorno and Pautz (published by the University of Nebraska Press in 1999) and will hereafter be cited by page number from volume 1 (1:244–45). Adorno and Pautz's three-volume study includes a facing-page English translation of the narrative as well as a study of the author's life, the multiple historical and ethnographic contexts in which the narrative emerged, and the relation of the narrative to other writings by Cabeza de Vaca as well as other accounts of the expedition. Of particular importance in this study is the 1555 Valladolid edition of Cabeza de Vaca's narrative, the *Relación y Comentarios*, which conjoined a new version of the 1542 narrative with an account by Pero

Hernández of Cabeza de Vaca's governorship of Río de la Plata. Readers may also wish to consult the shorter Adorno and Pautz paperback edition, *The Narrative of Cabeza de Vaca*.

48. Adorno 1993, 50.

49. Cabeza de Vaca 2003, 102–03; see Molloy 1987, 447.

50. Cabeza de Vaca 2003, 18–19. On this point, see especially Bauer 2003, 30–31.

51. On the production of the Joint Report, see Adorno and Pautz's account (2003, 22–24).

52. As Operé notes, there were in fact many captives who chose not to return (2008, 223). Gonzalo Guerrero, shipwrecked in the Yucatán in 1511, remained with the Maya and his wife and children, despite Cortés's requests that he return to the Spaniards and serve as a translator. See also Adorno's discussion in *Polemics* (2008, 220–45).

53. As I have argued elsewhere ("Cabeza de Vaca"), Cabeza de Vaca has been distinctly celebrated by U.S.-American literary studies for the criticism of the Spanish colonizers and the implied opposition to Spanish violence against the Natives that he famously voices at the end of his *Relación*, where he self-consciously presents himself returning from his New World captivity with a powerfully changed identity, and a putative understanding of and proximity to the indigenous inhabitants of Florida and northern Mexico. In the early 1990s, Cabeza de Vaca was lauded as the virtual inventor of "Chicano narrative," the inaugurator of a new autobiographical mode in which "ambiguity, the essence of *chicanismo*, is already present" (Leal 1993, 64; see also Bruce-Novoa 1990, 12–21). Later critics followed this lead, dubbing him "the first Latino author . . . an intercultural man creating an intergeneric literary form" (Augenbraum 2000, 4). By the first decade of the twenty-first century, not surprisingly, the purported *chicanismo* and *latinidad* of Cabeza de Vaca's *Relación* had evolved into the marks of its mainstream and representative Americanness, its status as "the first truly literary document of the Americas, written by a European who has been changed by his American experiences" (Augenbraum 2000, 4). In this light, its narrator emerges as "a curious and debatable hybrid . . . [a]nticipating many later heroes and heroines in American literature" (Gray 2004, 25); in "becoming American by experience," Cabeza de Vaca creates, "in essence, the story of America" itself (Reséndez 2007, 10). In these accounts, Cabeza de Vaca emerges heroically as a "literary pioneer [who not only] deserves the distinction of being called the Southwest's first writer," but also indeed provides the "prototype of much American writing to come" (Reséndez 2007, 250, citing William T. Pilkington).

Such critical accounts indirectly enable the early American field to retain its focus on New England, simply by establishing Cabeza de Vaca's narrative as the hispanophone exception to the larger Anglo-American tradition. In *The Cambridge History of American Literature*, Cabeza de Vaca serves as a benevolent foil to his seventeenth-century counterpart, Mary Rowlandson, the Puritan ex-captive author of the enormously popular narrative *The Sovereignty and Goodness of God* (1682). While Rowlandson fails at cross-cultural identification, "insist[ing] that she has been transported beyond the human pale," Cabeza de Vaca recognizes "linguistic difference" and thereby "makes [the Indians] commensurate with himself, people with whom he can communicate, if not always actually, then potentially" (Jehlen 1994, 50). Cabeza de Vaca's quintessential American strength in such accounts is his ability to "occupy a border area between one culture, one version of experience, and another": he and the three fellow captives who accompany him are "mixed, New World beings . . . and their tale, finally, is about neither conquest nor captivity but about the making of Americans" (Gray 2004, 25).

Scholars in colonial Latin American studies have emphasized other, more faithfully historical interpretive contexts for the *Relación*, particularly its participation in the new discourse of imperial "pacification" and its function as the author's "narrative curriculum vitae" for a leadership role in future conquests (see Adorno and Pautz, "Introduction," 25; Bauer 2003, 33–48; Rabasa 1994, 31–32). The Cabeza de Vaca of these studies appears as a figure wholly unlike the celebrated border dweller of American literary studies. This more fully historicized Cabeza de Vaca—the one seen from the vantage of colonial Latin American literary history—is no oppositional hero: instead, his call for a "peaceful" colonization in seeming opposition to those he casts as greedy, slave-catching conquistadors in Nueva Galicia appears not only utterly conventional and in keeping with emergent Spanish imperial policy but also quite self-serving given his interest in future colonial endeavors and his eventual, short-lived appointment as governor of the South American colony Río de la Plata, where he was ultimately arrested under allegations of (among other things) mistreatment of the Indians (see Bauer 2003, 36–46; Pupo-Walker 1993, 129). In this light, to read Cabeza de Vaca as an icon of early American multilingualism is at best absurd, and at worst, as José Rabasa argues, a kind of scholarly "perpetuat[ion of] the culture of conquest" (1994, 31; and see Ferens)—or, at the least, a reinscription of its rhetorical violence.

54. See previous note.

55. As Voigt notes, Garcilaso "valorizes Álvar Núñez Cabeza de Vaca as a textual source" while also "chastis[ing] him for his desire to return [to Spain]" rather than to stay in Florida (2008, 142–43).

56. See Bauer 2003, 36–46; Pupo-Walker 1993, 129.

57. See the brief discussion on Garcilaso's Juan Ortiz in Chapter 1.

58. The page is numbered 39 in *La Florida*, but occurs after 29. On El Inca and Cervantes, see Suárez 2005. I disagree with Lee Dowling, who sees Garcilaso as representative of the "era's confusion" over the differences between fiction and history, while Cervantes is "the genius who managed to shape" this confusion into his masterwork in *Don Quixote* (1997, 105).

59. The passage appears on 42–42v of *La Florida*, but the page is misnumbered as 43, the first of two pages numbered as such.

60. As Galloway points out, Garcilaso would surely have known Castiglione's *Il Cortegiano*, for the man whose name El Inca chose as his own and upon whom he modeled his own career—the poet Garcilaso de la Vega, who introduced Renaissance Italian forms to Spanish literature—had written the introduction to a famous Spanish translation of *The Courtier* (29). Castanien suggests that Garcilaso would have known Machiavelli as well, as an influence upon what emerged as "a kind of standard approach to the historian's task" during this period (1969, 133). Greenblatt's classic reading of Machiavelli's work as the "mocking and demonic counterpart" to Castiglione's occurs in *Sir Walter Raleigh* (1973, 38).

61. On the phenomenon of exemplarity in crisis, see Rigolet 1998.

62. It is worth noting that in the second part of Book 2, a group of Indian captives shout Ortiz's name, "without uttering another word." El Inca suggests that the name is meant to remind the Spaniards of the good treatment Ortiz received in his own captivity, but the use of the translator's name to indicate a refusal to speak, and to be translated, also registers a certain irony (221).

63. Mignolo 1991, 9.

64. On the romanticization of captivity, see Strong 2000; on primitivism and the appropriation of indigeneity across American history, see Deloria 1999.

65. This argument about the emergence of modernity is made most forcefully by Quijano and Wallerstein 1992; for critiques of the "Americas" focus and a shift toward a broader (non-Americas-centric) hemispheric studies, see Taylor 2007b and Dimock 2009.

66. Carbado 2005, 639. Carbado is discussing black subjectivity and the law.

67. Mignolo 2000, esp. 2–11.

Chapter 4

1. Today we call him, incorrectly, by the name *Fontaneda* because of an early edition of the castaway's account—translated by David O. True, *Memoir of Do. d'Escalente* [sic] *Fontaneda Respecting Florida*, written in Spain, about the year 1575—which bequeathed to us this tradition rather than the normative Spanish practice, which would refer to him as Escalante or, in Menéndez's usage, Descalante.

2. The English version of the title comes from Buckingham Smith, the nineteenth-century U.S. scholar who first transcribed and translated Fontaneda's text in 1854. Contemporary scholars such as Greenblatt have largely followed the lead of Quinn, who retitled Smith's English translation of text in 1979 as *Memorial of Hernando de Escalante Fontaneda on the Florida Indians*. See Quinn 1979, 5:7. The Spanish text can be found in Hernando de Escalante Fontaneda, *Memoria*. This edition follows the transcription made by Juan Bautista Muñoz in the late eighteenth century and retains its original orthography, including lack of accents that are normative in contemporary Spanish. Throughout this chapter, citations hereafter will appear parenthetically. I have consulted the English translation of the text—"Memorial of Hernando de Escalante Fontaneda on the Florida Indians"—which may be found in Quinn, 1979, 5: 7–14. Like most contemporary scholars, Quinn reproduces the nineteenth-century Buckingham Smith (1854) translation in *A Letter of Hernando de Soto and Memoir of Hernando de Escalante Fontaneda*. For a recent examination of the original Fontaneda materials that are housed in the Archivo General de Indias in Seville—including the discovery of three new documents in Fontaneda's hand—see Worth 1995.

3. Ethnographic studies drawing upon Fontaneda's memoir include Swanton 1922; Griffin 1996; Santos Granero 2009; McGoun 1993; Purdy 1991; and Sturtevant 2005.

4. See, e.g., Jehlen 1994, 49–51; Reséndez 2007; Bruce-Novoa 1990; Glantz 1993; Voigt 2008; and Santos Granero 2009.

5. Bridenbaugh offers the classic example of this formulation in *Jamestown* (1980, 15–18).

6. Lisa Voigt (2008) makes the case for this kind of knowledge with particular clarity throughout *Writing Captivity*.

7. On the idea of an emergent narrative voice—the voice of the "dominated yet privileged colonial subject"—in the early modern era, see Mazzotti 1996.

8. As of August 1, 1566, Don Luis was with Menéndez at Fort San Mateo in Florida (see Quinn 1979, 5:550); in 1566, Menéndez was also entering into alliance with Carlos (Hoffman 2004, 241).

9. Menéndez had sent his only son to Mexico to command a treasure fleet bound for Spain; Juan's vessel apparently wrecked near the Bermudas, and nothing more was

heard from him again (though Fontaneda does mention him in his account, as discussed below). See Lowery 1995, 138–39.

10. On Menéndez's career in Florida, see Lyon 1976; as well as Milanich 1999; Hoffman 2002, 51–62, and 2004, 231–66; Galgano 2005, 40–42; and Axtell 1997, 5–24. On the Calusa Indians and especially their Atlantic castaways, see Swanton 1952, 125–28; Marquardt and Payne 1992, 327–54; and Hann 1994, 327–54.

11. The translation of the letter appears in Hann 1991, 301; the letter is also discussed in Landers 2005, 55. Lyon's reading of the letter is more specific than Hann's in *Missions*: the five *mestizo* women are from Peru, the five men are Spaniards (1976, 264). I have chosen here to use the term "Spanish Creole" rather than "Spaniard" because the castaways' desire to remain with the Calusa so aptly illustrates the potential ambivalence at the core of *criollismo*. My thanks go to Bianca Premo for this suggestion.

12. Hann 1991, 301.

13. *Pedro Menéndez de Avilés to the King, October 20, 1566*, from Hann 1991, 301. Hann also notes that the writing clipped off just before the phrase "a strong desire to help" includes the syllable "*ban*" from which he deduces that the missing word may have been "*mostraban*" or "they showed." See 301, n.21.

14. The phrase "was very good looking" is taken from Lyon's transcription; Hann's photo-reproduction was out of focus, but he had initially transcribed this portion as "of very good character"; see 301, n.22.

15. Hann 1991, 301.

16. See, e.g., McCarthy and Trotter 1992, 11; Voigt 2008, 152; Heard 1987, 156; Santos Granero 2009, 233; Grunwald 2007, 27; Griffin 1996, 188. Karen Ordahl Kupperman likewise appears to assume a rescue when she cites Fontaneda's account as exemplifying the "plight of shipwrecked Spaniards among the Florida Indians" (2007, 85–86). Most of these scholars have probably followed the lead of David B. Quinn (1985, 5:7), who refers explicitly to Fontaneda's rescue from Carlos.

17. As noted later in this chapter, Fontaneda writes in the memoir that he and his brother had been "sent . . . to Spain to be educated; when we were wrecked on Florida . . ." (541).

18. The wording is confusing, but Fontaneda seems to suggest that Menéndez's son was probably *not* in one of the ships that sank off the coast of Florida.

19. Adorno and Pautz 2003, 162.

20. Greenblatt 1991, 98.

21. Voigt 2008, 152. On Garcilaso and his *La Florida del Inca*, see especially Chang-Rodríguez 2006.

22. See Elliot 2007, 19.

23. The full text of the *requerimiento* in Spanish appears in Suess 2002, 327–28. For an English translation, see Grewe 2000, 238–39.

24. Grewe 2000, 239.

25. Suess 2002, 328; Grewe 2000, 239.

26. Grewe 2000, 239.

27. See Mann and Grinde Jr 2001, 3.

28. Connor 1925–30, 1:34–35.

29. See especially Rabasa 2000, 84–137.

30. Connor 1925–30, 1:80. English translation available on facing page.

31. Díaz 2005, 4. See also 2008, 2.

32. See also Greenblatt, who similarly notes that "Escalante's story would seem to be a sly, displaced critique of Spanish linguistic colonialism" (*Marvelous Possessions*, 98).

33. The phrase from the *requerimiento* can be found in Grewe 2000, 239. On the trope of Spanish apotheosis, see Restall 2004, 108–20; and Townsend 2003, 659–87.

34. The use of the term "free negro" suggests, of course, that this Afro-Caribbean castaway had a very different status living among the Calusa than he would likely have had living in the Spanish-settled parts of the Americas (from which he presumably came before his arrival in coastal Florida). On this subject, see Landers 1999, 14–15; and 2005, 53–57.

35. Adorno 2008, 24.

36. Adorno 2008, 25.

37. Thanks to Bianca Premo for pointing out that what Fontaneda is suggesting here is essentially the Portuguese *feitoria* model—a coastal fortress used for trade and protection from rivals—as opposed to the Spanish conquest model that attempted to acculturate the Native population of the interior. Thus, even if we take Fontaneda at his word here, the suggestion effects another model of unsettlement, a last ditch effort to persuade the Spaniards not to encroach beyond the Floridian coast if they did in the end remain there.

38. Thanks again to Bianca Premo for this observation.

39. Quinn 1979, 5:13.

40. On the effect of Fontaneda's narrative upon further colonization, see McCarthy and Trotter 1992, 11. On the rapid decline of a Spanish foothold in La Florida, which Don Luis's act of unsettlement helped to launch, see Weber 2009, 72–75. By 1587, St. Augustine was the only Spanish settlement left in all of La Florida.

41. Father Juan Rogel to Father Didacus Avellaneda, November 1566 to January 1567. The letter appears in Document 41 from "Monumenta Antiquae Floridae (1566–1572)" (Zubillaga 1946, 101–40). Translation in Hann 1991, 278–85.

42. Zubillaga 1946, 132.

43. Ibid., 133–35.

44. See especially Solís de Meras's account of the episode.

45. Zubillaga 1946, 135.

46. Ibid., 133.

47. Ibid., 133–34.

48. Ibid., 134.

49. Ibid.

50. Ibid.

51. Ibid., 135.

52. Ibid., 134.

53. Ibid., 134.

54. Ibid., 135–36.

55. Ibid., 138.

56. Ibid., 138–39.

57. Ibid., 136.

58. Father Juan Rogel to Father Jerónimo Ruiz del Portillo, April 25, 1568. The letter appears in Document 85 from Zubillaga 1946, 276; the emphasis is mine. See also the translation in Hann 1991, 235.

59. Zubillaga 1946, 291–92.

60. Ibid.

61. Ibid., 291.

62. Ibid., 280.

63. See Zubillaga, 1946, 134–35 n. 134.

64. Zubillaga 1946, 282–83.

65. See "Montezuma and Signs," in Todorov 1996, 63–97.

66. Zubillaga 1946, 285, 283.

67. Todorov 1996, 81–82.

68. Zubillaga 1946, 279.

69. Todorov 1996, 85.

70. Marquardt 1992, 2.

71. Hann 1991, 4–5.

72. Granberry, *A Grammar and Dictionary of the Timucua Language*, cited in Hann 1991, 5.

73. See, e.g., Rogel, *Father Jerónimo Ruiz del Portillo, April 25, 1568,* where he speaks of Carlos's "great hate against me especially because I discredited and spoke evil about his idols" (Hann 1991, 266).

74. "Statement by the Ensign Francisco Romero" (1698) in Hann 1991, 184–85.

75. On Fray Andrés's life and career, see García 1902, xviii–xxvii; and Hann 2001; his writings on architecture, hydraulics and technology may be found in Eduardo Báez Macías, ed., *Obras de Fray Andrés de San Miguel.*

76. San Miguel, *Relación de los trabajos que la gente de una nao llamada nra señora de la merced padeció y algunas cosas que en aquella flota sucedieron* in García, ed., *Dos antiguas relaciones*, translated into English by Hann (2001). Where relevant I have modified Hann's translations slightly. All citations of Andrés are from *Dos antiguas relaciones*.

77. San Miguel 1902, 198.

78. Lezama's classic essay on the American baroque, "La curiosidad barroca," appears in *La expresión Americana*; for an English translation, see Zamora and Kaup 2010, 212–40.

79. The concept of "the written church" comes from Chapter Five of Brentano 1988.

80. On the topos of *desengaño*, see Maravall 1986, 202–03; see also Beverly 2008, 1–22. On the baroque as a counterconquest mode, see especially the introduction to Zamora and Kaup 2010; and More 2010, 1–28.

81. Based on the manuscript's position in between two other writings within a bound volume, Hann believes that it was most likely penned while Andrés was living in Mexico City in the 1630s (2001, 9).

82. San Miguel 1902, 162–63.

83. Ibid., 166.

84. The workmanlike "good purser" (*buen escrivano*) becomes the de facto leader, but drops out of the narrative soon after the survivors make it to land.

85. San Miguel 1902, 177.

86. Ibid., 174, 185–86.

87. On the shipwreck's rupturing of narrative certainty, especially in the context of empire, see Blackmore 2002, 28.

88. San Miguel 1902, 189–90.

89. Ibid., 190.

90. Ibid.

91. Ibid., 190–91.

92. Ibid., 191.

93. Ibid., 195.

94. Ibid., 195–96.

95. Ibid.

96. Ibid., 196.

97. Ibid., 197.

98. Felipe was executed in 1570; see Lowery 1905, 346.

99. After Don Luis's unsettlement of Ajacán, Rogel went to New Spain, and from 1579 to 1619 worked in the port of Vera Cruz; see Lewis and Loomie 71.

100. San Miguel 1902, 197.

101. Ibid., 205.

102. On the prophet Neolin and the drinking of purgative tea, see Malcolmson 2010, 54–55.

103. San Miguel 1902, 199.

104. Ibid., 200.

105. Thomas 2011, 13.

106. Thomas 2011, xi and 13.

107. John T. Worth, for example, assumes two separate individuals, the Guale leader Don Juan and the Timucuan leader Don Juan (1998, 1: 52).

108. See Torquemada 3:350–54. This material was composed between 1609 and 1613 and drew on accounts Torquemada had been collecting since the late sixteenth century. See Franch 1973, 13: 256–75.

109. San Miguel 1902, 198.

110. Ibid., 207.

111. Ibid., 209–10.

112. Adorno 1994, 378.

113. On the chain of revolts, and the indigenous transmission of information regarding them, from the 1576 "Escamacu Revolt," to the unsettlement of Santa Elena by the Oristan Indians, to an early Guale revolt, as well as related revolts running from the 1570s through the 1590s, see Rowland et al. 1996, 1:37–47. On the Guale uprising, see Francis et al. 2011; as well as Mann and Grinde 2001, 70–72; and Stojanowski 2008, 8–11.

114. The slave-hunting missions in La Florida began because the indigenous labor force in nearby Cuba was declining too quickly to reproduce itself (Axtell 1997, 101).

115. See Diana Taylor's critique of scholarship's tendency, beginning with J. L. Austin, to restrict the role of the "performative" to the realm of discourse rather than performance (2007a, 5–6).

116. In this sense, the name "Don Luis" deploys a rhetorical force similar to what Robert McKee Irwin (citing José Manuel Valenzuela Arce) identifies in the ubiquitous nineteenth-century figure of Joaquín Murrieta, whose "social functionality" endures wherever particular cultural conflicts remain unresolved (2007, 39).

Chapter 5

1. The Black Legend refers (derogatively) to a complex of anti-Catholic, anti-Iberian attitudes, assumptions, and rhetorical maneuvers structuring historical writing about the

Spanish conquest of the Americas and Spanish colonialism more broadly. The master narrative of the Black Legend hinges upon the supposed bloodthirstiness and rapine of the Spanish conquerors (as opposed, at least implicitly, to the temperate chastity and moderation of English settlers). Scholars trace the origins of the Black Legend to the writings of Bartolomé de las Casas, discussed in Chapter 1 and elsewhere, which protested Spanish atrocities against indigenous Americans during the conquest. When translated into English shortly after their initial publication, these texts provided anti-Spanish propaganda for those who wished to promote English colonization (or simply to demonize Spanish Catholics); see Gibson 1971. In the nineteenth century, the Black Legend persisted as a historiographical mode but provided ideological cover for new imperial aspirations, particularly those of the United States; see DeGuzmán 2005. The Black Legend arguably continues to exert its influence on historical understanding today, especially as a mode of implicit racialization; see Mignolo and Quilligan 1988.

2. The first English translation of Las Casas's *Brevisima Relación* appeared in 1583 as *The Spanish Colonie*. Later translations of Las Casas include titles such as *Spanish Cruelties* and *Tears of the Indians*; see Clark 2003, 2.

3. The phrase "all-devouringe Spaniard" is from the First Report of Council in Jamestown, signed by Edward Maria Wingfield, John Smith et al. on June 22, 1607. As Cañizares-Esguerra notes throughout *Puritan Conquistadors*, however, the English were often modeling themselves *upon* the Spanish, even as they claimed them as a rhetorical, moral foil. Moreover, the signs that Spaniards had preceded the English were unmistakable. When the Chickahominy Indians in Virginia negotiated a treaty with the Jamestown settlers, for example, they apparently agreed to supply military forces "against the Spaniards, whose name is odious among them, for Powhatan's father was driven by them from the west-Indies into these parts" (Hamor 1957, 13). The Jamestown settlers believed they had achieved the agreement through their own diplomatic virtuosity, exploiting an inter-indigenous conflict between the Chickahominy and the Powhatan Indians to an English advantage (just as Cortés claimed to have done with the Tlaxcalans and the Mexica in his self-serving accounts of the conquest of Mexico): the Chickahominies would fight the Spaniards, in other words, simply because Spaniards were responsible for bringing their enemy's leader into Virginia. It never occurred to the English that, seen from the Chickahominy and perhaps also the Powhatan point of view, the treaty took advantage of an inter-European conflict as well, ensuring that a potential return of Spanish colonial forces to Ajacán would face an allied front of English settlers and natives. Some historians have wondered whether this Powhatan leader brought by Spaniards to Virginia might have been Don Luis himself, known to the English as Opechancanaugh (see especially Bridenbaugh 1980, chap. 2; see also the discussion in Chapter 2). As Lewis and Loomie note, Robert Beverley's *History and Present State of Virginia* is remarkably suggestive in describing Opechancanaugh as "a Prince of a Foreign Nation, and came to them a great Way from the South-West . . . from the Spanish Indians, some-where near Mexico . . ." (LL 59).

4. Scheckel 1998, 45.

5. Shea 1877, 343.

6. Blackman 2005, 141–44. On Greenhow's life and personality more generally, see Blackman 2005, 94–100; and Burger 1967, 14–18.

7. See *On the Use and Abuse of History for Life*, esp. section III (25–29) and 75–76.

8. Blackman 2005, 94. As I have argued elsewhere, Greenhow is overshadowed in contemporary historical scholarship by the figure of his far more famous and flamboyant wife, Rose O'Neal Greenhow: "Wild Rose," the "Confederate Spy," as her biographers have dubbed her in telling the story of her larger-than-life career as a secret agent for the South during the Civil War, a decade after her husband's death in 1854. See, e.g., Blackman 2005; Burger 1967.

9. On the advent of history as a profession, see Novick 1988, esp. 21–60. On nineteenth-century history and the New World, see Burrow 2008, 423–52; on U.S. history during the first half of the nineteenth century, especially Romantic history and antiquarianism, see Callcott 1970.

10. Novick 1988, 45.

11. Inconsistencies in the literature-versus-history divide abound during the period. Prescott, later (and still often) known as the chief of the romancers, sided with the "professed skeptics" when, writing under the influence of Black Legend historiography, he criticized one of his major Spanish sources, the seventeenth-century historian Solís, for putting made-up speeches into the mouths of his historical subjects: "There is something like deception in it," he complained. "The reader is unable to determine what are the sentiments of the characters, and what those of the author. History assumes the air of romance, and the bewildered student wanders about in an uncertain light, doubtful whether he is treading on fact or fiction" (2:294).

12. This characterization of the antiquary comes from Theodore Parker's 1849 review essay, "The Character of Mr. Prescott as an Historian," cited in Ernest 1993, 231. See Ernest more generally for a brilliant reading of what he calls Prescott's "self-reflexive understanding" and his "demonstration of truth as a perspectival methodology and corresponding mode of representation" in *Conquest of Mexico* (1993, 233).

13. "Memoir, Historical and Political, on the Northwest Coast of North America, and the Adjacent Territories; Illustrated by a Map and a Geographical View of Those Countries. By Robert Greenhow, Translator and Librarian to the Department of State. February 10, 1840. Submitted by Mr. [Lewis F.] Linn, from the Select Committee on the Oregon Territory; and ordered to be printed, and that 2,500 additional copies be sent to the Senate. Washington: Blair and Rives, Printers. 1840." U.S. Senate Document of the 26th Cong., 1st Sess., Vol. IV (1839–40), 140–41. See Jackson 1974, 47.

14. There are some interesting differences between the wording of the *Memoir* and that of the *History*, including greater emphasis on the fictionality of those accounts Greenhow dismisses.

15. Greenhow 1840, 200. Citations hereafter are internal.

16. Greenhow 1845, 78.

17. Greenhow 1845, 86. Greenhow's generic designation was not a foregone conclusion for everyone. The English reviewer of Greenhow's book for the London-based *Quarterly Review*, for example, insisted upon the term "fable" for Fuca's account, and placed it in the category of "fables . . . circumstantially and plausibly told" which exacted a particular reader response: they "excited a strong desire to discover the supposed passages" (310).

18. Whether or not Greenhow and Poe ever met in person is unknown, but it is certain they knew of each other. In 1811, when Greenhow was a ten-year-old boy, his parents took him to a benefit show in Richmond, a play whose proceeds were to help support a newly orphaned boy named Edgar, son of the late Elizabeth Arnold Poe.

A fire broke out in the theater, and Greenhow's mother's last words to her husband were, according to his father's later account, a plea to save her child at all costs. Greenhow and his father barely made it out of the theater alive; Greenhow's mother died in the fire. Greenhow and Poe were thus uncannily connected from their childhoods by a shared tragedy that left Greenhow, like Poe, bereft of a mother. For an account of the fire and Greenhow's near death, see Blackman 2005, 95–96. As this section of my chapter argues, their written paths, too, would intersect when the two motherless boys grew up to become writers.

19. *Memoir* 1840, 140. Greenhow eliminated the Rodman account from his 1845 *History*; sometime between the publication of the *Memoir* in 1840 and the "revised, corrected, and enlarged" *History* in 1845, Greenhow decided, probably after reading the ensuing installments of *Julius Rodman*, that the Poe text would not stand up as historical evidence.

20. As advertised on the rear cover of the February 1840 installment of *The Journal of Julius Rodman*. On *Rodman* as a parody, see Teunissen and Hinz; on Rodman and U.S. imperial ideology, see Rowe 2000, 55–70.

21. Edgar Allan Poe to William E. Burton, June 1, 1840 (LTR-093).

22. Poe was, of course, actually court-martialed and thrown out of West Point within six months; see Quinn 1998, 173–74.

23. Kennedy 2002, 2005. Both provide an excellent overview of the *Rodman*-era changes occurring in Poe's fiction.

24. On Greenhow's trip to Mexico, see Blackman 2005, 103–07; and Phipps 2003, 41–43.

25. On Greenhow's conflict with Trist, see Blackman 2005, 135–36, 142. On Trist and the Mexican War, see Ohrt 1998.

26. The Virginia Philosophical and Historical Society was founded in 1831 to gather and house natural history specimens, historical artifacts, and written materials.

27. Cushing 1833, 33.

28. The memoir is collected in Robinson 1848.

29. Greenhow 1848, 481.

30. Andrés González de Barcia Carballido Zuñiga, *Ensayo cronológico para la historia general de la Florida* (Madrid 1723). Citations hereafter are internal.

31. On González de Barcia's scholarly career and contributions to Enlightenment historiography, see Carlyon 2005.

32. Carlyon 2005, 7.

33. As I discuss later, he may have learned about González de Barcia's text from John Gilmary Shea.

34. Not surprisingly, in Greenhow's *Memoir, Historical and Political,* he disparages Humboldt, perhaps because he supported an independent Mexico and believed in local knowledge; he did not, as some Anglophone historians did, dismiss Spanish sources (44).

35. Calhoun addressing the Senate on January 8, 1848; cited in Niven 1993, 54.

36. On Greenhow's support of Narciso López, and his work for the California Land Commission, see Blackman 2005, 143 and 162–64.

37. See Ford 2011, 136.

38. On the history of the discovery doctrine and its far-reaching implications for American Indian law, see Miller et al. 2010 as well as Deloria 2010, 85–112; and Newcomb (2008) argues that U.S. federal Indian law originates in Old testament narratives, and shows how *Johnson v. M'Intosh* violates the separation of church and state. For background

on the larger Western religious and legal frameworks shaping early European ideas about the rights of non-Christian peoples, see Muldoon 1977.

39. *Johnson v. M'Intosh*, 21 U.S. (1883): 573–74. Scholarship on this landmark case as well as the other two included in the Marshall Trilogy and the effect upon future Indian law and U.S. imperial ventures includes Watson 2012, Robertson 2005, Deloria Jr. and Lyttle 2010, Garrison 2002, Wilkins 2010, Williams, Jr. 1992 and 1995. See also the analysis of the Marshall Trilogy and "quasi-sovereigns" by Cho and Gott (2010, 194–204).

40. Robertson 2005, 4.

41. The classic source on racial discourse and U.S. imperialism during this period is Horsman 1986; for an analysis of the literary dimensions of this problem, see also Rowe 2000.

42. On Shea's life and career as a Catholic historian, see Guilday 1926; Pasquier 2010, 480–81; and Franchot 1994, 62–63.

43. On Rose Greenhow's Catholicism, see Blackman 2005, 99–100.

44. *United States Catholic Magazine*, 5:538.

45. Jorge Cañizares-Esguerra 2002, 5.

46. "Our Martyrs, No. III," *United States Catholic Magazine*, 5:604–07.

47. We know this because Campbell's *History of the Colony* cites a "MS. letter of John Gilmary Shea, Esq., author of *History of the Catholic Missions among the Indians of the United States*, citing Barcia and Alegambe" (1860, 18). Campbell cites the source as a reference for his statement that the Spaniards avenged the deaths of the Jesuits.

48. On Pocahontas's role in sectional conflict and the eagerness of northern historians to debunk John Smith's writings, see Tilton 1994, 162.

49. Shea 1865.

50. Shea gave frequent addresses to the New York Historical Society; see Kelby 1905.

51. Shea 1877, 333–43. Citations hereafter are internal.

52. On the role of capitol art and the emergence of U.S. discourse, see Fryd 2001.

53. On Bryant and Gay's *Popular History* and reactions to the popular history genre in the United States more generally, see Bold 2012, 624–25. See also the biography of Bryant in Muller 2010, 323–24, 329.

54. On the collaboration of Gay and Bryant, see the excellent chapter in Pfitzer 2008, 73–122.

55. Bryant and Gay 1876–1881, 1:xxi. On the reception of British popular history in the United States, see Pfitzer's account 2008, 74.

56. On the Maximilian Affair in relation to the U.S. Civil War, see Ridley 1992 as well as Cornish 2002, 1268–69.

57. David Allen Nichols' *Lincoln and the Indians* was among the first studies to recognize the intertwinement of the Civil War and American Indian policy.

58. Bryant 1893, 50–51.

59. Bryant 1893, 52. See especially Kirsten Silva Gruesz's reading of Bryant's poem in the context of nineteenth-century theories about the Mound Builders and her speculation that they may have resonated with U.S. interest in other, more southerly "pyramid-builders—Aztecs, Mayans, Incans" (2001, 49–52).

60. See Cortés's famous depiction of Montezuma's alleged speech in the Second Letter (*Letters from Mexico*, 85). As José Rabasa points out, "In legal terms, this amounts to a self-denial of a natural right to power; hence the conquest of a conqueror

under the banner of Christianity is more than justifiable" (1994, 108). On the late nineteenth-century U.S. in the context of Indian violence and brutality, see also Deloria 2004, 21–22.

61. In Greeson's subtle reading, Bryant's perspective is not merely expansionist, however. The poem marks a shift in the "temporal valences" of the U.S. South in the cultural imagination, which now figures as "an ominous herald—a foreshadowing—of a dystopic national future" (2010, 116).

62. For general background on this theory and its surrounding controversy, see especially Silverberg 1986.

63. On U.S. literary interest in the Native peoples of Mexico and South America, as sharply differentiated from North American Indians, see Wertheimer 1998.

64. Pfitzer 2008, 91. Bryant and Gay's history does, however, call into question what it calls "the romantic story of John Smith and Pocahontas," even noting that it is "anticipate[d] in the experience of . . . Juan Ortiz" (158).

65. On the relation between the Black Legend and settler colonialism, see Altamirano-Jiménez 2013, 27–44.

66. On the "ontological conservatism" of alternative history and counterfactual history in the nineteenth century, see Dannenberg 2008, 200–01.

67. Fletcher 1888. Citations hereafter are internal.

68. On John Eaton as Commissioner of Education, see Trafzer, Keller, and Sisquoc 2006, 12–13; on his involvement in the creation of the report on Indian Education, see Mark 1989, 115.

69. On the history of the Bureau of American Indians, see Sturtevant 1989, 4: 255–57.

70. On settler colonialism and the logic of elimination, see Wolfe 2013, 102. See also Wolfe 1999 and 2006.

71. The major source on Alice Fletcher's life and career is Mark 1989; see also Jacobs 2011, 98–101, 196–210.

72. Mark 1989, 280.

73. On Fletcher's interest in eugenicist thought, see Mark 1989, 105 and 280.

74. On the relation of the exposition to the charges leveled by Jackson, see Viswaswaran 1998, 102. On the exposition more generally, see Mark 1989, 109–15.

75. See, for example, her description in *Indian Education and Civilization* of Virginia, where Indians were "enslaved, degraded by law, impoverished by the loss of their homes and by the greater loss of their own rude laws and government" (1888, 32) versus records in Massachusetts, which "show a uniform desire to confirm the Indians in all their rights" (1888, 41).

76. See Mark 1989, 116–17.

77. On the history of the Dawes Act and its effects, see Otis 1973; Washburn 1986; and Hoxie 2001. I have been especially influenced by the subtle arguments against historical inevitability outlined in Genetin-Pilawa 2012, 134–55. On the effects of Dawes on the Omaha in particular, see Boughter 1998, 96–133.

78. Cited in Mark 1989, 118.

79. Fletcher 1886, 430.

80. See, for example, Deloria 2010, 6.

81. Dawes as quoted in the *Proceedings of the Tenth Annual Lake Mohonk Conference of Friends of the Indian* (1892, 126); also cited in Mark 1989, 119.

82. The first quotation comes from Susette La Flesche's Introduction to Harsha 1881, 4; she writes under the name "Inshta Theamba (Bright Eyes)"; the second is Wolfe 2006, 387.

83. La Flesche 1881, 4.

84. On Susette La Flesche's life and career, see Wilson 1974 and Peterson 2006, 47–70.

85. La Flesche 1881, 4.

86. On Fletcher's adoption of Francis La Flesche, see Mark 1989, 153, 348.

87. On the strained relations of the La Flesche siblings to their respective partners, see (regarding Susette la Flesche and Thomas Tibbles) Peterson 2006, 61–66; and (regarding Francis La Flesche and Fletcher) Mark 1989, 271–74.

88. Tibbles 1972, 17–18. Citations hereafter are internal. On Tibbles's role in Indian reform, see also Mathis and Lowitt 2003, 55–87, 175–80.

89. Fletcher 1885, 3. Cited in Mark 1989, 13.

90. On Francis La Flesche's anthropological contributions, see especially *The Osage and the Invisible World*, which includes a short biographical chapter on La Flesche (1999, 10–26); Elliott, particularly his reading of La Flesche's novel *The Middle Five* (2002, 143–63); and Liberty 2002, 51–69.

91. See Mark's account of Fletcher's growing intellectual reliance on Francis La Flesche, and his gradual resistance to collaboration, particularly when his contributions went unrecognized (1989, 79–89, 212, 216, 271–74).

92. La Flesche 1905, 13.

93. Cabell makes this pronouncement about the story of Don Luis as told in his own novel, *The First Gentleman of America*, in "Myths of the Old Dominion," in the 1947 collection *Let Me Lie*. Both texts are discussed in the next chapter.

Chapter 6

1. Letter from Rose Greenhow to John C. Calhoun, August 29, 1849, Washington. *The Papers of John C. Calhoun*, ed. William Edwin Hemphill. Rose's letter appended a translation, probably made by Greenhow and purportedly from a Spanish-language newspaper published in New York, which warned that Spain planned, in the event of British intervention in Cuba, to "arm her Africans . . . and grant them freedom as a reward for their aid"; the excerpt therefore "implore[d] the interference of the Government of the United States to whom, from institutions and Character, such a generous and humane service appertains more than anyone else" (40–42).

2. Ambrosias 1990, 16–22.

3. Wilson is cited in *Current Opinion* 71 (December 1921): 714.

4. The text of the January 16, 1917, telegram, decoded and translated, can be found in Stacy 2002, 883. On the history of the episode, see Tuchman 1985.

5. See especially Greeson's reading of Crevecoeur in "The Problem of the Plantation" (2010, 19–32); on the intertwined histories of the U.S. South and the "New World" South, see the essays collected in Cohn and Smith 2004.

6. The phrase comes from Samuel Guy Inman in his *Problems in Pan Americanism* (1921).

7. Whitaker's 1954 study, *The Western Hemisphere Idea: Its Rise and Decline*, locates the decline at 1940. The Pan-American movement and the "Bolton thesis" are discussed later.

8. Cited in "Latin America in 1899," an unsigned report in *Pan American Union* in 1900.

9. Roosevelt is cited in Schulman 1994, 3. Narratives of Virginia exceptionalism spring largely from the cavalier myth, the (fallacious) idea that Virginia was largely settled by fugitive English nobility who brought their titles and their aristocratic culture to the New World and created a uniquely genteel and courtly culture in the Old Dominion that set it apart from the South and the nation at large. For an excellent overview of the cavalier myth and a sampling of the primary texts that propounded it, see Watson 2001, 131–33.

10. Mencken 1920, 138. Citations hereafter internal. On the wider context of this essay as well as Mencken's complex attitudes toward the U.S. South, see Hobson 1974.

11. On the political milieu in which this collection was produced, see Rubin's Introduction to the 1977 LSU edition of *I'll Take My Stand* (1977); Kreyling 1998, esp. 3–18; and Hobson 197, 147–84.

12. See Cash's analysis of the Agrarian version of the cavalier myth (1941, esp. 3–10). The authors of *I'll Take My Stand* also sometimes criticized the cavalier myth. Frank Lawrence Owsley, in "The Irrepressible Conflict," for example, noted that "All who came to Virginia were not gentlemen . . . in fact, only a few were of the gentry. Most of them were of the yeomanry" (in Davidson et al. 2006, 69). But more often than not, the collection finds traction in comparisons of Southern-ness to English gentility, and a shared set of qualities presumed to have originated during Virginia settlement. Thus we find Stark Young, in "Not in Memoriam but in Defense," asserting that the "English get on better with Southerners than with other Americans, the better classes especially" and that "the Duke of This or That" has "a culture very much the same" as "Southern culture" (341–42). The opening essay by John Crowe Ransom, "Reconstructed but Unregenerate" sets the tone by describing the "unadulterated Europeanism" of Southern culture and its perpetuation of the "human life of English provinces" and the "squirearchy" of "Southern society (5, 13–14).

13. Cash 1941, 8.

14. Cited in Hobson 1974, 11. As Hobson notes, this comparison of the South to Yucatán did not come from the original Sahara essay, but from a Mencken letter to an editor (194).

15. On anti-Darwinism, see, e.g., Mencken 2001, 94.

16. The third section of Greeson's *Our South*—"The Question of Empire/The Reconstruction South"—makes this point powerfully.

17. Tate 1998, 80; Faulkner 1929, 234.

18. Roosevelt's remarks are quoted on the commemorative program from 1937; see Jaffe 1958, 7.

19. Green, "The Beginning of *The Lost Colony*," 2001, 149. Hereafter cited internally from the 1937 edition.

20. For a cultural history of the Jamestown exposition, see Yarsinske 1999.

21. On this phrase, see, e.g., Page 1907.

22. The play has run continuously with the exception of the four years of U.S. participation in World War II. On various cultural representations of Roanoke, including Green's, see Harkin 2008, 103–17.

23. Green 39. On Raleigh's Irish experience, see Sir John Pope Hennessy's 1883 *Sir Walter Raleigh in Ireland*, as well as Miller 1998, 50–85.

24. Cash's book is approached from a variety of perspectives in Eagles 1992.

25. See Kupperman's account of Wanchese's transatlantic visit and subsequent betrayal in *Roanoke* (1984, 82, 113) as well as Vaughn 2008, 21–27. Wanchese is discussed in the context of other "treasonous translators" in Chapter 1.

26. On the larger legal context of Elizabeth's patent, see Williams 1992.

27. Brown 2000, 3–4; Hawthorne 1862, 50.

28. On the history of U.S. interpretations of Noah's curse in relation to race and slavery, see Haynes 2002.

29. See Kupperman 1984, 87, 91; the slaves included Indians brought from the Caribbean as well.

30. The Introduction to the 1954 edition is included in *The Lost Colony*, ed. Avery 2000, 148–49.

31. George Alfred Townsend, *Swamp Outlaws*, as cited in Heinegg 2007, 790.

32. Heinegg 2007, 26; see also McMillan 1988.

33. On the actual history of the lost English colonists and their possible flight to the Croatan Indians, see Kupperman 1984, 137–40.

34. Heinegg 2007, 26.

35. On the history of the Lumbees and their racial designation and pursuit of tribal status, see Lowery 2010 and Sider 1994.

36. Mooney, "Croatans," in Hodge 1907, 365.

37. Fiedler's famous observation comes from his reading of Cooper's *Last of the Mohicans* in *Love and Death in the American Novel* (1966, 204).

38. On Roosevelt's relation to the U.S. South as a political region, see McMahon 2003.

39. The firsthand account of John White, "Fourth Voyage Made to Virginia" (1904), casts Fernandes as suspicious based largely upon his refusal to leave off privateering and get to Roanoke to relieve the colonists. On Fernandes, see also Horn 2007, 518–21.

40. As Jorge Cañizares-Esguerra argues in *Puritan Conquistadors*, even in the wake of the "transnational turn" in the various fields of American Studies, scholars are still reluctant to "treat the South as normative," or to cast Spanish America as "more than a background to narratives of the British Atlantic" (2006, 223).

41. On Raleigh's obsession with Spanish colonial models, see Whitehead 1995, 17–24; and Pérez 1973.

42. All quotes will come from the annotated edition by Whitehead, *Sir Walter Raleigh: The Discoverie of the Large, Rich, and Bewtiful Empyre of Guiana* (1995).

43. On racial "Anglo-Saxonism" and the ascription of a racially mixed and therefore ostensibly inferior historical destiny to Latin America, see especially Horsman 1986.

44. Numerous firsthand accounts suggest that the warrior and prophet known as Nemattanew (or Jack of the Feathers to the English) played an important role among the Powhatan leadership. As J. Frederick Fausz suggests, Nemattanew helped to engineer a "military renaissance" and "psychological revitalization" of the Powhatans, and was intimately connected to the 1622 massacre that nearly destroyed Jamestown (1982, 30). Cabell explains his positing of Nemattanew as the later identity of Don Luis, after his return to Ajacán, in the Editorial Note at the end of the novel (283–84). It is worth noting that his proposition closely resembles the historical theory that Don Luis became Opechancanaugh, Powhatan's brother and successor (see Chapter 2) as outlined most notably by Carl Bridenbaugh (1980, 10–33; 1981, 5–49). In fact, Nemattanew and Opechancanaugh worked closely together; it is likely that Opechanancanaugh orchestrated both the 1622 and the 1644 attacks against the English. If Opechancanaugh were in

fact Don Luis, the 1644 attack would have been his third attempt at large-scale unsettlement of European colonization.

45. Cabell 2003, 284. Smith's description can be found in *The Generall Historie* (2:293).

46. Cabell 1947, 35–36.

47. Cabell's letter to his publisher is cited in MacDonald 1993, 308.

48. On Cabell's ancestry, see MacDonald 1993, 3–10. On James Lawrence Cabell and his eugenicist work, see Dorr 2008, 21–47.

49. On the *Jurgen* obscenity trial, see Sova 2006, 125–28. The notoriety worked in Cabell's favor for a time.

50. "Cabell Minor" and "Cabell Major" are the first two sections of Carl Van Doren's 1925 study *James Branch Cabell*; the quotation is from the first section (5).

51. See Kazin 2013, xxi. On Cabell's changing literary fortunes, see Hobson 1974, 121–46.

52. See MacDonald 1993, 300–15.

53. Cabell 2003, 183. Earlier in the sentence, I am quoting from John Conington's 1867 translation of the *Aeneid*, which would have been readily available to Cabell (Virgil 1867, 1).

54. On the WPA funding of various aspects of Green's drama, see Glassberg 1990, 275.

55. "Myths of the Old Dominion" is included in *Let Me Lie* (Cabell 2001, 43–76).

56. Cabell 2003, 214–16; compare to Quirós and Segura letter (LL 85–86). See the discussion of the entire Quirós and Segura letter in Chapter 2.

57. The quote comes from Bolton's famous 1932 speech delivered to the American Historical Association (Bolton 1933, 448; citations hereafter will be internal). There is a great deal of excellent scholarship on the so-called Bolton thesis; see, e.g., Hanke 1965, and particularly the essay of the same title in this volume, by Edmundo O'Gormon, originally published in Spanish as "*Hegel y el moderno panamericanismo.*"

58. On Cabell's well-known FFV status, see, e.g., Kunitz and Haycraft 1973, 233. On the FFV more generally, see Heuvel 2007, 263–65.

59. On Roosevelt and the Good Neighbor Policy, see Pike 2010; Ruano de la Haza 2007; Hart 2012; and Grandin 2010, 27–39.

60. See *TIME*, November 15, 1948 (cover article); and "Trujillo: Portrait of a Dictator," *CBS Reports*: Season 1, Episode 7, March 17, 1960. Recent sources citing Roosevelt's alleged remark about Nicaraguan dictator Anastasio Somoza García include Dent 1995, 404; Kagan 1996, 394; and Black 2007, 150. Schmitz argues that Roosevelt likely never made the statement (1999, 4–5); Andrew Crawley argues in *Somoza and Roosevelt* that the myth of Roosevelt's statement likely originated with Somoza himself (2007, 153).

61. *The Public Papers and Addresses of Franklin D. Roosevelt* 2:129–33. On the Pan-American Union, see González and Rydell 2011, 1–18; McCoy and Scarano 2009, 179, 185; and on Pan-Americanism more generally, see Brown 2008, 1–34.

62. A number of scholars have written on Roosevelt's virtuosic casuistry; see Black 2007, 229; Kammen 1997, 339; and Jasinski 2001, 89–91.

63. Roosevelt's attitude toward European colonialism has been differently interpreted by historians; for a good overview, see Kimball (with Fred E. Pollock) 1994, 127–58.

64. For the text of the letter see Roosevelt 1948, 550; also cited and discussed in Pike 2010, 132.

65. On Doña Catalina de Tapia's descent and marriage, see Himmerich y Valencia 1996, 70.

66. Ribault was the second leader of the earliest French colony in what is now the United States, Fort Caroline, established in Florida in 1564; he succeeded René de Laudonnière and governed for less than a month before Menéndez found and destroyed the settlement. On the history of the colony and its attendant documents, see Bennett 2001.

67. Quetzal evokes the Nahua deity Quetzalcoatl, the so-called feathered serpent; see below in this chapter for later interpretations of the figure and its connection to Atlantism.

68. The story of Lerma originally comes from Bernal Díaz del Castillo's sixteenth-century account of the Conquest of Mexico; see *Historia verdadera de la conquista de la Nueva España: Manuscrito "Guatemala,"* Part 1 (2005, 789), where he tells of a valiant solider who saved Cortés's life but incurred his wounded pride and hatred in the process, and eventually ran away to live with Indians. But it was popularized in the United States in Robert Montgomery Bird's 1835 novel *The Infidel, or the Fall of Mexico*, whose hero Juan Lerma takes his name from the figure in Bernal Díaz; the novel begins with the Lerma episode, as told in *Historia verdadera*, as its epigraph. The episode also appears in an 1844 review of Prescott's *Conquest of Mexico*, published in the *U.S. Magazine and Democratic Review* (vol. 14 February), which quoted Bernal Díaz's sketch in translation (192).

69. See also Stacy-Judd 1939 (rpt. 1999).

70. On Lope de Oviedo, see Chapter 3.

71. Cabell 2003, 110–11. On late nineteenth- and early twentieth-century theories of Atlantis and its relation to Phoenicia, divination, and prophecy, see especially the works of Lewis Spence published from the 1920s through the 1940s, including *Occult Sciences in Atlantis* (1943), *The History of Atlantis* (1924), *The Problem of Atlantis* (1924), and *Atlantis in America* (1925); as well as the Braghine and Donnelly sources cited earlier. An account of Menéndez's marriage to the Calusa woman known as Antonia can also be found in Solís de Merás 2010.

72. See, e.g., Brewer 2011, 87–140.

73. Cabell 2001, 41–42. As Cabell notes in this essay, he even published a magazine article outlining his use of historical sources in writing *First Gentleman*—"to no purpose" (42), as critics continued to see the novel as a fantasy. See "Factual Fiction," *The Saturday Review of Literature*, April 11, 1942 (15).

74. Alfred Jackson Hanna's *Flight Into Oblivion* was first published in 1938. Hanna and Cabell met in Florida and together co-authored *St. John's: A Paradise of Diversities* in 1943.

Epilogue

1. Cabell 2001, 34.

2. Ibid., 267.

3. "America's 400th Anniversary Jamestown 2007 Steering Committee Report," House Document No. 13 (121). The document records the decade-long planning and implementation of the 2007 quadricentennial celebration of the English settlement of Jamestown.

4. Garcilaso de la Vega 1985 1:15; see also Zamora's discussion (2005, 67–68). This episode is discussed briefly in Chapter 1.

5. On the significance of Aztlán in Chicano cultural history, a good place to begin is the collected work in Anaya and Lomelí 1991. See also Brady, who notes that "the proclamation of Aztlán successfully called attention to the naturalizing work of the geopolitical

narrative of the United States" (2002, 146) as well as Pérez-Torres 2000 and 2006, 145–56; Arteaga 1997, esp. 1–20); and Alarcón 1997.

6. See Holmes 1829, 1:563.

7. As Kartunnen and Lockhart note, "16th-century Nahuatl orthography primarily adopted . . . x for [š] in native words" (1994, 5)—though because the pronunciation of "x" in mid-sixteenth-century Spanish was in the process of yielding to the velar sound represented now by j, any argument about the spelling of Axacán remains purely speculative.

8. Luis Leal's classic essay, "In Search of Aztlán" parses the Nahuatl sources for these details (Anaya and Lomelí 1991, 8–10).

9. While Fray Bernardino Sahagún's Native informants reported these details suggesting the mystical power of the toponym Aztlán, I am taking a cue here from Alarcón's conception of Aztlán as a "palimpsest" encoding "the nexus of power, empire, and discourse" (1997, 4).

10. On the "Aztlán Reconquista," see Buchanan 2006, esp. ch. 8; Huntington 2004; and Gilchrist and Corsi 2006, chapter 10.

11. See Horsman 1986. For a contemporary example of racial Anglo-Saxonism, see Huntington 2004 as well as *Clash of Civilizations*, which opposes "Anglo-American North America" to "Spanish Indian Mexico" and draws on Octavio Paz to suggest essential incompatibility (149–50).

12. Garcilaso 1982, Book II, part 1, Ch. 1, 30v (incorrectly paginated as 39).

{ BIBLIOGRAPHY }

Primary Sources

Adams, Martha D., ed. *Proceedings of the Tenth Annual Lake Mohonk Conference of Friends of the Indian*. Lake Mohonk, NY: Lake Mohonk Conference of Friends of the Indian, 1892.

America's 400th Anniversary Jamestown 2007 Steering Committee Report. Virginia House of Delegates Document 13. Virginia: Jamestown-Yorktown Foundation, 2007.

Barreiro, José. *The Indian Chronicles*. Houston: Arte Público, 1993.

Bird, Robert Montgomery. *The Infidel, or the Fall of Mexico*. 2 vols. Philadelphia: Carey, Lea and Blanchard, 1835.

Bolton, Herbert E. "The Epic of Greater America." *American Historical Review* 38 (1933): 448–74.

Bourne, Edward Gaylord, ed. *Narratives of the Career of Hernando de Soto*. 2 vols. New York: A.S. Barnes, 1904.

Bradford, William. *Of Plymouth Plantation 1620–1647*. Ed. Samuel Eliot Morison. New York: McGraw-Hill, 1981.

Brown, William Wells. *Clotel: or, The President's Daughter*. New York: Random House, 2000.

Bryant, William Cullen. *Poems: With a Biographical Sketch by Nathan Haskell Dole*. New York: Thomas Y. Crowell & Co., 1893.

Bryant, William Cullen and Sydney Howard Gay. *A Popular History of the United States: From the First Discovery of the Western Hemisphere by the Northmen, to the End of the Civil War, Preceded by a Sketch of the Pre-Historic Period and the Age of the Mound Builders*. 4 vols. New York: Scribner, Armstrong, 1876–1881.

Cabell, James Branch. "Factual Fiction." *The Saturday Review of Literature* (April 11, 1942).

———. *The First Gentleman of America: A Comedy of Conquest*. Reprint Edition. Rockville, MD: Wildside Press, 2003.

———. *Let Me Lie: Being in the Main an Ethnological Account of the Remarkable*. Charlottesville: University Press of Virginia, 2001.

Cabell, James Branch and Alfred Jackson Hanna. *The St. Johns: A Paradise of Diversities*. New York: Farrar and Rinehart, 1943.

Cabeza de Vaca, Álvar Núñez. *His Account, His Life and the Expedition of Pánfilo de Narváez*. Ed. and trans. Rolena Adorno and Charles Pautz. 3 vols. Lincoln: University of Nebraska Press, 1999.

———. *The Narrative of Cabeza de Vaca*. Trans. Rolana Adorno and Patrick Charles Pautz. Lincoln: University of Nebraska Press, 2003.

Calhoun, John C. *The Papers of John C. Calhoun*. Vol. V: 1820–1821. Ed. W. Edwin Hemphill. Columbia: University of South Carolina Press, 1971.

Campbell, Charles. *History of the Colony and Ancient Dominion of Virginia*. Philadelphia: Lippincott, 1860.

Cash, W. J. *The Mind of the South.* New York: Knopf, 1941.

Cecil, Jane ed. *Select Documents Illustrating the Four Voyages of Columbus.* Vol. 1. Surrey, UK: Ashgate, 2010.

Chanca, Dr. Diego Álvarez. "Carta de Diego Álvarez Chanca." In Francisco Morales Padrón, ed. *Primeras cartas sobre América (1492–1503).* Seville: Raimundo, 1990. 109–38.

———. "The Letter Written by Dr. Chanca to the City of Seville." *The Four Voyages of Christopher Columbus.* Ed. and trans. J. M. Cohen. London: Penguin, 1969.

Clark, Michael, ed. *The Eliot Tracts: With Letters from John Eliot to Thomas Thorowgood and Richard Baxter.* Westport, CT: Praeger, 2003.

Clayton, Lawrence et al., ed. and trans. *The De Soto Chronicles: The Expedition of Hernando de Soto to North America in 1539–1543.* 3 vols. Tuscaloosa: University of Alabama Press, 1993.

Colombo, Fernando. *Le Historie della vita e dei fatti di Cristoforo Colombo per D. Fernando Colombo su figlio.* Ed. Rinaldo Caddeo. 2 vols. Milan: 1930.

Colón, Hernando. *Historia del almirante de Hernando Colón.* Ed. Luis Arranz. Océano: Instituto Gallach, 1988.

———. *The Life of the Admiral Christopher Columbus by His Son Ferdinand.* Trans. and ed. Benjamin Keen. New Brunswick, NJ: Rutgers University Press, 1992.

Columbus, Christopher. *The* Diario *of Christopher Columbus's First Voyage to America 1492–1493, abstracted by Fray Bartolomé de las Casas.* Ed. and trans. Oliver Dunn and James E. Kelley, Jr. Norman: University of Oklahoma Press, 1989.

———. *The Four Voyages of Christopher Columbus.* Trans. J. M. Cohen. London: Penguin, 1969.

———. *Textos y documentos completos.* Ed. Consuelo Varela. Madrid: Alianza, 1982.

———. *The Voyage of Christopher Columbus: Columbus' Own Journal of Discovery Newly Restored and Translated.* Ed. John Cummins. New York: St. Martin's, 1922.

Connor, Jeanette Thurber. *Colonial Records of Spanish Florida, 1570–1580.* 2 vols. DeLand: Florida State Historical Society, 1925–30.

Cortés, Hernán. *Cartas de relación.* Ed. Ángel Delgado Gómez. Madrid: Castalia, 1993.

———. *Letters from Mexico.* Trans. Anthony Pagden. New Haven: Yale University Press, 1970.

"Critics on Mexico." *United States Catholic Magazine* 5 (October, 1846): 521–43.

Cushing, Jonathan P. "President's Cushing's Address." *Collections of the Virginia Historical and Philosophical Society,* vol. 1. Richmond: Thomas W. White, 1833.

Davidson, Donald et al. *I'll Take My Stand: The South and the Agrarian Tradition.* 75th Anniversary Edition. Baton Rouge: Louisiana State University Press, 2006.

Díaz del Castillo, Bernal. *The History of the Conquest of New Spain.* Abridged trans. David Carrasco. Albuquerque: University of New Mexico Press, 2008.

———. *Historia verdadera de la conquista de la Nueva España.* Ed. José Antonio Barbón Rodríguez. Mexico City: Colegio de México et al., 2005.

Elvas, Fidalgo de. *True Relation of the Hardships Suffered by Governor Fernando de Soto & Certain Portuguese Gentlemen During the Discovery of the Province of Florida, Now Newly Set Forth by a Gentleman of Elvas.* 2 vols. Facsimile and translation ed. and trans. James A. Robertson. DeLand: Florida State Historical Society, 1932–33.

———. *The Worthye and Famous History, of the Travailes, Discovery, and Conquest, of That Great Continent Terra Florida, Being Lively Paraleld, with That of Our Now Inhabited Virginia.* Trans. Richard Hakluyt. London: Mathew Lownes, 1611.

Faulkner, William. *The Sound and the Fury*. New York: Jonathan Cape and Harrison Smith, 1929.

Fletcher, Alice Cunningham. "Between the Lines." *Lend a Hand* 1 (1886): 430.

———. "The Crowning Act." *Morning Star* 7 (March 1887): 1.

———. "The Indian Bureau at the New Orleans Exposition." Report to the Commissioner of Indian Affairs, May 6, 1885. Carlisle, PA: Carlisle Indian School Print, 1885.

———. *Indian Education and Civilization: A Report Prepared in Answer to Senate Resolution of February 23, 1885*. Washington, DC: U.S. Department of Education, 1888.

Fontaneda, Hernando de Escalante. *A Letter of Hernando de Soto and Memoir of Hernando de Escalante Fontaneda*. Trans. Buckingham Smith. Washington, DC: n.p., 1854.

———. *Memoria de las cosas y costa y indios de la Florida, que ninguno de cuantos la han costeado, no lo han sabido declarar*. In Joaquín Francisco Pacheco, Francisco de Cárdenas, and Luis Torres de Mendoza, eds. *Colección de documentos inéditos relativos al descubrimiento, conquista y organizacion de las antiguas posesiones españolas en América y Oceanía, sacados de los archivos del reino, y muy especialmente del de Indias*. Vol. 5. Madrid: Frías y compaña, 1866. 532–48.

———. *Memoir of Do. d'Escalante Fontaneda Respecting Florida*. Ed. David O. True. Coral Gables, FL: Glade House, 1945.

Forster, Johann Reinhold. *History of the Voyages and Discoveries Made in the North*. Anonymous translation. Dublin: White and Byrne, 1786.

Garcilaso de La Vega, El Inca. *Comentarios reales de los Incas*. 2 vols. Ed. Miró Quesada Sosa. Caracas: Fundacion Biblioteca Ayacuch, 1985.

———. *La Florida del Inca*. Ed. Pedro Crasbeek. Lisbon, 1605. Facsimile edition by Sylvia-Lyn de Hilton. Madrid, 1982.

———. *The Florida of the Inca*. Trans. Jeannette Varner and John Varner. Austin: University of Texas Press, 1981.

———. *Royal Commentaries of the Incas, and General History of Peru*. 2 vols. Ed. Harold J. Livermore. Austin: University of Texas Press, 1989.

González de Barcia, Andrés. *Ensayo cronológico para la historia general de la Florida*. Madrid: Nicolas Rodriguez Franco, 1723.

Gorges, Ferdinando. *Sir Ferdinando Gorges and His Province of Maine*. 2 vols. Ed. James Phinney Baxter. Boston: The Prince Society, 1890.

Green, Paul. *The Lost Colony: A Symphonic Drama of American History*. Ed. Laurence G. Avery. Chapel Hill: University of North Carolina Press, 2000.

Greenhow, Robert. *The History of Oregon and California and Other Territories of the North-West Coast of North America*. Boston: Charles C. Little and James Brown, 1845.

———. *Memoir on the First Discovery of the Chesapeake Bay. Communicated to the Virginia Historical Society*. Richmond: Virginia Historical Society, 1848.

———. *Memoir, Historical and Political, on the Northwest Coast of North America*. Washington, DC: Blair and Rives, 1840.

Hamor, Ralph. *A True Discourse of the Present State of Virginia* (London, 1615); Richmond: Virginia State Library, 1957.

Hann, John H., ed. and trans. *Missions to the Calusa*. Gainesville: University Press of Florida, 1991.

Hanna, Alfred Jackson. *Flight into Oblivion* (1938). Reprint Edition. Baton Rouge: Louisiana State University Press, 1999.

Harriot, Thomas. *A Briefe and True Report of the New Found Land of Virginia.* Facsimile of 1590 London edition. New York: Dover, 1972.

Hawthorne, Nathaniel. "Chiefly about War Matters: By a Peacable Man." *Atlantic Monthly* 10 (1862): 43–61.

Hennessy, Sir John Pope. *Sir Walter Raleigh in Ireland.* London: Keegan Paul, 1883.

Holmes, Abiel. *The Annals of America: From the Discovery by Columbus in the Year 1492, to the Year 1826.* 2 vols. Cambridge: Hilliard and Brown, 1829.

Ignatius of Loyola. *Letters of Ignatius of Loyola.* Selected and trans. William J. Young. Chicago: Loyola Press, 1959.

Inman, Samuel Guy. *Problems in Pan Americanism.* New York: Doran, 1921.

Johnson, Robert. *Nova Brittania: Offering Most Excellent Fruits by Planting in Virginia.* London: Samual Macham, 1609.

Johnson v. M'Intosh. 21 U.S. (8 Wheat.) 543 (1823).

La Flesche, Francis. *The Osage and the Invisible World: From the Works of Francis la Flesche.* Ed. Garrick Bailey. Norman: University of Oklahoma Press, 1999.

———. *Who Was the Medicine Man?* Hampton, VA: Hampton Institute Press, 1905.

La Flesche, Susette, writing as Inshta Theamba (Bright Eyes). "Introduction." In William Justin Harsha, ed. *Ploughed Under: The Story of an Indian Chief, Told by Himself.* New York: Fords, Howard, and Hulbert, 1881. 3–6.

Las Casas, Bartolomé de. *Brevísima relación de la destrucción de las Indias.* Ed. Jean-Paul Duviols. Buenos Aires: Stockcero, 2006.

———. *Brevísima relación de la destrucción de las Indias.* Seville, 1552.

———. *Historia de las Indias.* 3 vols. Ed. Augustín Millares Carlo and Lewis Hanke. Mexico City: Mexico, 1965.

———. *Obras completas.* Madrid: Alianza, 1992–1998. Vol. 13: *Cartas Memoriales,* 1995.

———. *Obras escogidas de Fray Bartolomé de Las Casas: Opúsculos, Cartas y Memoriales.* 5 vols. Ed. Juan Pérez de Tudela y Bueso. Madrid: Biblioteca de Autores Españoles. 1958.

———. *Short Account of the Destruction of the Indies.* Trans. Anthony Pagden. New York: Penguin, 2004.

"Latin America in 1899—A Review." *Bulletin of the Pan American Union* 8 (1900): 75–111.

Lewis, Clifford M. and Albert J. Loomie, eds. *The Spanish Jesuit Mission in Virginia, 1570–1572.* Chapel Hill: University of North Carolina Press, 1953.

McMillan, Hamilton. *Sir Walter Raleigh's Lost Colony: An Historical Sketch of the Attempts of Sir Walter Scott to Establish a Colony in Virginia . . .* Wilson, NC: Advance Presses, 1888.

Mencken, H. L. *H. L. Mencken's Smart Set Criticism.* Ed. William H. Nolte. New York: Gateway Editions, 2001.

———. "Sahara of the Bozart." *Prejudices: Second Series,* 1920.

Menéndez de Avilés, Pedro. *Cartas sobre la Florida.* Ed. Juan Carlos Mercado. Madrid: Vervuert, 2002.

M.M. "On the Word 'Canada'." *British American Magazine* 1 (1863): 490–93.

Nebrija, Antonio de. *Gramática de la lengua castellana.* Salamanca, n.p., 1492.

Nietzsche, Friedrich. *On the Use and Abuse of History for Life.* Trans. New York: Cosimo, 2010.

Percy, George. "A Trewe Relacyon of the Procedeinges and Occurrences of Moment which have happened in Virginia." [1609–1612] *Tylers Quarterly Magazine* 3 (1922): 275–76.

Poe, Edgar Allan. "Edward Lytton Bulwer." In G. R. Thompson, ed. *Edgar Allan Poe: Essays and Reviews.* New York: Library of America, 1984. 142–46.

———. "The Journal of Julius Rodman." *Burton's Gentlemen's Magazine* 6 (Jan.–June 1840): 44–47, 80–85, 109–13, 178–83, 206–10, 255–59.

———. *The Narrative of Arthur Gordon Pym.* In Patrick F. Quinn, ed. *Edgar Allan Poe: Poetry and Tales.* New York: Library of America, 1984. 1003–1182.

Prescott, William Hickling. *Mexico and the Life of the Conqueror, Hernando Cortés.* 2 vols. New York: Collier and Son, 1898.

Quinn, David B., ed. *New American World: A Documentary History of North America to 1612.* Vol. 2. New York: Arno Press, 1979.

Raleigh, Sir Walter. *The Discoverie of the Large, Rich, and Bewtiful Empyre of Guiana.* Transcribed, annotated, and introduced by Neil Whitehead. Manchester: Manchester University Press, 1995.

Ribadeneyra, Pedro de. *Historias de la contrareforma.* Ed. Eusebio Rey. Madrid: Editorial Catolica, 1950.

———. "Tratado de la religión y virtudes que debe tener el príncipe cristiano para gobernar y conservar sus estados: contra lo que Nicolás Maquiavelo y los políticos de este tiempo enseñan." In Don Vicente de la Fuente, ed. *Obras escogidas del Padre Pedro Ribadeneyra.* Madrid: Pantaleon Zanar, 1868.

———. *Vita Francisci Borgiae.* Madrid: n.p., 1592.

Robinson, Conway. *An Account of Discoveries in the West Until 1519, and of Voyages to and along the Atlantic Coast of North America from 1520 to 1573.* Richmond: Shepherd and Colin, 1848.

Roosevelt, Franklin Delano. *F.D.R.: His Personal Letters, 1905–1928.* New York: Duell, 1948.

———. *The Public Papers and Addresses of Franklin D. Roosevelt.* Vol. 2: *The Year of Crisis, 1933.* Ed. Samuel I. Rosenman. New York: Random House, 1969.

Rubin, Louis D., ed. *I'll Take My Stand: The South and the Agrarian Tradition* (1930). Reprint Edition. Baton Rouge: Louisiana State University Press, 1977.

Ruidíaz y Caravia, Eugenio. *La Florida; su conquista y colonización por Pedro Menéndez de Avilés.* Madrid: Hijos de J.A. García, 1893.

San Miguel, Fray Andrés de. *An Early Florida Adventure Story.* Trans. John H. Hann. Gainesville: University Press of Florida, 2001.

———. *Obras de Fray Andrés de San Miguel.* Ed. Eduardo Báez Macías. Mexico City: Universidad Nacional Autonóma de México, 2008.

———. "Relación de los trabajos que la gente de una nao llamada Nra Señora de la Merced padeció y algunas cosas que en aquella flota sucedieron." In Genaro García, ed. *Dos Antiguas Relaciones de la Florida.* Charleston, SC: Nabu Press, 1902.

Shakespeare, William. *King Lear.* Ed. Barbara Mowat. New York: Simon and Schuster, 2005.

Shea, John Gilmary. *The Lincoln Memorial: A Record of the Life, Assassination, and Obsequies of the Martyred President.* New York: Bunce and Huntington, 1865.

———. "The Log Chapel on the Rappahannock." *The Catholic World* 20 (March 1875): 847–56.

———. "Our Martyrs." Parts I-IV. *The United States Catholic Magazine* 5 (1846–47): 497–99; 561–68; 604–07; 665–69.

———. "The Spanish Mission Colony on the Rappahannock; The First European Settlers in Virginia." In W.W. Beach, ed. *The Indian Miscellany: Containing Papers on* the History, Antiquities, Arts, Languages, Religions, Traditions and Superstitions of the American Aborigines; with Descriptions of Their Domestic Life, Manners, Customs, Traits, Amusements and Exploits; Travels and Adventures in the Indian Country; Incidents of Border Warfare; Missionary Relations, Etc. Albany: J. Munsell, 1877. 333–43.

Simms, William Gilmore. *Views and Reviews in American Literature, History and Fiction.* New York: Wiley and Putnam, 1845.

Smith, John. *The Complete Works of Captain John Smith, 1580–1631.* Ed. Philip L. Barbour and Thad W. Tate. Chapel Hill: University of North Carolina Press, 1986.

Solís de Merás, Gonzalo. *Menéndez de Avilés and la Florida: Chronicles of His Expeditions.* Ed. Juan Carlos Mercado and trans. Laura Callahan. New York: Edwin Mellen, 2010.

Spence, Lewis. *Atlantis in America.* London: Ernest Benn, 1925.

———. *The History of Atlantis.* London: Ernest Benn, 1924.

———. *Occult Sciences in Atlantis.* Reprint Edition. Mokelumne, CA: Mokelumne Hill Press, 1976.

———. *The Problem of Atlantis.* London: William Rider and Son, 1924.

Stavig, Ward and Ella Schmidt, eds. *The Tupac Amaru and Catarista Rebellions: An Anthology of Sources.* Indianapolis: Hackett Publishing, 2008.

Suess, Paolo. *La conquista espiritual de la América Espanõla: Doscientos documentos del siglos XVI.* Quito, Ecuador: Editorial Abya Yala, 2002.

Tanner, Mathias. *Societas Jesu Usque ad Sanguinis et Vitae Profusionem Militans.* Prague, 1675.

Thurber, Jeannette Connor, ed. and trans. *Pedro Menéndez de Avilés, Adelantado, Governor and Captain-General of Florida. Memorial.* Publications of the Florida State Historical Society no. 3. Gainesville: University Press of Florida, 1964.

Torquemada, Juan de. *Monarquía Indiana: de los veinte y un libros rituales y monarquía indiana, con el origen y guerras de los Indios Occidentales, de sus poblazones, descubrimiento, conquista, conversión y otras cosas maravillosas de la mesma tierra.* 7 vols. Ed. M. León-Portilla. Mexico City: Universidad Nacional Autónoma de México, 1975–1983.

Townsend, Camilla, ed. *American Indian History: A Documentary Reader.* New York: Wiley-Blackwell, 2009.

"Trujillo: Portrait of a Dictator." *CBS Reports*: Season 1, Episode 7, March 17, 1960.

Van Doren, Carl. *James Branch Cabell.* New York: Robert M. McBridge and Co., 1925.

Virgil. *The Aeneid of Virgil.* Trans. John Conington. New York: W.J. Widdleton, 1867.

"We Can't Seem to Get Away from Mr. Wilson." *Current Opinion* 71 (December 1921): 711–15.

White, John. "Fourth Voyage Made to Virginia." In Richard Hakluyt, ed. *The Principal Navigations Voyages Traffiques & Discoveries of the English Nation Made by Sea or Over-land to the Remote and Farthest Distant Quarters of the Earth at Any Time Within the Compasse of These 1600 Yeeres.* New York: Macmillan, 1904.

Zubillaga, Felix, S. J., ed. *Monumenta antiquae Floridae (1566–1572).* Rome: Monumenta Historica Soc. Iesu, 1946.

Secondary Studies

Adorno, Rolena. *Guaman Poma: Writing and Resistance in Colonial Peru.* Austin: University of Texas Press, 1986.

————. "The Indigenous Ethnographer: The *Indio Ladino* and Cultural Mediation." In Stuart B. Schwartz, ed. *Implicit Understandings: Observing, Reporting, and Reflecting on the Encounters.* Cambridge: Cambridge University Press, 1994. 378–402.

————. "The Negotiation of Fear in Cabeza de Vaca's *Naufragios*." In Stephen Greenblatt, ed. *New World Encounters.* Berkeley: University of California Press, 1993. 48–84.

————. "The Polemics of Possession: Spain on America, Circa 1550." In Linda Gregerson and Susan Juster, eds. *Empires of God: Religious Encounters in the Early Modern Atlantic.* Philadelphia: University of Pennsylvania Press, 2011. 19–36.

————. *The Polemics of Possession in Spanish American Narrative.* New Haven: Yale University Press, 2008.

Adorno, Rolena and Patrick Charles Pautz. "Introduction." In Cabeza de Vaca, *The Narrative of Cabeza de Vaca.* Lincoln: University of Nebraska Press, 2003. 1–42.

Agamben, Giorgio. *The Time That Remains: A Commentary on the Letter to the Romans.* Trans. Patricia Dailey. Stanford, CA: Stanford University Press, 2005.

Alarcón, Daniel Cooper. *The Aztec Palimpsest: Mexico in the Modern Imagination.* Tempe: University of Arizona Press, 1997.

Altamirano-Jiménez, Isabel. "Indigeneity and Transnational Routes." In Julián Castro Rea, ed. *Our North America.* Farnham, Surrey, UK: Ashgate, 2013. 27–44.

Alva, Jorge Klor de. "The Postcolonization of the (Latin) American Experience: A Reconsideration of 'Colonialism,' 'Postcolonialism,' and 'Mestijzaje'." In Gyan Prakash, ed. *After Colonialism: Imperial Histories and Postcolonial Displacements.* Princeton, NJ: Princeton University Press, 1995. 241–75.

Ambrosias, Lloyd E. *Woodrow Wilson and the American Diplomatic Tradition.* Cambridge: Cambridge University Press, 1990.

Anaya, Rudolfo and Francisco A. Lomelí, eds. *Aztlán: Essays on the Chicano Homeland*, Albuquerque: University of New Mexico Press, 1991.

Apter, Emily. *The Translation Zone: A New Comparative Literature.* Princeton, NJ: Princeton University Press, 2005.

Arteaga, Alfred. *Chicano Poetics: Heterotexts and Hybridities.* Cambridge: Cambridge University Press, 1997.

Augenbraum, Harold. "Literary Strategies in Álvar Núñez Cabeza de Vaca's *Account*." In Harold Augenbraum and Margarite Fernández Olmos, eds. *U.S. Latino Literature: A Critical Guide for Students and Teachers.* New York: Mercantile Library Association of the City of New York/Greenwood, 2000. 1–9.

Axtell, James. "Babel of Tongues: Communicating with the Indians in Eastern North America." In Edward G. Gray and Norman Fiering, eds. *The Language Encounter in the Americas, 1492–1800: A Collection of Essays.* New York: Berghahn Books, 2001. 15–60.

————. *The European and the Indian: Essays in the Ethnohistory of Colonial North America.* Oxford: Oxford University Press, 1982.

————. *The Indians' New South: Cultural Change and the Colonial Southeast.* Baton Rouge: Louisiana State University Press, 1997.

————. *The Rise and Fall of the Powhatan Empire: Indians in Seventeenth-Century Virginia.* Williamsburg, VA: Colonial Williamsburg Foundation, 1995.

Bassnett, Susan. *Translation Studies.* London: Methuen and Co., 1980.

Bauer, Ralph. *The Cultural Geography of Colonial American Literatures: Empire, Travel, Modernity*. Cambridge: Cambridge University Press, 2003.

———. "Early American Literature and American Literary History at the 'Hemispheric' Turn." *American Literary History* 22 (2010): 250–65.

Bauer, Ralph and José Antonio Mazzotti, eds. *Creole Subjects in the Colonial Americas: Empires, Texts, Identities*. Published for Omohundro Institute of Early American History and Culture. Chapel Hill: University of North Carolina Press, 2009.

Baym, Nina, ed. *The Norton Anthology of American Literature: Literature to 1860*. 6th Edition. New York: W.W. Norton, 2002.

Bellin, Joshua and Laura Mielke, eds. *Native Acts: Indian Performance: 1603–1832*. Lincoln: University of Nebraska Press, 2012.

Benjamin, Walter. "The Task of the Translator." In Walter Benjamin, ed. *Illuminations: Essays and Reflections*. New York: Harcourt Brace Jovanovich, 1968. 69–82.

Bennett, Charles. *Laudonnière and Fort Caroline: History and Documents*. Tuscaloosa: University of Alabama Press, 2001.

Berry, Wendell. *The Unsettling of America: Culture and Agriculture*. San Francisco: Sierra Club, 1977.

Beverly, John. *Essays on the Literary Baroque in Spain and Spanish America*. Woodbridge, Suffolk, UK: Tamesis Books, 2008.

Bilinkoff, Jodi. "The Many 'Lives' of Pedro Ribadeneyra." *Renaissance Quarterly* 52 (1999): 180–96.

Boruchoff, David A. "Piety, Patriotism, and Empire: Lessons for England, Spain, and the New World in the Works of Richard Hakluyt." *Renaissance Quarterly* 62 (2009): 809–58.

Black, Conrad. *Richard M. Nixon: A Life in Full*. New York: Public Affairs, 2007.

Blackman, Ann. *Wild Rose: Rose O'Neale Greenhow, Civil War Spy*. New York: Random House, 2005.

Blackmore, Josiah. *Manifest Perdition: Shipwreck Narrative and the Disruption of Empire*. Minneapolis: University of Minnesota Press, 2002.

Bold, Christine. *The Oxford History of Popular Print Culture* vol. 6: *US Popular Print Culture, 1860–1920*. Oxford: Oxford University Press, 2012.

Boughter, Judith A. *Betraying the Omaha Nation, 1790–1916*. Norman: University of Oklahoma Press, 1998.

Brady, Mary Pratt. *Extinct Lands, Temporal Geographies: Chicana Literature and the Urgency of Space*. Durham, NC: Duke University Press, 2002.

Bragdon, Kathleen J. *Native People of Southern New England, 1500–1650*. Norman: University of Oklahoma Press, 1999.

Brentano, Robert. *Two Churches: England and Italy in the Thirteenth Century*. Berkeley and Los Angeles: University of California Press, 1988.

Brewer, Susan. *Why America Fights: Patriotism and War Propaganda from the Philippines to Iraq*. Oxford: Oxford University Press, 2011.

Brickhouse, Anna. *Transamerican Literary Relations and the Nineteenth Century Public Sphere*. Cambridge: Cambridge University Press, 2004.

Bridenbaugh, Carl. *Early Americans*. Oxford: Oxford University Press, 1981.

———. *Jamestown, 1544–1699*. Oxford: Oxford University Press, 1980.

Brooks, Lisa. *The Common Pot: The Recovery of Native Space in the Northeast.* Minneapolis: University of Minnesota Press, 2008.

———. "Digging at the Roots: Locating an Ethical, Native Criticism." In Janice Acoose et al., eds. *Reasoning Together: The Native Critics Collective.* Norman: University of Oklahoma Press, 2008. 234–64.

Bross, Kristina and Hilary E. Wyss, eds. *Early Native Literacies in New England: A Documentary and Critical Anthology.* Amherst: University of Massachusetts Press, 2008.

Brown, David Luis. *Waves of Decolonization: Discourses of Race and Hemispheric Citizenship in Cuba, Mexico, and the United States.* Durham, NC: Duke University Press, 2008.

Bruce-Novoa, Juan. "Naufragios en los mares de la significación: de *La Relación* de Cabeza de Vaca a la literatura Chicana." *Plural* 221 (1990): 12–21.

Buchanan, Patrick. *State of Emergency: The Third World Invasion and the Conquest of America.* New York: Thomas Dunne Books, 2006.

Burger, Nash K. *Confederate Spy: Rose O'Neale Greenhow.* Danbury, CT: Franklin Watts, 1967.

Burns, Kathryn. "Unfixing Race." In Margaret Greer, Walter D. Mignolo, and Maureen Quilligan, eds. *Rereading the Black Legend: Discourses of Religious and Racial Difference in the Renaissance Empires.* Chicago: University of Chicago Press, 1988. 188–203.

Burrow, John. *A History of Histories: Epics, Chronicles, Romances, and Inquiries from Herodotus and Thucydides to the Twentieth Century.* New York: Vintage, 2008.

Bushnell, Amy Turner. "A Requiem for Lesser Conquerors: Honor and Oblivion on a Maritime Periphery." In Raquel Chang-Rodríguez, ed. *Beyond Books and Borders: Garcilaso de la Vega and La Florida del Inca.* Cranbury, NJ: Rosemont Publishing, 2006. 66–74.

Callcott, George H. *History in the United States, 1800–1860: Its Practice and Purpose.* Baltimore: Johns Hopkins University Press, 1970.

Calloway, Colin G. "Indian History from the End of the Alphabet: What Now?" *Ethnohistory* 58 (2011): 197–211.

Cañizares-Esguerra, Jorge. *How to Write the History of the New World.* Stanford, CA: Stanford University Press, 2002.

———. *Puritan Conquistators: Iberianizing the Atlantic, 1550–1700.* Stanford, CA: Stanford University Press, 2006.

Carbado, Devon. "Racial Naturalization." *American Quarterly* 57 (2005): 633–58.

Carlyon, Jonathan Earl. *Andrés González de Barcia and the Creation of the Colonial Spanish American Library.* Toronto: University of Toronto Press, 2005.

Castanien, Donald Garner. *El Inca Garcilaso de la Vega.* New York: Twayne Publishing, 1969.

Castro, Daniel. *Another Face of Empire: Bartolomé de Las Casas, Indigenous Rights, and Ecclesiastical Imperialism.* Durham, NC: Duke University Press, 2007.

Castronovo, Russ. *Beautiful Democracy: Aesthetics and Anarchy in a Global Era.* Chicago: University of Chicago Press, 2007.

Castronovo, Russ and Susan Gillman, eds. *States of Emergency: The Object of American Studies.* Chapel Hill: University of North Carolina Press, 2009.

Cave, Alfred. *Lethal Encounters: Englishmen and Indians in Colonial Virginia.* Lincoln: University of Nebraska Press, 2013.

Chang-Rodríguez, Raquel, ed. *Beyond Books and Borders: Garcilaso de la Vega and La Florida del Inca*. Cranbury, NJ: Rosemont Publishing, 2006.

Cheyfitz, Eric. *The Poetics of Imperialism: Translation and Colonization from* The Tempest *to* Tarzan. Philadelphia: University of Pennsylvania Press, 1997.

Cho, Sumi and Gil Gott. "The Racial Sovereign." In Austin Sarat, ed. *Sovereignty, Emergency, Legality*. Cambridge: Cambridge University Press, 2010. 194–204.

Clifford, James. *Routes: Travel and Translation in the Late Twentieth Century*. Cambridge: Harvard University Press, 1997.

Cline, Sarah. "The Spiritual Conquest Re-examined: Baptism and Christian Marriage in Mexico." In John F. Schwaller, ed. *The Church in Colonial Latin America*. New York: Rowman and Littlefield, 2000. 73–102.

Cohen, Matt. *The Networked Wilderness: Communicating in Early New England*. Minneapolis: University of Minnesota Press, 2010.

Cohn, Deborah and Jon Smith, eds. *Look Away! The U.S. South in New World Studies*. Durham, NC: Duke University Press, 2004.

Cornish, Rory T. "Maximilian." In David Stephen Heidler, ed. *Encyclopedia of the American Civil War*. New York: W.W. Norton, 2002. 1268–69.

Coronado, Raúl. *A World Not to Come: A History of Latino Writing and Print Culture*. Cambridge, MA: Harvard University Press, 2013.

Crawley, Andrew. *Somoza and Roosevelt: Good Neighbour Diplomacy in Nicaragua, 1933–1945*. Oxford: Oxford University Press, 2007.

Cronin, Michael. "The Empire Talks Back: Orality, Heteronomy, and the Cultural Turn in Interpretation Studies." In Maria Tymoczko and Edwin Gentzler, eds. *Translation and Power*. Amherst: University of Massachusetts Press, 2002. 45–62.

Cypess, Sandra Messinger. *La Malinche in Mexican Literature: From History to Myth*. Austin: University of Texas Press, 1991.

Dannenberg, Hilary P. *Coincidence and Counterfactuality: Plotting Time and Space in Narrative and Fiction*. Lincoln: University of Nebraska Press, 2008.

Davis, David Brion. *The Problem of Slavery in Western Culture*. Oxford: Oxford University Press, 1988.

Davis, Jeffrey E. *Hand Talk: Sign Language among American Indian Nations*. Cambridge: Cambridge University Press, 2010.

DeGuzmán, María. *Spain's Long Shadow: The Black Legend, Off-Whiteness, and Anglo-American Empire*. Minneapolis: University of Minnesota Press, 2005.

Deloria, Philip J. *Indians in Unexpected Places*. Lawrence: University of Kansas Press, 2004.

———. *Playing Indian*. New Haven: Yale University Press, 1999.

Deloria, Philip J. and Neal Salisbury. *A Companion to American Indian History*. New York: Wiley-Blackwell, 2004.

Deloria, Vine Jr. *Behind the Trail of Broken Treaties: An Indian Declaration of Independence*. Austin: University of Texas Press, 2010.

Deloria, Vine Jr. and Clifford Lyttle. *American Indians, American Justice*. Austin: University of Texas Press, 2010.

Demos, John. *The Unredeemed Captive: A Family Story from Early America*. New York: Vintage, 1995.

Dent, David W. *U.S.-Latin American Policymaking*. Westport, CT: Greenwood, 1995.

Dimock, Wai Chee. "Hemispheric Islam: Continents and Centuries for American Literature." *American Literary History* 21 (2009): 28–52.

Doherty, Craig A. and Katherine M. Doherty. *Massachusetts.* New York: Facts on File, 2005.

Donaldson, Laura. "Making a Joyful Noise: William Apess and the Search for Postcolonial Method(ism)." In Malini Johar Schueller and Edward Watts, eds. *Messy Beginnings: Postcoloniality and Early American Studies.* Newark: Rutgers University Press, 2003. 29–44.

Dorr, Gregory Michael. *Segregation's Science: Eugenics and Society in Virginia.* Charlottesville: University of Virginia Press, 2008.

Dowling, Lee. "*La Florida del Inca*: Garcilaso's Literary Sources." In Patricia Galloway, ed. *The Hernando de Soto Expedition: History, Historiography, and "Discovery" in the Southeast.* Lincoln: University of Nebraska Press, 1997. 98–154.

Durand, José. *El Inca Garcilaso, Clásico de América.* Mexico City: SEP, 1976.

Eagles, Charles W., ed. *The Mind of the South: Fifty Years Later.* Oxford: University Press of Mississippi, 1992.

Elbl, Martin Malcolm and Ivana Elbl. "The Gentleman of Elvas and His Publishers." In Patricia Galloway, ed. *The Hernando de Soto Expedition: History, Historiography, and "Discovery" in the Southeast.* Lincoln: University of Nebraska Press, 1997.

Elliott, John H. *Empires of the Atlantic World: Britain and Spain in America 1492–1830.* New Haven and London: Yale University Press, 2007.

——. "The Iberian Atlantic and Virginia." In Peter C. Mancall, ed. *The Atlantic World and Virginia, 1550–1624.* Omohundro Institute of Early American History and Culture. Chapel Hill: University of North Carolina Press, 2007. 541–57.

Elliott, Michael. *The Culture Concept: Writing and Difference in the Age of Realism.* Minneapolis: University of Minnesota Press, 2002.

Ernest, John. "Reading the Romantic Past: William H. Prescott's History of the Conquest of Mexico." *American Literary History* 5 (1993): 231–49.

Fabian, Johannes. *Time and the Other: How Anthropology Makes Its Object.* New York: Columbia University Press, 2000.

Fausz, J. Frederick. "Opechancanough: Indian Resistance Leader." In David G. Sweet and Gary B. Nash, eds. *Struggle and Survival in Colonial America.* Berkeley and Los Angeles: University of California Press, 1982. 21–37.

Ferens, Dominika. "Wayward Conquistador or Transcultural Hybrid? Commentaries on Álvar Núñez Cabeza de Vaca's *The Account.*" *Anglica Wratislaviensia* 36 (2001): 21–34.

Fernández-Armesto, Felipe. *Columbus on Himself.* Indianapolis, IN: Hackett, 2010.

Fernández-Santamaría, J.A. *Natural Law, Constitutionalism, Reason of State, and War: Counter-Reformation Spanish Political Thought Volume 1.* New York: Peter Lang, 2005.

Fiedler, Leslie. *Love and Death in the American Novel.* New York: Stein and Day, 1966.

Flores Galindo, Alberto. *In Search of an Inca: Identity and Utopia in the Andes.* Trans. Carlos Aguirre et al. Cambridge: Cambridge University Press, 2010.

Forbes, Jack D. *Africans and Native Americans: The Language of Race and the Evolution of Red-Black Peoples.* Urbana: University of Illinois Press, 1993.

Ford, Lisa. *Settler Sovereignty: Jurisdiction and Indigenous People in America and Australia, 1788–1836.* Cambridge, MA: Harvard University Press, 2011.

Foster, David William and Daniel Altamiranda. *Theoretical Debates in Spanish American Literature*, vol. 1: *Spanish American Literature—20th Century*. New York and London: Routledge, 1997.

Franch, José Alcina. "Juan De Torquemada, 1564–1624." In Howard Francis Cline, ed. *Handbook of Middle American Indians*, vol. 13: *Guide to Ethnohistorical Sources*. Austin: University of Texas Press, 1973. 256–75.

Franchot, Jenny. *Roads to Rome: The Antebellum Protestant Encounter with Catholicism*. Berkeley and Los Angeles: University of California Press, 1994.

Francis, John Michael et al., eds. *Murder and Martyrdom in Spanish Florida: Don Juan and the Guale Uprising*. Washington, DC: American Museum of Natural History, 2011.

Fryd, Vivien Green. *Art & Empire: The Politics of Ethnicity in the United States Capitol, 1815–1860*. Athens: Ohio University Press, 2001.

Fuller, Mary C. *Remembering the Early Modern Voyage: English Narratives in the Age of European Expansion*. New York: Palgrave Macmillan, 2008.

Galgano, Robert C. *Feast of Souls: Indians and Spaniards in the Seventeenth-Century Mission of Florida and New Mexico*. Albuquerque: University of New Mexico Press, 2005.

Gallay, Alan. *Indian Slavery in Colonial America*. Lincoln: University of Nebraska Press, 2010.

Galloway, Patricia, ed. *The Hernando de Soto Expedition: History, Historiography, and "Discovery" in the Southeast*. Lincoln: University of Nebraska Press, 1997.

Garrison, Tim Alan. *The Legal Ideology of Removal: The Southern Judiciary and the Sovereignty of Native American Nations*. Athens: University of Georgia Press, 2002.

Genetin-Pilawa, Joseph. *Crooked Paths to Allotment: The Fight over Federal Indian Policy after the Civil War*. Chapel Hill: University of North Carolina Press, 2012.

Gentzler, Edwin. *Translation and Identity in the Americas*. New Brunswick, NJ: Routledge University Press, 2007.

Gibson, Charles. *The Black Legend: Anti-Spanish Attitudes in the Old World and the New*. New York: Random House, 1971.

Gilchrist, Jim and Jerome R. Corsi. *Minutemen: The Battle to Secure America's Borders*. New York: World Ahead Publishing, 2006.

Gillman, Susan. "Otra Vez Caliban/Encore Caliban: Adaptation, Translation, Americas Studies." *American Literary History* 20 (2008): 187–209.

Glantz, Margot. *Notas y comentarios sobre Álvar Núñez Cabeza de Vaca*. Mexico City: Grijalbo, 1993.

Glassberg, David. *American Historical Pageantry: The Uses of Tradition in the Early Twentieth Century*. Chapel Hill: University of North Carolina Press, 1990.

Gleach, Frederick W. *Powhatan's World and Colonial Virginia: A Conflict of Cultures*. Lincoln: University of Nebraska Press, 2000.

Glick, Thomas. *Islamic and Christian Spain in the Early Middle Ages*. Princeton, NJ: Princeton University Press, 1979.

González, Robert Alexander and Robert Rydell, eds. *Designing Pan-America: US Architectural Visions for the Western Hemisphere*. Austin: University of Texas Press, 2011.

González Echevarría, Roberto. *Myth and Archive: A Theory of Latin American Narrative*. Durham, NC: Duke University Press, 1998.

Gradie, Charlotte. "The Powhatans in the Context of the Spanish Empire." In Helen Rountree, ed. *Powhatan Foreign Relations, 1500–1722*. Charlottesville: University Press of Virginia, 1993. 154–72.

Granberry, Julian. *A Grammar and Dictionary of the Timucua Language.* Tuscaloosa: University of Alabama Press, 1993.

Grandin, Greg. *Empire's Workshop: Latin America, the United States, and the Rise of the New Imperialism.* New York: Empire Books, 2010.

Granero, Fernando Santos. *Vital Enemies: Slavery, Predation, and the Amerindian Political Economy of Life.* Austin: University of Texas Press, 2009.

Gray, Edward G. and Norman Fiering, eds. *The Language Encounter in the Americas, 1492–1800: A Collection of Essays.* New York: Berghahn Books, 2001.

Gray, Richard. *A History of American Literature.* Oxford: Blackwell, 2004.

Greenblatt, Stephen. *Learning to Curse: Essays in Early Modern Culture.* New York: Routledge, 1990.

———. *Marvelous Possessions: The Wonder of the New World.* Chicago: University of Chicago Press, 1992.

———, ed. *New World Encounters.* Berkeley and Los Angeles: University of California Press, 1993.

———. *Shakespearean Negotiations: The Circulation of Social Energy in Renaissance England.* Berkeley and Los Angeles: University of California Press, 1989.

———. *Sir Walter Raleigh: The Renaissance Man and His Roles.* New Haven: Yale University Press, 1973.

Greer, Margaret, Walter D. Mignolo, and Maureen Quilligan, eds. *Rereading the Black Legend: Discourses of Religious and Racial Difference in the Renaissance Empires.* Chicago: University of Chicago Press, 1988.

Greeson, Jennifer. *Our South: Geographic Fantasy and the Rise of National Literature.* Cambridge: Harvard University Press, 2010.

Grewe, Wilhelm. *The Epochs of International Law.* Trans. and ed. Michael Byers. Berlin: Walter de Gruyter, 2000.

Griffin, John W. *Fifty Years of Southeastern Archaeology: Selected Works of John W. Griffin.* Gainesville: University of Florida Press, 1996.

Gruesz, Kirstin Silva. "Alien Speech, Incorporated: On the Cultural History of Spanish in the US." *American Literary History* 25 (2012): 18–32.

———. *Ambassadors of Culture: The Transamerican Origins of Latino Writing.* Princeton, NJ: Princeton University Press, 2001.

———. "Translation: A Keyword into the Language of America(nists)." *ALH* 16 (2004): 85–92.

Grunwald, Michael. *The Swamp: The Everglades, Florida, and the Politics of Paradise.* New York: Simon and Schuster, 2007.

Guilday, Peter. *John Gilmary Shea: Father of American Catholic History 1824–1892.* New York: The American Catholic Historical Society, 1926.

Hamlin, William M. "Imagined Apotheoses: Drake, Harriot, and Raleigh in the Americas." *Journal of the History of Ideas* 57 (1996): 405–28.

Hanke, Lewis, ed. *Do the Americas Have a Common History? A Critique of the Bolton Theory.* New York: Alfred A. Knopf, 1965.

Hann, John H. "The Apalachee of the Historic Era." In Charles M. Hudson and Carmen Chaves Tesser, eds. *The Forgotten Centuries: Indians and Europeans in the American South, 1521–1704.* Athens: University of Georgia Press, 1994. 327–54.

———. "Introduction." In Fray Andrés de San Miguel, ed. *An Early Florida Adventure Story.* Trans. John H. Hann. Gainesville: University Press of Florida, 2001. 3–10.

Harkin, Michael. "Performing Paradox: Narrativity and the Lost Colony of Roanoke." In John Sutton Lutz, ed. *Myth and Memory: Stories of Indigenous-European Contact*. Vancouver: University of British Columbia Press, 2008. 103–17.

Hart, Justin. *Empire of Ideas: The Origins of Public Diplomacy and the Transformation of U.S. Foreign Policy*. Oxford: Oxford University Press, 2012.

Haynes, Stephen R. *Noah's Curse: The Biblical Justification of American Slavery*. Oxford: Oxford University Press, 2002.

Heard, Joseph Norman. *Handbook of the American Frontier: Four Centuries of Indian-White Relationships*. Lanham, MD: Scarecrow Press, 1987.

Heinegg, Paul. *Free African Americans of North Carolina, Virginia, and South Carolina from the Colonial Period to about 1820*. Clearfield, PA: Clearfield Co., 2007.

Henige, David P. *In Search of Columbus: The Sources for the First Voyage*. Tucson: University of Arizona Press, 1991.

Heuvel, Lisa L. "First Families of Virginia." In Robert E. Weir, ed. *Class in America* vol. 1. Westport, CT: Greenwood Press, 2007. 263–65.

Hill, Ruth. *Hierarchy, Commerce, and Fraud in Bourbon Spanish America: A Postal Inspector's Exposé*. Vanderbilt, TN: Vanderbilt University Press, 2006.

———. *Sceptres and Sciences in the Spains: Four Humanists and the New Philosophy (ca. 1680–1740)*. Liverpool: Liverpool University Press, 2000.

Himmerich y Valencia, Robert. *The Encomenderos of New Spain, 1521–1555*. Austin: University of Texas Press, 1996.

Hinderaker, Eric. "Translation and Cultural Brokerage." In Philip J. Deloria and Neal Salisbury, eds. *A Companion to American Indian History*. New York: Wiley-Blackwell, 2004. 357–75.

Hine, Robert V. and John Mack Faragher. *The American West: An Interpretive History*. New Haven and London: Yale University Press, 2000.

Hobson, Fred. *Serpent in Eden: H. L. Mencken and the South*. Chapel Hill: University of North Carolina Press, 1974.

Hodge, Frederick Webb. *Handbook of American Indians North of Mexico*. New York: Rowman and Littlefield, 1907.

Hoffman, Paul E. *Florida's Frontiers*. Bloomington: Indiana University Press, 2002.

———. *A New Andalucia and a Way to the Orient: The American Southeast During the Sixteenth Century*. Baton Rouge: Louisiana State University Press, 2004.

Höpfl, Harro. *Jesuit Political Thought: The Society of Jesus and the State, c. 1540–1630*. Cambridge: Cambridge University Press, 2008.

Horn, James. "Imperfect Understandings: Rumor, Knowledge, and Uncertainty in Early Virginia." In Peter C. Mancall, eds. *The Atlantic World and Virginia, 1550–1624*. Chapel Hill: University of North Carolina Press, 2007. 513–40.

———. *A Land as God Made It: Jamestown and the Birth of America*. New York: Basic Books, 2006.

Horsman, Reginald. *Race and Manifest Destiny: Origins of American Racial Anglo-Saxonism*. Cambridge, MA: Harvard University Press, 1986.

Householder, Michael. *Inventing America in the Age of Discovery: Narratives of Encounter*. Surrey, UK: Ashgate, 2011.

Hoxie, Frederick E. *A Final Promise: The Campaign to Assimilate the Indians, 1880–1920*. Lincoln: University of Nebraska Press, 2001.

Hsia, R. Po-Chia. *The World of Catholic Renewal, 1540–1770*. Cambridge: Cambridge University Press, 2005.

Hulme, Peter. *Colonial Encounters: Europe and the Native Caribbean 1492–1797*. New York: Routledge, 1992.

Huntington, Samuel P. *The Clash of Civilizations and the Remaking of World Order*. New York: Simon and Schuster, 2007.

———. "The Hispanic Challenge." *Foreign Policy* 141 (2004): 30–45.

Irwin, Robert McKee. *Bandits, Captives, Heroines, and Saints: Cultural Icons of Mexico's Northwest Borderlands*. Minneapolis: University of Minnesota Press, 2007.

Jackson, David K. "A Poe Hoax Comes Before the U.S. Senate." *Poe Studies* 7 (1974): 47–48.

Jacobs, Margaret D. *White Mother to a Dark Race: Settler Colonialism, Maternalism, and the Removal of Indigenous Children in the American West and Australia, 1880–1940*. Lincoln: University of Nebraska Press, 2011.

Jaffe, Bernard. *Men of Science in America: The Story of American Science Told Through the Lives of Twenty Outstanding Men from Earliest Colonial Times to the Present Day*. New York: Simon and Schuster, 1958.

Jasinski, James. *Sourcebook on Rhetoric*. New York: Sage Publications, 2001.

Jehlen, Myra. "The Literature of Colonization." In Sacvan Bercovitch, ed. *The Cambridge History of American Literature: Volume 1. 1590–1820*. Cambridge: Cambridge University Press, 1994. 11–168.

Kagan, Robert. *Twilight Struggle: American Power and Nicaragua, 1977–1990*. New York: Free Press, 1996.

Kammen, Michael. "Some Patterns and Meanings of Memory Distortion in American History." In Daniel Schachter, ed. *Memory Distortion: How Minds, Brains, and Societies Reconstruct the Past*. Cambridge, MA: Harvard University Press, 1997. 329–43.

Kartunnen, Frances E. *Between Worlds: Interpreters, Guides, and Survivors*. New Brunswick, NJ: Rutgers University Press, 1994.

———. "Interpreters Snatched from the Shore: The Successful and Others." In Edward G. Gray and Norman Fiering, eds. *The Language Encounter in the Americas, 1492–1800: A Collection of Essays*. New York: Berghahn Books, 2001. 215–30.

Kartunnen, Frances E. and James M. Lockhart. *Nahuatl in the Middle Years: Language Contact Phenomena in Texts of the Colonial Period*. Berkeley: University of California Press, 1977.

Kazin, Alfred. *On Native Grounds: An Interpretation of Modern American Prose Literature*. New York: Houghton Mifflin Harcourt, 2013.

Kelby, Robert Hendre. *The New York Historical Society, 1804–1904*. Washington DC: Library of Congress, 1905.

Kelton, Paul. *Epidemics and Enslavement: Biological Catastrophe in the Native Southeast, 1492–1715*. Lincoln: University of Nebraska Press, 2007.

Kennedy, J. Gerald. "'A Mania for Composition': Poe's Annus Mirabilis and the Violence of Nation-Building." *ALH* 17 (2005): 1–35.

———. *The American Turn of Edgar Allan Poe*. Baltimore: Edgar Allan Poe Society and the Library of the University of Baltimore, 2002.

Kenny, Michael. *Romance of the Floridas: The Finding and the Founding*. Milwaukee, WI: The Bruce Publishing Company, 1934.

Kimball, Warren F. (with Fred E. Pollock). *The Juggler: Franklin Roosevelt as Wartime Statesman*. Princeton, NJ: Princeton University Press, 1994.

King, C. Richard. *Unsettling America: The Uses of Indianness in the 21st Century*. Philadelphia: Rowman and Littlefield, 2013.

Knapp, Jeffrey. *An Empire Nowhere: England, America, and Literature from Utopia to The Tempest*. Berkeley and Los Angeles: University of California Press, 1991.

Kreyling, Michael. *Inventing Southern Literature*. Oxford: University of Mississippi Press, 1998.

Krupat, Arnold. *The Turn to the Native: Studies in Criticism and Culture*. Lincoln: University of Nebraska Press, 1996.

Kunitz, Stanley and Howard Haycraft. *Twentieth-Century Authors: A Biographical Dictionary of Modern Literature*. New York: H.W. Wilson Co., 1973.

Kupperman, Karen Ordahl. *Indians and English: Facing Off in Early America*. Ithaca and London: Cornell University Press, 2000.

———. *The Jamestown Project*. Cambridge, MA: Belknap Press of Harvard University, 2007.

———. *Roanoke: The Abandoned Colony*. New York: Rowman and Littlefield, 1984.

Lamana, Gonzalo. "Of Books, Popes, and Huacas; or, the Dilemmas of Being Christian." In Margaret Greer, Walter D. Mignolo, and Maureen Quilligan, eds. *Rereading the Black Legend: Discourses of Religious and Racial Difference in the Renaissance Empires*. Chicago: University of Chicago Press, 1988. 117–49.

Landers, Jane. "Africans and Native Americans on the Spanish Florida Frontier." In Matthew Restall, ed. *Beyond Black and Red: African-Native Relations in Colonial Latin America*. Albuquerque: University of New Mexico Press, 2005. 53–80.

———. *Black Society in Spanish Florida*. Urbana-Champaign: University of Illinois Press, 1999.

Leal, Luis. "In Search of Aztlán." Trans. Gladys Leal. In Rudolfo Anaya and Francisco A. Lomelí, eds. *Aztlán: Essays on the Chicano Homeland*, Albuquerque: University of New Mexico Press, 1991. 6–13.

———. "Pre-Chicano Literature: Process and Meaning." In Nicolás Kanellos, Claudio Esteva Febregat, and Francisco Lomelí, eds. *Handbook of Hispanic Cultures in the United States*. Houston, TX: Arte Publico, 1993. 62–85.

Lerner, Isaías. "Spanish Colonization and the Indigenous Languages of America." In Edward G. Gray and Norman Fiering, eds. *The Language Encounter in the Americas, 1492–1800: A Collection of Essays*. New York: Berghahn Books, 2001. 281–92.

Levine, Robert S. *Dislocating Race and Nation: Episodes in Nineteenth-Century American Literary Nationalism*. Chapel Hill: University of North Carolina Press, 2008.

Liberty, Margot. *American Indian Intellectuals of the Nineteenth and Early Twentieth Centuries*. Norman: University of Oklahoma Press, 2002.

Lima, José Lezama. "Baroque Curiosity" (1957). In Lois Parkinson Zamora and Monika Kaup, eds. *Baroque New Worlds: Representation, Transculturations, Counterconquest*. Durham, NC: Duke University Press, 2010. 212–40.

Lima, José Lezama. *La expresión Americana*. Mexico City: Fondo de Cultura Económica, 2010.

López, Kimberle S. "Naked in the Wilderness: The Transculturation of Cabeza de Vaca in Abel Posse's *El Largeo atardecer del caminante*." In Santiago Juan-Navarro and Theodore Robert Young, eds. *A Twice-Told Tale: Reinventing the Encounter in Iberian/Iberian American Literature.* Newark: University of Delaware Press, 2001. 149–65.

Losada, Angel. "The Controversy between Sepúlveda and Las Casas in the Junta of Valladolid." In Juan Friede and Benjamin Keen, eds. *Bartolomé de las Casas in History: Toward an Understanding of the Man and His Work.* DeKalb: Northern Illinois University Press, 1979. 284–89.

Lowery, Melinda Maynard. *Lumbee Indians in the Jim Crow South: Race, Identity, and the Making of a Nation.* Chapel Hill: University of North Carolina Press, 2010.

Lowery, Woodbury. *The Spanish Settlements within the Present Limits of the United States.* New York and London: Putnam's, 1905.

Luebering, J. E. *The Literature of Spain and Latin America.* New York: Rosen Education Service, 2010.

Lyon, Eugene. *The Enterprise of Florida: Pedro Menéndez de Avilés and the Spanish Conquest of 1565–1568.* Gainesville: University of Florida Press, 1976.

Lyons, Scott Richard. "Rhetorical Sovereignty: What Do American Indians Want from Writing?" *CCC* 51 (2000): 447–68.

MacCormack, Sabine. "Ethnography in South America: The First Two Hundred Years." In Frank Salomon and Stuart B. Schwartz, eds. *The Cambridge History of the Native Peoples of the Americas.* Vol. 3: South America, Part 1. Cambridge: Cambridge University Press, 1996. 96–187.

———. *Religion in the Andes: Vision and Imagination in Early Colonial Peru.* Princeton, NJ: Princeton University Press, 1993.

Malcolmson, Scott. *One Drop of Blood: The American Misadventure of Race.* New York: Farrar, Straus and Giroux, 2010.

Maltby, William S. *The Black Legend in England: The Development of Anti-Spanish Sentiment, 1558–1660.* Durham, NC: Duke University Press, 1971.

Mann, Barbara Alice and Donald A. Grinde Jr. "'Now the Friar Is Dead': Sixteenth-Century Spanish Florida and the Guale Revolt." In Barbara Alice Mann, ed. *Native American Speakers of the Eastern Woodlands: Selected Speeches and Critical Analyses.* Westport, CT: Greenwood, 2001. 1–33.

Maravall, José Antonio. *Culture of the Baroque: Analysis of a Historical Structure.* Minneapolis: University of Minnesota Press, 1986.

Mark, Joan T. *A Stranger in Her Native Land: Alice Fletcher and the American Indians.* Lincoln: University of Nebraska Press, 1989.

Marquardt, William H. and Claudia Payne. *Culture and Environment in the Domain of the Calusa.* Gainesville: University of Florida Press, 1992.

Maryks, Robert A. *The Jesuit Order as a Synagogue of Jews.* Leiden: Brill, 2009.

MacDonald, Edgar. *James Branch Cabell and Richmond-in-Virginia.* Oxford: University of Mississippi Press, 1993.

McCarthy, Kevin M. and William L. Trotter. *Thirty Florida Shipwrecks.* Sarasota, FL: Pineapple Press, 1992.

McCoy, Alfred W. and Francisco Scarano, eds. *Colonial Crucible: Empire in the Making of the Modern Atlantic State.* Madison: University of Wisconsin Press, 2009.

McGoun, William E. *Prehistoric Peoples of South Florida.* Tuscaloosa: University of Alabama Press, 1993.

McGrath, John T. *The French in Early Florida: In the Eye of the Hurricane.* Gainesville: University of Florida Press, 2000.

McMahon, Kevin J. *Reconsidering Roosevelt on Race: How the Presidency Paved the Road to Brown.* Chicago: University of Chicago Press, 2003.

Mancall, Peter C. *The Atlantic World and Virginia, 1550–1624.* Chapel Hill: University of North Carolina Press, 2007.

Mathis, Valerie Sherer and Richard Lowitt. *The Standing Bear Controversy: Prelude to Indian Reform.* Champaign-Urbana: University of Illinois Press, 2003.

Mazzotti, José Antonio. *Incan Insights: El Inca Garcilaso's Hints to Andean Readers.* Madrid: Iberoamericana/Vervuert, 2008.

———. "The Lightning Bolt Yields to the Rainbow: Indigenous History and Colonial Semiosis in the Royal Commentaries of the Inca Garcilaso de le Vega." *Modern Language Quarterly* 57 (1996): 197–211.

Merrim, Stephanie. "The First Fifty Years of Hispanic New World Historiography: The Caribbean, Mexico, and Central America." In Roberto González Echevarría and Enrique Pupo-Walker, eds. *The Cambridge History of Latin American Literature*, vol. 1. Cambridge: Cambridge University Press, 1996. 58–100.

Mignolo, Walter. *The Darker Side of the Renaissance: Literacy, Territoriality and Colonization.* Ann Arbor: University of Michigan Press, 1995.

———. *The Darker Side of Western Modernity: Global Futures, Decolonial Options.* Durham and London: Duke University Press, 2011.

———. *The Idea of Latin America.* Oxford: Wiley-Blackwell, 1991.

———. *Local Histories/Global Designs.* Princeton, NJ: Princeton University Press, 2000.

Mignolo, Walter and Freya Schiwy. "Double Translation: Transculturation and Colonial Difference." In Tullio Maranhão and Bernhard Streck, eds. *Translation and Ethnography: The Anthropological Challenge of Intercultural Understanding.* Tempe: University of Arizona Press, 2003. 3–29.

Milanich, Jerald T. "A New World: Indians and Europeans in Sixteenth-Century La Florida." In Raquel Chang-Rodríguez, ed. *Beyond Books and Borders: Garcilaso de la Vega and La Florida del Inca.* Cranbury, NJ: Rosemont Publishing, 2006. 47–65.

———. *The Timucua.* Oxford: Wiley-Blackwell, 1999.

Miller, Robert et al., eds. *Discovering Indigenous Lands: The Doctrine of Discovery in the English Colonies.* Oxford: Oxford University Press, 2010.

Miller, Shannon. *Invested with Meaning: The Raleigh Circle in the New World.* Philadelphia: University of Pennsylvania Press, 1998.

Molloy, Sylvia. "Alteridad y reconocimiento en los Naufragios de Álvar Núñez Cabeza de Vaca." *Nueva Revista de Filología Hispánica* 35, no. 2 (1987): 425–49.

Moraña, Mabel, Enrique Dussel, and Carlos A. Jáuregui, eds. *Coloniality at Large: Latin America and the Postcolonial Debate.* Durham, NC: Duke University Press, 2008.

More, Anna. *Baroque Sovereignty: Carlos de Siguenza y Gongora and the Creole Archive of Colonial Mexico.* Philadelphia: University of Pennsylvania Press, 2010.

Morgan, Edmund S. *American Slavery, American Freedom.* New York: W.W. Norton, 2003.

Muldoon, James, ed. *The Expansion of Europe: The First Phase.* Philadelphia: University of Pennsylvania Press, 1977.

———. *Popes, Lawyers, and Infidels: The Church and the Non-Christian World, 1250–1550.* Philadelphia: University of Pennsylvania Press, 1979.

Muller, Gilbert H. *William Cullen Bryant: Author of America*. Binghamton: SUNY Press, 2010.

Newcomb, Steven T. *Pagans in the Promised Land: Decoding the Doctrine of Christian Discovery*. New York: Fulcrum Publishing, 2008.

Nicholas, David Allen. *Lincoln and the Indians: Civil War Policy and Politics*. Minneapolis: Minnesota Historical Society, 2012.

Niven, John. *John C. Calhoun and the Price of Union: A Biography*. Baton Rouge: Louisiana State University Press, 1993.

Novick, Peter. *That Noble Dream: The 'Objectivity Question' and the American Historical Profession*. Cambridge: Cambridge University Press, 1988.

Ohrt, Wallace. *Defiant Peacemaker: Nicholas Trist in the Mexican War*. College Station: Texas A&M University Press, 1998.

Olson, James S. and Heather Olson Beal. *The Ethnic Dimension in American History*. New York: Wiley-Blackwell, 2010.

Operé, Fernando. *Indian Captivity in Spanish America: Frontier Narratives*. Trans. Gustavo Pellón. Charlottesville: University of Virginia Press, 2008.

Otis, D. S. *The Dawes Act and the Allotment of Indian Lands*. Norman: University of Oklahoma Press, 1973.

Owensby, Brian Philip. *Empire's Law and Indian Justice in Colonial Mexico*. Stanford, CA: Stanford University Press, 2008.

Pagden, Anthony. *The Fall of Natural Man: The American Indian and the Origins of Comparative Ethnology*. Cambridge: Cambridge University Press, 1987.

Page, Thomas Nelson. *Jamestown: Cradle of American Civilization*. New York: Scribner, 1907.

Parratt, John. *An Introduction to Third World Theologies*. Cambridge: Cambridge University Press, 2004.

Pasquier, Michael. "Catholicism to 1945." In Philip Goff, ed. *The Blackwell Companion to Religion in America*. Oxford: Wiley-Blackwell, 2010. 478–90.

Pérez-Torres, Rafael. *Mestizaje: Critical Uses of Race in Chicano Culture*. Minneapolis: University of Minnesota Press, 2006.

———. "Refiguring Aztlán." In Amritjit Singh and Peter Schmidt, eds. *Postcolonial Theory and the United States: Race, Ethnicity, and Literature*. Oxford: University of Mississippi Press, 2000. 103–21.

Peterson, Nancy M. *Walking in Two Worlds: Mixed-Blood Indian Women Seeking Their Paths*. Lincoln, NE: Caxton Press, 2006.

Peyer, Bernd. *The Tutor'd Mind: Indian Missionary-Writers in Antebellum America*. Amherst: University of Massachusetts Press, 1997.

Pfitzer, Gregory M. *Popular History and the Literary Marketplace, 1840–1920*. Amherst: University of Massachusetts Press, 2008.

Phipps, Sheila R. *Genteel Rebel: The Life of Mary Greenhow Lee*. Baton Rouge: Louisiana State University Press, 2003.

Pike, Fredrick B. *F.D.R.'S Good Neighbor Policy: Sixty Years of Generally Gentle Chaos*. Austin: University of Texas Press, 2010.

Pratt, Mary Louise. *Imperial Eyes: Travel Writing and Transculturation*. New York: Routledge, 1992.

Pupo-Walker, Enrique. *Castaways: The Narrative of Álvar Núñez Cabeza de Vaca*. Berkeley: University of California Press, 1993.

Purdy, Barbara A. *The Art and Archaeology of Florida's Wetlands.* Boca Raton, FL: CRC Press, 1991.

Quijano, Aníbal and Immanuel Wallerstein. "Americanity as a Concept; or the Americas in the Modern World-System." *International Journal of Social Sciences* 134 (1992): 249–57.

Quinn, Arthur Hobson. *Edgar Allan Poe: A Critical Biography.* Reprint. Baltimore: Johns Hopkins University Press, 1998.

Quinn, David Beers, ed. *New American World: A Documentary History of North America to 1612.* 5 vols. New York: Arno Press, 1979.

———. *Set Fair for Roanoke: Voyages and Colonies, 1584–1606.* Chapel Hill: University of North Carolina Press, 1985.

Rabasa, José. *Inventing America: Spanish Historiography and the Formation of Eurocentrism.* Norman: University of Oklahoma Press, 1994.

———. *Writing Violence on the Northern Frontier: The Historiography of Sixteenth-Century New Mexico and Florida and the Legacy of Conquest.* Durham, NC: Duke University Press, 2000.

Rama, Ángel. *The Lettered City.* Trans. John Charles Chasteen. Durham, NC: Duke University Press, 1996.

Ramos Pérez, Demetrio. *El Mito del Dorado: Su génesis y su proceso.* Caracas: Academia Nacional De La Historia, 1973.

Reséndez, Andrés. "Cabeza de Vaca and the Problem of First Encounters." *Historically Speaking* 10 (2009): 36–38.

———. *A Land So Strange: The Epic Journey of Cabeza de Vaca: The Extraordinary Tale of a Shipwrecked Spaniard Who Walked Across America in the Sixteenth Century.* New York: Basic Books, 2007.

Restall, Matthew. *Seven Myths of the Spanish Conquest.* Oxford: Oxford University Press, 2004.

Richter, Daniel. *Before the Revolution: America's Ancient Pasts.* Cambridge, MA: Belknap Press of Harvard University, 2011.

———. *Facing East from Indian Country: A Native History of Early America.* Cambridge, MA: Harvard University Press, 2003.

———. *Trade, Land, Power: The Struggle for Eastern North America.* Philadelphia: University of Pennsylvania Press, 2013.

———. "Tsenacommacah and the Atlantic World." In Peter C. Mancall, ed. *The Atlantic World and Virginia, 1550–1624.* Chapel Hill: University of North Carolina Press, 2007. 29–65.

Ridley, Jasper. *Maximilian and Juárez.* New York: Ticknor and Fields, 1992.

Rigolet, François. "The Renaissance Crisis of Exemplarity." *Journal of the History of Ideas* 49 (1998): 557–63.

Roa-de-la-Carrera, Cristián. *Histories of Infamy: Francisco López de Gómara and the Ethics of Spanish Imperialism.* Trans. Scott Sessions. Boulder: University of Colorado Press, 2005.

Robbins, Bruce. "Solidarity and Worldliness: For Edward Said." *Logos* 3 (2004). n.p.

Robertson, Lindsay G. *Conquest by Law: How the Discovery of America Dispossessed Indigenous Peoples of Their Lands.* Oxford: Oxford University Press, 2005.

Round, Philip. *Removable Type: Histories of the Book in Indian Country, 1663–1880.* Chapel Hill: University of North Carolina Press, 2010.

Rountree, Helen. *Pocahontas's People: The Powhatan Indians of Virginia through Four Centuries.* Norman: University of Oklahoma Press, 1996.

Rowe, John. "El movimiento nacional inca del siglo XVIII." In Alberto Flores Galindo, ed. *Tupac Amaru II. 1780.* Lima: Retablo de papel, 1976.

Rowe, John Carlos. *Literary Culture and US Imperialism: From the Revolution to World War II.* Oxford: Oxford University Press, 2000.

Rowland, Lawrence et al., eds. *The History of Beaufort County, South Carolina.* Vol. 1: 1514–1861. Columbia: University of South Carolina Press, 1996.

Ruano de la Haza, Jonathan C. *The Good Neighbor Policy in a Geopolitical Context.* Ottawa, Ontario, Canada: University of Ottawa Press, 2007.

Rumeu de Armas, Antonio. *Hernando Colón, historiador del descubrimiento de América.* Madrid: Instituto de Cultura Hispánica, 1973.

Said, Edward W. *The World, The Text, and the Critic.* Cambridge, MA: Harvard University Press, 1983.

St. George, Robert Blair, ed. *Possible Pasts: Becoming Colonial in Early America.* Ithaca and London: Cornell University Press, 2000.

Saldívar, José Davíd. *Trans-americanity: Subaltern Modernities, Global Coloniality, and the Cultures of Greater Mexico.* Durham, NC: Duke University Press, 2011.

Salisbury, Neal. *Manitou and Providence: Indians, Europeans, and the Making of New England, 1500–1643.* Oxford: Oxford University Press, 1984.

———. "Squanto: Last of the Patuxets." In David G. Sweet and Gary B. Nash, eds. *Struggle and Survival in Colonial America.* Berkeley and Los Angeles: University of California Press, 1981. 228–46.

Scheckel, Susan. *The Insistence of the Indian: Race and Nationalism in Nineteenth-Century American Culture.* Princeton, NJ: Princeton University Press, 1998.

Schmitz, David W. *Thank God They're On Our Side: The United States and Right-Wing Dictatorships.* Chapel Hill: University of North Carolina Press, 1999.

Schueller, Malini Johar and Edward Watts. *Messy Beginnings: Postcoloniality and Early American Studies.* New Brunswick, NJ: Rutgers University Press, 2003.

Schulman, Bruce J. *From Cotton Belt to Sun Belt: Federal Policy, Economic Development, and the Transformation of the South 1938–1980.* Durham, NC: Duke University Press, 1994.

Schwartz, Stuart B. *Implicit Understandings: Observing, Reporting, and Reflecting on the Encounters between Europeans and Other Peoples in the Early Modern Era.* Cambridge: Cambridge University Press, 1994.

Seed, Patricia. *American Pentimento: The Invention of Indians and the Pursuit of Riches.* Minneapolis: University of Minnesota Press, 2001.

Shannon, Timothy J. *Iroquois Diplomacy on the Early American Frontier.* New York: Penguin, 2008.

Shuffleton, Frank. "Indian Devils and Pilgrim Fathers: Squanto, Hobomok, and the English Conception of Indian Religion." *New England Quarterly* 49 (1976): 108–16.

Sider, Gerald M. *Lumbee Indian Histories: Race, Ethnicity, and Indian Identities in the Southern United States.* Cambridge: Cambridge University Press, 1994.

Silva, Alan J. "Conquest, Conversion, and the Hybrid Self in Cabeza de Vaca's *Relacion*." *Post Identity* 2, no. 1 (1999): 123–46.

Silva, Cristobal. *Miraculous Plagues: An Epidemiology of Early New England Narrative.* Oxford and New York: Oxford University Press, 2011.

Silverberg, Robert. *Mound Builders of Ancient America: The Archaeology of a Myth.* Athens: Ohio University Press, 1986.

Silverman, David J. *Faith and Boundaries: Colonists, Christianity, and Community among the Wampanoag Indians of Martha's Vineyard, 1600–1871.* Cambridge: Cambridge University Press, 2007.

Skinner, Quentin. *The Foundations of Modern Political Thought.* 2 vols. Cambridge: Cambridge University Press, 1978.

Smith, Verity. *The Encyclopedia of Latin American Literature.* London: Fitzroy Dearborn, 2009.

Soler, Daniel Wasserman. "Language and Communication in the Spanish Conquest of America." *History Compass* 8, no. 6 (2010): 491–502.

Sommer, Doris. *Proceed with Caution, When Engaged by Minority Writing in the Americas.* Cambridge, MA: Harvard University Press, 1999.

Sosa, Aurelio Miró Quesada Sosa. *El Inca Garcilaso.* Lima: Pontificia Universidad Católica del Perú, 1994.

Sova, Dawn B. *Literature Suppressed on Sexual Grounds.* New York: Facts on File, 2006.

Stacy, Lee. *Mexico and the United States.* London: Marshall Cavendish, 2002.

Stacy-Judd, Robert B. *Atlantis: Mother of Empires.* Kempton, IL: Adventures Unlimited, 1999.

Stavans, Ilan. *Art and Anger: Essays on Politics and the Imagination.* New York: Palgrave, 2001.

Stavig, Ward. *The World of Túpac Amaru: Conflict, Community, and Identity in Colonial Peru.* Lincoln: University of Nebraska Press, 1999.

Steigman, Jonathan. *La Florida del Inca and the Struggle for Social Equality in Colonial Spanish America.* Tuscaloosa: University of Alabama Press, 2005.

Stojanowski, Christopher M. and William M. Duncan. "Anthropological Contributions to the Cause of the Georgia Martyrs." *Occasional Papers of the Georgia Southern Museum.* Statesboro: Georgia Southern Museum, 2008.

Strong, Pauline. *Captive Selves, Captivating Others: The Politics and Poetics of Colonial American Captivity Narratives.* Boulder, CO: Westview Press, 2000.

Sturtevant, William C. *Handbook of North American Indians, Vol. 4: History of Indian-White Relations.* Washington, DC: Smithsonian Institution, 1989.

———. "History of Research on the Native Languages of the Southeast." In Heather Hardy and Janine Scancarelli, eds. *Native Languages of the Southeastern United States.* Lincoln: University of Nebraska Press, 2005. 8–68.

Suárez, Silvia B. "Perspectives on Mestizaje in the Early Baroque: Inca Garcilaso and Cervantes." In Nicholas Spalding and Luis Martín-Estudillo, eds. *Hispanic Baroques: Reading Cultures in Context.* Vanderbilt, TN: Vanderbilt University Press, 2005. 187–204.

Swanton, John Reed. *Early History of the Creek Indians and Their Neighbors.* Smithsonian Institution Bureau of American Ethnology Bulletin 73. Washington, DC: Smithsonian Institution, 1922.

———. *The Indian Tribes of North America.* Washington, DC: Smithsonian Institution, 1952.

Sweet, David G. and Gary B. Nash. *Struggle and Survival in Colonial America.* Berkeley and Los Angeles: University of California Press, 1981.

Takaki, Ronald. "*The Tempest* in the Wilderness: The Racialization of Savagery." *Journal of American History* 79 (1992): 892–912.

Tate, Allen. *Jefferson Davis: His Rise and Fall.* Nashville: J.S. Sanders, 1998.

Taylor, Diana. *The Archive and the Repertoire: Performing Cultural Memory in the Americas.* Durham, NC: Duke University Press, 2007-a.

———. "Remapping Genre Through Performance: From 'American' to 'Hemispheric' Studies." *PMLA* 122 (2007-b): 1416–30.

Teunissen, John J. and Evelyn J. Hinz. "Poe's *Journal of Julius Rodman* as Parody." *Nineteenth-Century Fiction* 27 (1972): 317–38.

Teuton, Sean. "Cities of Refuge: Indigenous Cosmopolitan Writers and the International Imaginary." *American Literary History* 25 (2013): 33–53.

Thomas, David Hurst. *St. Catherine's: An Island in Time.* Athens: University of Georgia Press, 2011.

Thomas, Hugh. *The Slave Trade: The Story of the Atlantic Slave Trade: 1440–1870.* New York: Simon and Schuster, 1999.

Tibbles, Thomas H. *The Ponca Chiefs: An Account of the Trial of Standing Bear.* Norman: University of Oklahoma Press, 1972.

Tilton, Robert S. *Pocahontas: The Evolution of an American Narrative.* Cambridge: Cambridge University Press, 1994.

Todorov, Tzvetan. *The Conquest of America.* New York: Harper, 1996.

Townsend, Camilla. "Burying the White Gods: New Perspectives on the Conquest of Mexico." *American Historical Review* 108 (2003): 659–87.

———. Commentary on Soler, "Language and Communication." *History Compass* 8, no. 6 (2010).

———. *Malintzin's Choices: An Indian Woman in the Conquest of Mexico.* Albuquerque: University of New Mexico Press, 2006.

———. "Mutual Appraisals: The Shifting Paradigms of the English, Spanish, and Powhatans in Tsenacomoco, 1560–1622." In Douglas Bradburn and John C. Coombs, eds. *Early Modern Virginia: Reconsidering the Old Dominion.* Charlottesville: University of Virginia Press, 2011. 57–90.

———. *Pocahontas and the Powhatan Dilemma.* New York: Hill and Wang, 2005.

Trafzer, Clifford, Jean A. Keller, and Lorraine Sisquoc, eds. *Boarding School Blues: Revisiting American Indian Educational Experiences.* Lincoln: University of Nebraska Press, 2006.

Tuchman, Barbara Wertheim. *The Zimmerman Telegram.* New York: Random House, 1985.

Van Zandt, Cynthia J. *Brothers Among Nations: The Pursuit of Intercultural Alliances in Early America, 1580–1660.* Oxford: Oxford University Press, 2008.

Varner, John Grier. *El Inca: The Life and Times of Garcilaso de la Vega.* Austin: University of Texas Press, 2012.

Vaughn, Alden T. "Shakespeare's Indian: The Americanization of Caliban." *Shakespeare Quarterly* 39 (1988): 137–53.

———. *Transatlantic Encounters: American Indians in Britain, 1500–1776.* Cambridge: Cambridge University Press, 2008.

———. "Trinculo's Indian: American Natives in Shakespeare's England." In Peter Hulme and William H. Sherman, eds. *'The Tempest' and Its Travels.* Philadelphia: University of Pennsylvania Press, 2000. 49–59.

Venuti, Lawrence. *The Translator's Invisibility: A History of Translation*. London: Routledge, 2005.

Villaverde, Leila E. and Joe L. Kincheloe. "Engaging Students as Researchers: Researching and Teaching Thanksgiving in the Elementary Classroom." In S. R. Steinberg and J. L. Kincheloe, eds. *Students as Researchers: Creating Classrooms that Matter*. London: Falmer, 1998.

Viswaswaran, Kamala. "'Wild West' Anthropology and the Disciplining of Gender." In Helene Silverberg, ed. *Gender and American Social Science: The Formative Years*. Princeton, NJ: Princeton University Press, 1998.

Voigt, Lisa. *Writing Captivity in the Early Modern Atlantic: Circulations of Knowledge and Authority in the Iberian and English Imperial Worlds*. Chapel Hill: University of North Carolina Press, 2008.

Waldman, Carl. *Atlas of the North American Indian*. New York: Facts on File, 2009.

Warner, Michael. "What's Colonial About Colonial America?" In Robert Blaire St. George, ed. *Possible Pasts: Becoming Colonial in Early America*. Ithaca and London: Cornell University Press, 2000. 49–70.

Warrior, Robert Allen. *The People and the Word: Reading Native Nonfiction*. Minneapolis: University of Minnesota Press, 2005.

———. *Tribal Secrets: Recovering American Indian Intellectual Traditions*. Minneapolis: University of Minnesota Press, 1995.

Washburn, Wilcomb E. *The Assault on Indian Tribalism: The General Allotment Act (Dawes Act) of 1887*. New York: Krieger Publishing Company, 1986.

Watson, Blake A. *Buying American from the Indians: Johnson v. McIntosh and the History of Native Land Rights*. Norman: University of Oklahoma Press, 2012.

Watson, Ritchie D. "Cavalier." In Joseph M. Flora et al., eds. *The Companion to Southern Literature*. Baton Rouge: Louisiana State University Press, 2001. 131–33.

Weaver, Jace. "The Red Atlantic: Transoceanic Cultural Exchanges." *American Indian Quarterly* 35 (2011): 418–63.

Weber, David. J. *The Spanish Frontier in North America*. New Haven: Yale University Press, 2009.

Wertheimer, Eric. *Imagined Empires: Incas, Aztecs, and the New World of American Literature, 1771–1876*. Cambridge: Cambridge University Press, 1998.

Wey Gómez, Nicolás. *The Tropics of Empire: Why Columbus Sailed South to the Indies*. Boston: MIT Press, 2008.

Whitaker, *The Western Hemisphere Idea: Its Rise and Decline*. Ithaca, NY: Cornell University Press, 1954.

White, Richard. *The Middle Ground: Indians, Empires, and the Republic in the Great Lakes Region, 1650–1815*. 20th Anniversary Edition. Cambridge: Cambridge University Press, 2010.

Whitehead, Neil L. "The *Discoverie* as Enchanted Text." In Sir Walter Raleigh, ed. *The Discoverie of the Large, Rich, and Bewtiful Empyre of Guiana*. Transcribed, annotated, and introduced by Neil Whitehead. Manchester: Manchester University Press, 1995. 17–24.

Wilkins, David E. *American Indian Sovereignty and the US Supreme Court: The Masking of Justice*. Austin: University of Texas Press, 2010.

Williams, Robert A., Jr. *The American Indian in Western Legal Thought: The Discourses of Conquest*. Oxford: Oxford University Press, 1992.

———. *Like a Loaded Weapon: The Rehnquist Court, Indian Rights, and the Legal History of Racism in America*. Minneapolis: University of Minnesota Press, 2005.

Wilmer, Lambert A. *The life, travels and adventures of Ferdinand de Soto, discoverer of the Mississippi*. Philadelphia: J. T. Lloyd, 1859.

Wilson, Dorothy Clarke. *Bright Eyes: The Story of Susette La Flesche, an Omaha Indian*. New York: McGraw-Hill, 1974.

Wolfe, Patrick. "Settler Colonialism and the Elimination of the Native." *Journal of Genocide Research* 8 (2006): 387–409.

———. *Settler Colonialism and the Transformation of Anthropology: The Politics and Poetics of an Ethnographic Event*. London: Cassell, 1999.

———. "Structure and Event: Settler Colonialism, Time, and the Question of Genocide." In A. Dirk Moses, ed. *Empire, Colony, Genocide: Conquest, Occupation, and Subaltern Resistance in World History*. Oxford, NY: Berghahn Books, 2013.

Womack, Craig. "Theorizing American Indian Experience." In Janice Acoose et al., eds. *Reasoning Together: The Native Critics Collective*. Norman: University of Oklahoma Press, 2008. 353–409.

Woolley, Benjamin. *Savage Kingdom: The True Story of Jamestown, 1607, and the Settlement of America*. New York: Harper, 2008.

Worth, John E. "Fontaneda Revisited: Five Descriptions of Sixteenth-Century Florida." *Florida Historical Quarterly* 73 (1995): 339–52.

———. *The Timucuan Chiefdoms of Spanish Florida*. 2 vols. Gainesville: University of Florida Press, 1998.

Wyss, Hilary. *English Letters and Indian Literacies: Reading, Writing, and New England Missionary Schools, 1750–1830*. Philadelphia: University of Pennsylvania Press, 2012.

Yannakakis, Yanna. *The Art of Being In-Between: Native Intermediaries, Indian Identity, and Local Rule in Colonial Oaxaca*. Durham, NC: Duke University Press, 2008.

Yarsinske, Amy Waters. *Jamestown Exposition, Virginia: American Imperialism on Parade*. 2 vols. Charlottesville, VA: Arcadia, 1999.

Zamora, Lois Parkinson and Monika Kaup, eds. *Baroque New Worlds: Representation, Transculturation, Counterconquest*. Durham, NC: Duke University Press, 2010.

Zamora, Margarita. "Christopher Columbus's 'Letter to the Sovereigns': Announcing the Discovery." In Stephen Greenblatt, ed. *New World Encounters*. Berkeley: University of California Press, 1993. 1–11.

———. *Language, Authority, and Indigenous History in the* Comentarios Reales de los Incas. Cambridge: Cambridge University Press, 2005.

———. *Reading Columbus*. Berkeley: University of California Press, 1993.

{ INDEX }